STAR WARS POE DAMERON

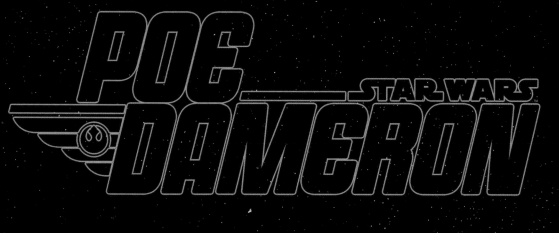

LEGEND FOUND

STAR WARS

Collection Editor JENNIFER GRÜNWALD
Assistant Editor CAITLIN O'CONNELL
Associate Managing Editor KATERI WOODY
Editor, Special Projects MARK D. BEAZLEY

VP Production & Special Projects JEFF YOUNGQUIST
SVP Print, Sales & Marketing DAVID GABRIEL
Book Designer ADAM DEL RE

DISNEY · LUCASFILM

STAR WARS: POE DAMERON VOL. 4 — LEGEND FOUND. Contains material originally published in magazine form as STAR WARS: POE DAMERON #20-25 and ANNUAL #1. First printing 2018. ISBN 978-1-302-90743-3. Published by MARVEL WORLDWIDE, INC., a subsidiary of MARVEL ENTERTAINMENT, LLC. OFFICE OF PUBLICATION: 135 West 50th Street, New York, NY 10020.

Printed in Canada. DAN BUCKLEY, President, Marvel Entertainment; JOHN NEE, Publisher; JOE QUESADA, Chief Creative Officer; TOM BREVOORT, SVP of Publishing; DAVID BOGART, SVP of Business Affairs & Operations, Publishing & Partnership; DAVID GABRIEL, SVP of Sales & Marketing, Publishing; JEFF YOUNGQUIST, VP of Production & Special Projects; DAN CARR, Executive Director of Publishing Technology; ALEX MORALES, Director of Publishing Operations; SUSAN CRESPI, Production Manager; STAN LEE, Chairman Emeritus. For information regarding advertising in Marvel Comics or on Marvel.com, please contact Vit DeBellis, Custom Solutions & Integrated Advertising Manager, at vdebellis@marvel.com. For Marvel subscription inquiries, please call 888-511-5480. **Manufactured between 3/9/2018 and 4/10/2018 by SOLISCO PRINTERS, SCOTT, QC, CANADA.**

LEGEND FOUND

ISSUES #20-25

Writer	CHARLES SOULE
Artist	ANGEL UNZUETA
Color Artist	ARIF PRIANTO
Cover Art	PHIL NOTO
Letterer	VC's JOE CARAMAGNA
Assistant Editor	HEATHER ANTOS
Editor	JORDAN D. WHITE

ANNUAL #1

Writer	ROBBIE THOMPSON
Artist	NIK VIRELLA
Color Artist	JORDAN BOYD
Cover Art	DAN MORA & MATT MILLA
Letterer	VC's JOE CARAMAGNA
Editor	HEATHER ANTOS

Editor in Chief	C.B. CEBULSKI
Chief Creative Officer	JOE QUESADA
President	DAN BUCKLEY

For Lucasfilm:

Assistant Editor	NICK MARTINO
Executive Editor	JENNIFER HEDDLE
Creative Director	MICHAEL SIGLAIN
Lucasfilm Story Group	JAMES WAUGH, LELAND CHEE, MATT MARTIN

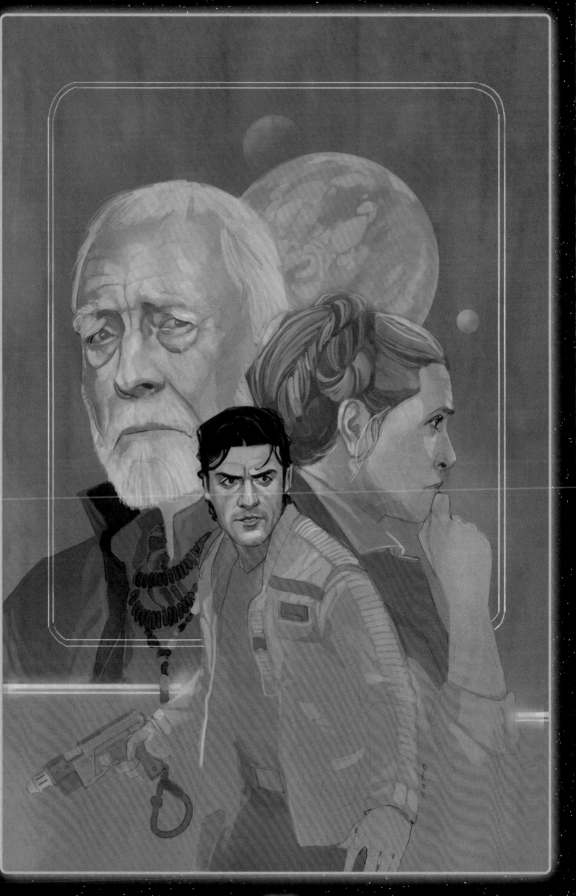

LEGEND FOUND

Insidious forces are at work across the galaxy. Officially, the First Order and the New Republic are at peace, but a cold war wages in secret between them.

General Leia Organa's brave Resistance works to fend off the First Order's efforts on all fronts. To that end, Poe Dameron has been put in charge of Black Squadron, an elite team of X-Wing pilots.

One of Black Squadron's ongoing missions has been tracking down Lor San Tekka, believing the explorer holds the key to finding Organa's missing brother, the Jedi and former rebel Luke Skywalker....

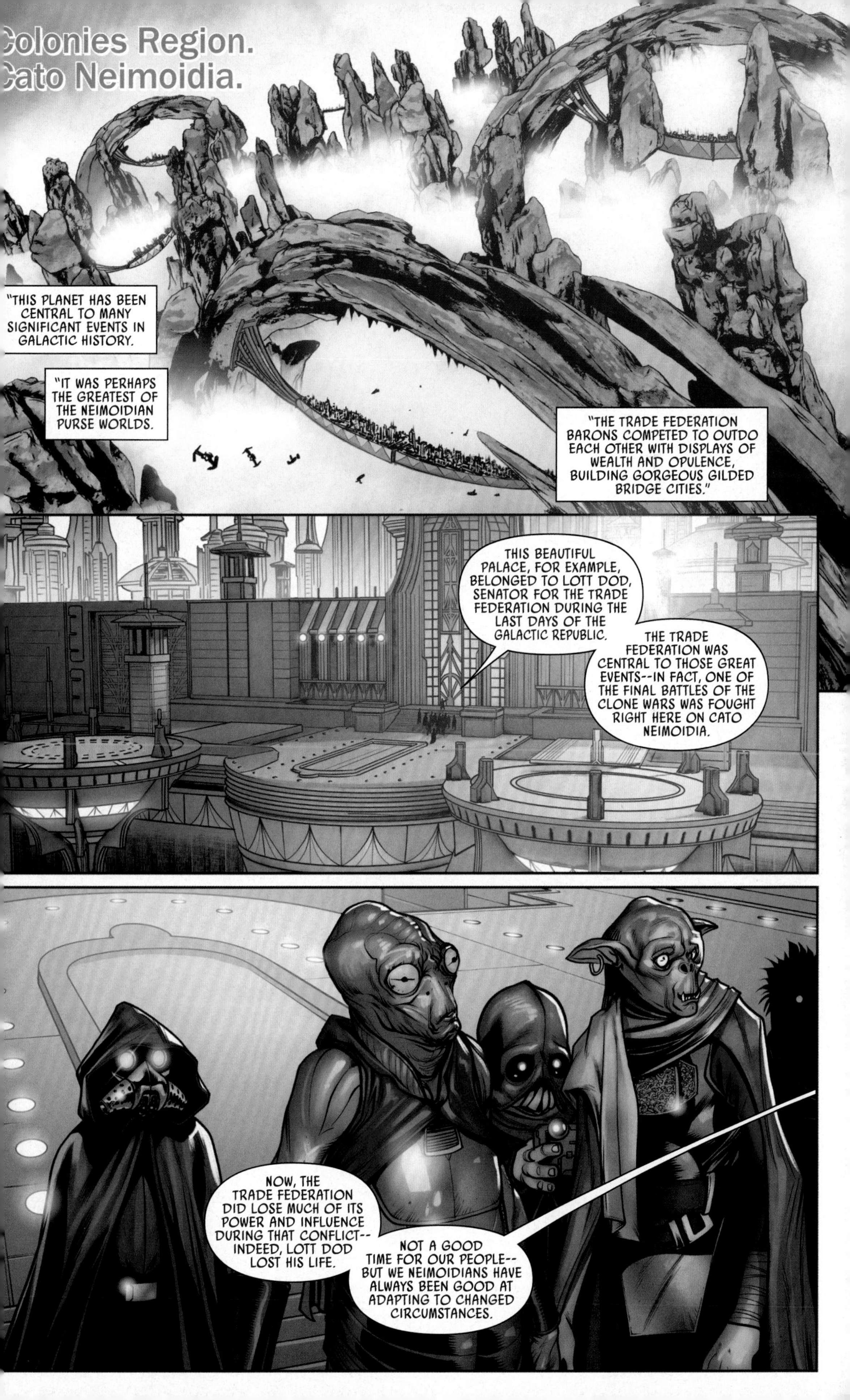

Colonies Region.
Cato Neimoidia.
"THIS PLANET HAS BEEN CENTRAL TO MANY SIGNIFICANT EVENTS IN GALACTIC HISTORY.
"IT WAS PERHAPS THE GREATEST OF THE NEIMOIDIAN PURSE WORLDS.
"THE TRADE FEDERATION BARONS COMPETED TO OUTDO EACH OTHER WITH DISPLAYS OF WEALTH AND OPULENCE, BUILDING GORGEOUS GILDED BRIDGE CITIES."
THIS BEAUTIFUL PALACE, FOR EXAMPLE, BELONGED TO LOTT DOD, SENATOR FOR THE TRADE FEDERATION DURING THE LAST DAYS OF THE GALACTIC REPUBLIC.
THE TRADE FEDERATION WAS CENTRAL TO THOSE GREAT EVENTS--IN FACT, ONE OF THE FINAL BATTLES OF THE CLONE WARS WAS FOUGHT RIGHT HERE ON CATO NEIMOIDIA.
NOW, THE TRADE FEDERATION DID LOSE MUCH OF ITS POWER AND INFLUENCE DURING THAT CONFLICT--INDEED, LOTT DOD LOST HIS LIFE.
NOT A GOOD TIME FOR OUR PEOPLE--BUT WE NEIMOIDIANS HAVE ALWAYS BEEN GOOD AT ADAPTING TO CHANGED CIRCUMSTANCES.

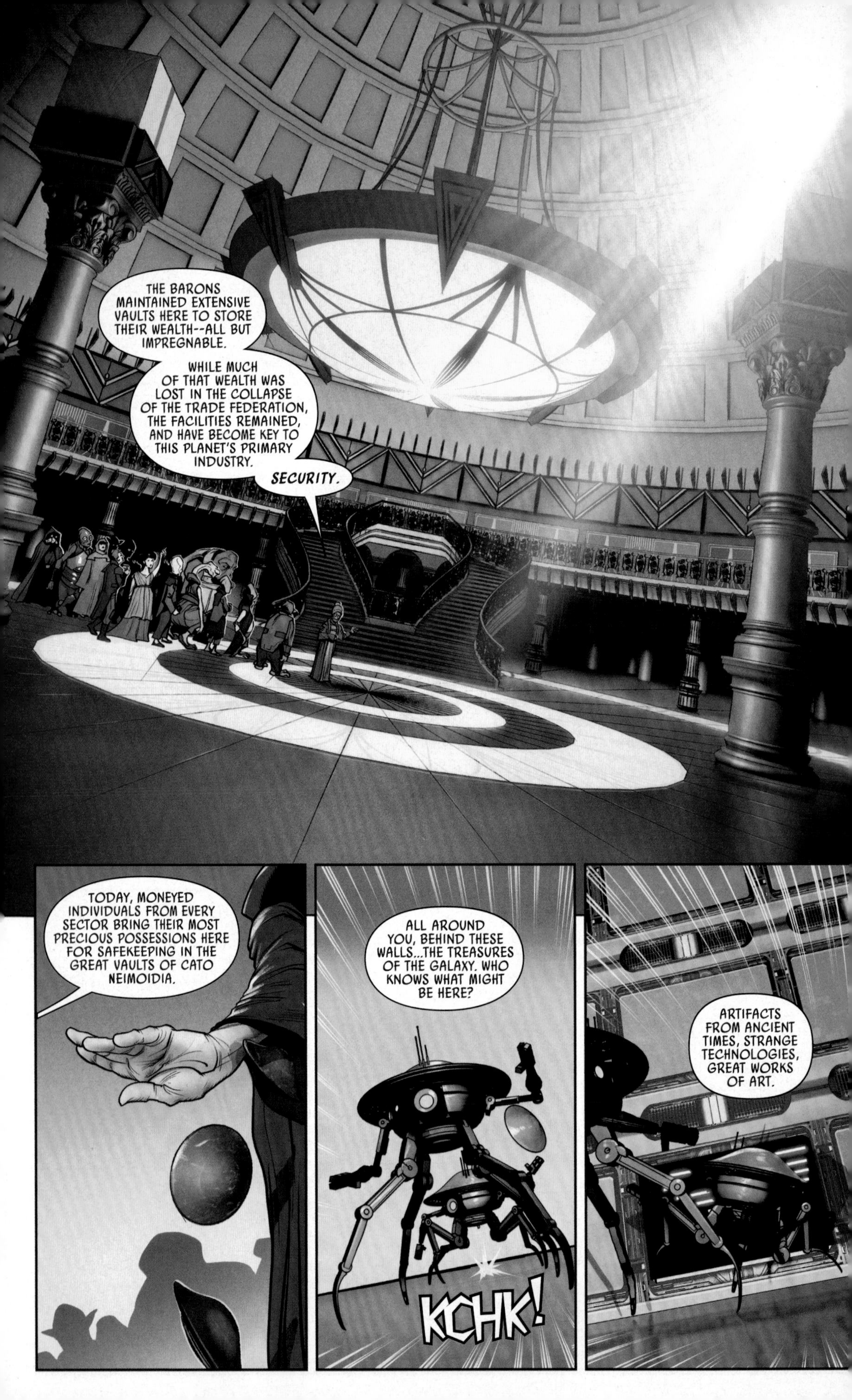
THE BARONS MAINTAINED EXTENSIVE VAULTS HERE TO STORE THEIR WEALTH--ALL BUT IMPREGNABLE.
WHILE MUCH OF THAT WEALTH WAS LOST IN THE COLLAPSE OF THE TRADE FEDERATION, THE FACILITIES REMAINED, AND HAVE BECOME KEY TO THIS PLANET'S PRIMARY INDUSTRY.
SECURITY.
TODAY, MONEYED INDIVIDUALS FROM EVERY SECTOR BRING THEIR MOST PRECIOUS POSSESSIONS HERE FOR SAFEKEEPING IN THE GREAT VAULTS OF CATO NEIMOIDIA.
ALL AROUND YOU, BEHIND THESE WALLS...THE TREASURES OF THE GALAXY. WHO KNOWS WHAT MIGHT BE HERE?
KCHK!
ARTIFACTS FROM ANCIENT TIMES, STRANGE TECHNOLOGIES, GREAT WORKS OF ART.

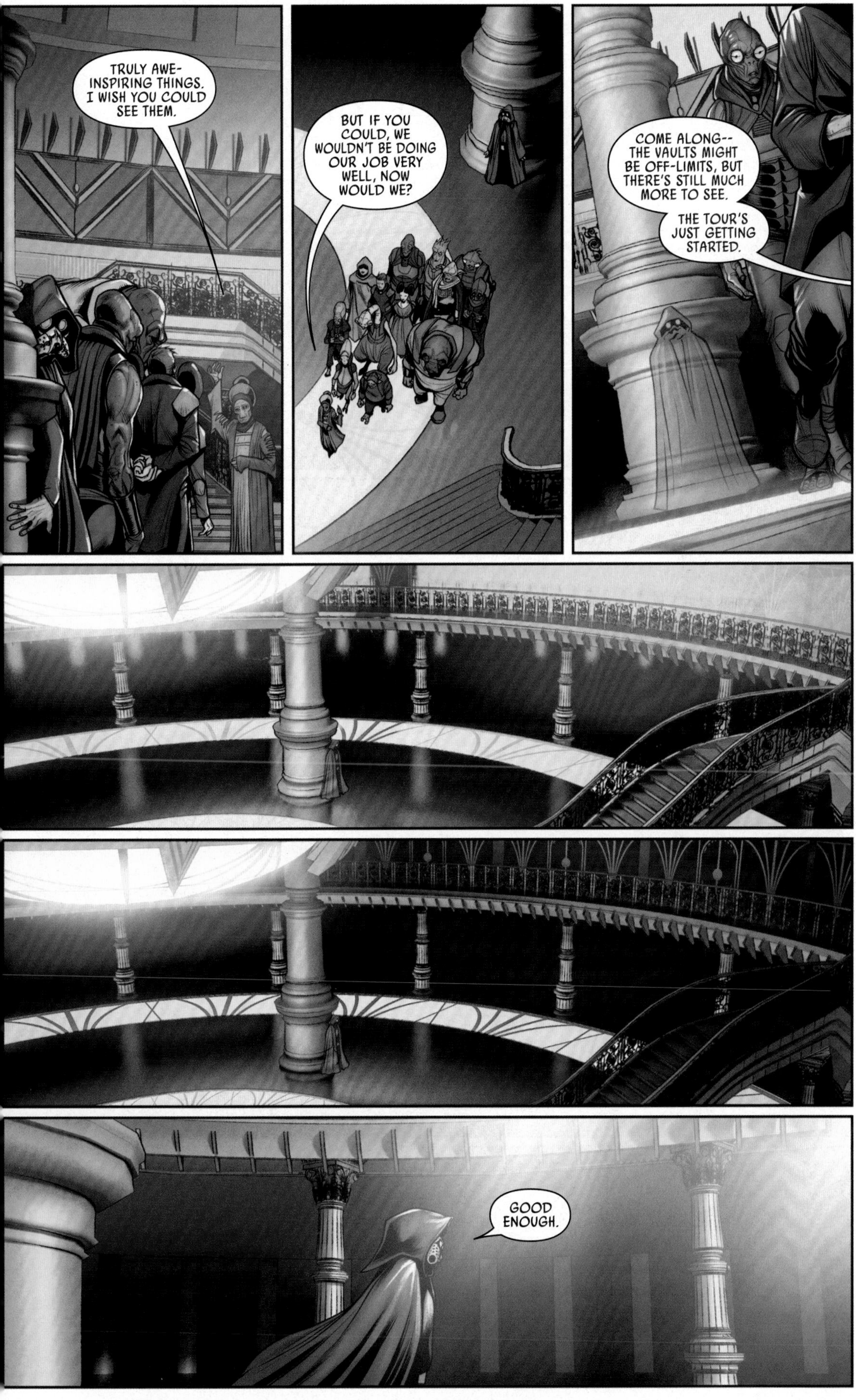
TRULY AWE-INSPIRING THINGS. I WISH YOU COULD SEE THEM.
BUT IF YOU COULD, WE WOULDN'T BE DOING OUR JOB VERY WELL, NOW WOULD WE?
COME ALONG-- THE VAULTS MIGHT BE OFF-LIMITS, BUT THERE'S STILL MUCH MORE TO SEE.
THE TOUR'S JUST GETTING STARTED.
GOOD ENOUGH.

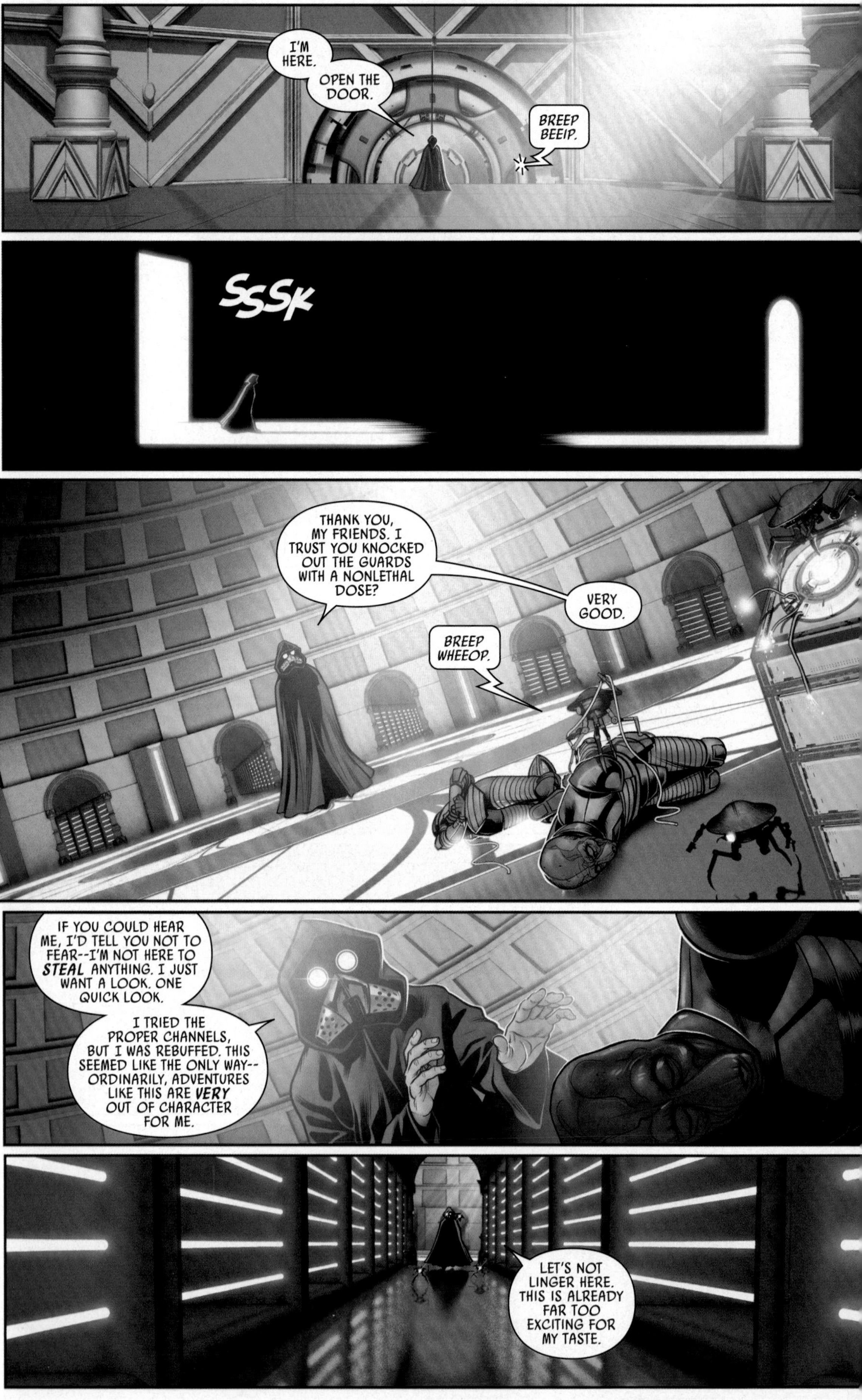
I'M HERE.
OPEN THE DOOR.
BREEP BEEIP.
SSSK
THANK YOU, MY FRIENDS. I TRUST YOU KNOCKED OUT THE GUARDS WITH A NONLETHAL DOSE?
VERY GOOD.
BREEP WHEEOP.
IF YOU COULD HEAR ME, I'D TELL YOU NOT TO FEAR--I'M NOT HERE TO STEAL ANYTHING. I JUST WANT A LOOK. ONE QUICK LOOK.
I TRIED THE PROPER CHANNELS, BUT I WAS REBUFFED. THIS SEEMED LIKE THE ONLY WAY-- ORDINARILY, ADVENTURES LIKE THIS ARE VERY OUT OF CHARACTER FOR ME.
LET'S NOT LINGER HERE. THIS IS ALREADY FAR TOO EXCITING FOR MY TASTE.

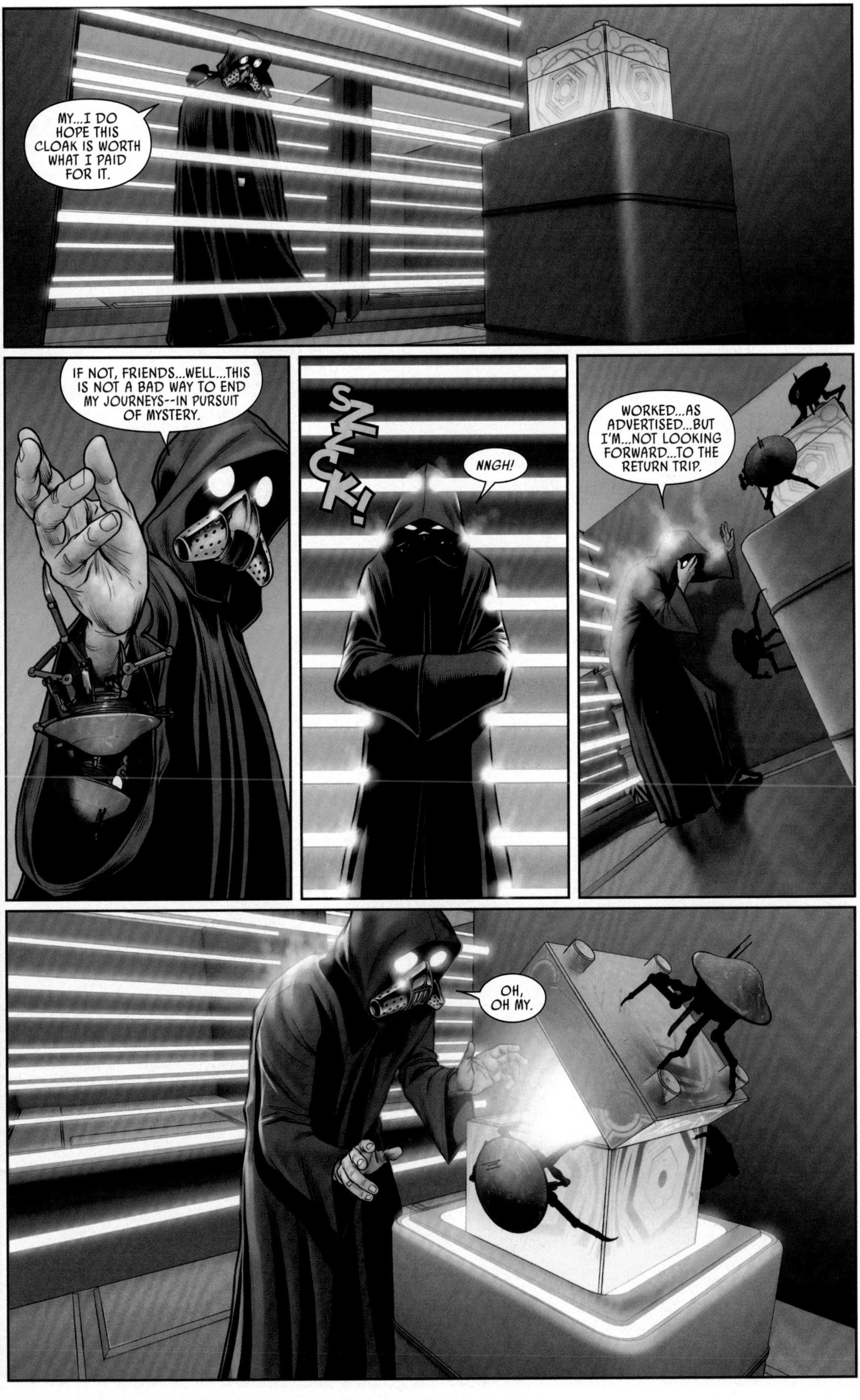
MY...I DO HOPE THIS CLOAK IS WORTH WHAT I PAID FOR IT.
IF NOT, FRIENDS...WELL...THIS IS NOT A BAD WAY TO END MY JOURNEYS--IN PURSUIT OF MYSTERY.
SZZCK!
NNGH!
WORKED...AS ADVERTISED...BUT I'M...NOT LOOKING FORWARD...TO THE RETURN TRIP.
OH, OH MY.

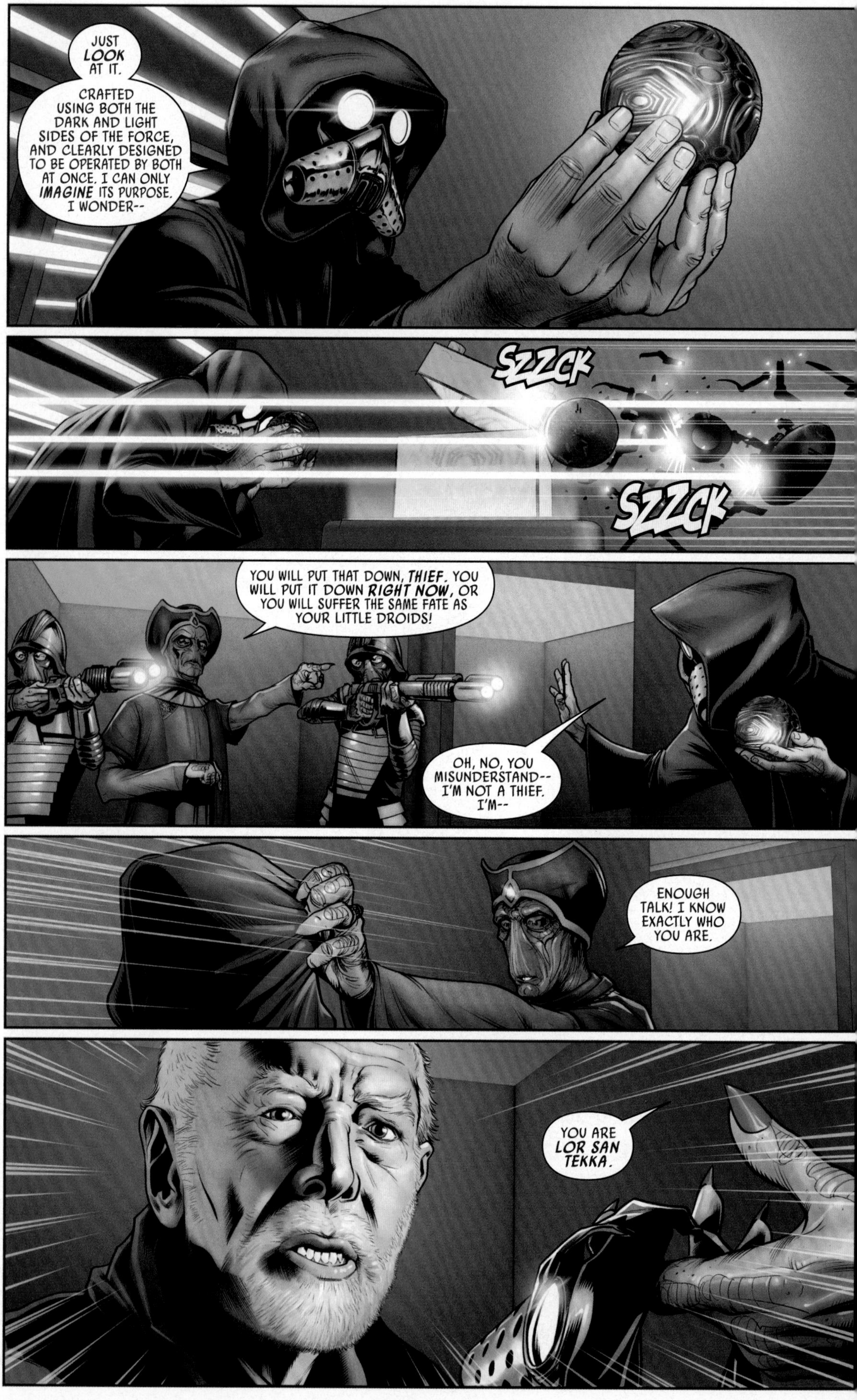
JUST LOOK AT IT.
CRAFTED USING BOTH THE DARK AND LIGHT SIDES OF THE FORCE, AND CLEARLY DESIGNED TO BE OPERATED BY BOTH AT ONCE. I CAN ONLY IMAGINE ITS PURPOSE. I WONDER--
SZZCK
SZZCK
YOU WILL PUT THAT DOWN, THIEF. YOU WILL PUT IT DOWN RIGHT NOW, OR YOU WILL SUFFER THE SAME FATE AS YOUR LITTLE DROIDS!
OH, NO, YOU MISUNDERSTAND-- I'M NOT A THIEF. I'M--
ENOUGH TALK! I KNOW EXACTLY WHO YOU ARE.
YOU ARE LOR SAN TEKKA.

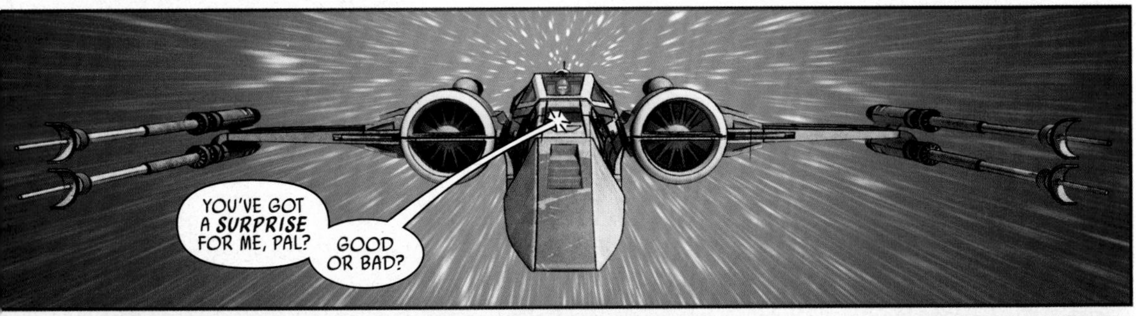
YOU'VE GOT A SURPRISE FOR ME, PAL?
GOOD OR BAD?

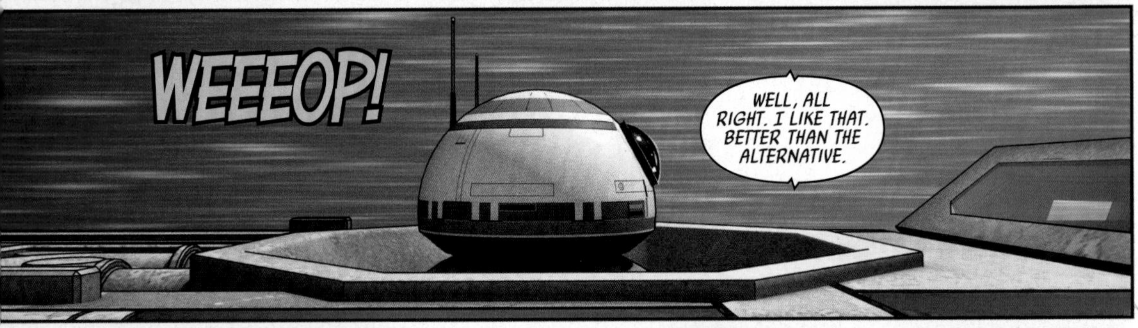
WEEEOP!
WELL, ALL RIGHT. I LIKE THAT. BETTER THAN THE ALTERNATIVE.

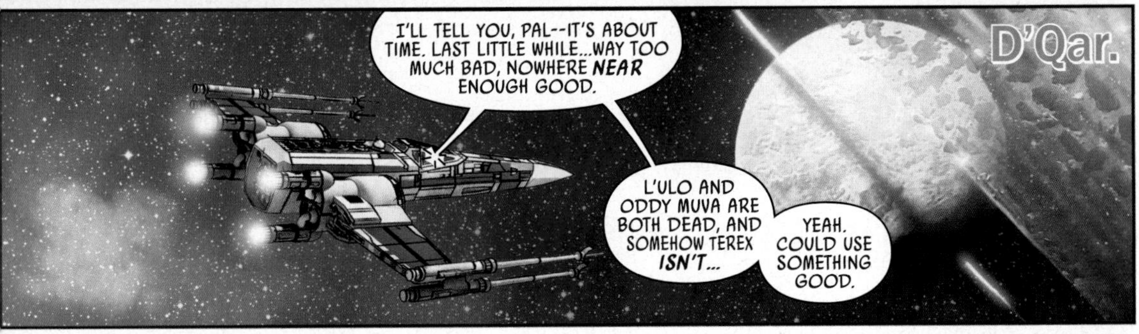
D'Qar.
I'LL TELL YOU, PAL--IT'S ABOUT TIME. LAST LITTLE WHILE...WAY TOO MUCH BAD, NOWHERE NEAR ENOUGH GOOD.
L'ULO AND ODDY MUVA ARE BOTH DEAD, AND SOMEHOW TEREX ISN'T...
YEAH. COULD USE SOMETHING GOOD.

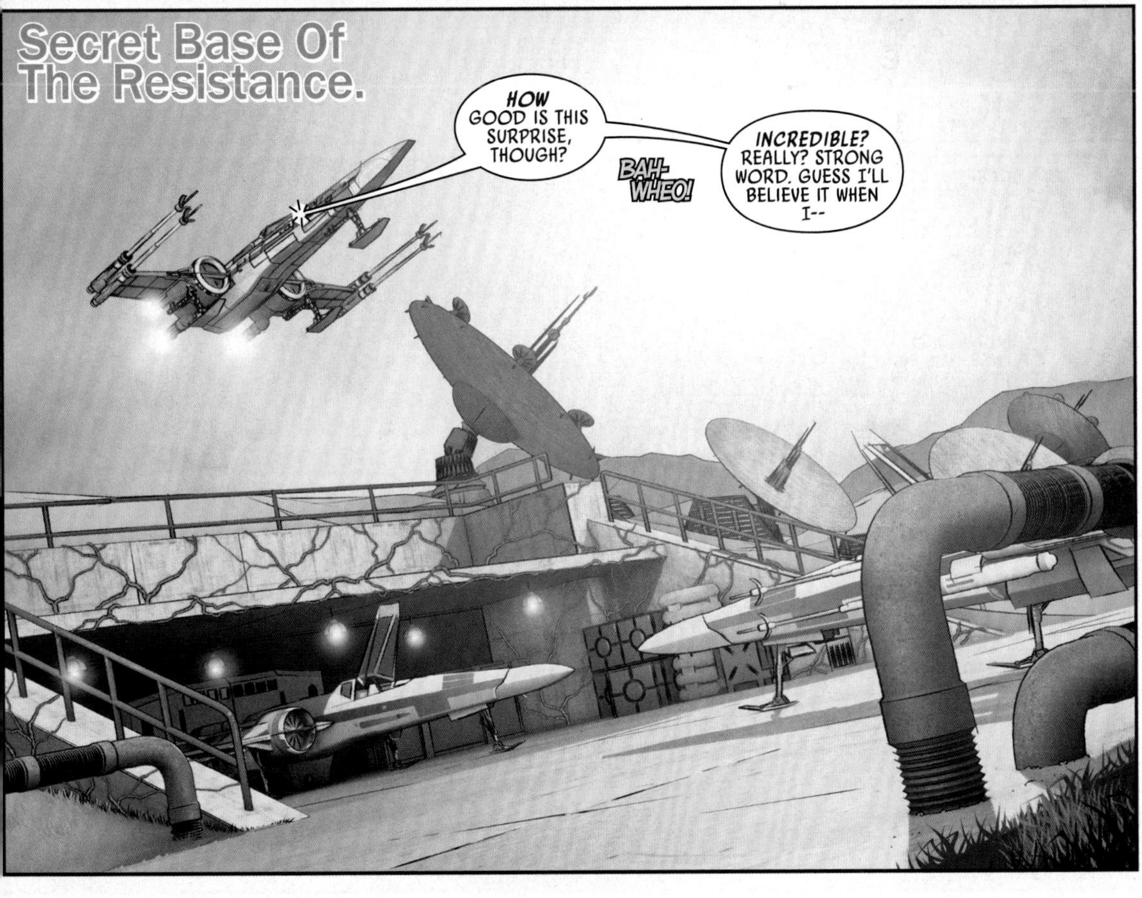
Secret Base Of The Resistance.
HOW GOOD IS THIS SURPRISE, THOUGH?
BAH-WHEO!
INCREDIBLE? REALLY? STRONG WORD. GUESS I'LL BELIEVE IT WHEN I--

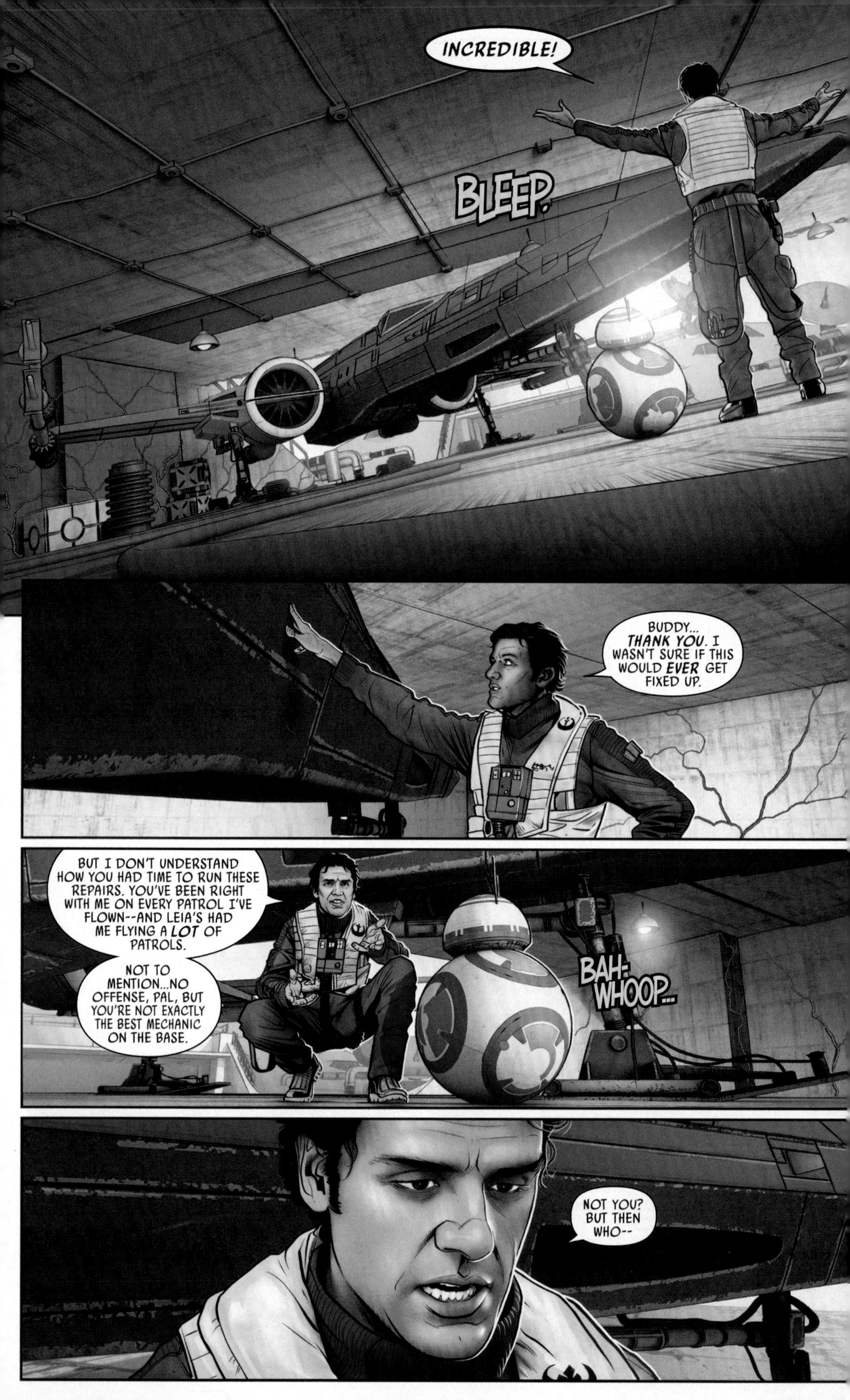
INCREDIBLE!
BLEEP.
BUDDY... THANK YOU. I WASN'T SURE IF THIS WOULD EVER GET FIXED UP.
BUT I DON'T UNDERSTAND HOW YOU HAD TIME TO RUN THESE REPAIRS. YOU'VE BEEN RIGHT WITH ME ON EVERY PATROL I'VE FLOWN--AND LEIA'S HAD ME FLYING A LOT OF PATROLS.
NOT TO MENTION...NO OFFENSE, PAL, BUT YOU'RE NOT EXACTLY THE BEST MECHANIC ON THE BASE.
BAH-WHOOP...
NOT YOU? BUT THEN WHO--

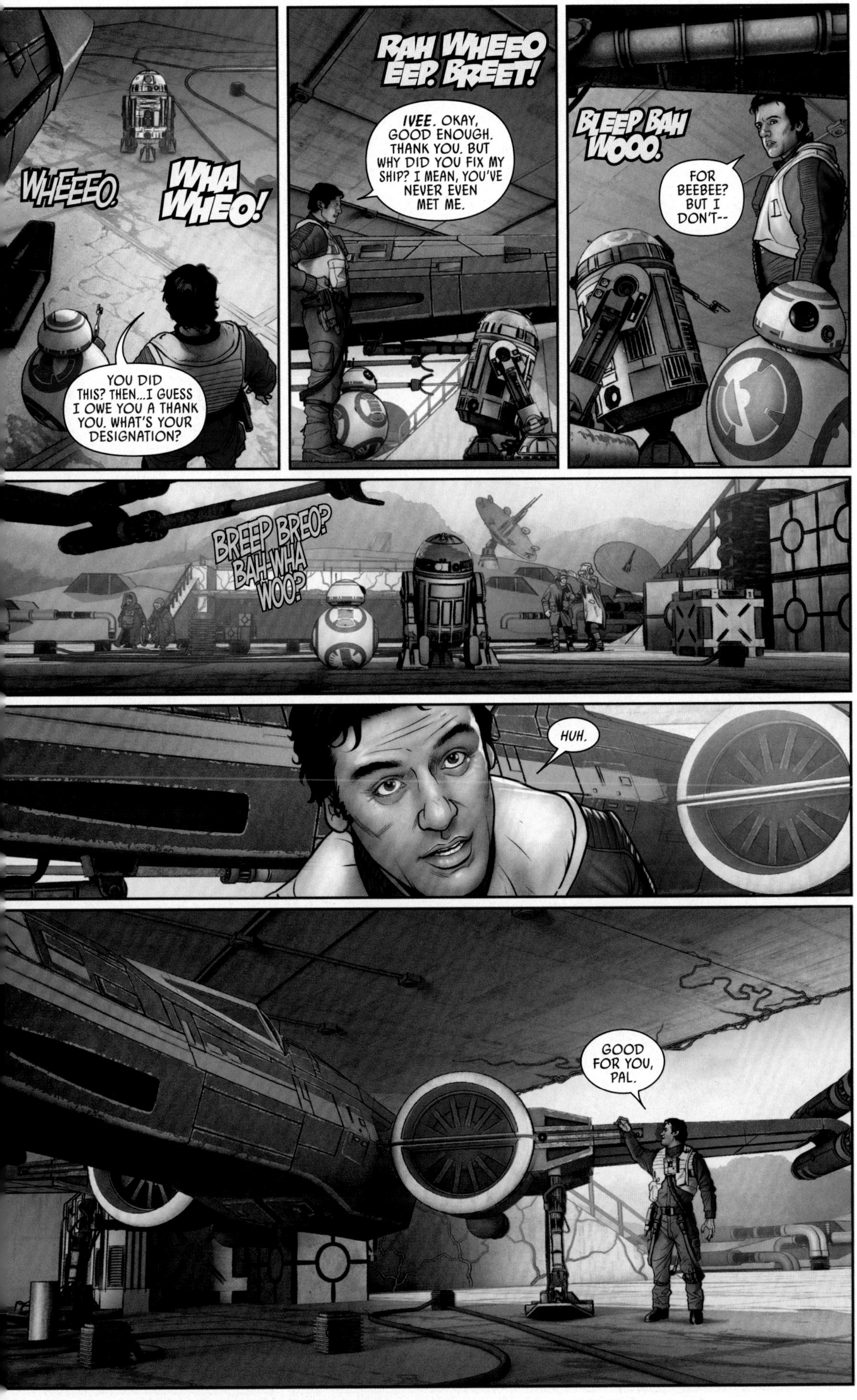
WHEEEO.
WHA WHEO!
YOU DID THIS? THEN...I GUESS I OWE YOU A THANK YOU. WHAT'S YOUR DESIGNATION?
RAH WHEEO EEP. BREET!
IVEE. OKAY, GOOD ENOUGH. THANK YOU. BUT WHY DID YOU FIX MY SHIP? I MEAN, YOU'VE NEVER EVEN MET ME.
BLEEP BAH WOOO.
FOR BEEBEE? BUT I DON'T--
BREEP BREO? BAH-WHA WOO?
HUH.
GOOD FOR YOU, PAL.

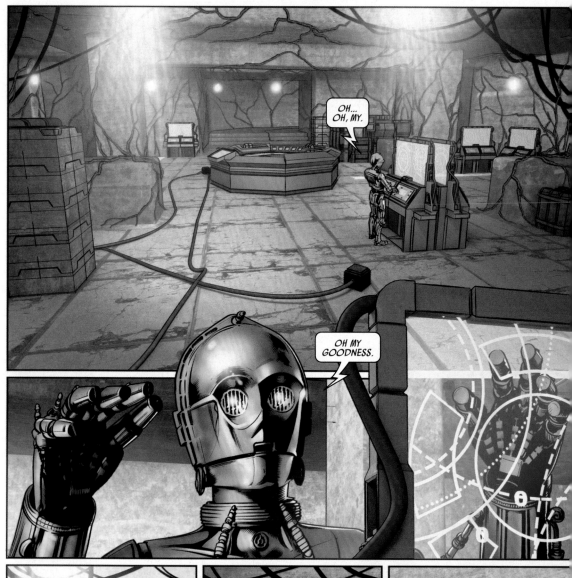

OH...
OH, MY.

OH MY
GOODNESS.

PARDON ME! EXCUSE ME! HAVE EITHER OF YOU SEEN GENERAL ORGANA? I MUST SPEAK WITH HER IMMEDIATELY.

BLEEP.
WRRRRRP
BEEP.

JESSIKA PAVA? I WAS ASKING ABOUT LEIA ORGANA!

BREEE
WWWRRRP!

OH, MY.

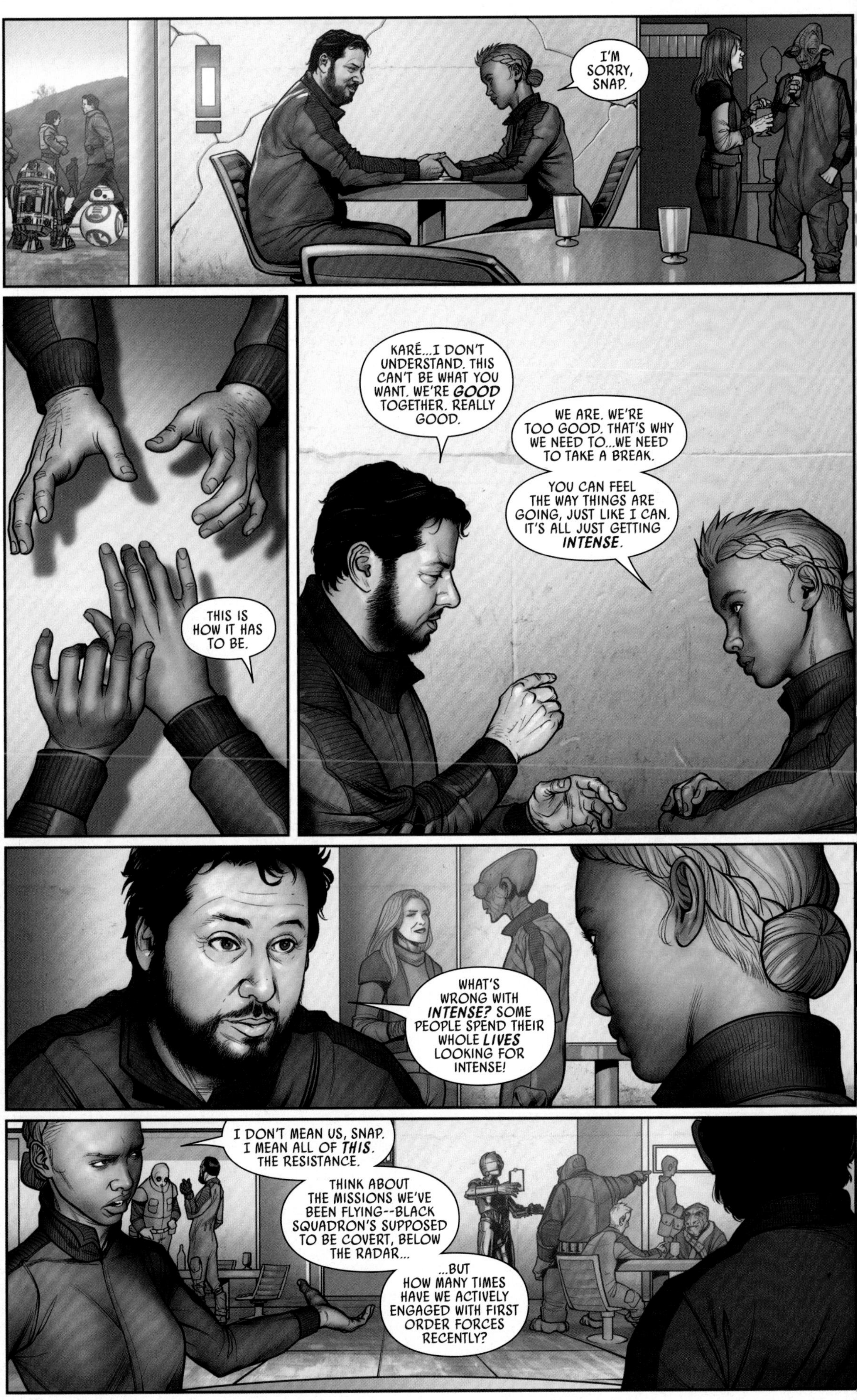
I'M SORRY, SNAP.
KARÉ...I DON'T UNDERSTAND. THIS CAN'T BE WHAT YOU WANT. WE'RE GOOD TOGETHER. REALLY GOOD.
WE ARE. WE'RE TOO GOOD. THAT'S WHY WE NEED TO...WE NEED TO TAKE A BREAK.
YOU CAN FEEL THE WAY THINGS ARE GOING, JUST LIKE I CAN. IT'S ALL JUST GETTING INTENSE.
THIS IS HOW IT HAS TO BE.
WHAT'S WRONG WITH INTENSE? SOME PEOPLE SPEND THEIR WHOLE LIVES LOOKING FOR INTENSE!
I DON'T MEAN US, SNAP. I MEAN ALL OF THIS. THE RESISTANCE.
THINK ABOUT THE MISSIONS WE'VE BEEN FLYING--BLACK SQUADRON'S SUPPOSED TO BE COVERT, BELOW THE RADAR...
...BUT HOW MANY TIMES HAVE WE ACTIVELY ENGAGED WITH FIRST ORDER FORCES RECENTLY?

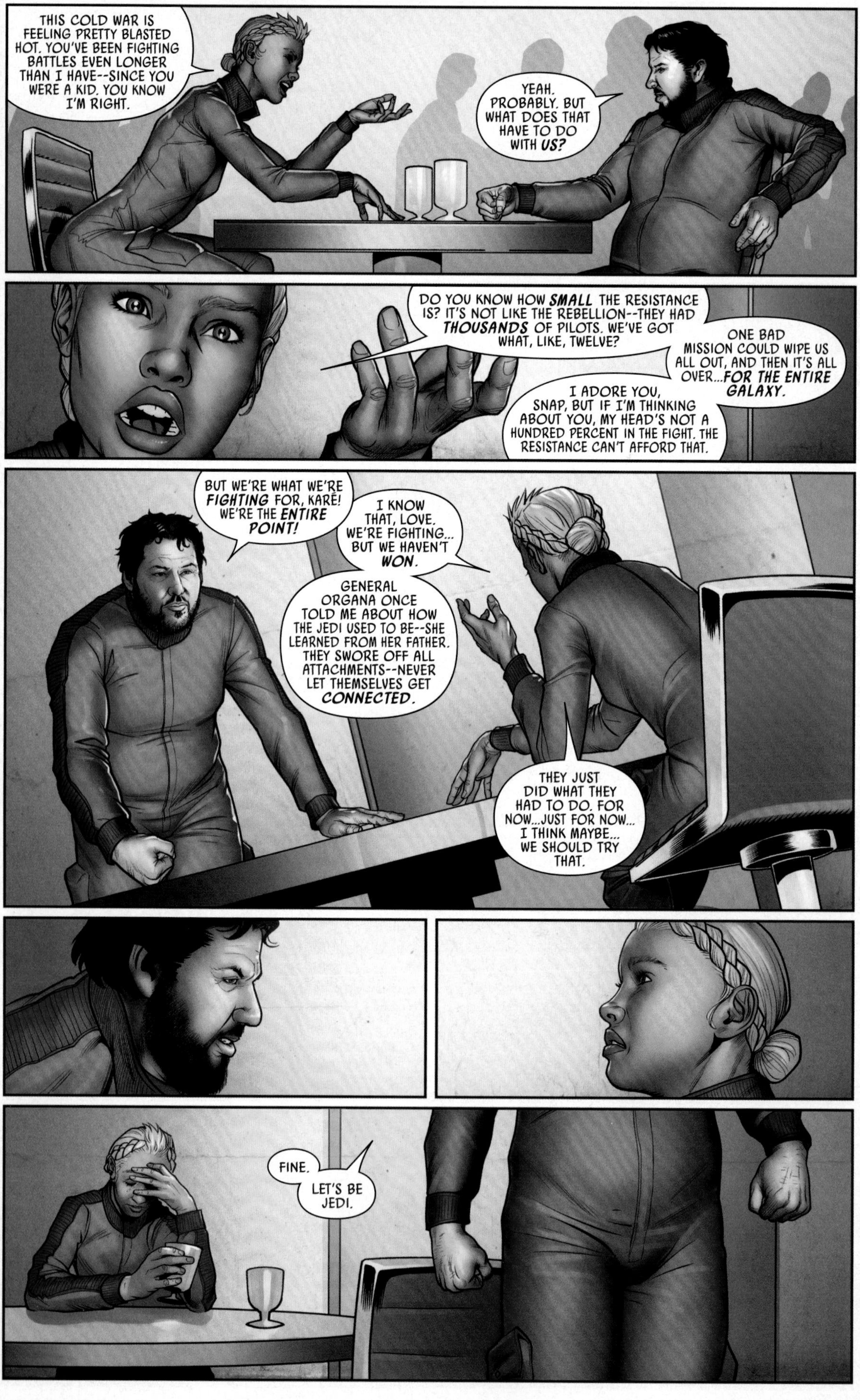
THIS COLD WAR IS FEELING PRETTY BLASTED HOT. YOU'VE BEEN FIGHTING BATTLES EVEN LONGER THAN I HAVE--SINCE YOU WERE A KID. YOU KNOW I'M RIGHT.
YEAH. PROBABLY. BUT WHAT DOES THAT HAVE TO DO WITH US?
DO YOU KNOW HOW SMALL THE RESISTANCE IS? IT'S NOT LIKE THE REBELLION--THEY HAD THOUSANDS OF PILOTS. WE'VE GOT WHAT, LIKE, TWELVE?
ONE BAD MISSION COULD WIPE US ALL OUT, AND THEN IT'S ALL OVER...FOR THE ENTIRE GALAXY.
I ADORE YOU, SNAP, BUT IF I'M THINKING ABOUT YOU, MY HEAD'S NOT A HUNDRED PERCENT IN THE FIGHT. THE RESISTANCE CAN'T AFFORD THAT.
BUT WE'RE WHAT WE'RE FIGHTING FOR, KARÉ! WE'RE THE ENTIRE POINT!
I KNOW THAT, LOVE. WE'RE FIGHTING... BUT WE HAVEN'T WON.
GENERAL ORGANA ONCE TOLD ME ABOUT HOW THE JEDI USED TO BE--SHE LEARNED FROM HER FATHER. THEY SWORE OFF ALL ATTACHMENTS--NEVER LET THEMSELVES GET CONNECTED.
THEY JUST DID WHAT THEY HAD TO DO. FOR NOW...JUST FOR NOW... I THINK MAYBE... WE SHOULD TRY THAT.
FINE.
LET'S BE JEDI.

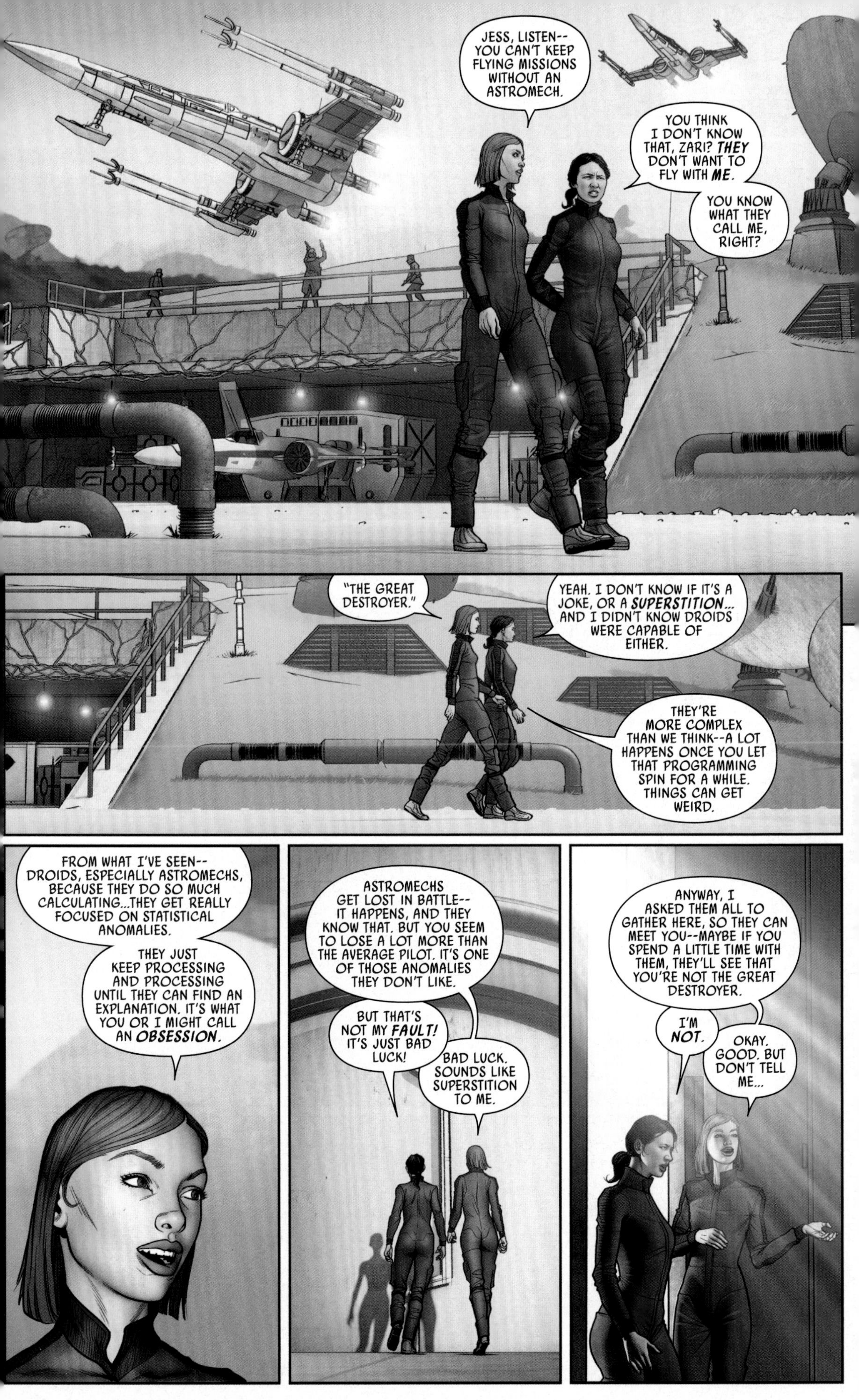
JESS, LISTEN--
YOU CAN'T KEEP FLYING MISSIONS WITHOUT AN ASTROMECH.
YOU THINK I DON'T KNOW THAT, ZARI? THEY DON'T WANT TO FLY WITH ME.
YOU KNOW WHAT THEY CALL ME, RIGHT?
"THE GREAT DESTROYER."
YEAH. I DON'T KNOW IF IT'S A JOKE, OR A SUPERSTITION... AND I DIDN'T KNOW DROIDS WERE CAPABLE OF EITHER.
THEY'RE MORE COMPLEX THAN WE THINK--A LOT HAPPENS ONCE YOU LET THAT PROGRAMMING SPIN FOR A WHILE. THINGS CAN GET WEIRD.
FROM WHAT I'VE SEEN--DROIDS, ESPECIALLY ASTROMECHS, BECAUSE THEY DO SO MUCH CALCULATING...THEY GET REALLY FOCUSED ON STATISTICAL ANOMALIES.
THEY JUST KEEP PROCESSING AND PROCESSING UNTIL THEY CAN FIND AN EXPLANATION. IT'S WHAT YOU OR I MIGHT CALL AN OBSESSION.
ASTROMECHS GET LOST IN BATTLE--IT HAPPENS, AND THEY KNOW THAT. BUT YOU SEEM TO LOSE A LOT MORE THAN THE AVERAGE PILOT. IT'S ONE OF THOSE ANOMALIES THEY DON'T LIKE.
BUT THAT'S NOT MY FAULT! IT'S JUST BAD LUCK!
BAD LUCK. SOUNDS LIKE SUPERSTITION TO ME.
ANYWAY, I ASKED THEM ALL TO GATHER HERE, SO THEY CAN MEET YOU--MAYBE IF YOU SPEND A LITTLE TIME WITH THEM, THEY'LL SEE THAT YOU'RE NOT THE GREAT DESTROYER.
I'M NOT.
OKAY. GOOD. BUT DON'T TELL ME...

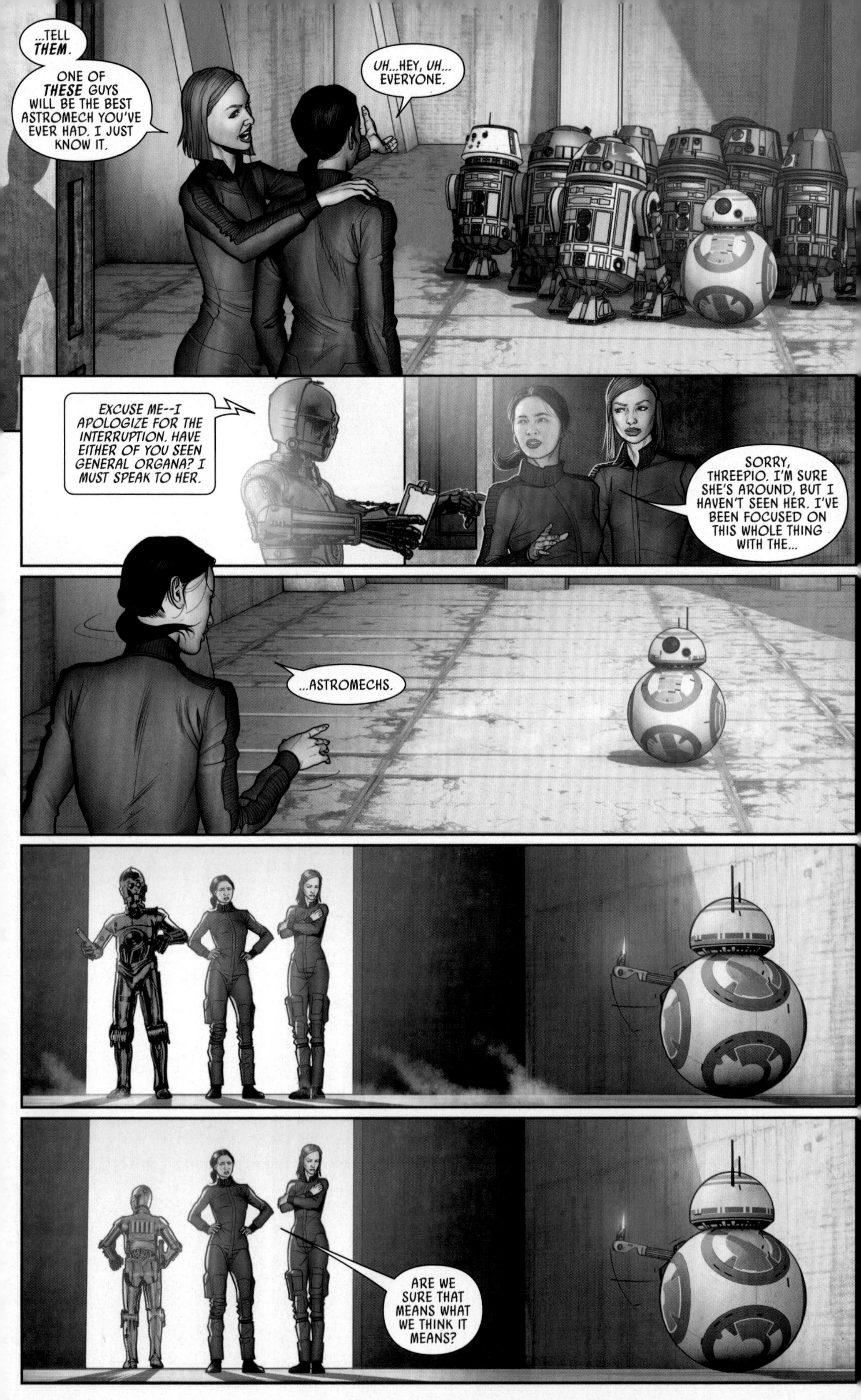
...TELL THEM.
ONE OF THESE GUYS WILL BE THE BEST ASTROMECH YOU'VE EVER HAD. I JUST KNOW IT.
UH...HEY, UH... EVERYONE.
EXCUSE ME--I APOLOGIZE FOR THE INTERRUPTION. HAVE EITHER OF YOU SEEN GENERAL ORGANA? I MUST SPEAK TO HER.
SORRY, THREEPIO. I'M SURE SHE'S AROUND, BUT I HAVEN'T SEEN HER. I'VE BEEN FOCUSED ON THIS WHOLE THING WITH THE...
...ASTROMECHS.
ARE WE SURE THAT MEANS WHAT WE THINK IT MEANS?

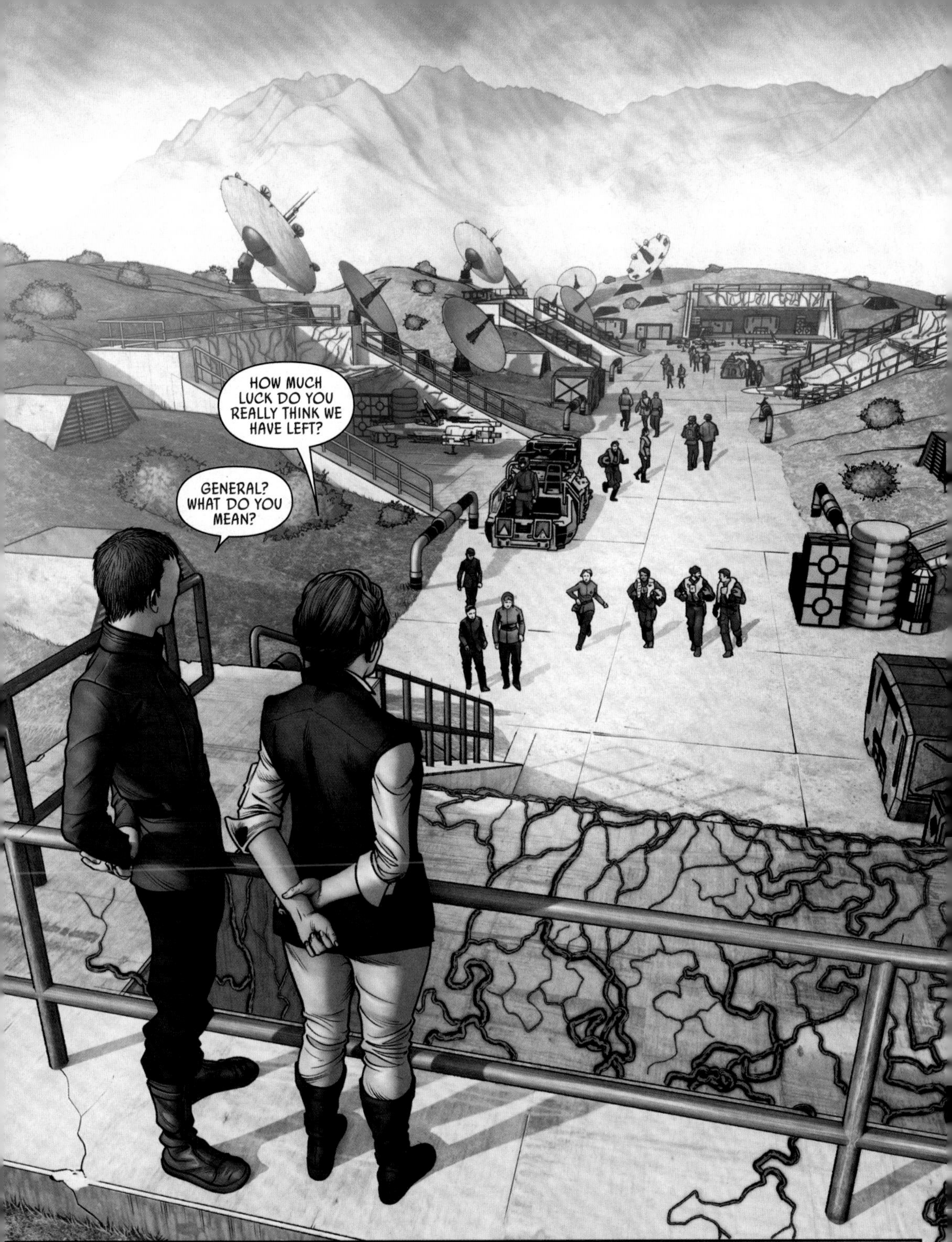
GENERAL? WHAT DO YOU MEAN?
HOW MUCH LUCK DO YOU REALLY THINK WE HAVE LEFT?

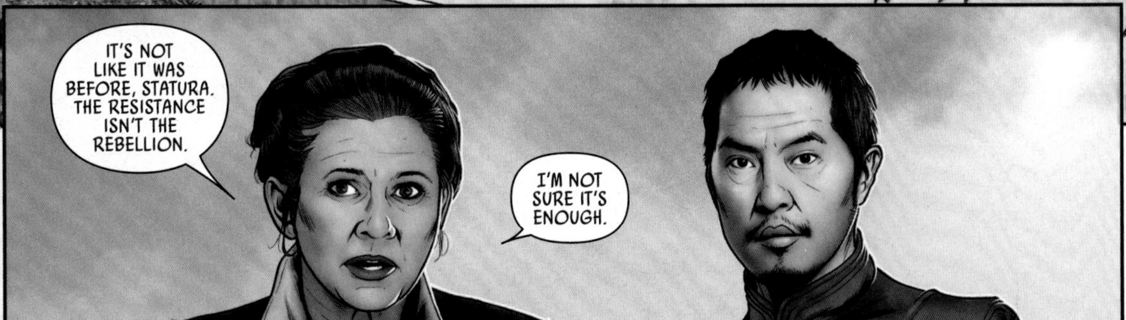
IT'S NOT LIKE IT WAS BEFORE, STATURA. THE RESISTANCE ISN'T THE REBELLION.
I'M NOT SURE IT'S ENOUGH.

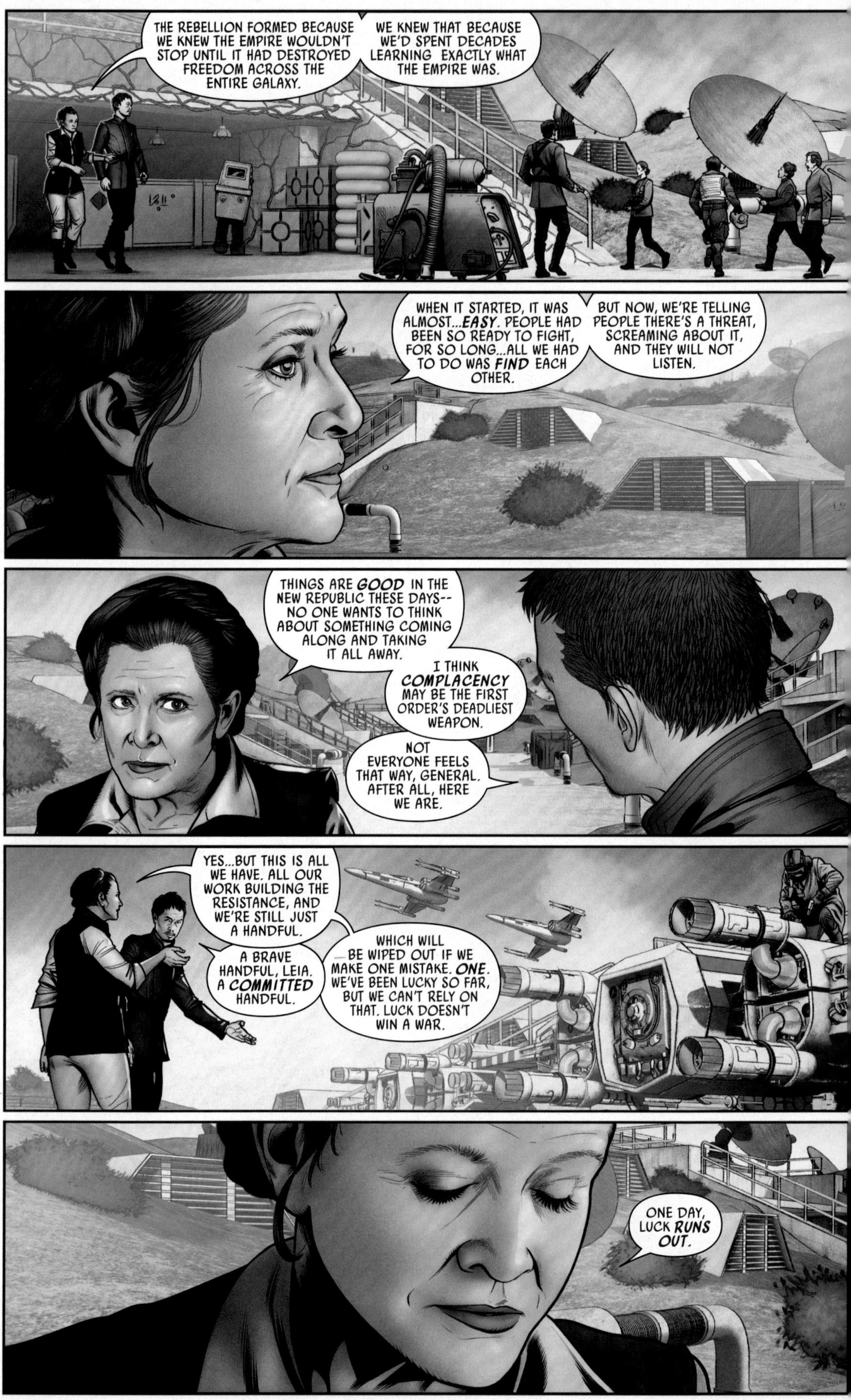
THE REBELLION FORMED BECAUSE WE KNEW THE EMPIRE WOULDN'T STOP UNTIL IT HAD DESTROYED FREEDOM ACROSS THE ENTIRE GALAXY.
WE KNEW THAT BECAUSE WE'D SPENT DECADES LEARNING EXACTLY WHAT THE EMPIRE WAS.
WHEN IT STARTED, IT WAS ALMOST...EASY. PEOPLE HAD BEEN SO READY TO FIGHT, FOR SO LONG...ALL WE HAD TO DO WAS FIND EACH OTHER.
BUT NOW, WE'RE TELLING PEOPLE THERE'S A THREAT, SCREAMING ABOUT IT, AND THEY WILL NOT LISTEN.
THINGS ARE GOOD IN THE NEW REPUBLIC THESE DAYS-- NO ONE WANTS TO THINK ABOUT SOMETHING COMING ALONG AND TAKING IT ALL AWAY.
I THINK COMPLACENCY MAY BE THE FIRST ORDER'S DEADLIEST WEAPON.
NOT EVERYONE FEELS THAT WAY, GENERAL. AFTER ALL, HERE WE ARE.
YES...BUT THIS IS ALL WE HAVE. ALL OUR WORK BUILDING THE RESISTANCE, AND WE'RE STILL JUST A HANDFUL.
A BRAVE HANDFUL, LEIA. A COMMITTED HANDFUL.
WHICH WILL BE WIPED OUT IF WE MAKE ONE MISTAKE. ONE. WE'VE BEEN LUCKY SO FAR, BUT WE CAN'T RELY ON THAT. LUCK DOESN'T WIN A WAR.
ONE DAY, LUCK RUNS OUT.

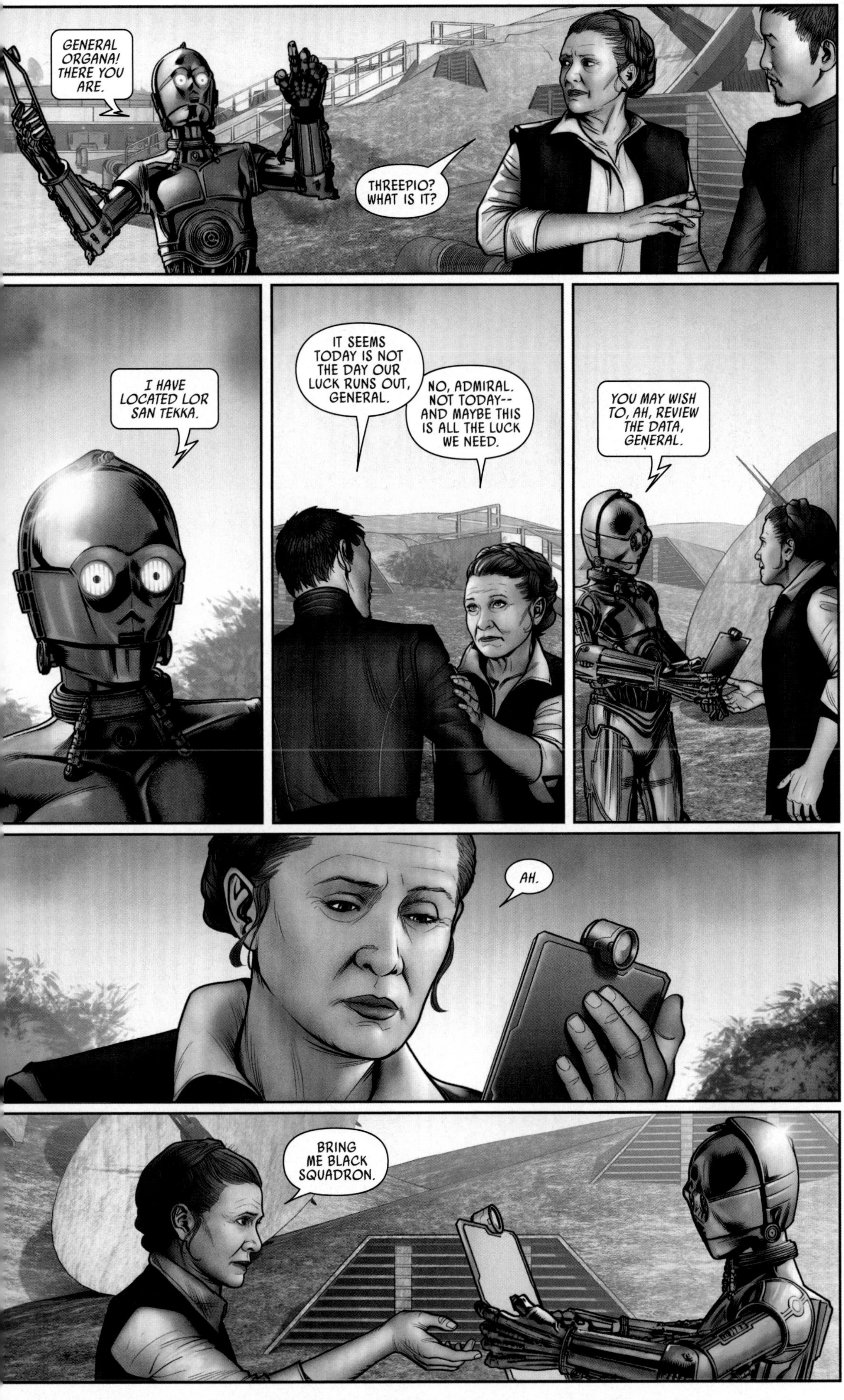

GENERAL ORGANA! THERE YOU ARE.
THREEPIO? WHAT IS IT?
I HAVE LOCATED LOR SAN TEKKA.
IT SEEMS TODAY IS NOT THE DAY OUR LUCK RUNS OUT, GENERAL.
NO, ADMIRAL. NOT TODAY-- AND MAYBE THIS IS ALL THE LUCK WE NEED.
YOU MAY WISH TO, AH, REVIEW THE DATA, GENERAL.
AH.
BRING ME BLACK SQUADRON.

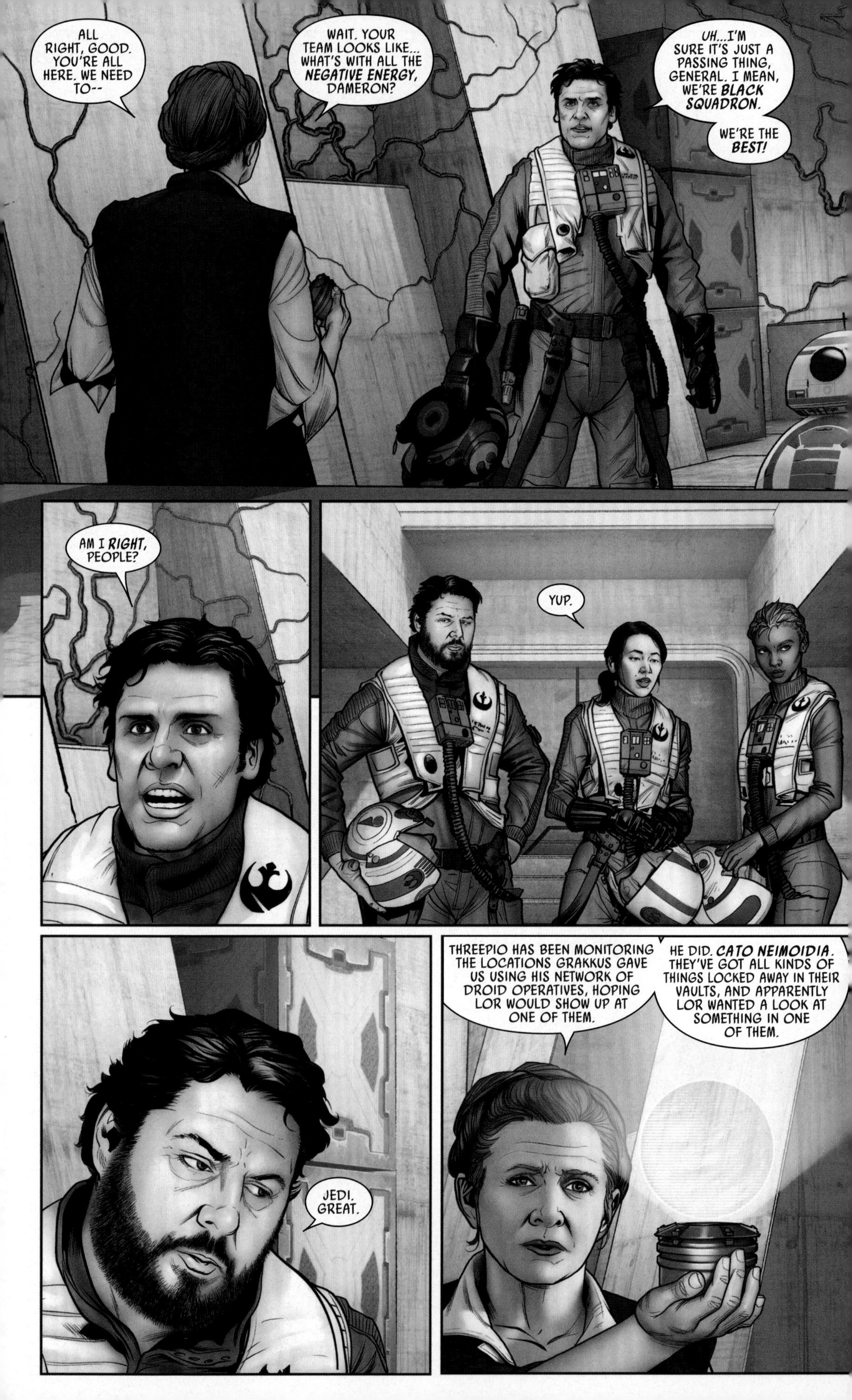
ALL RIGHT, GOOD. YOU'RE ALL HERE. WE NEED TO--
WAIT. YOUR TEAM LOOKS LIKE... WHAT'S WITH ALL THE NEGATIVE ENERGY, DAMERON?
UH...I'M SURE IT'S JUST A PASSING THING, GENERAL. I MEAN, WE'RE BLACK SQUADRON.
WE'RE THE BEST!
AM I RIGHT, PEOPLE?
YUP.
JEDI. GREAT.
THREEPIO HAS BEEN MONITORING THE LOCATIONS GRAKKUS GAVE US USING HIS NETWORK OF DROID OPERATIVES, HOPING LOR WOULD SHOW UP AT ONE OF THEM.
HE DID. CATO NEIMOIDIA. THEY'VE GOT ALL KINDS OF THINGS LOCKED AWAY IN THEIR VAULTS, AND APPARENTLY LOR WANTED A LOOK AT SOMETHING IN ONE OF THEM.

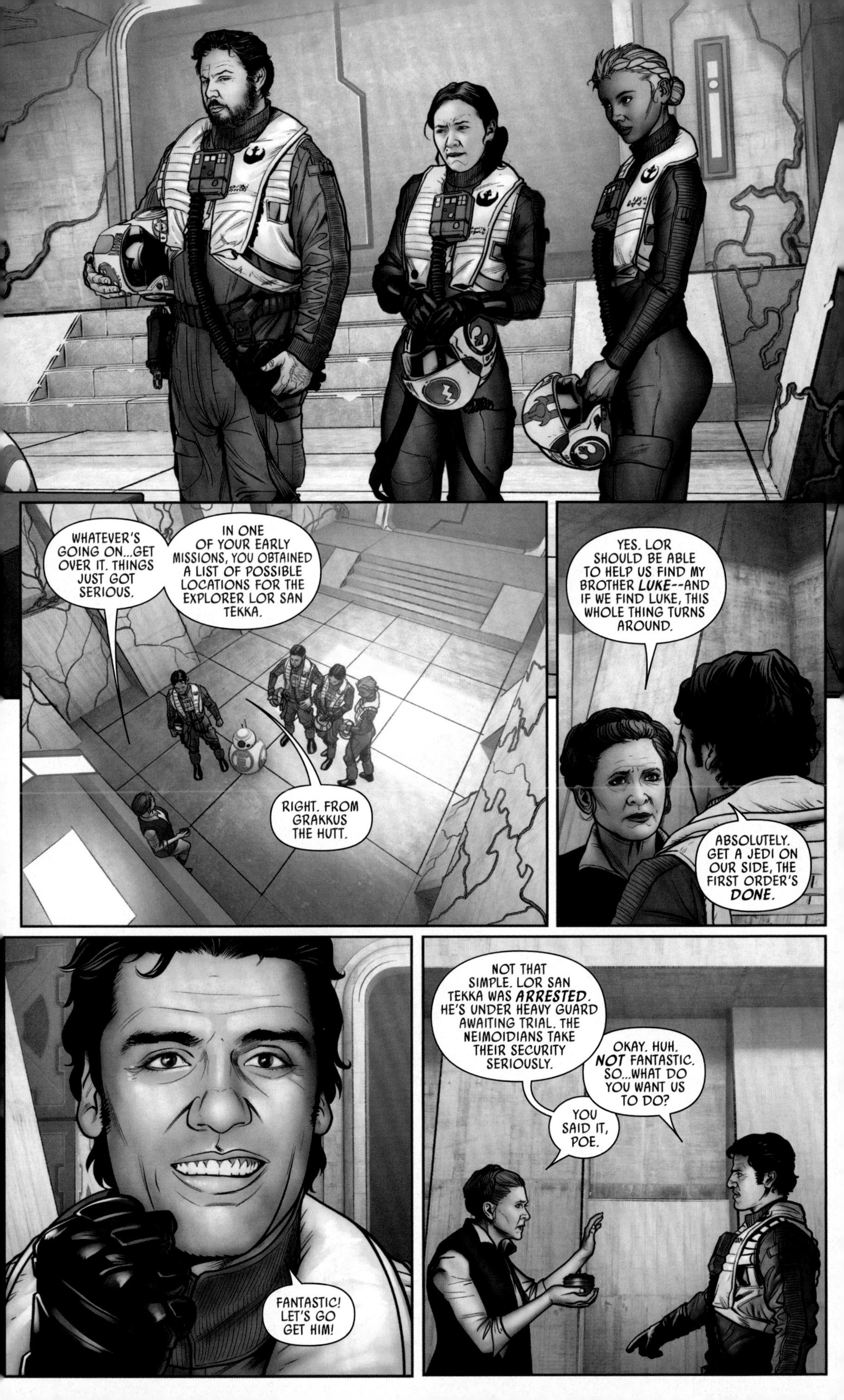
WHATEVER'S GOING ON...GET OVER IT. THINGS JUST GOT SERIOUS.
IN ONE OF YOUR EARLY MISSIONS, YOU OBTAINED A LIST OF POSSIBLE LOCATIONS FOR THE EXPLORER LOR SAN TEKKA.
RIGHT. FROM GRAKKUS THE HUTT.
YES. LOR SHOULD BE ABLE TO HELP US FIND MY BROTHER LUKE--AND IF WE FIND LUKE, THIS WHOLE THING TURNS AROUND.
ABSOLUTELY. GET A JEDI ON OUR SIDE, THE FIRST ORDER'S DONE.
FANTASTIC! LET'S GO GET HIM!
NOT THAT SIMPLE. LOR SAN TEKKA WAS ARRESTED. HE'S UNDER HEAVY GUARD AWAITING TRIAL. THE NEIMOIDIANS TAKE THEIR SECURITY SERIOUSLY.
OKAY. HUH. NOT FANTASTIC. SO...WHAT DO YOU WANT US TO DO?
YOU SAID IT, POE.

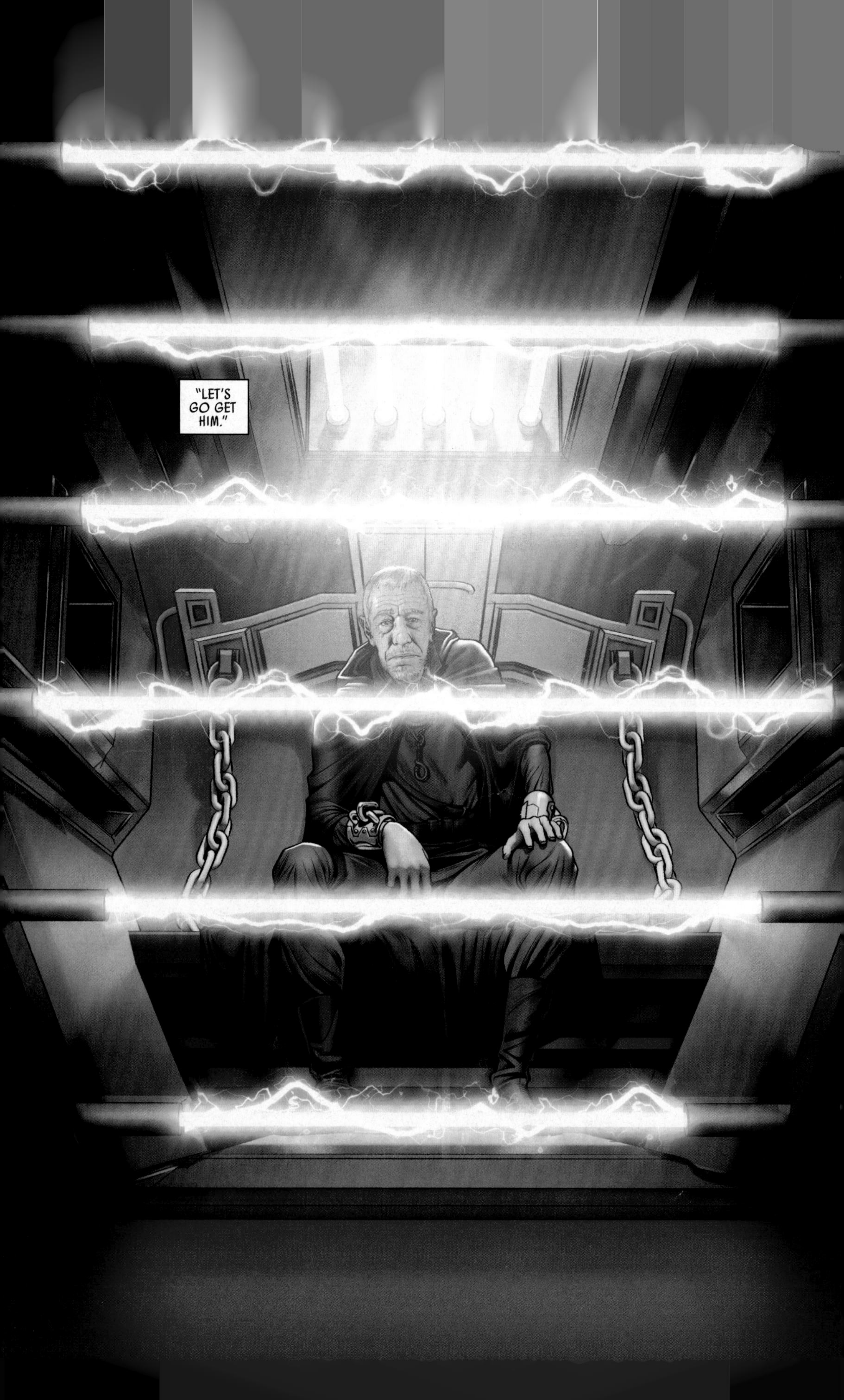
"LET'S GO GET HIM."

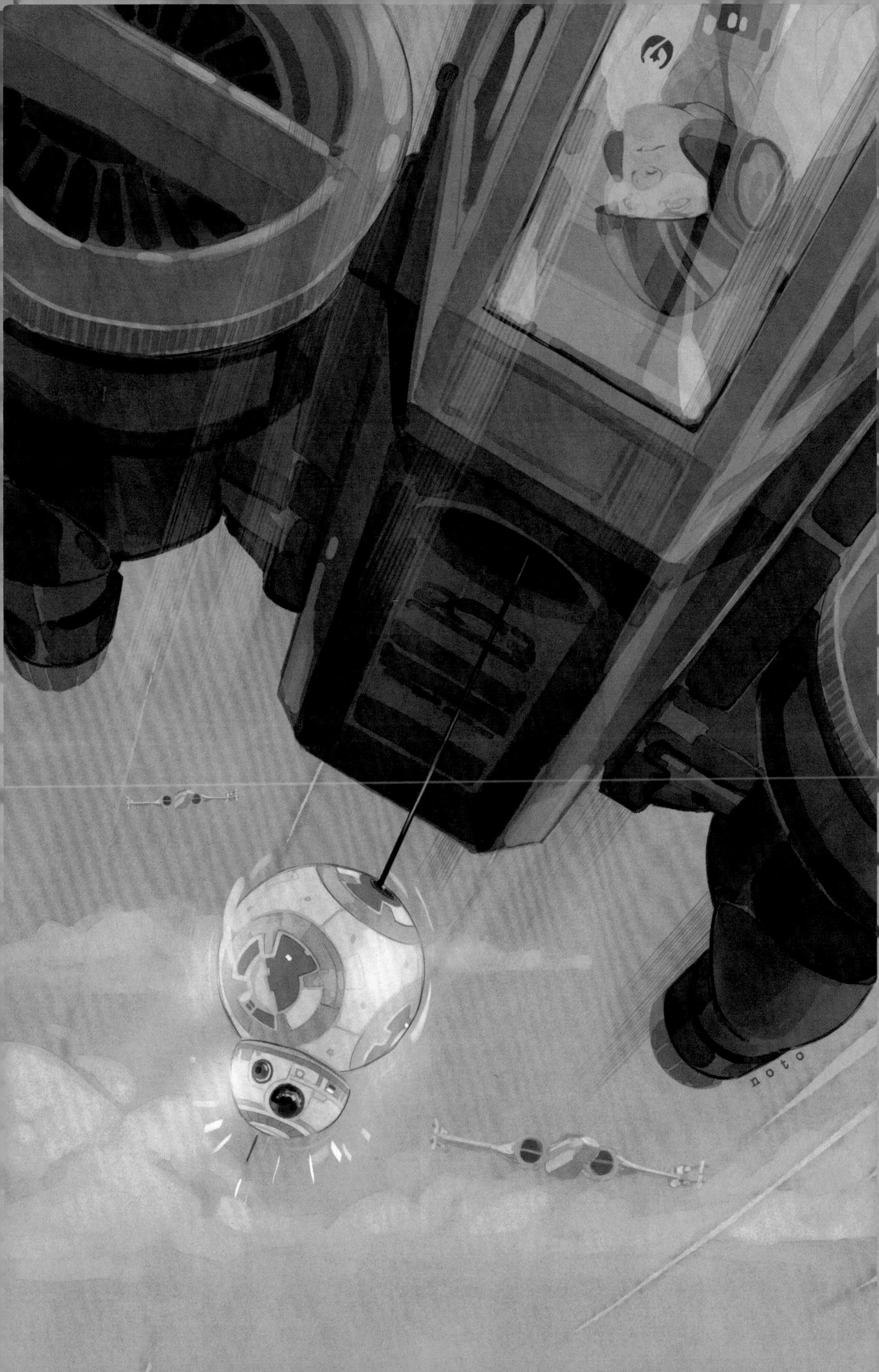
noto

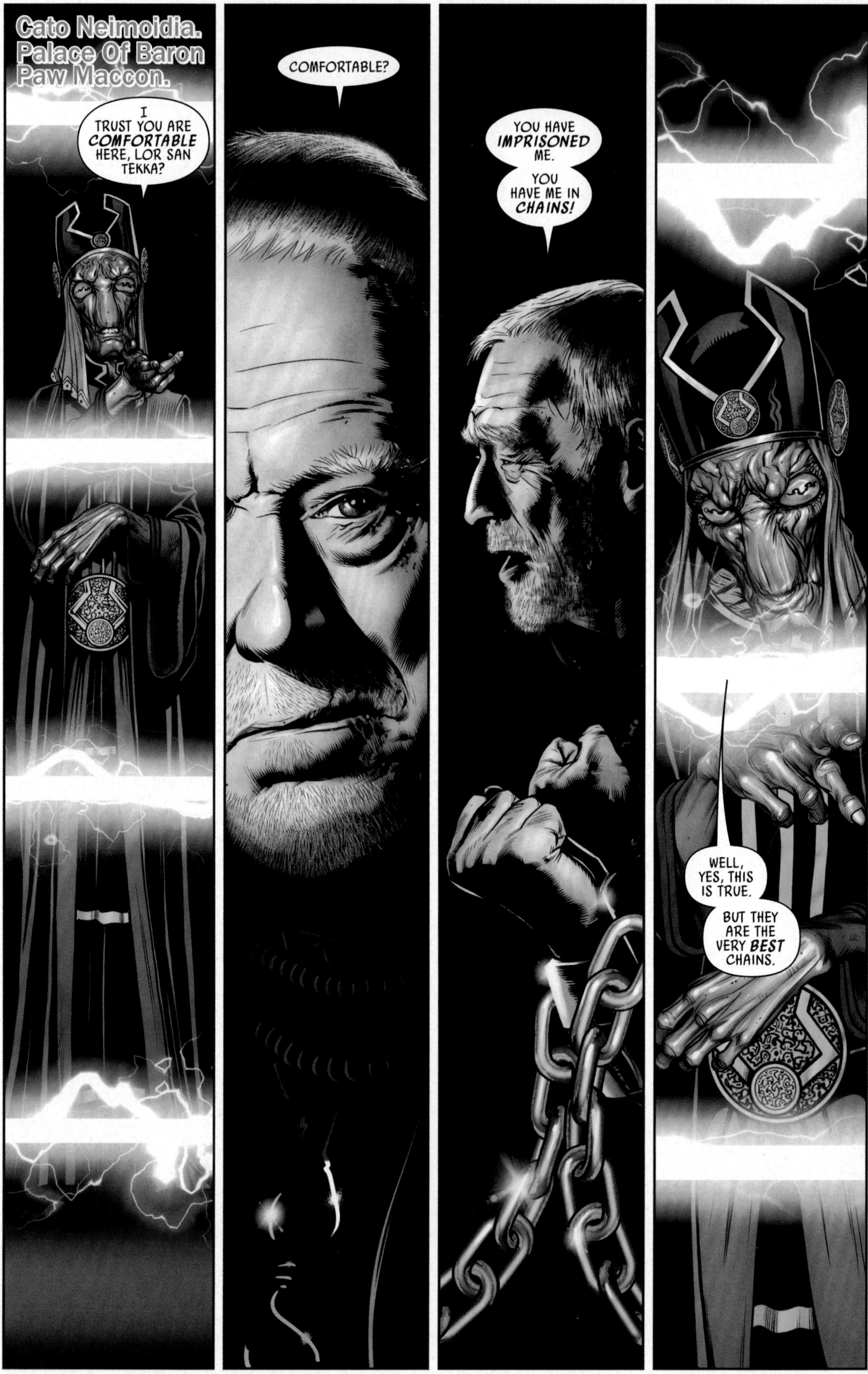
Cato Neimoidia. Palace Of Baron Paw Maccon.
I TRUST YOU ARE COMFORTABLE HERE, LOR SAN TEKKA?
COMFORTABLE?
YOU HAVE IMPRISONED ME.
YOU HAVE ME IN CHAINS!
WELL, YES, THIS IS TRUE.
BUT THEY ARE THE VERY BEST CHAINS.

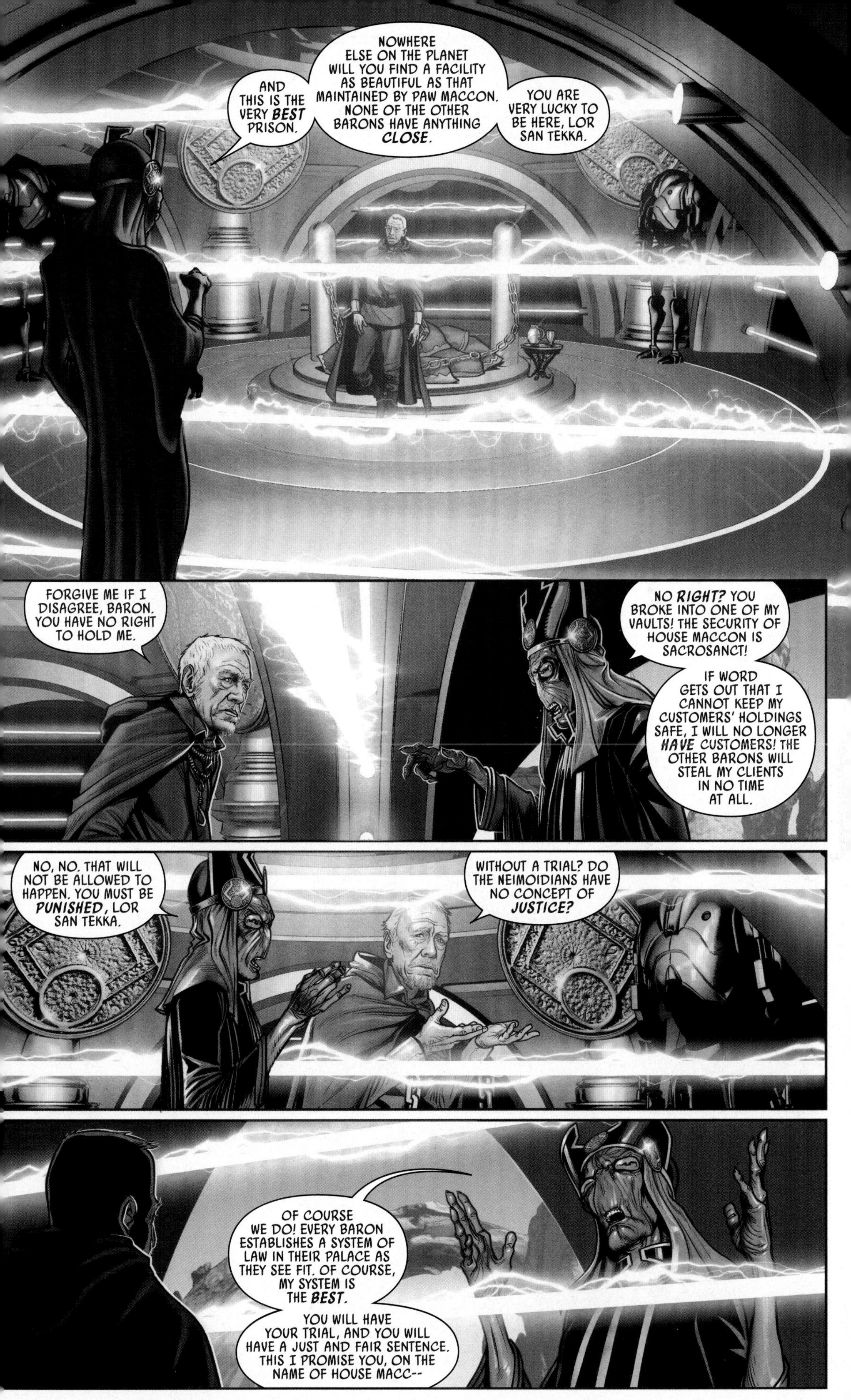
AND THIS IS THE VERY BEST PRISON.
NOWHERE ELSE ON THE PLANET WILL YOU FIND A FACILITY AS BEAUTIFUL AS THAT MAINTAINED BY PAW MACCON. NONE OF THE OTHER BARONS HAVE ANYTHING CLOSE.
YOU ARE VERY LUCKY TO BE HERE, LOR SAN TEKKA.
FORGIVE ME IF I DISAGREE, BARON. YOU HAVE NO RIGHT TO HOLD ME.
NO RIGHT? YOU BROKE INTO ONE OF MY VAULTS! THE SECURITY OF HOUSE MACCON IS SACROSANCT!
IF WORD GETS OUT THAT I CANNOT KEEP MY CUSTOMERS' HOLDINGS SAFE, I WILL NO LONGER HAVE CUSTOMERS! THE OTHER BARONS WILL STEAL MY CLIENTS IN NO TIME AT ALL.
NO, NO. THAT WILL NOT BE ALLOWED TO HAPPEN. YOU MUST BE PUNISHED, LOR SAN TEKKA.
WITHOUT A TRIAL? DO THE NEIMOIDIANS HAVE NO CONCEPT OF JUSTICE?
OF COURSE WE DO! EVERY BARON ESTABLISHES A SYSTEM OF LAW IN THEIR PALACE AS THEY SEE FIT. OF COURSE, MY SYSTEM IS THE BEST.
YOU WILL HAVE YOUR TRIAL, AND YOU WILL HAVE A JUST AND FAIR SENTENCE. THIS I PROMISE YOU, ON THE NAME OF HOUSE MACC--

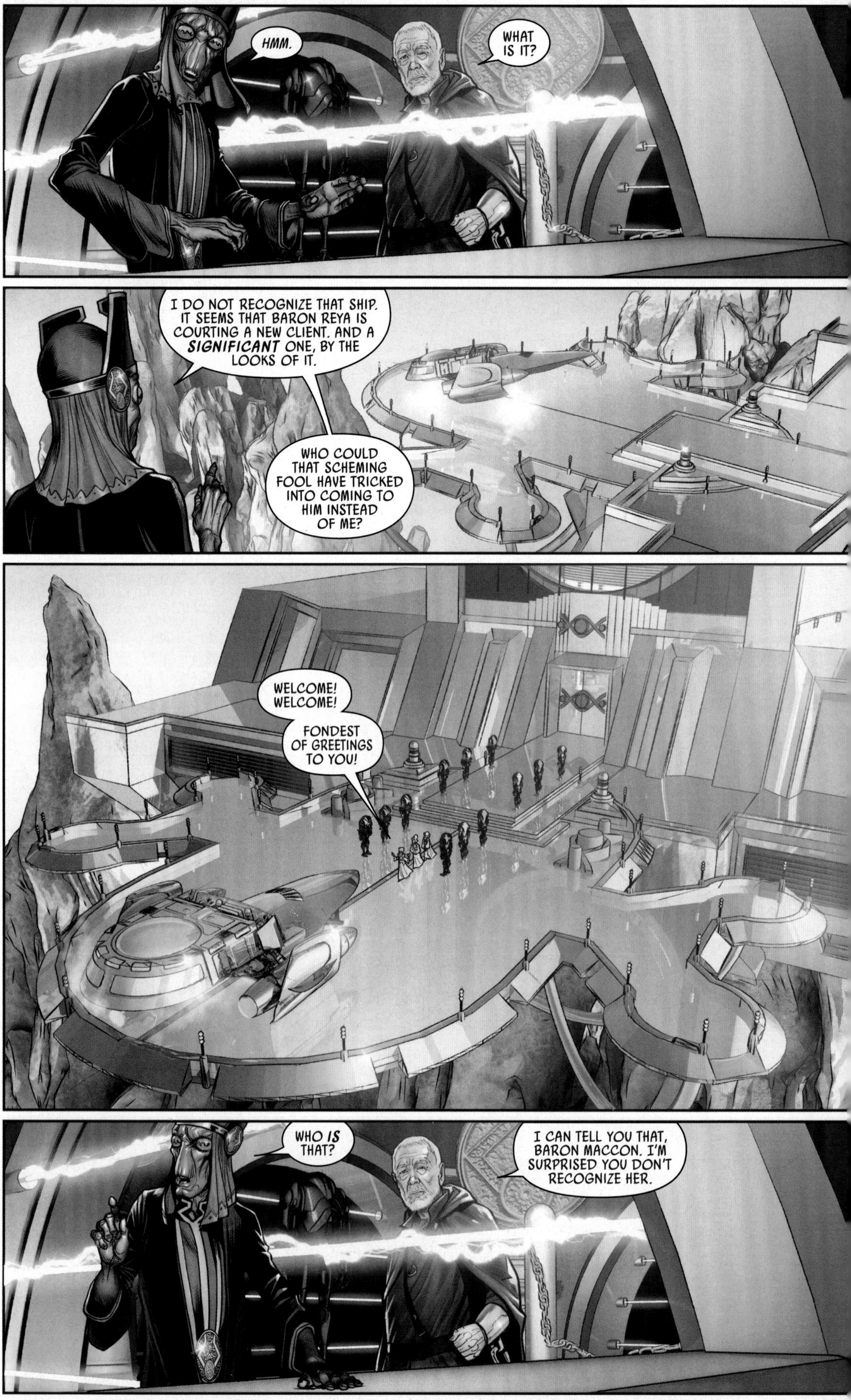
HMM.
WHAT IS IT?
I DO NOT RECOGNIZE THAT SHIP. IT SEEMS THAT BARON REYA IS COURTING A NEW CLIENT. AND A SIGNIFICANT ONE, BY THE LOOKS OF IT.
WHO COULD THAT SCHEMING FOOL HAVE TRICKED INTO COMING TO HIM INSTEAD OF ME?
WELCOME! WELCOME!
FONDEST OF GREETINGS TO YOU!
WHO IS THAT?
I CAN TELL YOU THAT, BARON MACCON. I'M SURPRISED YOU DON'T RECOGNIZE HER.

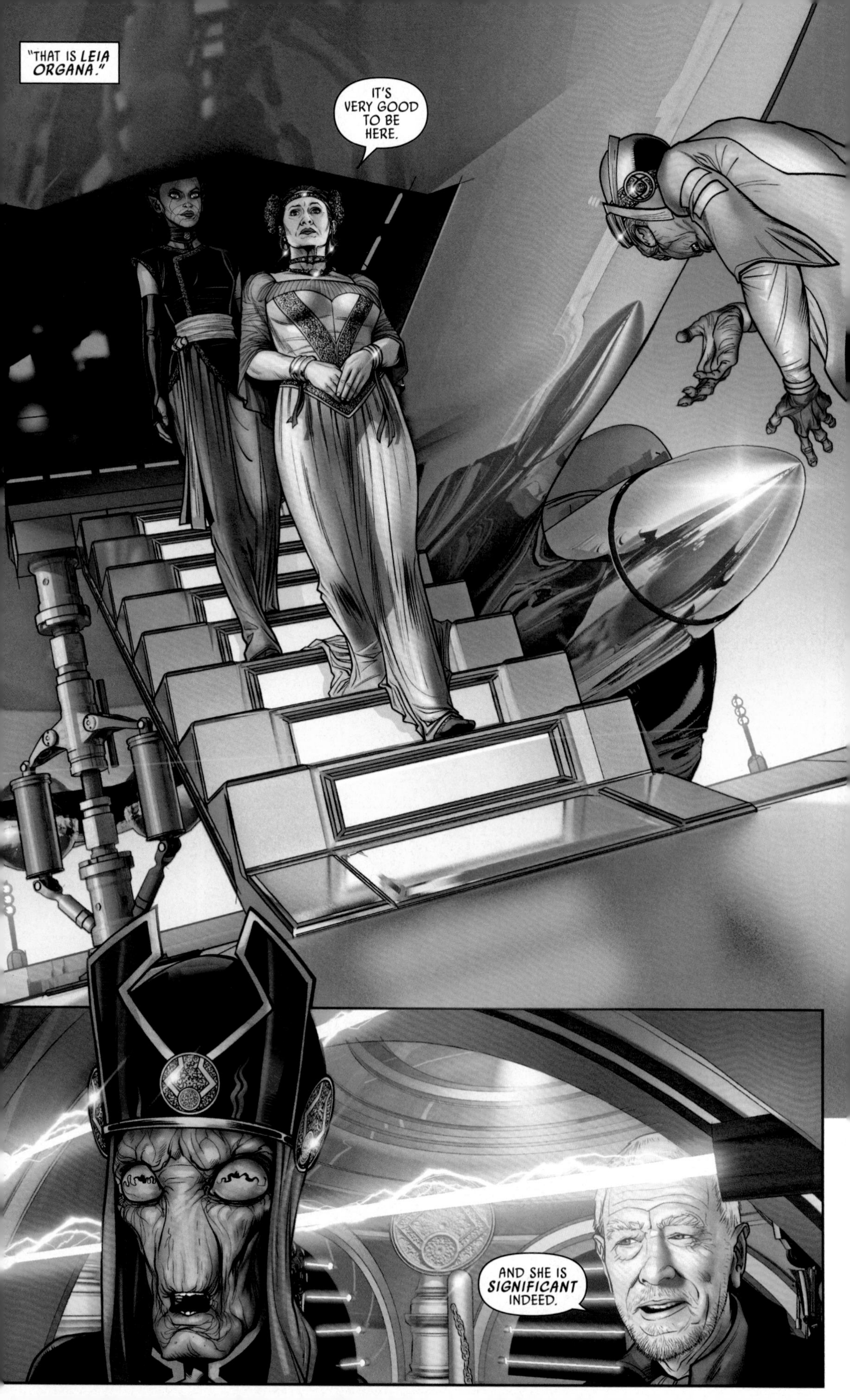
"THAT IS *LEIA ORGANA*."
IT'S VERY GOOD TO BE HERE.
AND SHE IS ***SIGNIFICANT*** INDEED.

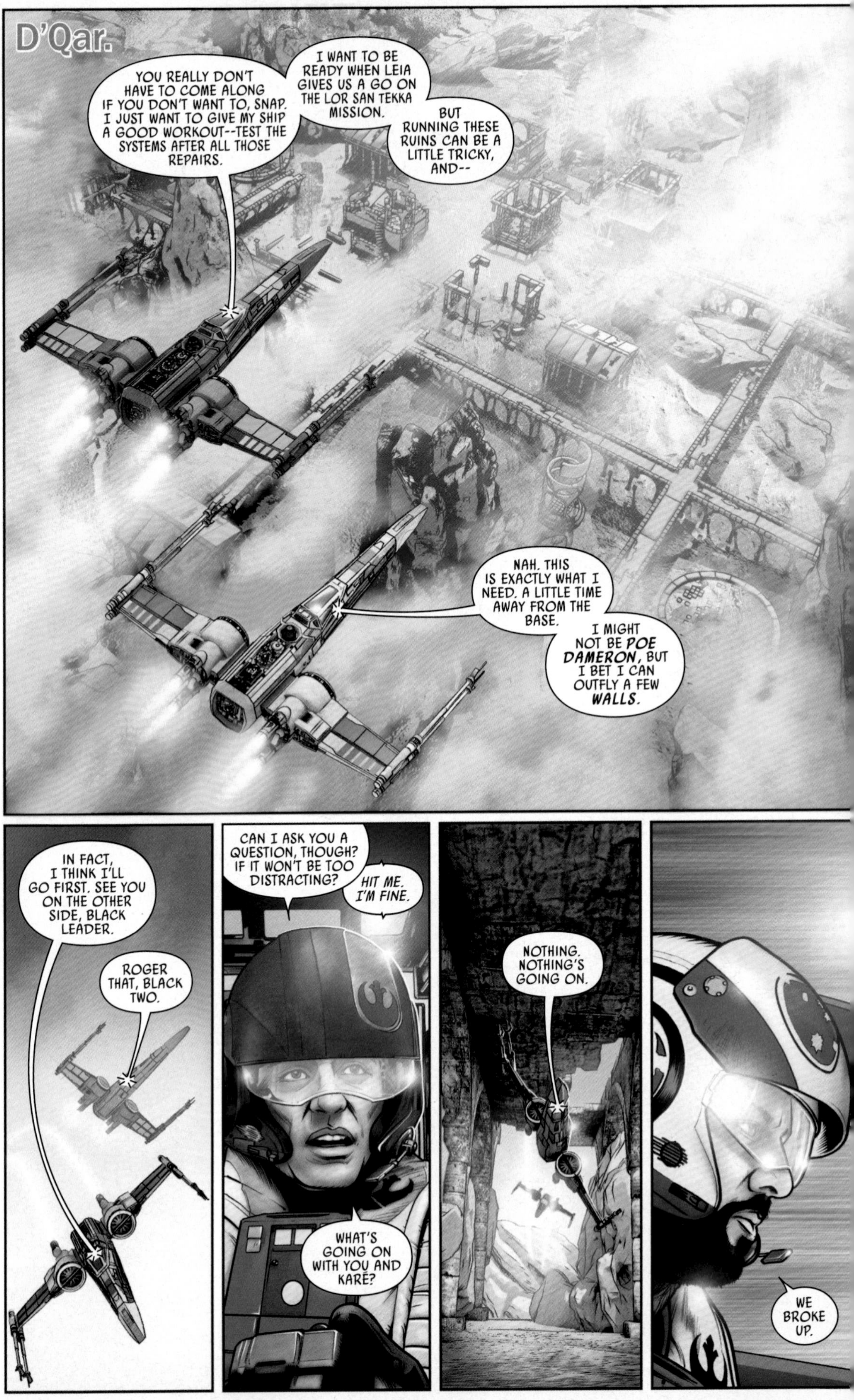
D'Qar.
YOU REALLY DON'T HAVE TO COME ALONG IF YOU DON'T WANT TO, SNAP. I JUST WANT TO GIVE MY SHIP A GOOD WORKOUT--TEST THE SYSTEMS AFTER ALL THOSE REPAIRS.
I WANT TO BE READY WHEN LEIA GIVES US A GO ON THE LOR SAN TEKKA MISSION.
BUT RUNNING THESE RUINS CAN BE A LITTLE TRICKY, AND--
NAH. THIS IS EXACTLY WHAT I NEED. A LITTLE TIME AWAY FROM THE BASE.
I MIGHT NOT BE POE DAMERON, BUT I BET I CAN OUTFLY A FEW WALLS.
IN FACT, I THINK I'LL GO FIRST. SEE YOU ON THE OTHER SIDE, BLACK LEADER.
ROGER THAT, BLACK TWO.
CAN I ASK YOU A QUESTION, THOUGH? IF IT WON'T BE TOO DISTRACTING?
HIT ME. I'M FINE.
WHAT'S GOING ON WITH YOU AND KARÉ?
NOTHING. NOTHING'S GOING ON.
WE BROKE UP.

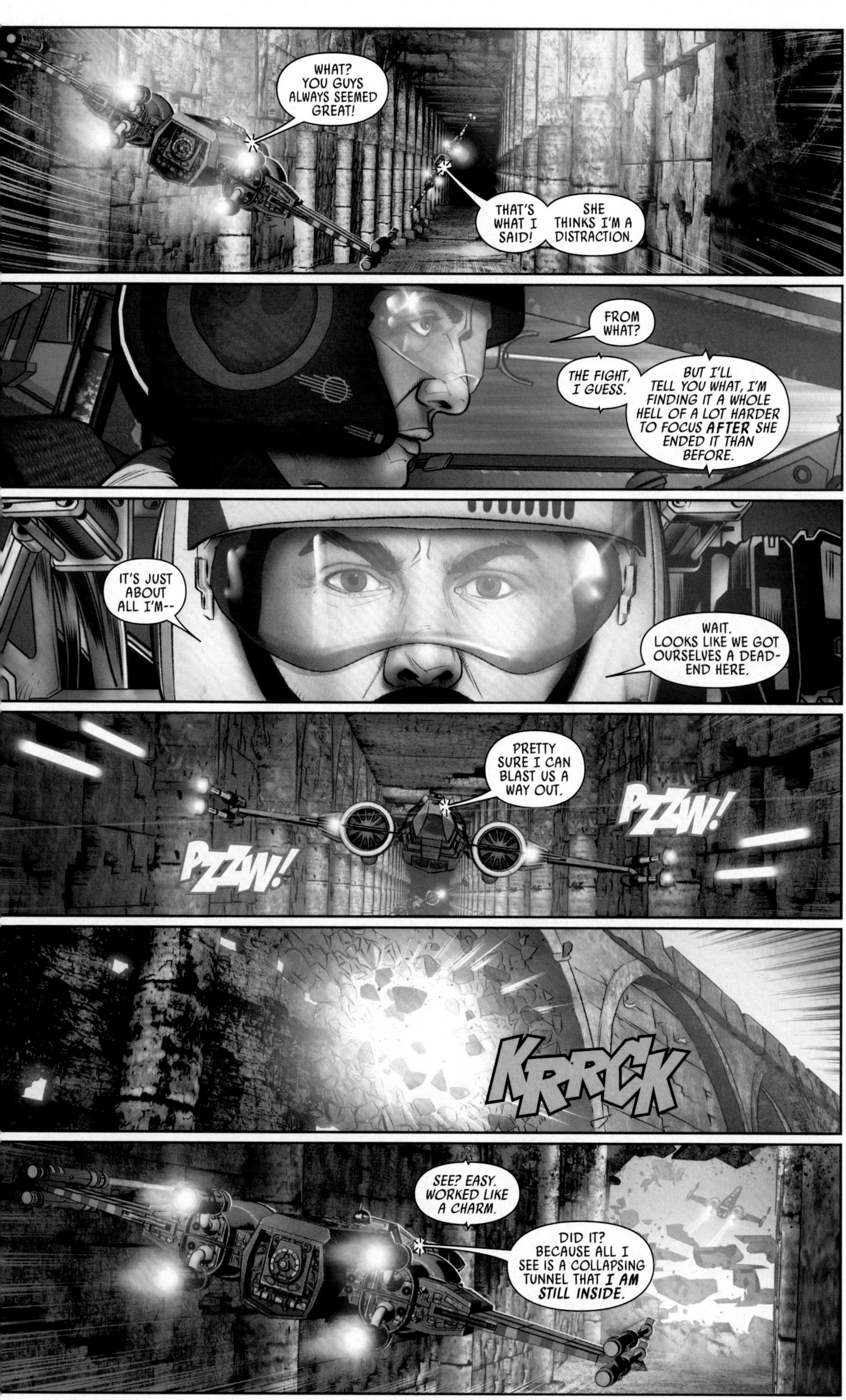
WHAT? YOU GUYS ALWAYS SEEMED GREAT!
THAT'S WHAT I SAID!
SHE THINKS I'M A DISTRACTION.
FROM WHAT?
THE FIGHT, I GUESS.
BUT I'LL TELL YOU WHAT, I'M FINDING IT A WHOLE HELL OF A LOT HARDER TO FOCUS AFTER SHE ENDED IT THAN BEFORE.
IT'S JUST ABOUT ALL I'M--
WAIT. LOOKS LIKE WE GOT OURSELVES A DEAD-END HERE.
PRETTY SURE I CAN BLAST US A WAY OUT.
PZZAW!
PZZAW!
KRRCK
SEE? EASY. WORKED LIKE A CHARM.
DID IT? BECAUSE ALL I SEE IS A COLLAPSING TUNNEL THAT I AM STILL INSIDE.

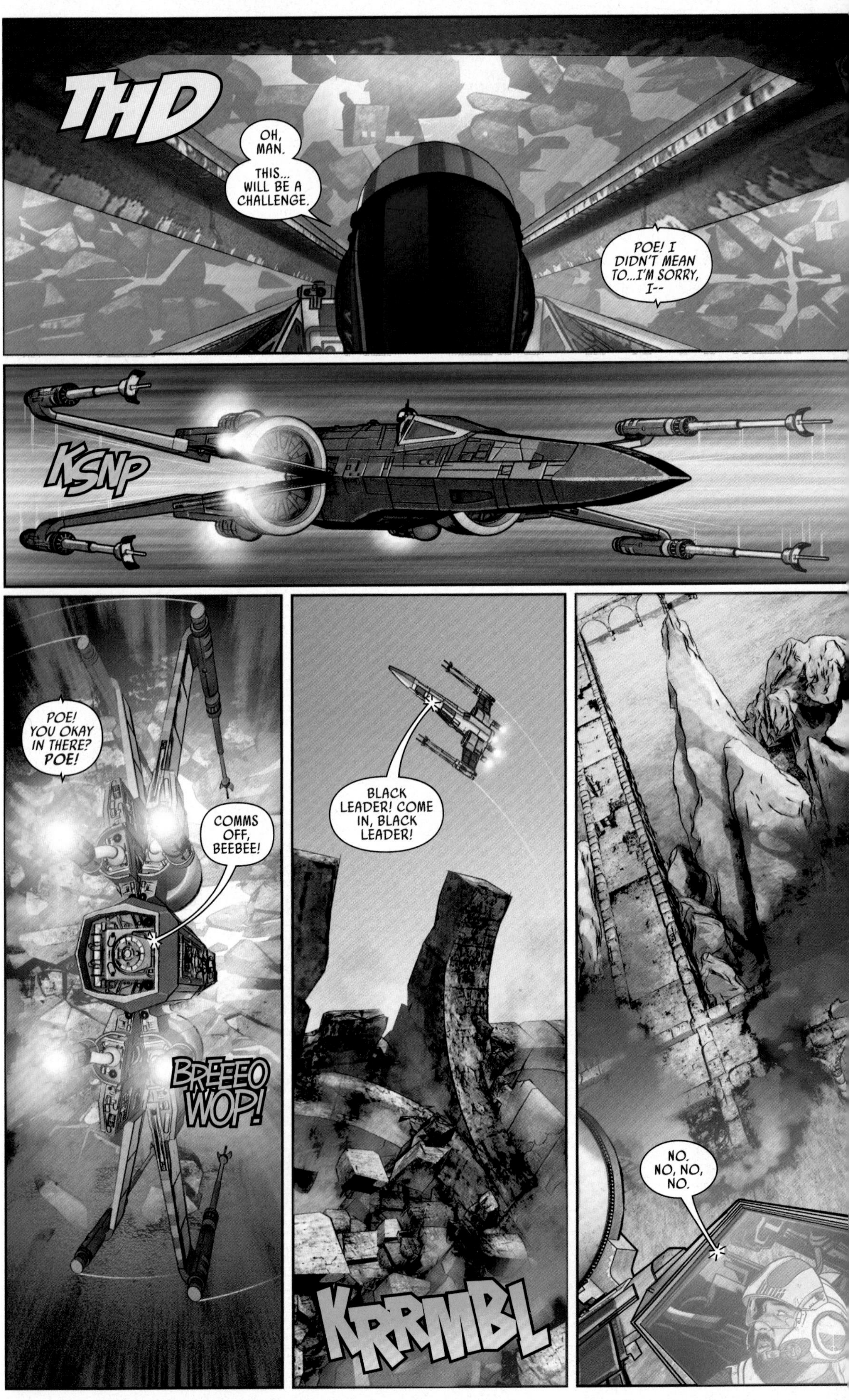
THD
OH, MAN.
THIS... WILL BE A CHALLENGE.
POE! I DIDN'T MEAN TO...I'M SORRY, I--
KSNP
POE! YOU OKAY IN THERE? POE!
COMMS OFF, BEEBEE!
BREEEO WOP!
BLACK LEADER! COME IN, BLACK LEADER!
KRRMBL
NO. NO, NO, NO.

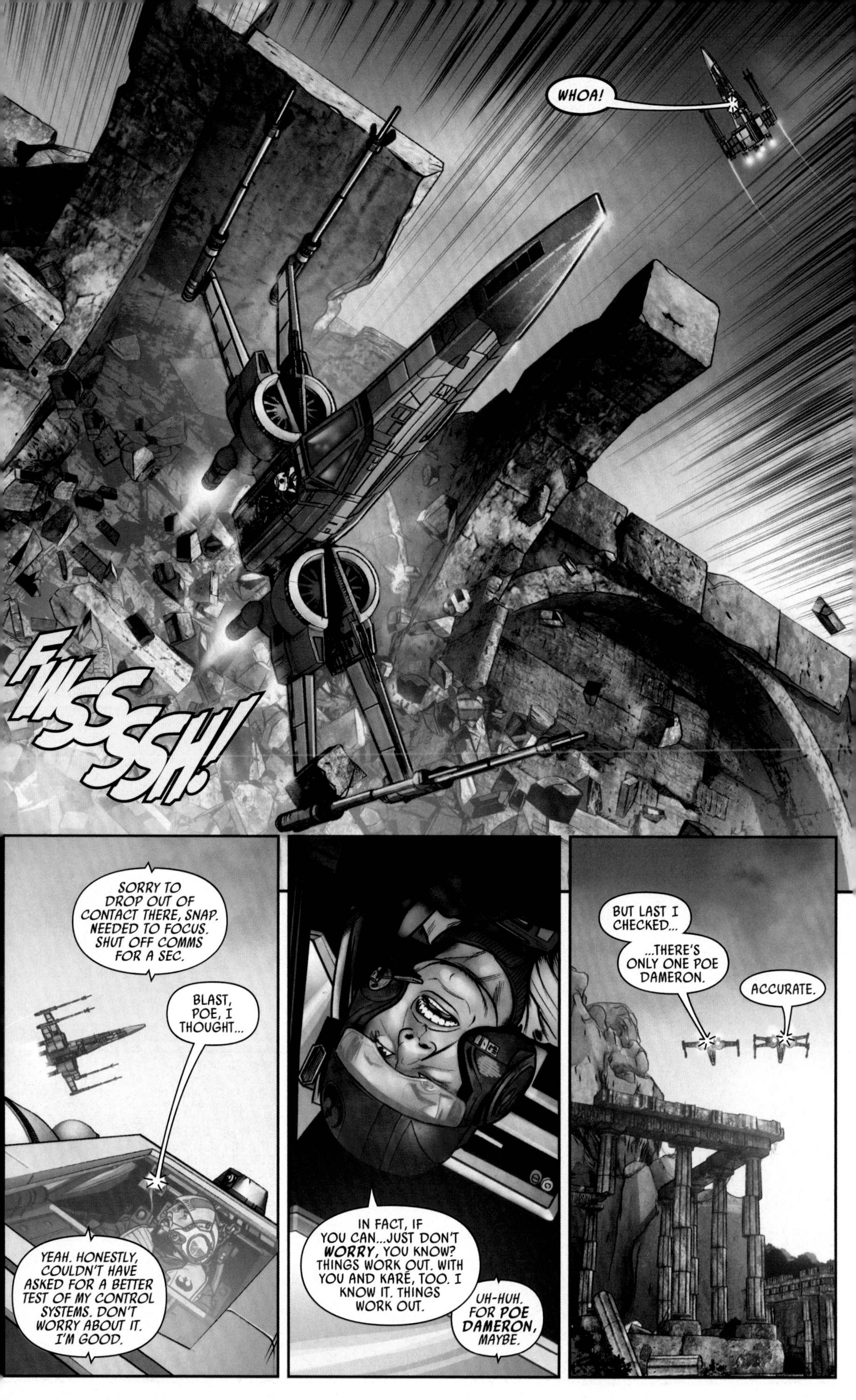
WHOA!
FWSSSH!
SORRY TO DROP OUT OF CONTACT THERE, SNAP. NEEDED TO FOCUS. SHUT OFF COMMS FOR A SEC.
BLAST, POE, I THOUGHT...
YEAH. HONESTLY, COULDN'T HAVE ASKED FOR A BETTER TEST OF MY CONTROL SYSTEMS. DON'T WORRY ABOUT IT. I'M GOOD.
IN FACT, IF YOU CAN...JUST DON'T WORRY, YOU KNOW? THINGS WORK OUT. WITH YOU AND KARÉ, TOO. I KNOW IT. THINGS WORK OUT.
UH-HUH. FOR POE DAMERON, MAYBE.
BUT LAST I CHECKED...
...THERE'S ONLY ONE POE DAMERON.
ACCURATE.

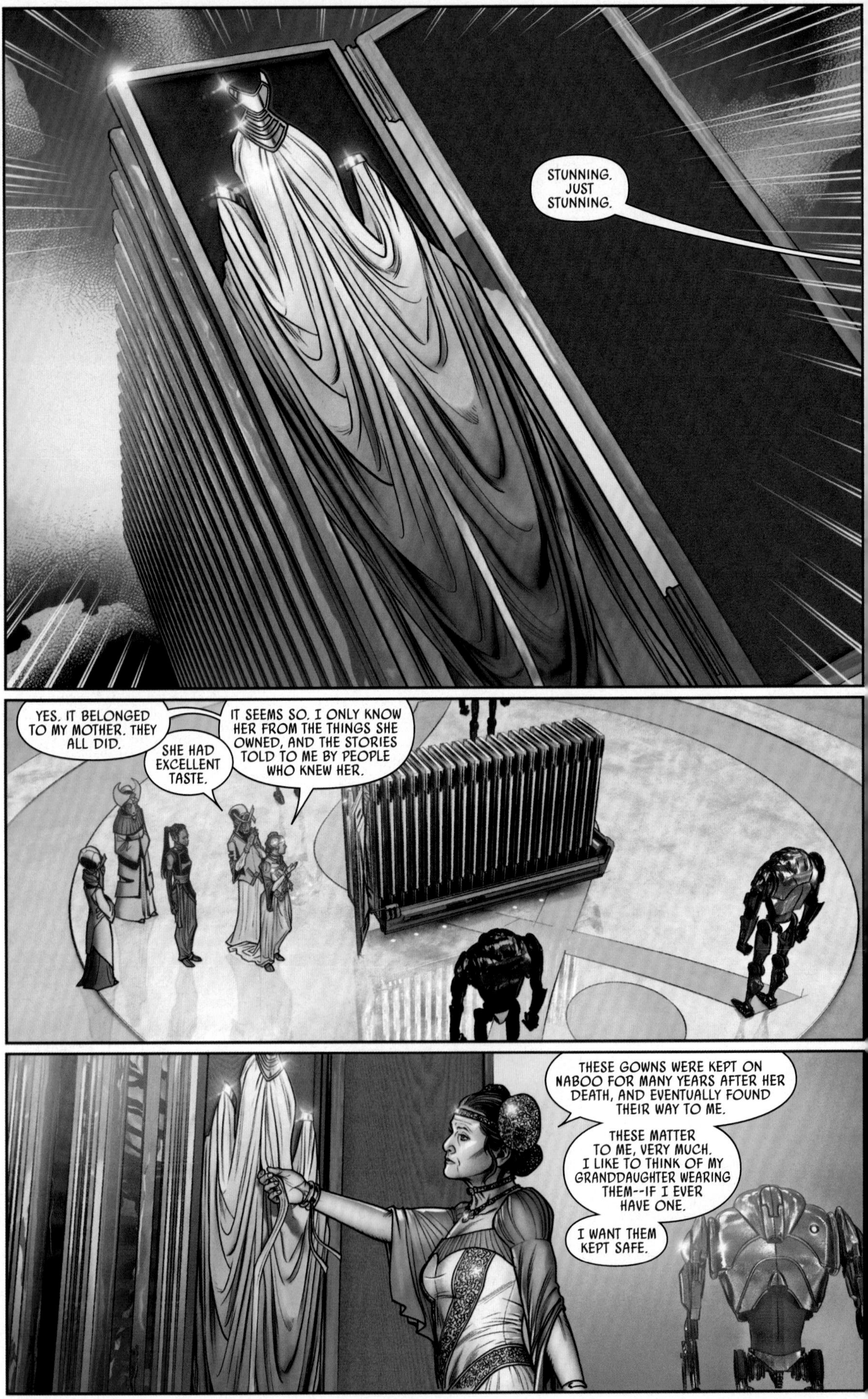
STUNNING. JUST STUNNING.
YES. IT BELONGED TO MY MOTHER. THEY ALL DID.
SHE HAD EXCELLENT TASTE.
IT SEEMS SO. I ONLY KNOW HER FROM THE THINGS SHE OWNED, AND THE STORIES TOLD TO ME BY PEOPLE WHO KNEW HER.
THESE GOWNS WERE KEPT ON NABOO FOR MANY YEARS AFTER HER DEATH, AND EVENTUALLY FOUND THEIR WAY TO ME.
THESE MATTER TO ME, VERY MUCH. I LIKE TO THINK OF MY GRANDDAUGHTER WEARING THEM--IF I EVER HAVE ONE.
I WANT THEM KEPT SAFE.

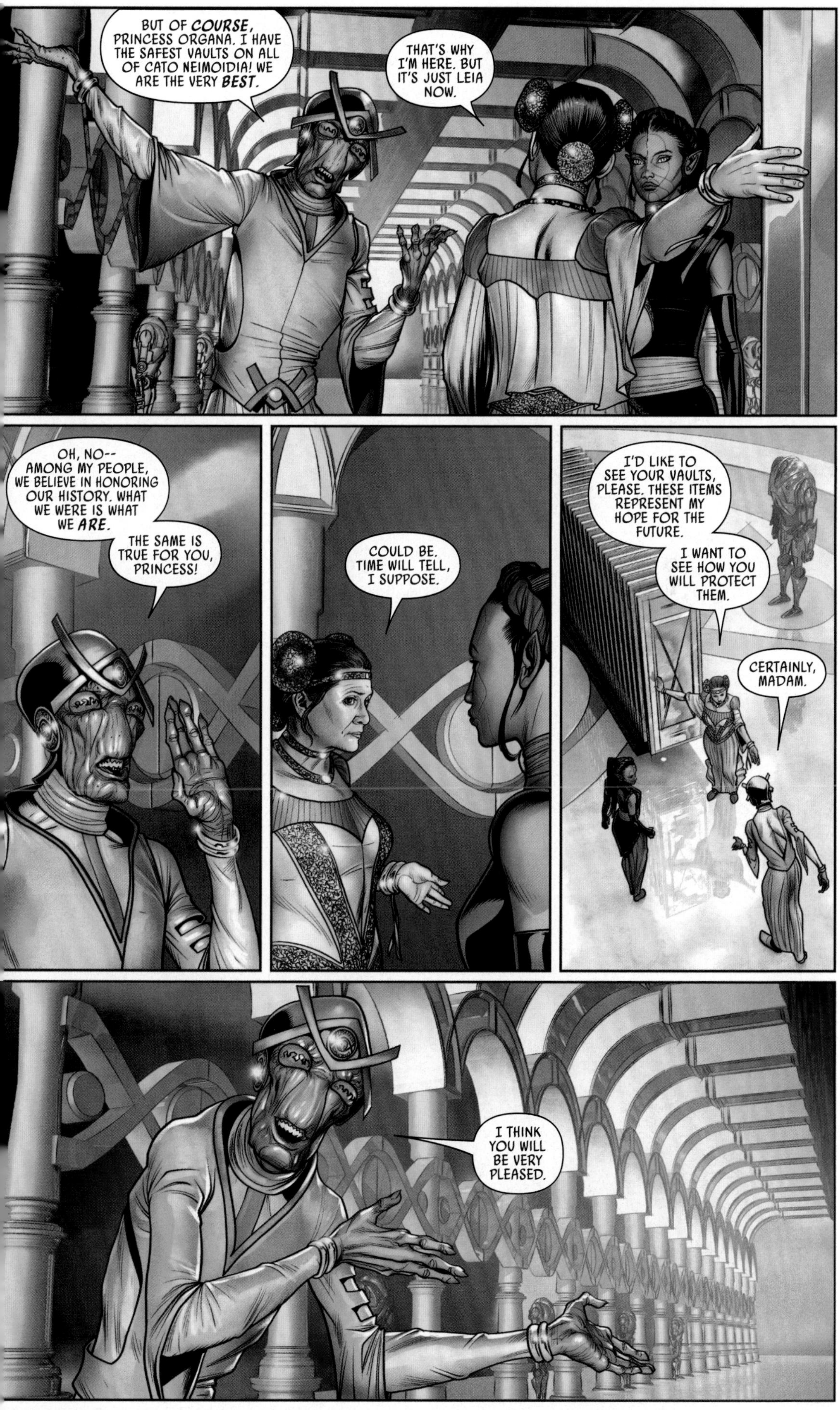

BUT OF COURSE, PRINCESS ORGANA. I HAVE THE SAFEST VAULTS ON ALL OF CATO NEIMOIDIA! WE ARE THE VERY BEST.
THAT'S WHY I'M HERE. BUT IT'S JUST LEIA NOW.
OH, NO-- AMONG MY PEOPLE, WE BELIEVE IN HONORING OUR HISTORY. WHAT WE WERE IS WHAT WE ARE.
THE SAME IS TRUE FOR YOU, PRINCESS!
COULD BE. TIME WILL TELL, I SUPPOSE.
I'D LIKE TO SEE YOUR VAULTS, PLEASE. THESE ITEMS REPRESENT MY HOPE FOR THE FUTURE.
I WANT TO SEE HOW YOU WILL PROTECT THEM.
CERTAINLY, MADAM.
I THINK YOU WILL BE VERY PLEASED.

COME ON, YOU...

BWIP BAH WOW?

OH, HEY, BEEBEE. I GUESS POE AND SNAP ARE BACK FROM THAT TEST FLIGHT, HUH?

WHEEO-WOO.

BARELY? WHAT DOES THAT M-- EH, NEVER MIND. IF THEY MADE IT BACK, THEY MADE IT BACK.

ANYWAY, I'M MODIFYING MY SHIP TO FLY WITHOUT AN ASTROMECH. IT'S NOT EASY, BUT I FIGURE IF I CAN PATCH IN SOME KIND OF NAVICOMPUTER... YOU KNOW.

WHEE BADA WIP?

OF *COURSE* IT WILL WORK.

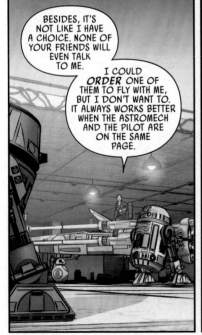

BESIDES, IT'S NOT LIKE I HAVE A CHOICE. NONE OF YOUR FRIENDS WILL EVEN TALK TO ME.

I COULD *ORDER* ONE OF THEM TO FLY WITH ME, BUT I DON'T WANT TO. IT ALWAYS WORKS BETTER WHEN THE ASTROMECH AND THE PILOT ARE ON THE SAME PAGE.

I HAVE TO FLY, THOUGH. YOU KNOW THE MISSION BLACK SQUADRON HAS COMING UP. *I HAVE TO FLY.*

IT'LL BE FINE. THIS WILL WORK.

I KNOW IT.

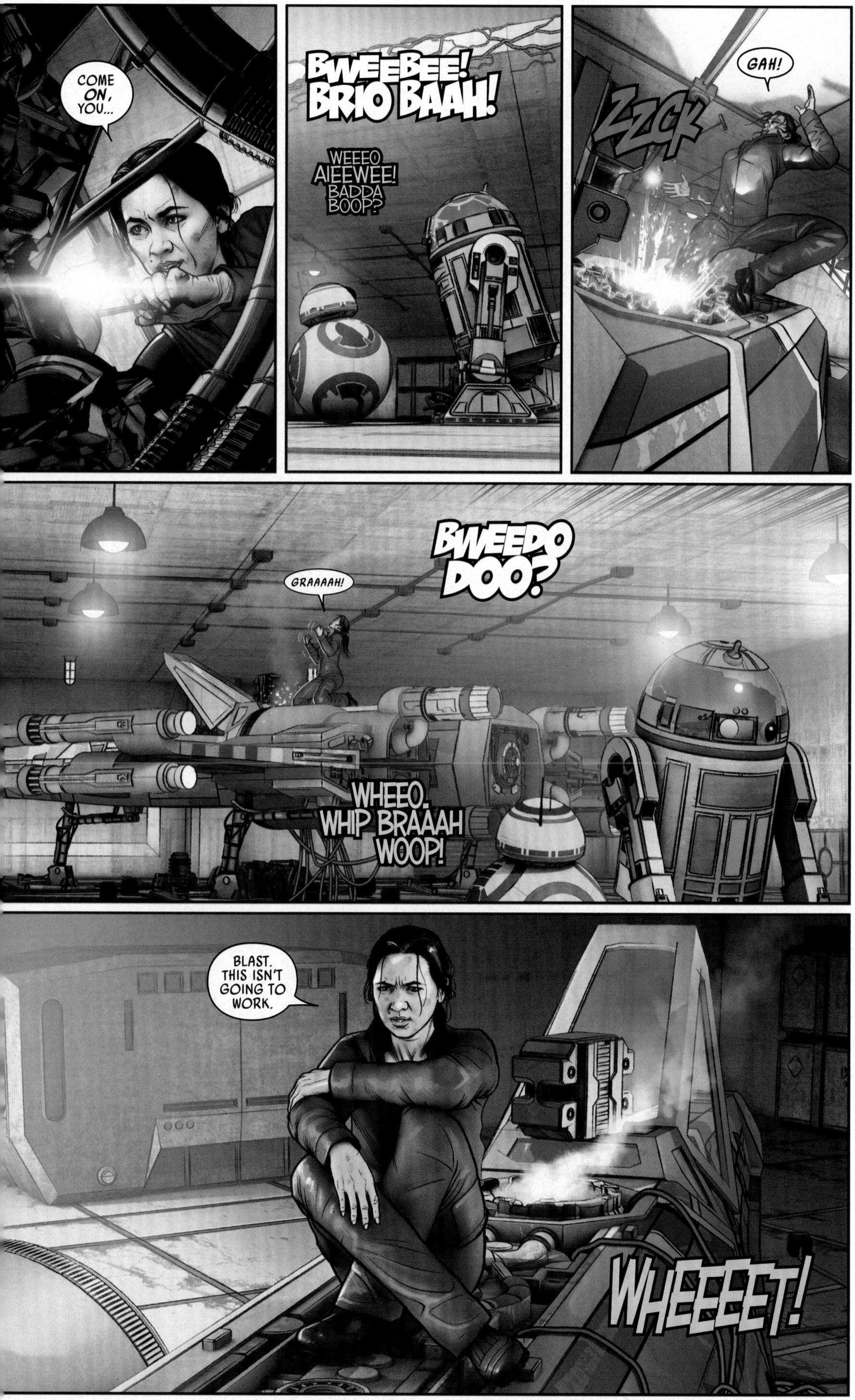
COME ON, YOU...
BWEEBEE! BRIO BAAH!
WEEEO AIEEWEE! BADDA BOOP?
GAH!
ZZZCK
GRAAAAH!
BWEEDO DOO?
WHEEO. WHIP BRAAAH WOOP!
BLAST. THIS ISN'T GOING TO WORK.
WHEEEET!

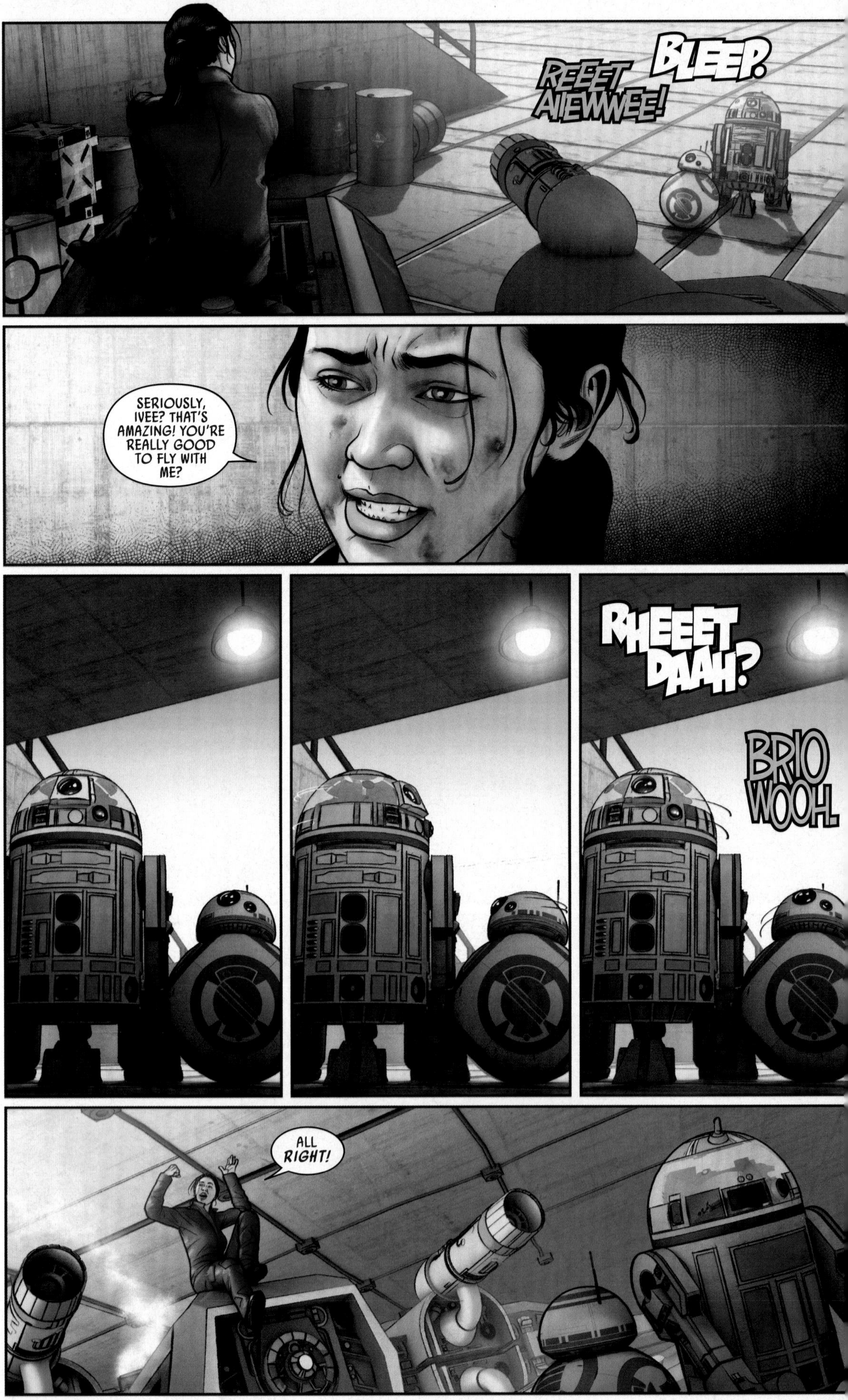
REEET AIEWWEE!
BLEEP.
SERIOUSLY, IVEE? THAT'S AMAZING! YOU'RE REALLY GOOD TO FLY WITH ME?
RHEEET DAAH?
BRIO WOOH.
ALL RIGHT!

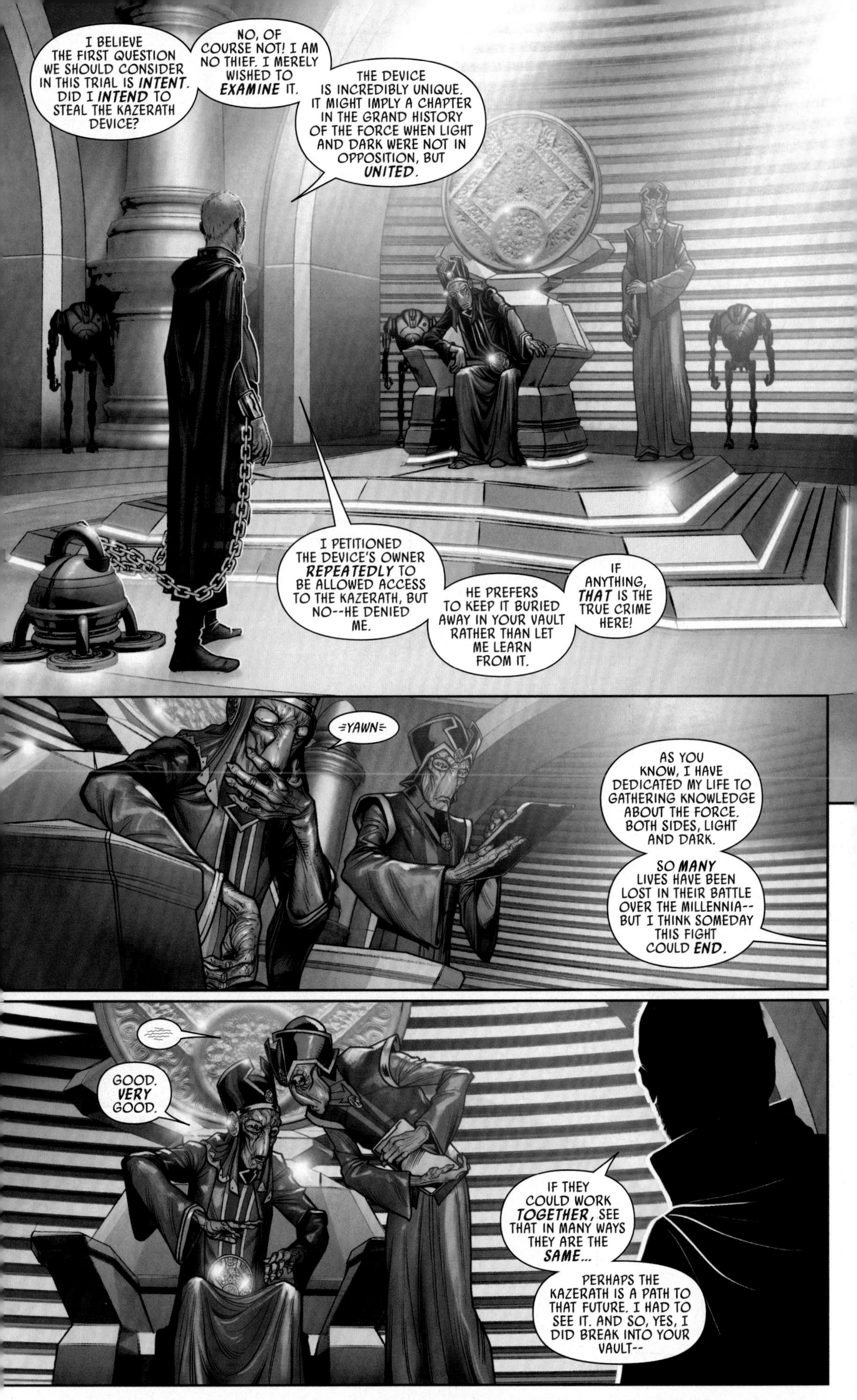
I BELIEVE THE FIRST QUESTION WE SHOULD CONSIDER IN THIS TRIAL IS INTENT. DID I INTEND TO STEAL THE KAZERATH DEVICE?
NO, OF COURSE NOT! I AM NO THIEF. I MERELY WISHED TO EXAMINE IT.
THE DEVICE IS INCREDIBLY UNIQUE. IT MIGHT IMPLY A CHAPTER IN THE GRAND HISTORY OF THE FORCE WHEN LIGHT AND DARK WERE NOT IN OPPOSITION, BUT UNITED.
I PETITIONED THE DEVICE'S OWNER REPEATEDLY TO BE ALLOWED ACCESS TO THE KAZERATH, BUT NO--HE DENIED ME.
HE PREFERS TO KEEP IT BURIED AWAY IN YOUR VAULT RATHER THAN LET ME LEARN FROM IT.
IF ANYTHING, THAT IS THE TRUE CRIME HERE!
=YAWN=
AS YOU KNOW, I HAVE DEDICATED MY LIFE TO GATHERING KNOWLEDGE ABOUT THE FORCE. BOTH SIDES, LIGHT AND DARK.
SO MANY LIVES HAVE BEEN LOST IN THEIR BATTLE OVER THE MILLENNIA-- BUT I THINK SOMEDAY THIS FIGHT COULD END.
GOOD. VERY GOOD.
IF THEY COULD WORK TOGETHER, SEE THAT IN MANY WAYS THEY ARE THE SAME...
PERHAPS THE KAZERATH IS A PATH TO THAT FUTURE. I HAD TO SEE IT. AND SO, YES, I DID BREAK INTO YOUR VAULT--

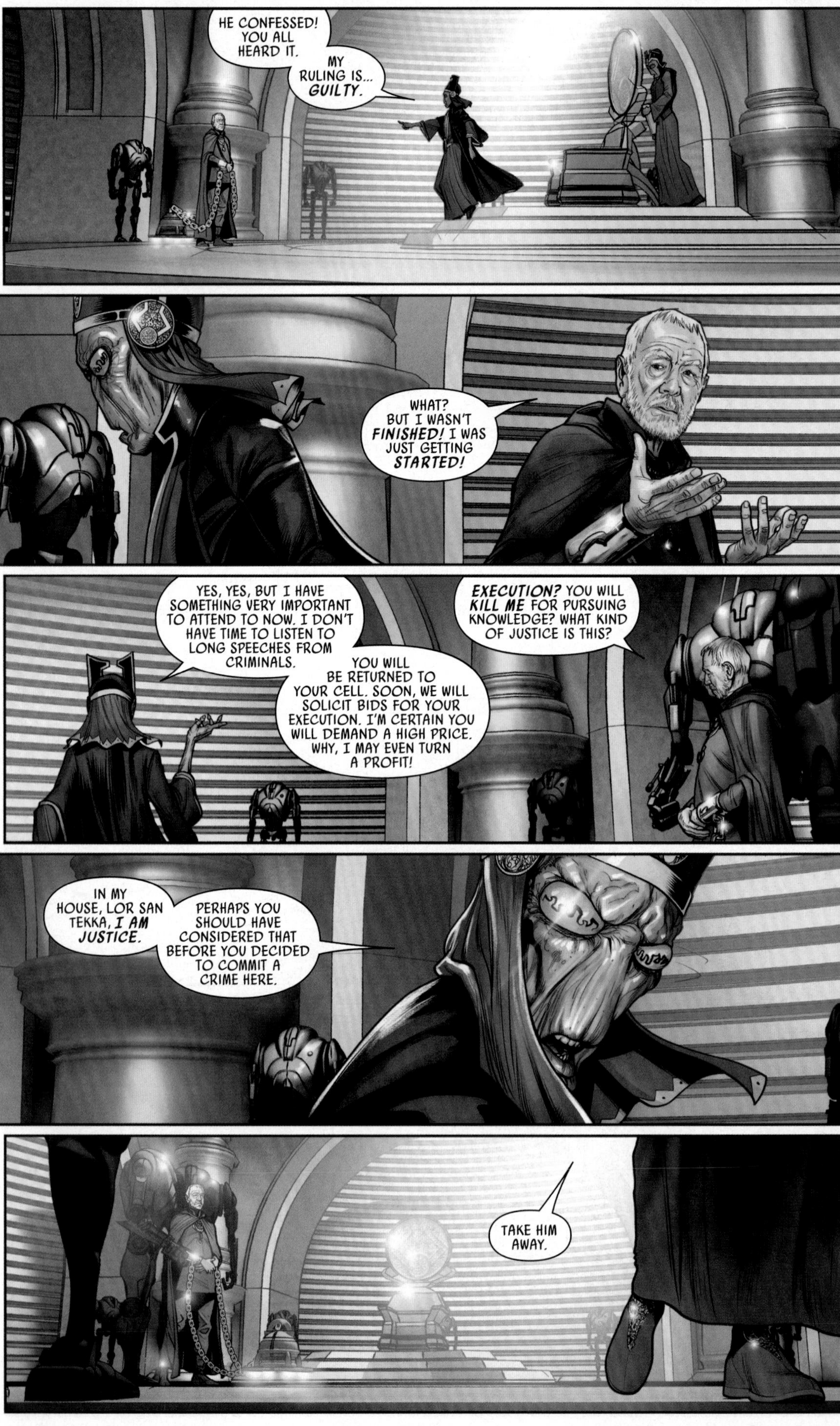
HE CONFESSED! YOU ALL HEARD IT.
MY RULING IS... GUILTY.
WHAT? BUT I WASN'T FINISHED! I WAS JUST GETTING STARTED!
YES, YES, BUT I HAVE SOMETHING VERY IMPORTANT TO ATTEND TO NOW. I DON'T HAVE TIME TO LISTEN TO LONG SPEECHES FROM CRIMINALS.
YOU WILL BE RETURNED TO YOUR CELL. SOON, WE WILL SOLICIT BIDS FOR YOUR EXECUTION. I'M CERTAIN YOU WILL DEMAND A HIGH PRICE. WHY, I MAY EVEN TURN A PROFIT!
EXECUTION? YOU WILL KILL ME FOR PURSUING KNOWLEDGE? WHAT KIND OF JUSTICE IS THIS?
IN MY HOUSE, LOR SAN TEKKA, I AM JUSTICE.
PERHAPS YOU SHOULD HAVE CONSIDERED THAT BEFORE YOU DECIDED TO COMMIT A CRIME HERE.
TAKE HIM AWAY.

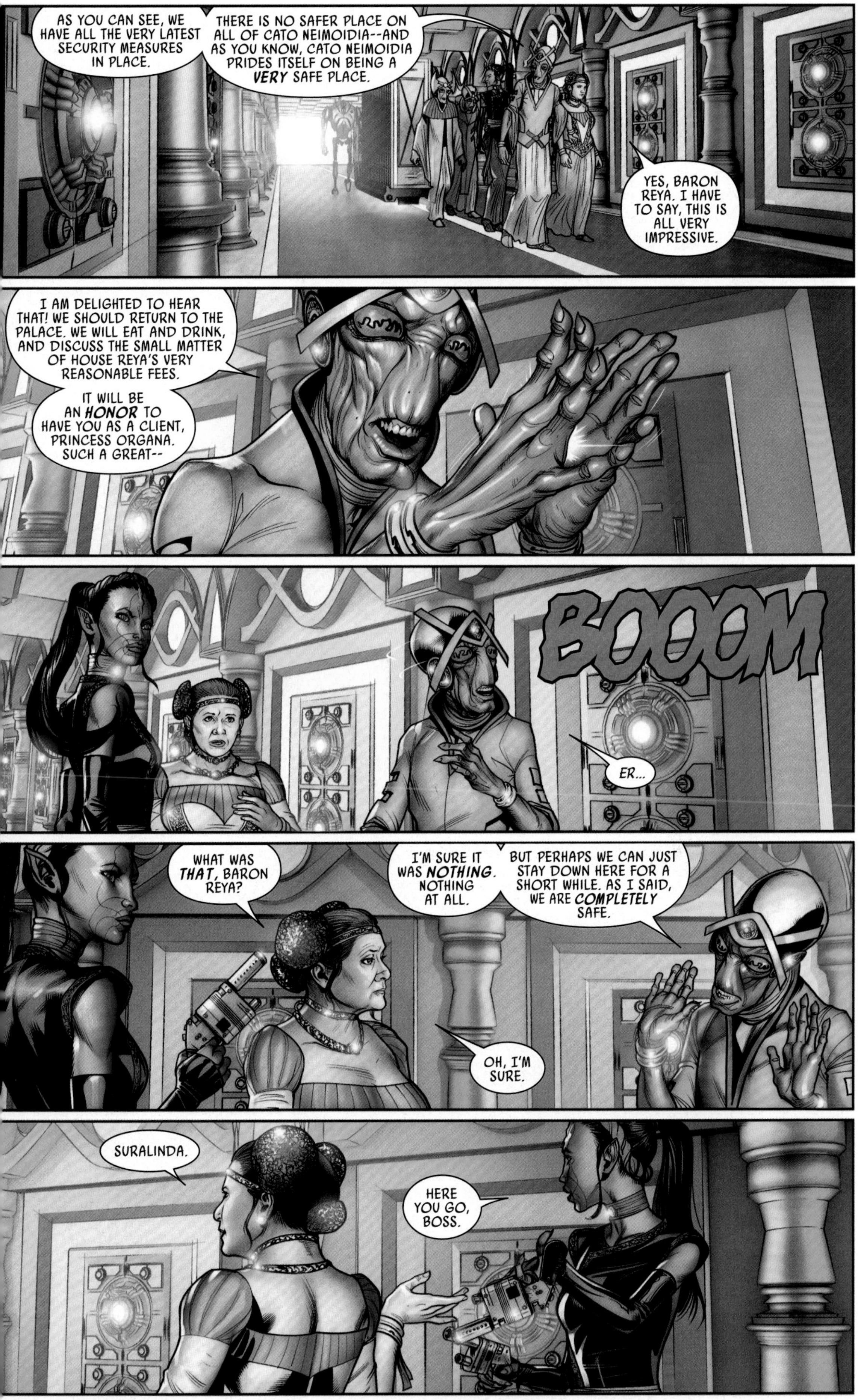
AS YOU CAN SEE, WE HAVE ALL THE VERY LATEST SECURITY MEASURES IN PLACE.
THERE IS NO SAFER PLACE ON ALL OF CATO NEIMOIDIA--AND AS YOU KNOW, CATO NEIMOIDIA PRIDES ITSELF ON BEING A VERY SAFE PLACE.
YES, BARON REYA. I HAVE TO SAY, THIS IS ALL VERY IMPRESSIVE.
I AM DELIGHTED TO HEAR THAT! WE SHOULD RETURN TO THE PALACE. WE WILL EAT AND DRINK, AND DISCUSS THE SMALL MATTER OF HOUSE REYA'S VERY REASONABLE FEES.
IT WILL BE AN HONOR TO HAVE YOU AS A CLIENT, PRINCESS ORGANA. SUCH A GREAT--
BOOOM
ER...
WHAT WAS THAT, BARON REYA?
I'M SURE IT WAS NOTHING. NOTHING AT ALL.
BUT PERHAPS WE CAN JUST STAY DOWN HERE FOR A SHORT WHILE. AS I SAID, WE ARE COMPLETELY SAFE.
OH, I'M SURE.
SURALINDA.
HERE YOU GO, BOSS.

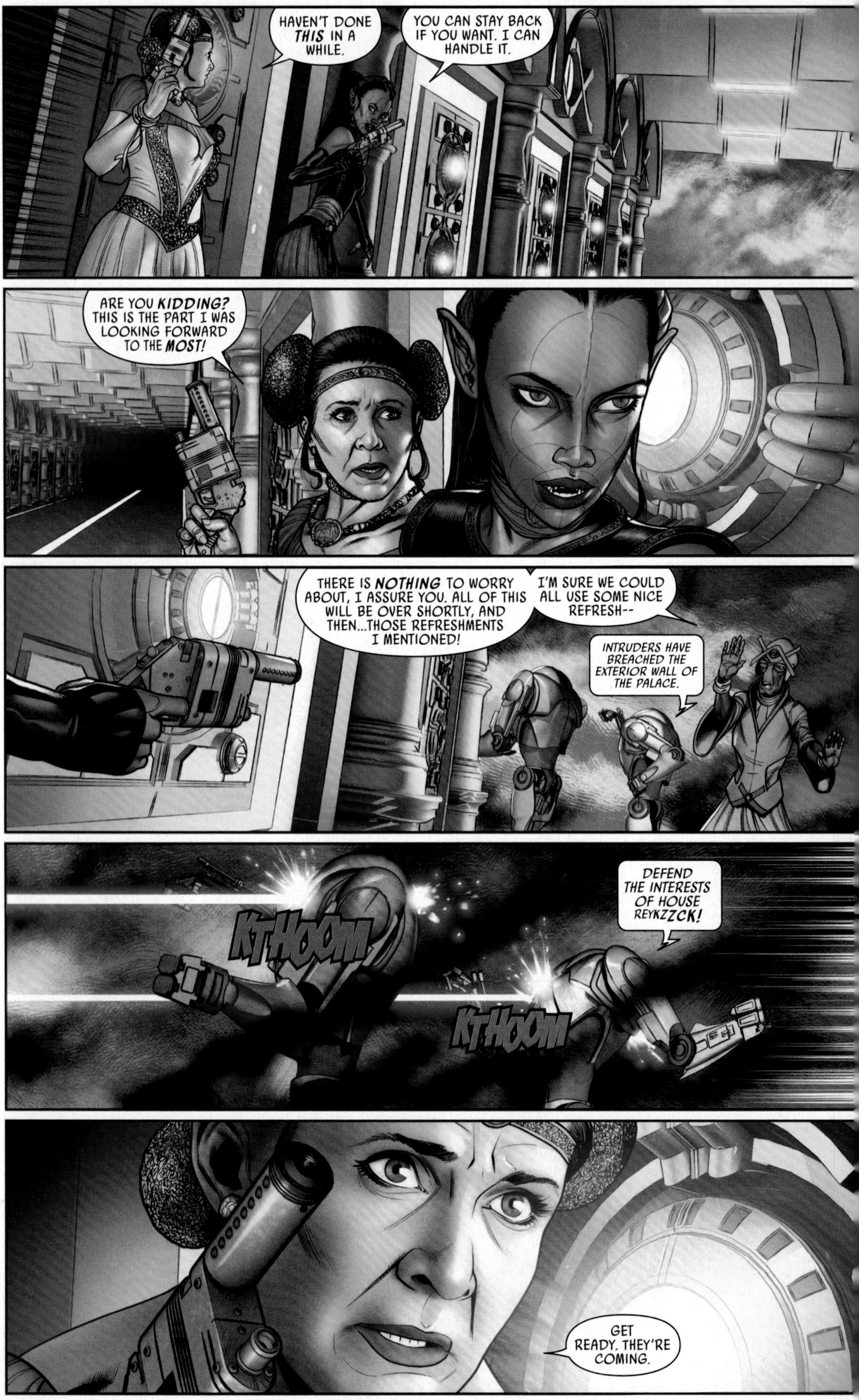
HAVEN'T DONE THIS IN A WHILE.
YOU CAN STAY BACK IF YOU WANT. I CAN HANDLE IT.
ARE YOU KIDDING? THIS IS THE PART I WAS LOOKING FORWARD TO THE MOST!
THERE IS NOTHING TO WORRY ABOUT, I ASSURE YOU. ALL OF THIS WILL BE OVER SHORTLY, AND THEN...THOSE REFRESHMENTS I MENTIONED!
I'M SURE WE COULD ALL USE SOME NICE REFRESH--
INTRUDERS HAVE BREACHED THE EXTERIOR WALL OF THE PALACE.
KTHOOM
KTHOOM
DEFEND THE INTERESTS OF HOUSE REYKZZCK!
GET READY. THEY'RE COMING.

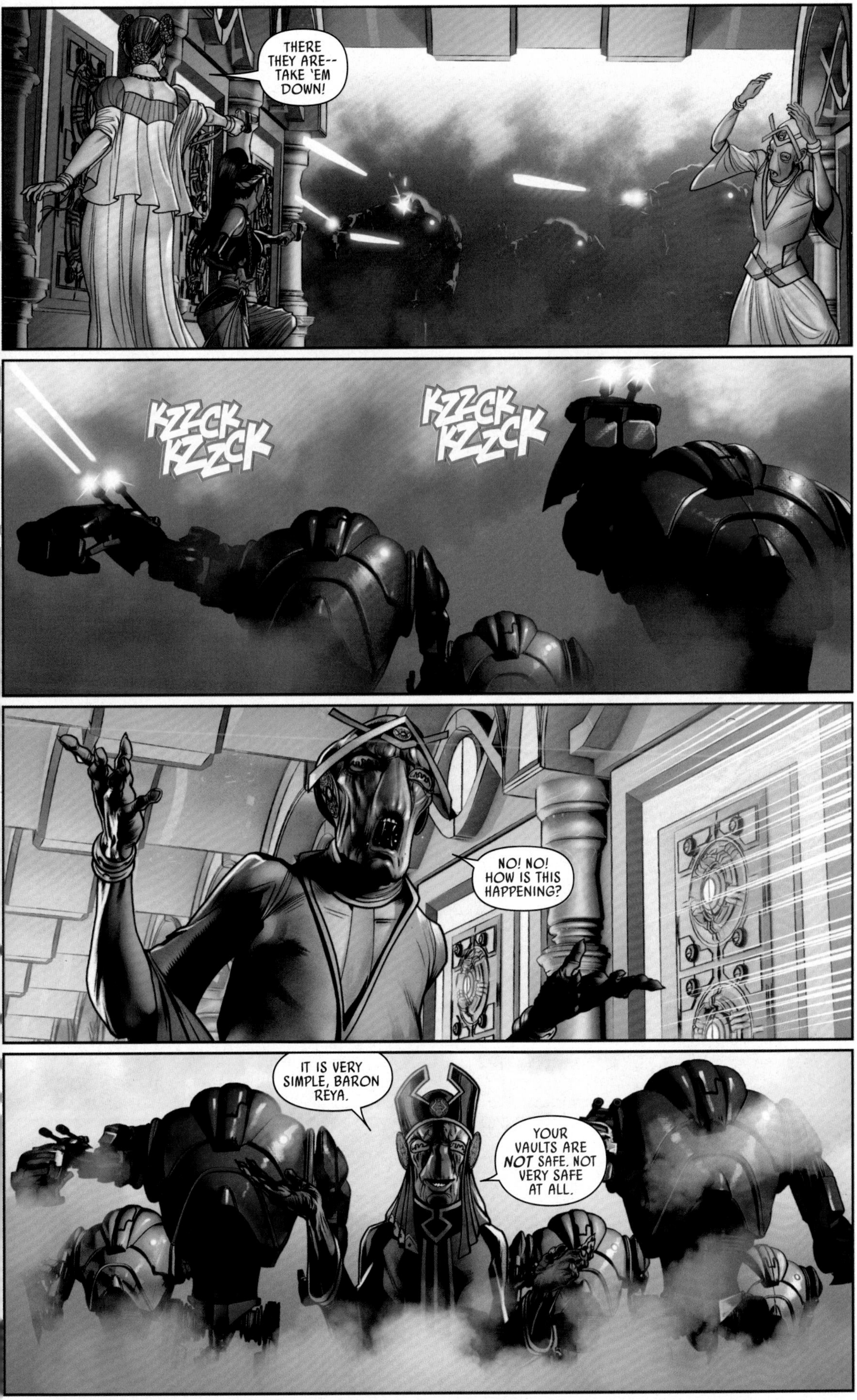
THERE THEY ARE-- TAKE 'EM DOWN!
KZZ-CK KZZCK
KZZ-CK KZZCK
NO! NO! HOW IS THIS HAPPENING?
IT IS VERY SIMPLE, BARON REYA.
YOUR VAULTS ARE NOT SAFE. NOT VERY SAFE AT ALL.

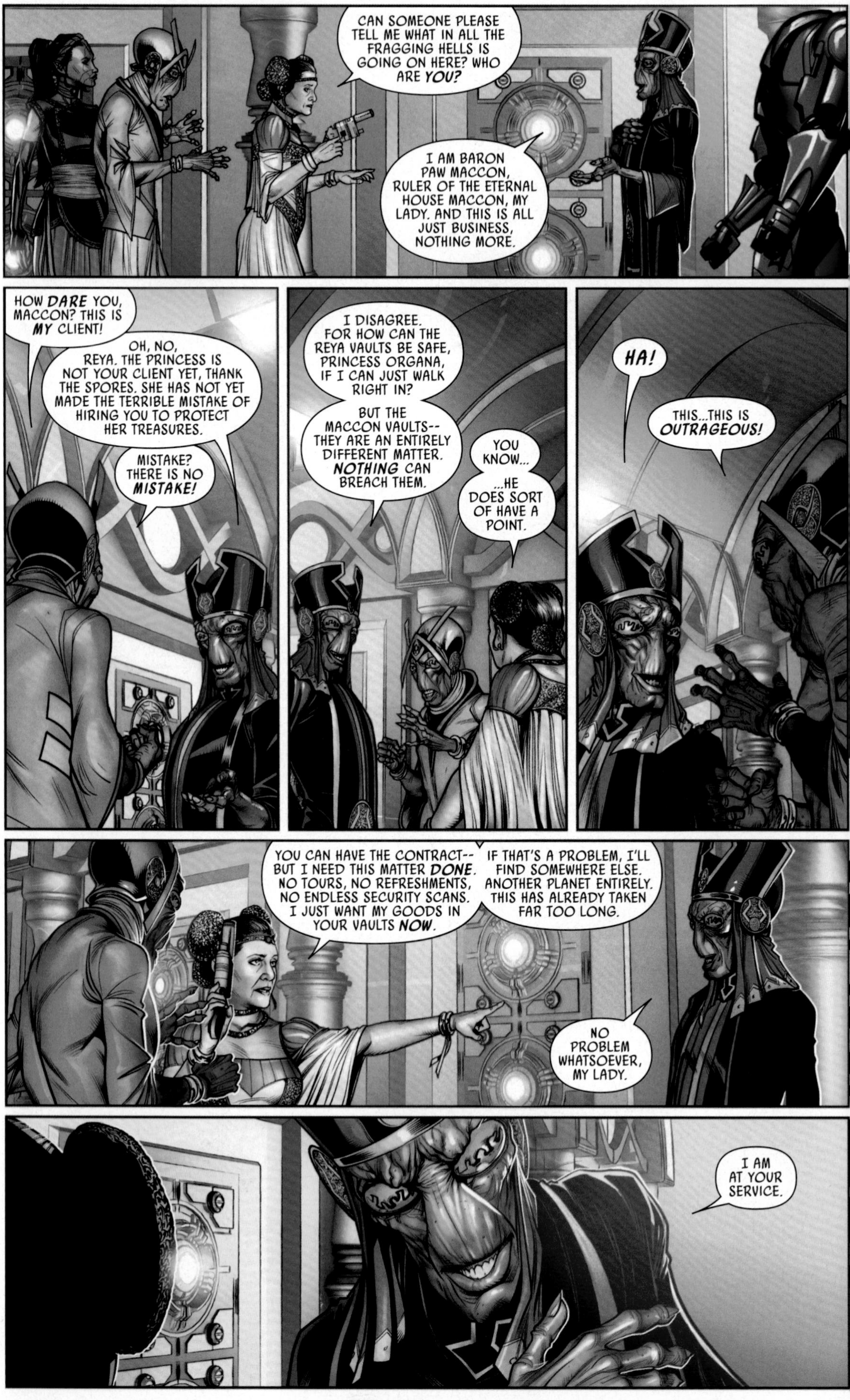

CAN SOMEONE PLEASE TELL ME WHAT IN ALL THE FRAGGING HELLS IS GOING ON HERE? WHO ARE *YOU?*
I AM BARON PAW MACCON, RULER OF THE ETERNAL HOUSE MACCON, MY LADY. AND THIS IS ALL JUST BUSINESS, NOTHING MORE.
HOW *DARE* YOU, MACCON? THIS IS *MY* CLIENT!
OH, NO, REYA. THE PRINCESS IS NOT YOUR CLIENT YET, THANK THE SPORES. SHE HAS NOT YET MADE THE TERRIBLE MISTAKE OF HIRING YOU TO PROTECT HER TREASURES.
MISTAKE? THERE IS NO *MISTAKE!*
I DISAGREE. FOR HOW CAN THE REYA VAULTS BE SAFE, PRINCESS ORGANA, IF I CAN JUST WALK RIGHT IN?
BUT THE MACCON VAULTS-- THEY ARE AN ENTIRELY DIFFERENT MATTER. *NOTHING* CAN BREACH THEM.
YOU KNOW...
...HE DOES SORT OF HAVE A POINT.
HA!
THIS...THIS IS *OUTRAGEOUS!*
YOU CAN HAVE THE CONTRACT-- BUT I NEED THIS MATTER *DONE*. NO TOURS, NO REFRESHMENTS, NO ENDLESS SECURITY SCANS. I JUST WANT MY GOODS IN YOUR VAULTS *NOW*.
IF THAT'S A PROBLEM, I'LL FIND SOMEWHERE ELSE. ANOTHER PLANET ENTIRELY. THIS HAS ALREADY TAKEN FAR TOO LONG.
NO PROBLEM WHATSOEVER, MY LADY.
I AM AT YOUR SERVICE.

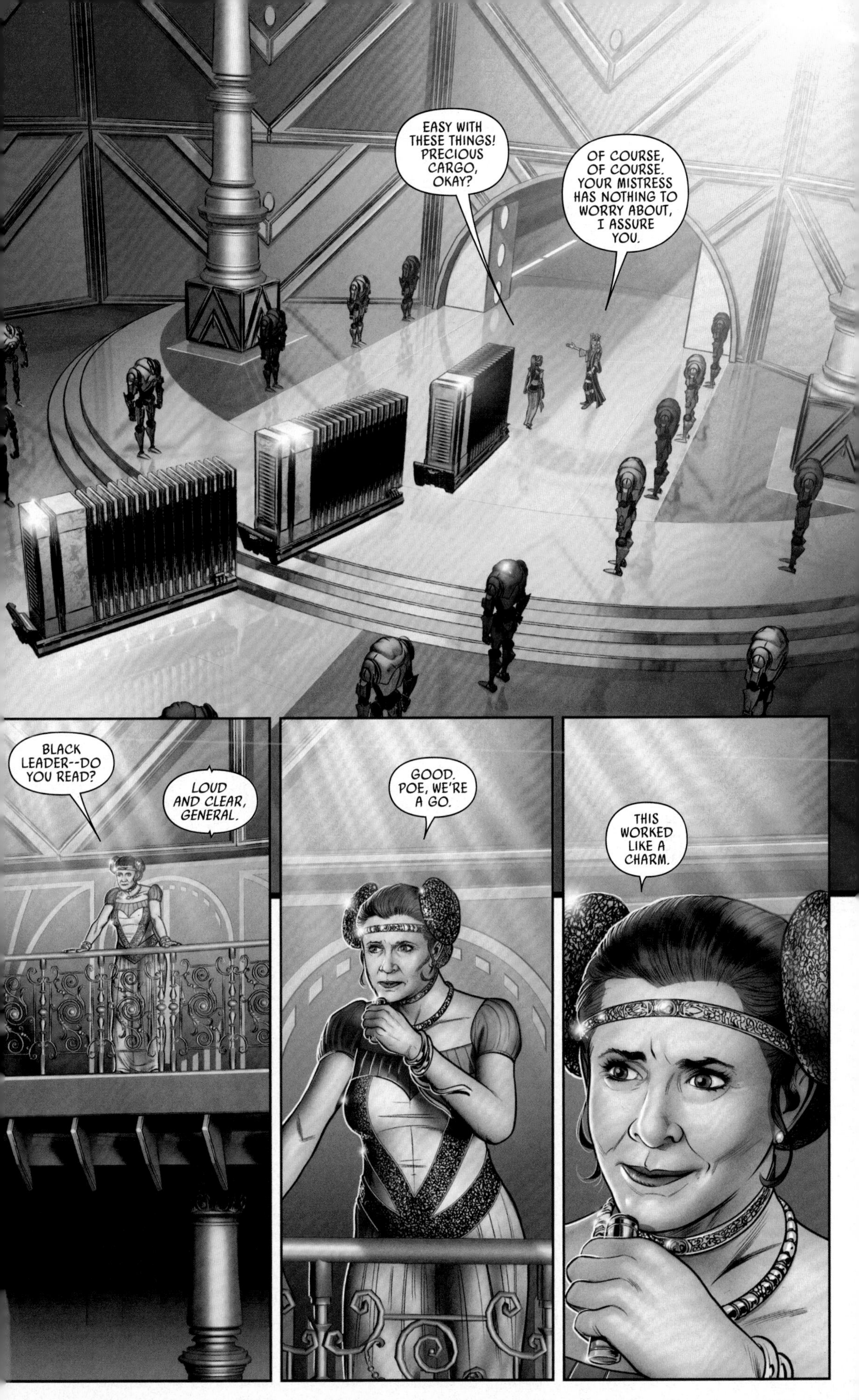
EASY WITH THESE THINGS! PRECIOUS CARGO, OKAY?
OF COURSE, OF COURSE. YOUR MISTRESS HAS NOTHING TO WORRY ABOUT, I ASSURE YOU.
BLACK LEADER--DO YOU READ?
LOUD AND CLEAR, GENERAL.
GOOD. POE, WE'RE A GO.
THIS WORKED LIKE A CHARM.

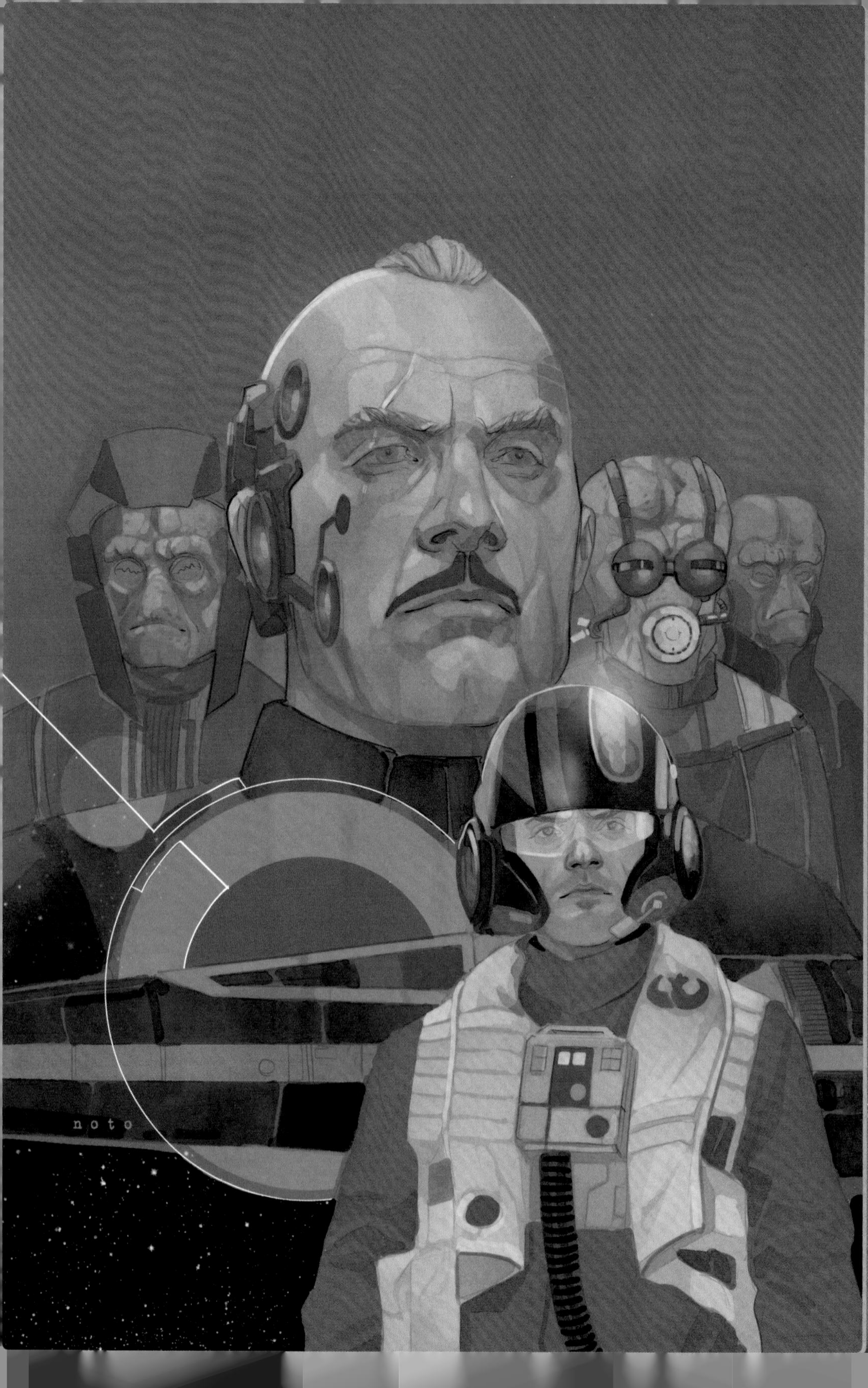
noto

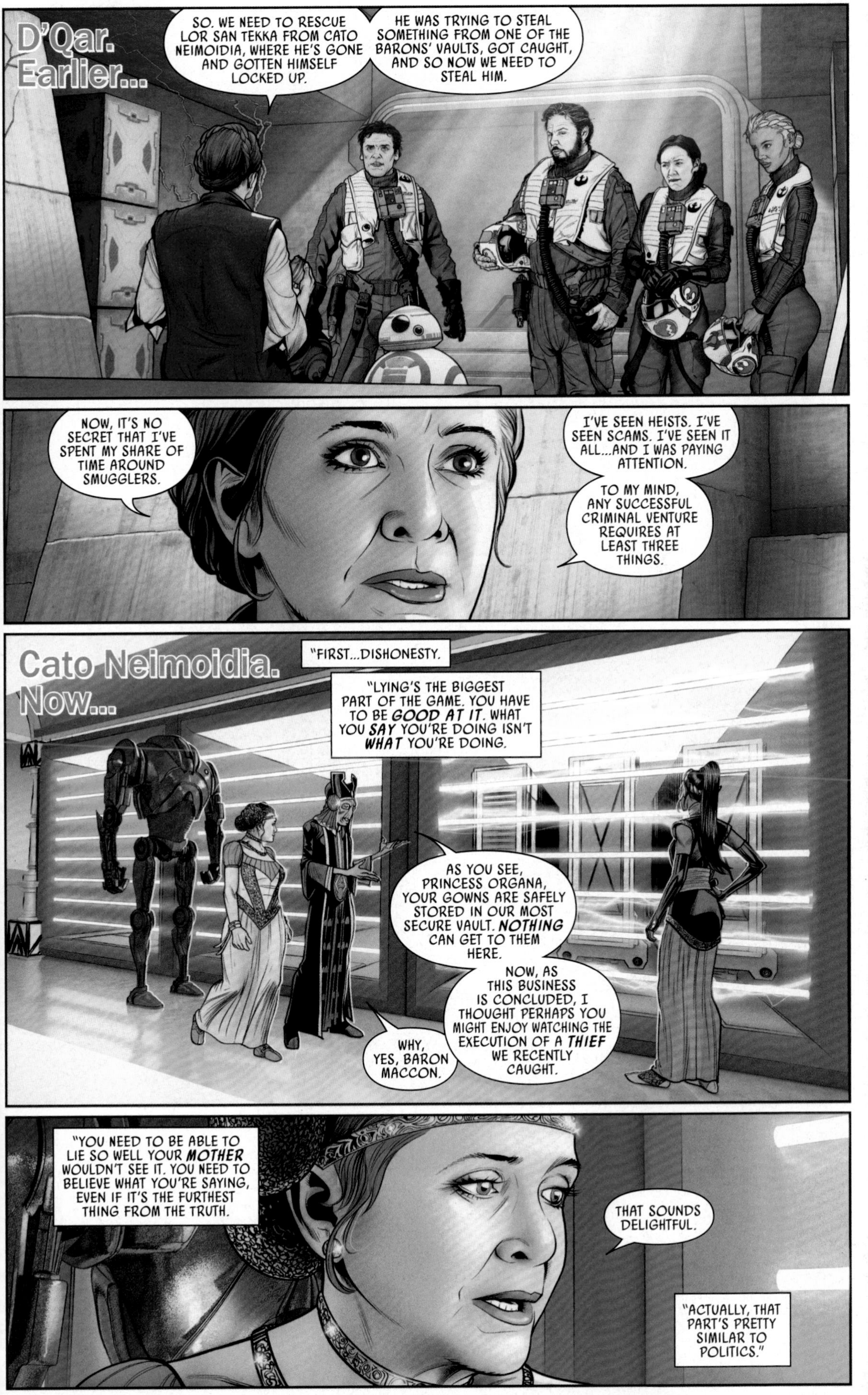
D'Qar. Earlier...
SO. WE NEED TO RESCUE LOR SAN TEKKA FROM CATO NEIMOIDIA, WHERE HE'S GONE AND GOTTEN HIMSELF LOCKED UP.
HE WAS TRYING TO STEAL SOMETHING FROM ONE OF THE BARONS' VAULTS, GOT CAUGHT, AND SO NOW WE NEED TO STEAL HIM.
NOW, IT'S NO SECRET THAT I'VE SPENT MY SHARE OF TIME AROUND SMUGGLERS.
I'VE SEEN HEISTS. I'VE SEEN SCAMS. I'VE SEEN IT ALL...AND I WAS PAYING ATTENTION.
TO MY MIND, ANY SUCCESSFUL CRIMINAL VENTURE REQUIRES AT LEAST THREE THINGS.
Cato Neimoidia. Now...
"FIRST...DISHONESTY.
"LYING'S THE BIGGEST PART OF THE GAME. YOU HAVE TO BE *GOOD AT IT*. WHAT YOU *SAY* YOU'RE DOING ISN'T *WHAT* YOU'RE DOING.
AS YOU SEE, PRINCESS ORGANA, YOUR GOWNS ARE SAFELY STORED IN OUR MOST SECURE VAULT. *NOTHING* CAN GET TO THEM HERE.
NOW, AS THIS BUSINESS IS CONCLUDED, I THOUGHT PERHAPS YOU MIGHT ENJOY WATCHING THE EXECUTION OF A *THIEF* WE RECENTLY CAUGHT.
WHY, YES, BARON MACCON.
"YOU NEED TO BE ABLE TO LIE SO WELL YOUR *MOTHER* WOULDN'T SEE IT. YOU NEED TO BELIEVE WHAT YOU'RE SAYING, EVEN IF IT'S THE FURTHEST THING FROM THE TRUTH.
THAT SOUNDS DELIGHTFUL.
"ACTUALLY, THAT PART'S PRETTY SIMILAR TO POLITICS."

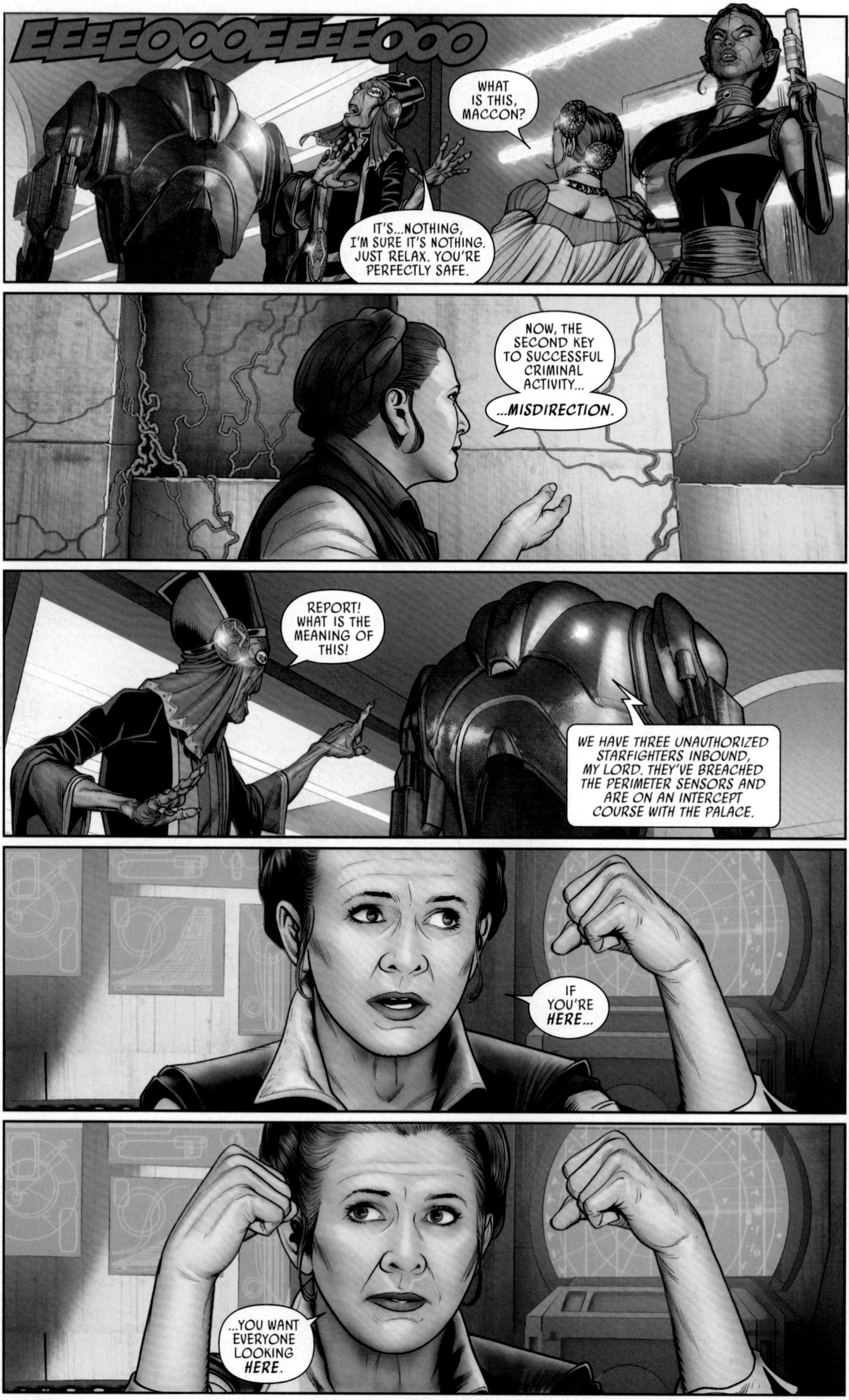
EEEEOOOEEEEOOO
WHAT IS THIS, MACCON?
IT'S...NOTHING, I'M SURE IT'S NOTHING. JUST RELAX. YOU'RE PERFECTLY SAFE.
NOW, THE SECOND KEY TO SUCCESSFUL CRIMINAL ACTIVITY...
...MISDIRECTION.
REPORT! WHAT IS THE MEANING OF THIS!
WE HAVE THREE UNAUTHORIZED STARFIGHTERS INBOUND, MY LORD. THEY'VE BREACHED THE PERIMETER SENSORS AND ARE ON AN INTERCEPT COURSE WITH THE PALACE.
IF YOU'RE HERE...
...YOU WANT EVERYONE LOOKING HERE.

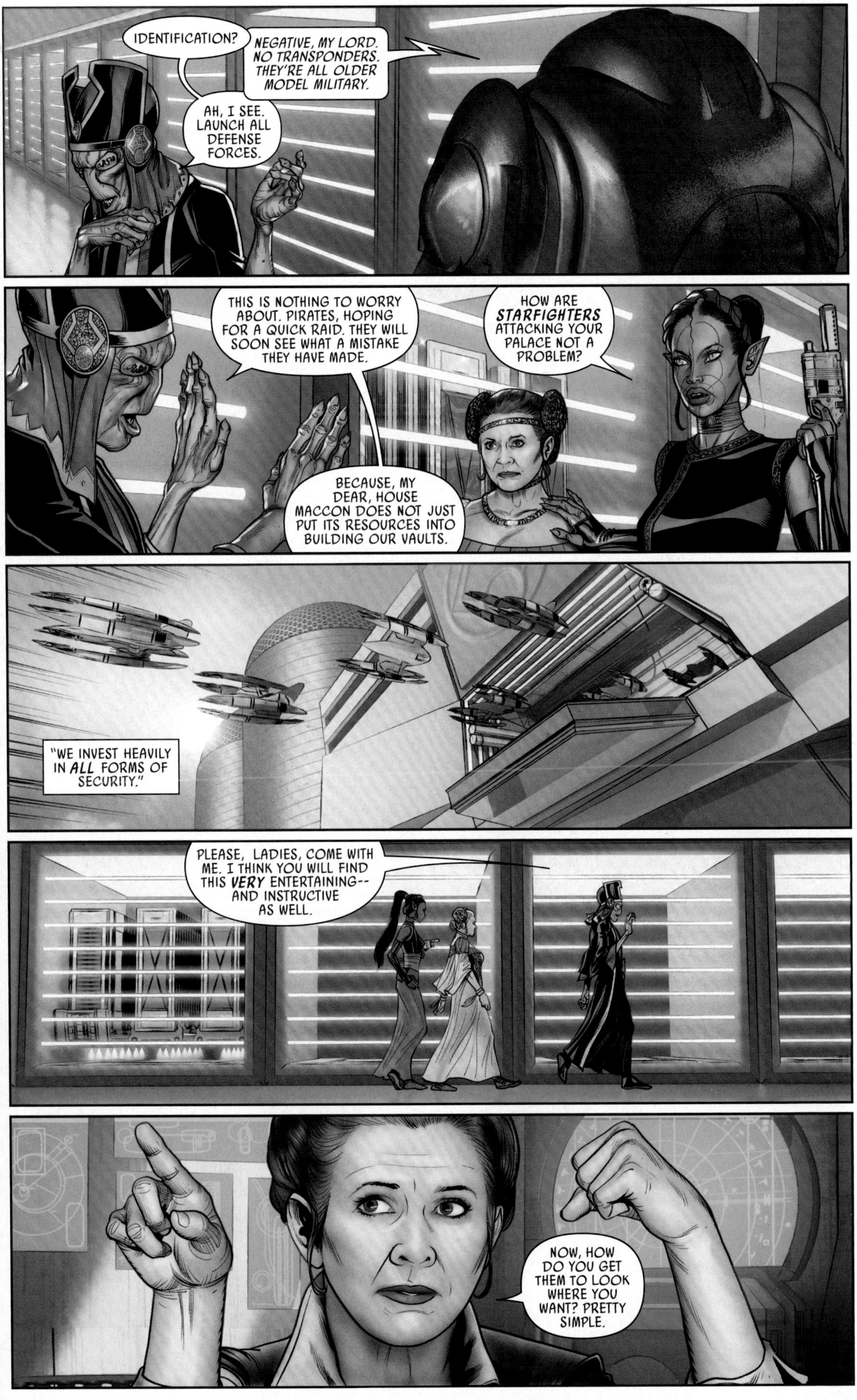
IDENTIFICATION?
NEGATIVE, MY LORD. NO TRANSPONDERS. THEY'RE ALL OLDER MODEL MILITARY.
AH, I SEE. LAUNCH ALL DEFENSE FORCES.
THIS IS NOTHING TO WORRY ABOUT. PIRATES, HOPING FOR A QUICK RAID. THEY WILL SOON SEE WHAT A MISTAKE THEY HAVE MADE.
HOW ARE STARFIGHTERS ATTACKING YOUR PALACE NOT A PROBLEM?
BECAUSE, MY DEAR, HOUSE MACCON DOES NOT JUST PUT ITS RESOURCES INTO BUILDING OUR VAULTS.
"WE INVEST HEAVILY IN ALL FORMS OF SECURITY."
PLEASE, LADIES, COME WITH ME. I THINK YOU WILL FIND THIS VERY ENTERTAINING-- AND INSTRUCTIVE AS WELL.
NOW, HOW DO YOU GET THEM TO LOOK WHERE YOU WANT? PRETTY SIMPLE.

"YOU GIVE THEM SOMETHING TO LOOK AT."

SO...WE'RE JUST SUPPOSED TO PLAY TARGET PRACTICE WITH THESE DROID FIGHTERS FOR A WHILE?

THAT'S THE ORDER, JESS. JUST STRING THINGS OUT AS LONG AS WE CAN. WE'RE THE DISTRACTION.

OH, IS THAT RIGHT?

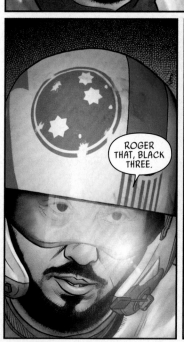

I THOUGHT DISTRACTIONS WERE A *BAD* THING IN A BATTLE, KARÉ.

COME ON, SNAP.

NOT IN EVERY SITUATION.

LADY, THAT IS WHAT I HAVE BEEN TRYING TO *TELL* YOU.

ROGER THAT, BLACK THREE.

S-FOILS LOCKED IN ATTACK POSITION.

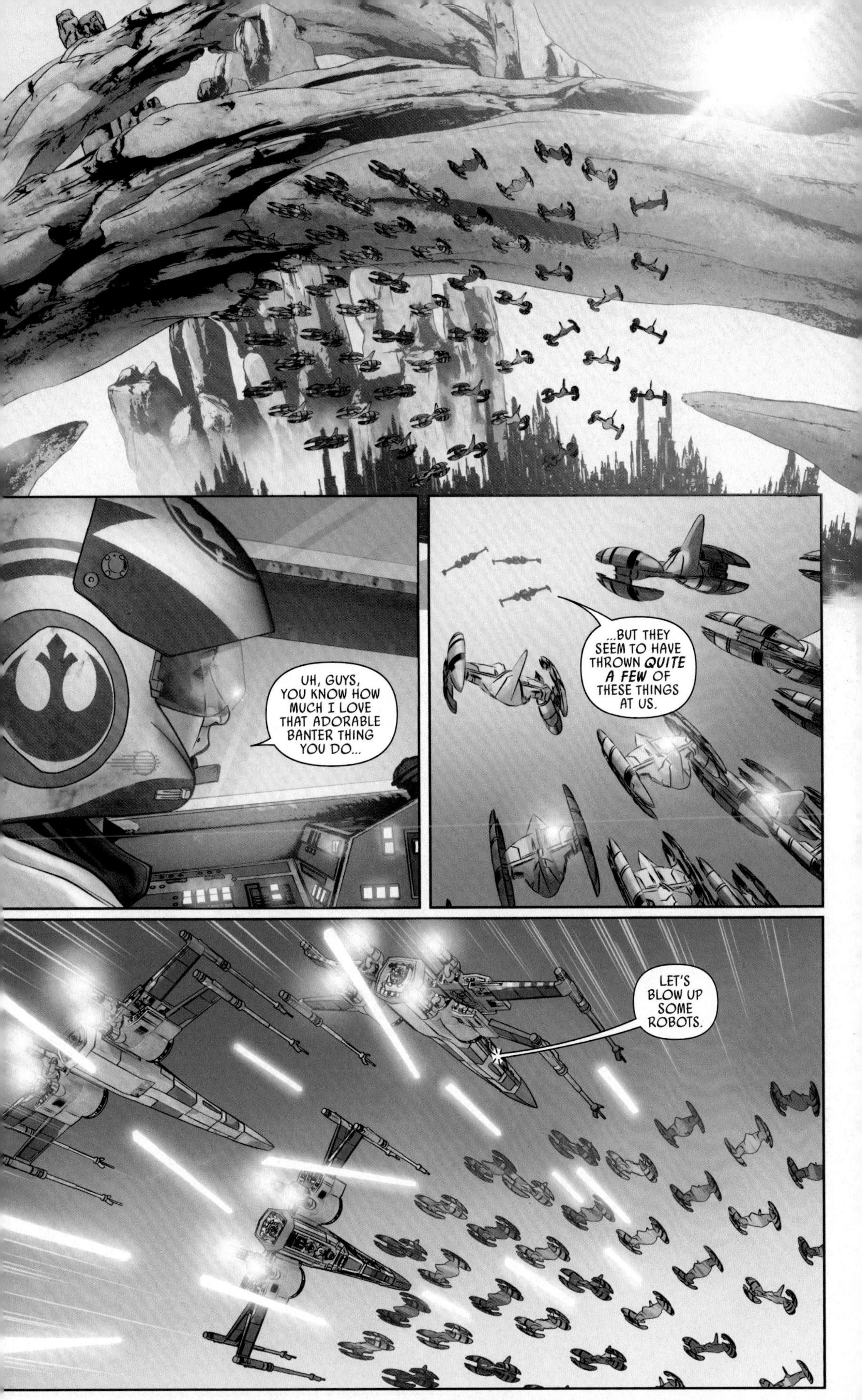
UH, GUYS, YOU KNOW HOW MUCH I LOVE THAT ADORABLE BANTER THING YOU DO...
...BUT THEY SEEM TO HAVE THROWN QUITE A FEW OF THESE THINGS AT US.
LET'S BLOW UP SOME ROBOTS.

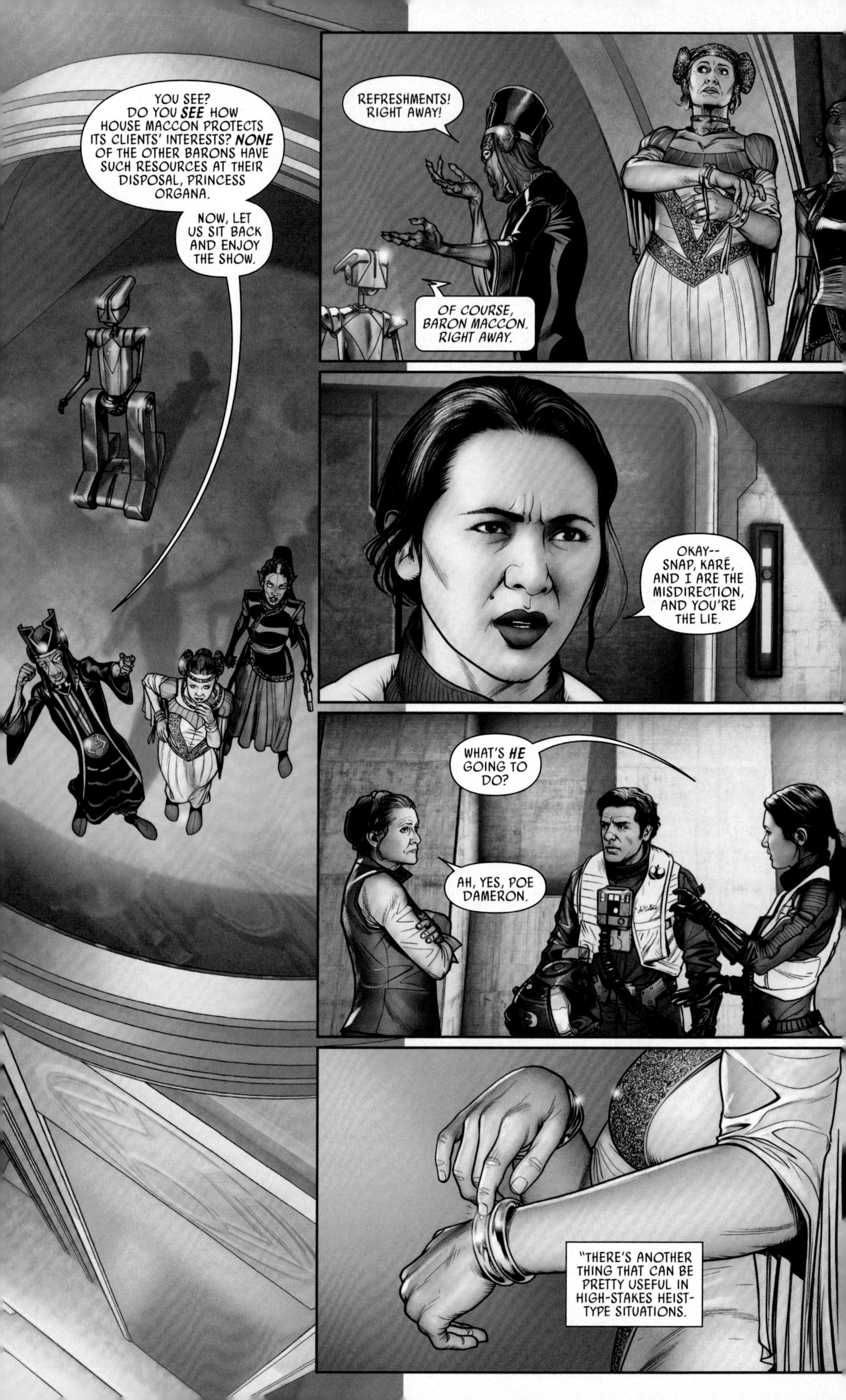
YOU SEE? DO YOU SEE HOW HOUSE MACCON PROTECTS ITS CLIENTS' INTERESTS? NONE OF THE OTHER BARONS HAVE SUCH RESOURCES AT THEIR DISPOSAL, PRINCESS ORGANA.
NOW, LET US SIT BACK AND ENJOY THE SHOW.
REFRESHMENTS! RIGHT AWAY!
OF COURSE, BARON MACCON. RIGHT AWAY.
OKAY-- SNAP, KARÉ, AND I ARE THE MISDIRECTION, AND YOU'RE THE LIE.
WHAT'S HE GOING TO DO?
AH, YES, POE DAMERON.
"THERE'S ANOTHER THING THAT CAN BE PRETTY USEFUL IN HIGH-STAKES HEIST-TYPE SITUATIONS.

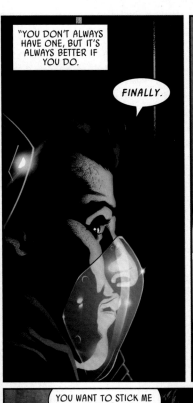

"YOU DON'T ALWAYS HAVE ONE, BUT IT'S ALWAYS BETTER IF YOU DO.

FINALLY.

"AN INSIDE MAN."

YOU WANT TO STICK ME IN A *CRATE?* WHAT IF THEY FIND ME?

YOU'LL BE FINE. I'LL GO TO A RIVAL OF HOUSE MACCON FIRST. IT'LL ALLAY SUSPICION, AND I CAN PLAY IT TO MAKE SURE YOU DON'T GET SCANNED ON THE WAY IN.

YOU SURE YOU WOULDN'T RATHER JUST HAVE ME FLYING? I'M *GOOD* AT FLYING.

YOU'RE GOOD AT LOTS OF THINGS, POE. I BET YOU'RE PRETTY GOOD AT CLIMBING, FOR INSTANCE.

"LET ME GIVE YOU THE WHOLE PLAN BEFORE YOU START THROWING OUT OBJECTIONS. THIS ALL MAKES SENSE, I PROMISE.

"PEOPLE TEND TO BUILD VAULTS SO THAT PEOPLE CAN'T BREAK INTO THEM.

"BREAKING OUT...LESS OF A CONCERN."

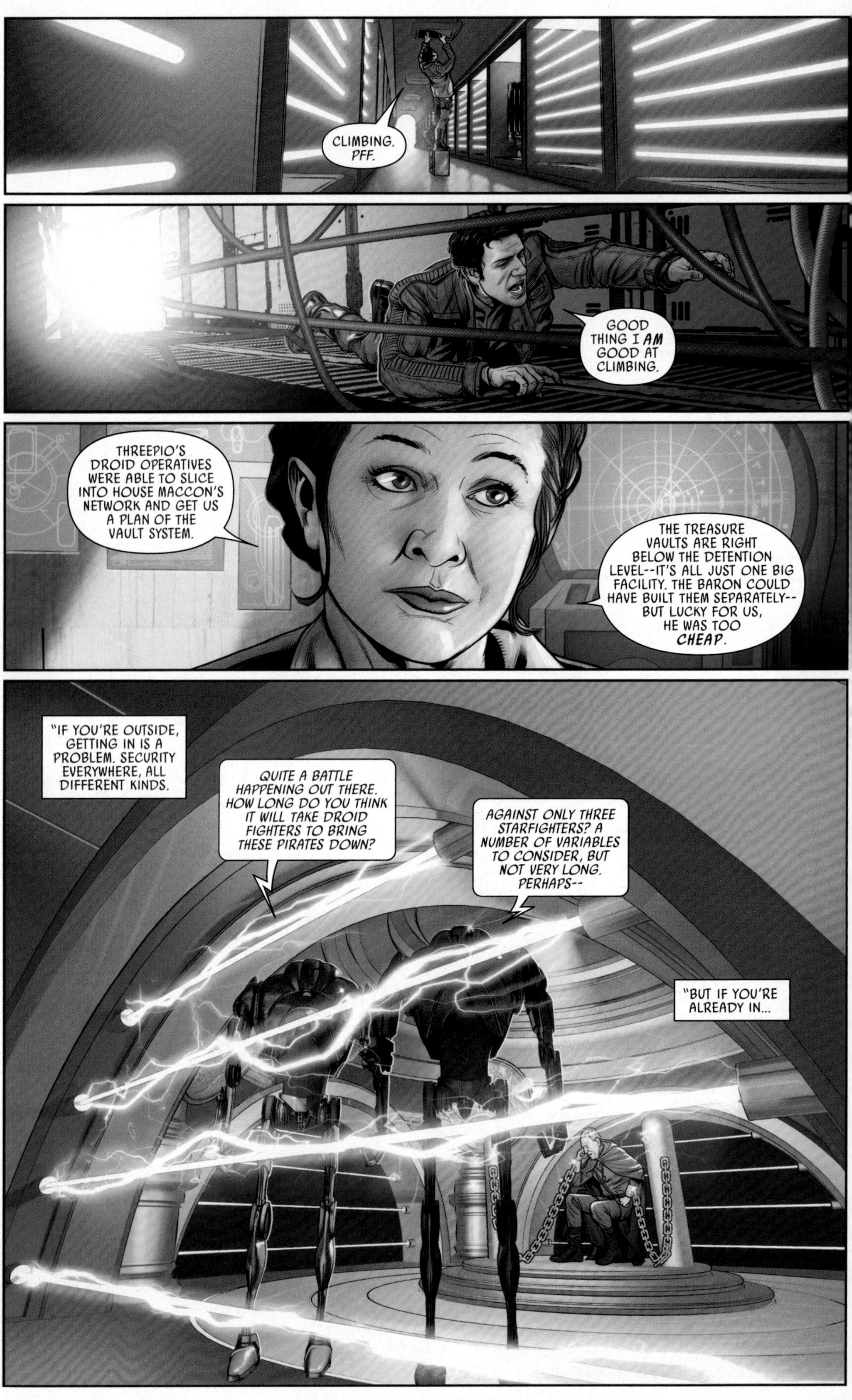
CLIMBING. PFF.
GOOD THING I AM GOOD AT CLIMBING.
THREEPIO'S DROID OPERATIVES WERE ABLE TO SLICE INTO HOUSE MACCON'S NETWORK AND GET US A PLAN OF THE VAULT SYSTEM.
THE TREASURE VAULTS ARE RIGHT BELOW THE DETENTION LEVEL--IT'S ALL JUST ONE BIG FACILITY. THE BARON COULD HAVE BUILT THEM SEPARATELY--BUT LUCKY FOR US, HE WAS TOO CHEAP.
"IF YOU'RE OUTSIDE, GETTING IN IS A PROBLEM. SECURITY EVERYWHERE, ALL DIFFERENT KINDS.
QUITE A BATTLE HAPPENING OUT THERE. HOW LONG DO YOU THINK IT WILL TAKE DROID FIGHTERS TO BRING THESE PIRATES DOWN?
AGAINST ONLY THREE STARFIGHTERS? A NUMBER OF VARIABLES TO CONSIDER, BUT NOT VERY LONG. PERHAPS--
"BUT IF YOU'RE ALREADY IN...

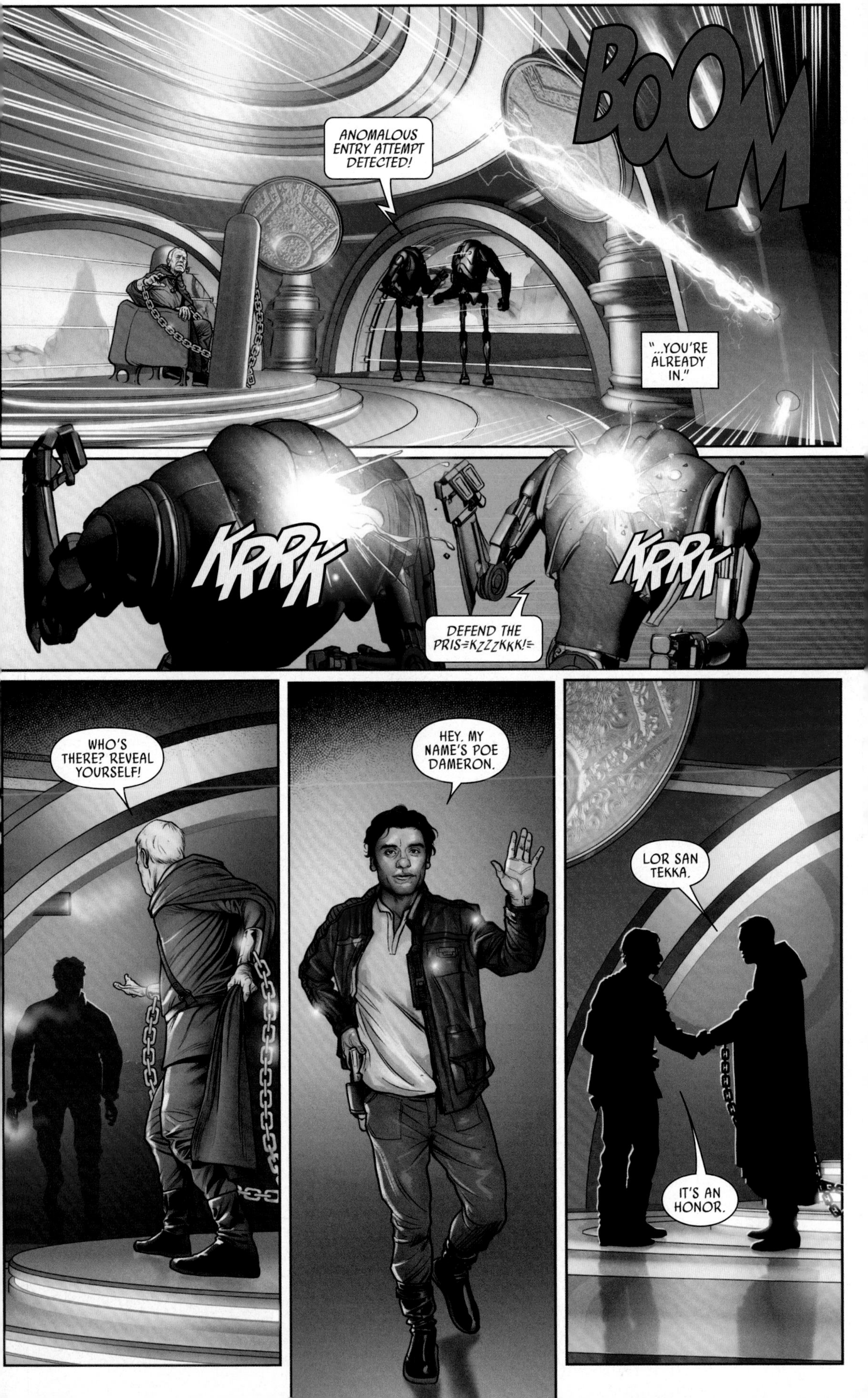
ANOMALOUS ENTRY ATTEMPT DETECTED!
BOOM
"...YOU'RE ALREADY IN."
KRRK
DEFEND THE PRIS=KZZZKKK!=
KRRK
WHO'S THERE? REVEAL YOURSELF!
HEY. MY NAME'S POE DAMERON.
LOR SAN TEKKA.
IT'S AN HONOR.

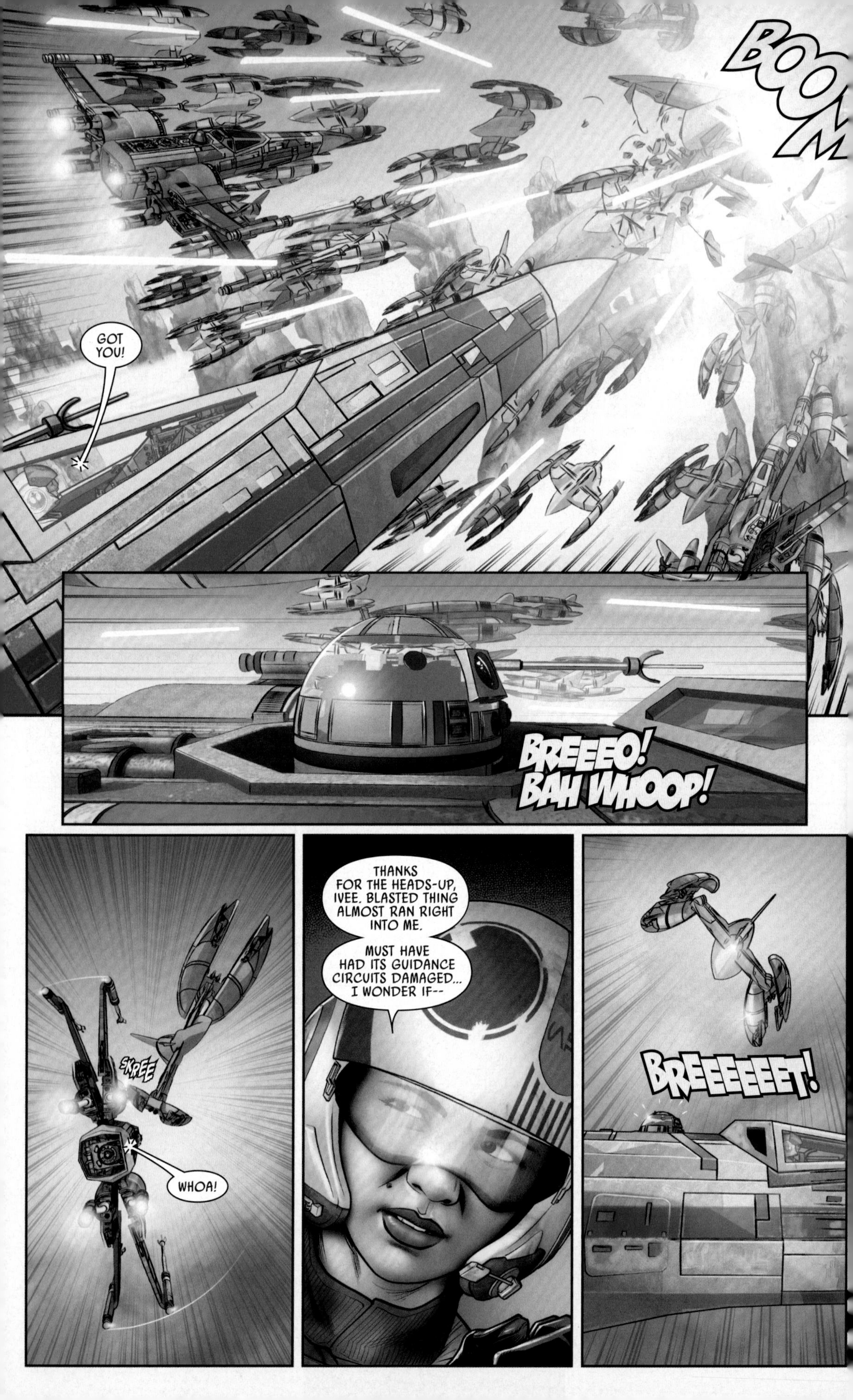
BOOM
GOT YOU!
BREEEO! BAH WHOOP!
SKREE
WHOA!
THANKS FOR THE HEADS-UP, IVEE. BLASTED THING ALMOST RAN RIGHT INTO ME.
MUST HAVE HAD ITS GUIDANCE CIRCUITS DAMAGED... I WONDER IF--
BREEEEEET!

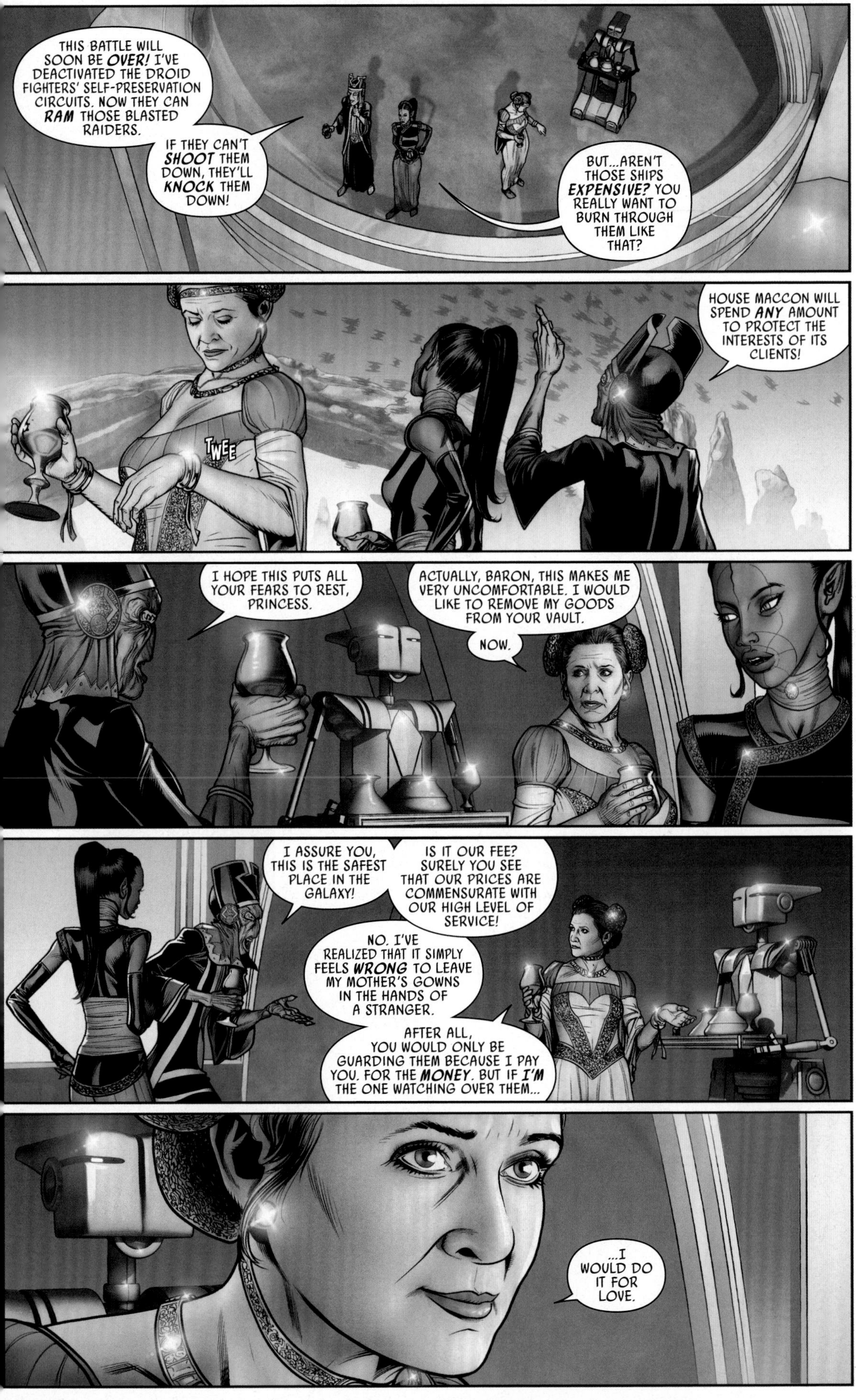

THIS BATTLE WILL SOON BE OVER! I'VE DEACTIVATED THE DROID FIGHTERS' SELF-PRESERVATION CIRCUITS. NOW THEY CAN RAM THOSE BLASTED RAIDERS.
IF THEY CAN'T SHOOT THEM DOWN, THEY'LL KNOCK THEM DOWN!
BUT...AREN'T THOSE SHIPS EXPENSIVE? YOU REALLY WANT TO BURN THROUGH THEM LIKE THAT?
HOUSE MACCON WILL SPEND ANY AMOUNT TO PROTECT THE INTERESTS OF ITS CLIENTS!
TWEE
I HOPE THIS PUTS ALL YOUR FEARS TO REST, PRINCESS.
ACTUALLY, BARON, THIS MAKES ME VERY UNCOMFORTABLE. I WOULD LIKE TO REMOVE MY GOODS FROM YOUR VAULT.
NOW.
I ASSURE YOU, THIS IS THE SAFEST PLACE IN THE GALAXY!
IS IT OUR FEE? SURELY YOU SEE THAT OUR PRICES ARE COMMENSURATE WITH OUR HIGH LEVEL OF SERVICE!
NO. I'VE REALIZED THAT IT SIMPLY FEELS WRONG TO LEAVE MY MOTHER'S GOWNS IN THE HANDS OF A STRANGER.
AFTER ALL, YOU WOULD ONLY BE GUARDING THEM BECAUSE I PAY YOU. FOR THE MONEY. BUT IF I'M THE ONE WATCHING OVER THEM...
...I WOULD DO IT FOR LOVE.

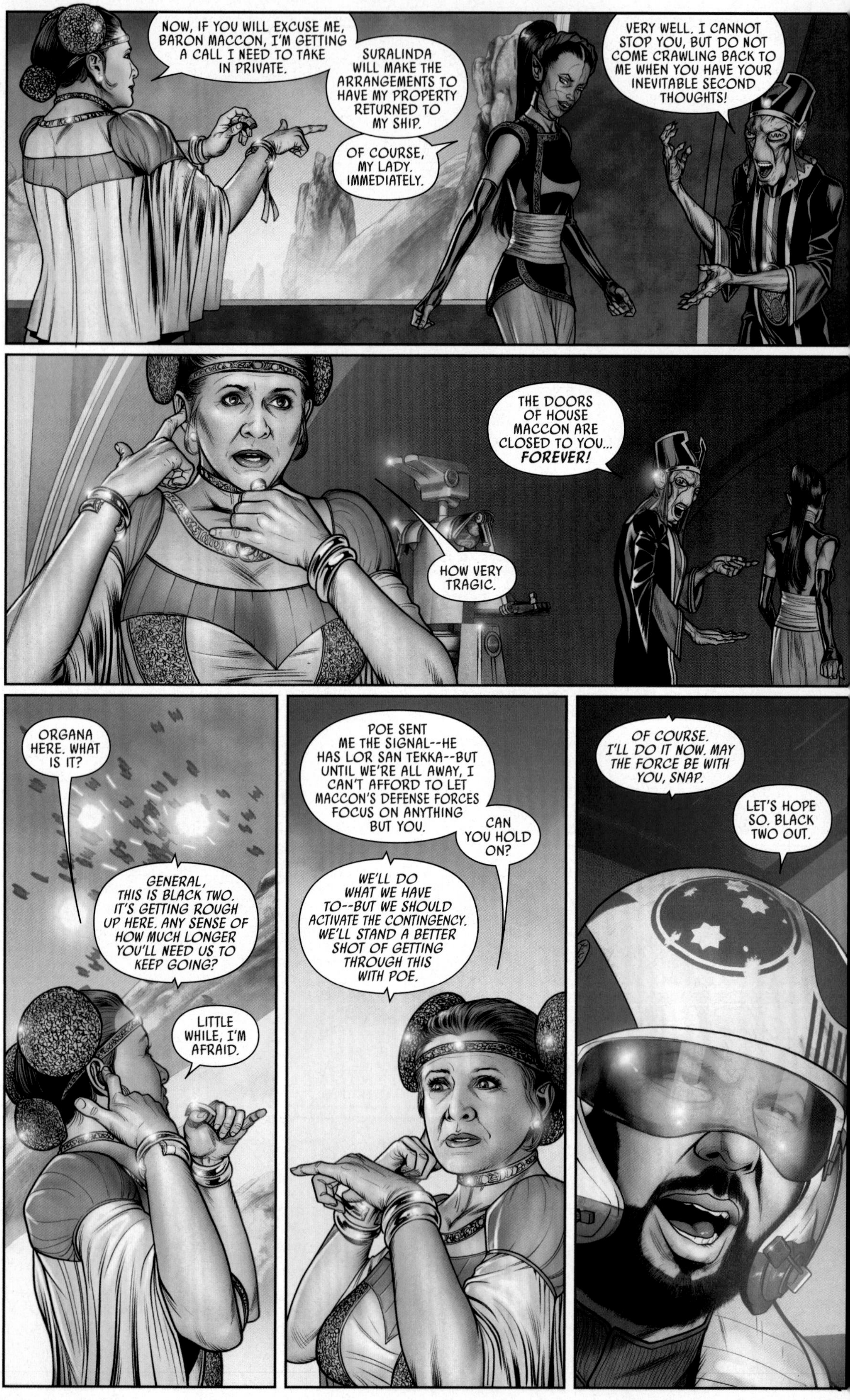
NOW, IF YOU WILL EXCUSE ME, BARON MACCON, I'M GETTING A CALL I NEED TO TAKE IN PRIVATE.
SURALINDA WILL MAKE THE ARRANGEMENTS TO HAVE MY PROPERTY RETURNED TO MY SHIP.
OF COURSE, MY LADY. IMMEDIATELY.
VERY WELL. I CANNOT STOP YOU, BUT DO NOT COME CRAWLING BACK TO ME WHEN YOU HAVE YOUR INEVITABLE SECOND THOUGHTS!
THE DOORS OF HOUSE MACCON ARE CLOSED TO YOU... FOREVER!
HOW VERY TRAGIC.
ORGANA HERE. WHAT IS IT?
GENERAL, THIS IS BLACK TWO. IT'S GETTING ROUGH UP HERE. ANY SENSE OF HOW MUCH LONGER YOU'LL NEED US TO KEEP GOING?
LITTLE WHILE, I'M AFRAID.
POE SENT ME THE SIGNAL--HE HAS LOR SAN TEKKA--BUT UNTIL WE'RE ALL AWAY, I CAN'T AFFORD TO LET MACCON'S DEFENSE FORCES FOCUS ON ANYTHING BUT YOU.
CAN YOU HOLD ON?
WE'LL DO WHAT WE HAVE TO--BUT WE SHOULD ACTIVATE THE CONTINGENCY. WE'LL STAND A BETTER SHOT OF GETTING THROUGH THIS WITH POE.
OF COURSE. I'LL DO IT NOW. MAY THE FORCE BE WITH YOU, SNAP.
LET'S HOPE SO. BLACK TWO OUT.

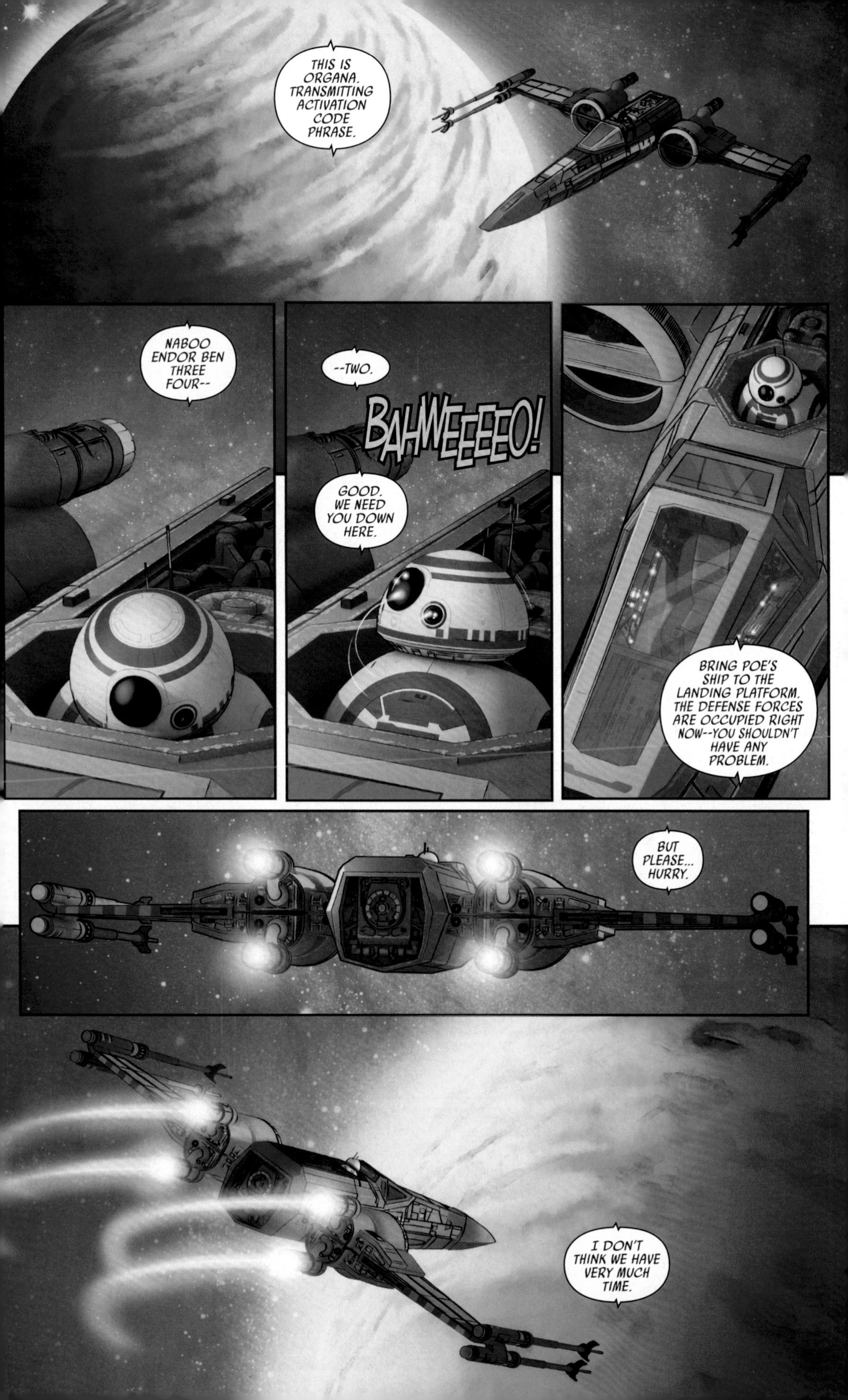
THIS IS ORGANA. TRANSMITTING ACTIVATION CODE PHRASE.
NABOO ENDOR BEN THREE FOUR--
--TWO.
BAHWEEEEEO!
GOOD. WE NEED YOU DOWN HERE.
BRING POE'S SHIP TO THE LANDING PLATFORM. THE DEFENSE FORCES ARE OCCUPIED RIGHT NOW--YOU SHOULDN'T HAVE ANY PROBLEM.
BUT PLEASE... HURRY.
I DON'T THINK WE HAVE VERY MUCH TIME.

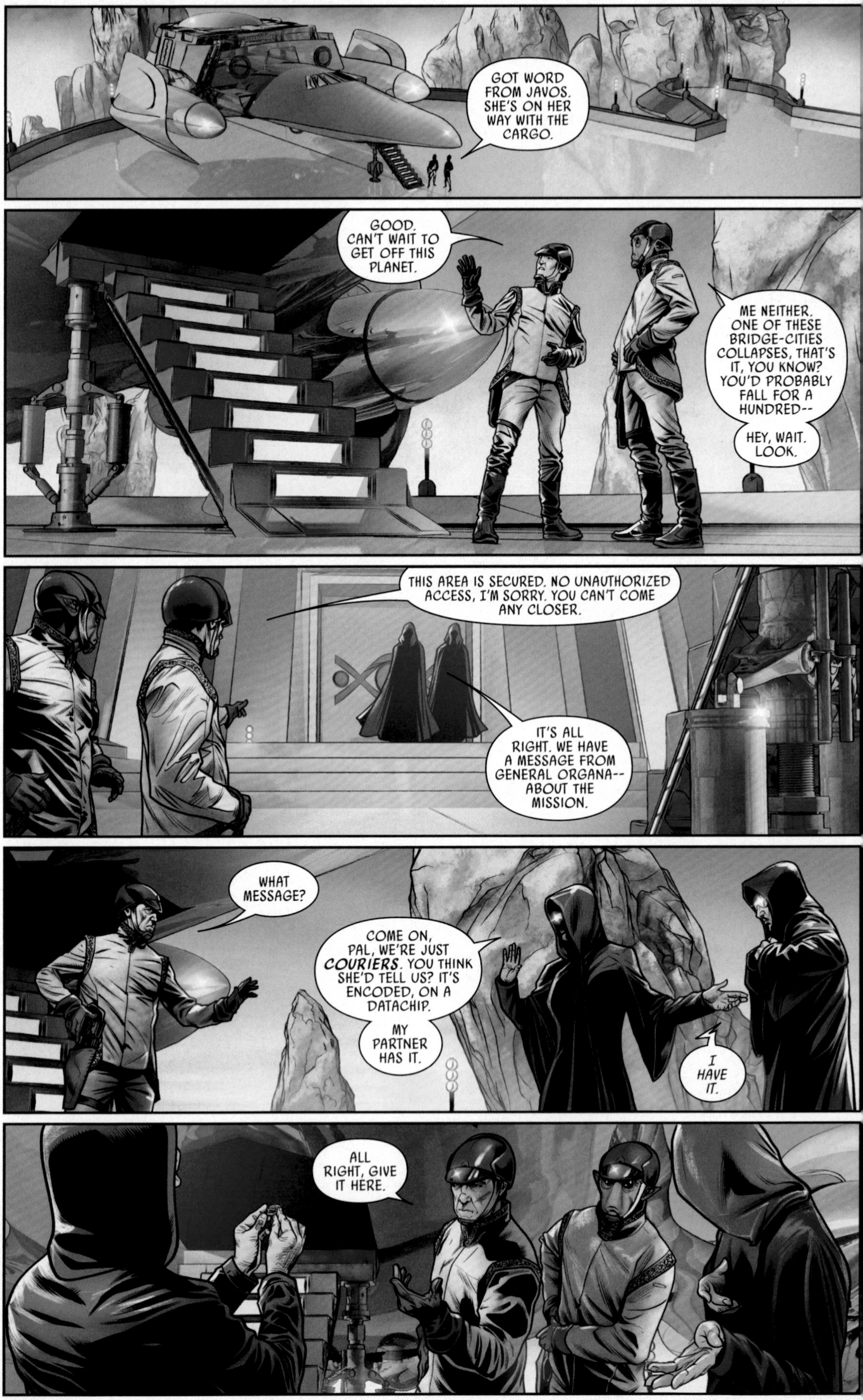
GOT WORD FROM JAVOS. SHE'S ON HER WAY WITH THE CARGO.
GOOD. CAN'T WAIT TO GET OFF THIS PLANET.
ME NEITHER. ONE OF THESE BRIDGE-CITIES COLLAPSES, THAT'S IT, YOU KNOW? YOU'D PROBABLY FALL FOR A HUNDRED--
HEY, WAIT. LOOK.
THIS AREA IS SECURED. NO UNAUTHORIZED ACCESS, I'M SORRY. YOU CAN'T COME ANY CLOSER.
IT'S ALL RIGHT. WE HAVE A MESSAGE FROM GENERAL ORGANA--ABOUT THE MISSION.
WHAT MESSAGE?
COME ON, PAL, WE'RE JUST **COURIERS**. YOU THINK SHE'D TELL US? IT'S ENCODED, ON A DATACHIP.
MY PARTNER HAS IT.
I HAVE IT.
ALL RIGHT, GIVE IT HERE.

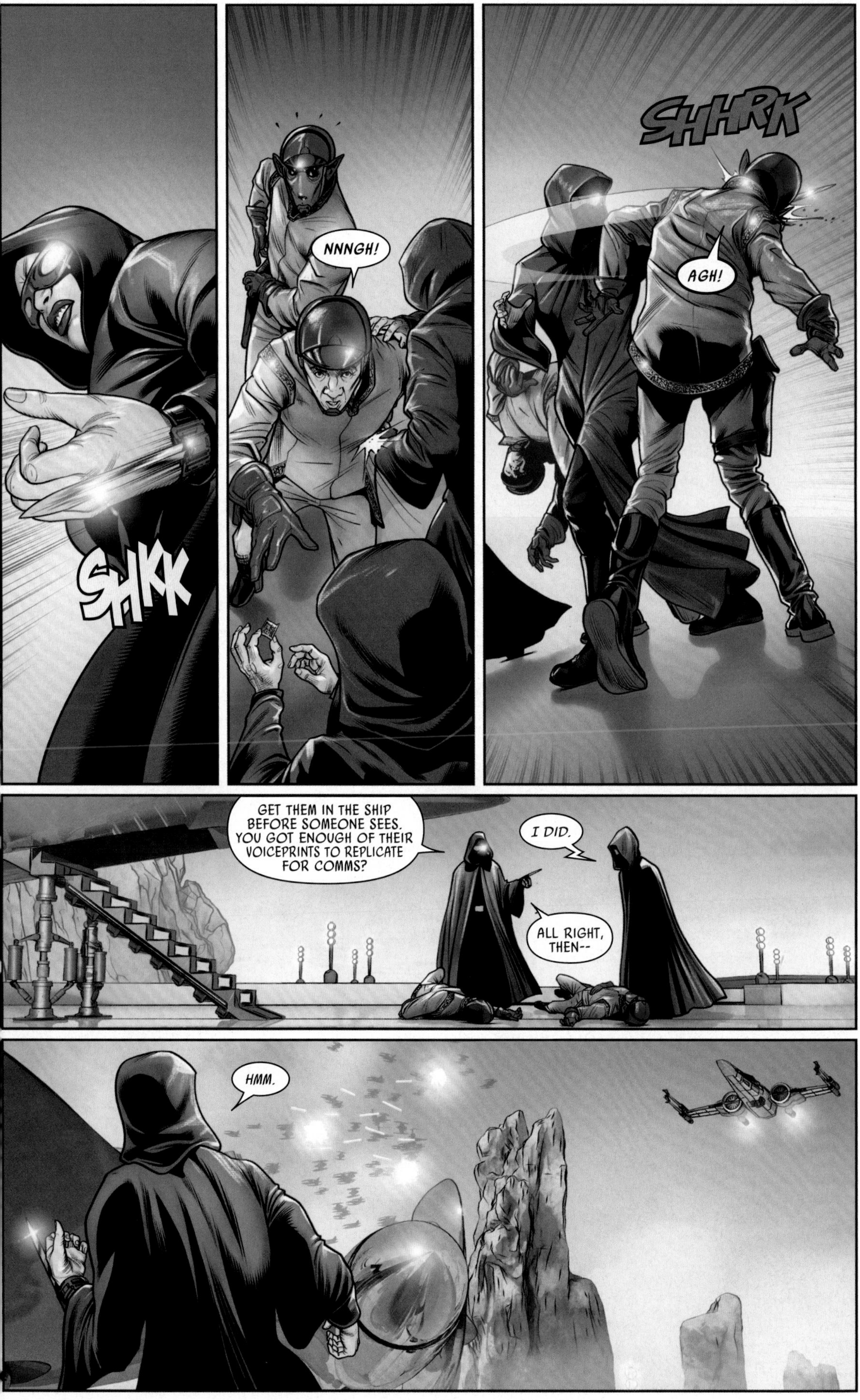
SHKK
NNNGH!
SHHRK
AGH!
GET THEM IN THE SHIP BEFORE SOMEONE SEES. YOU GOT ENOUGH OF THEIR VOICEPRINTS TO REPLICATE FOR COMMS?
I DID.
ALL RIGHT, THEN--
HMM.

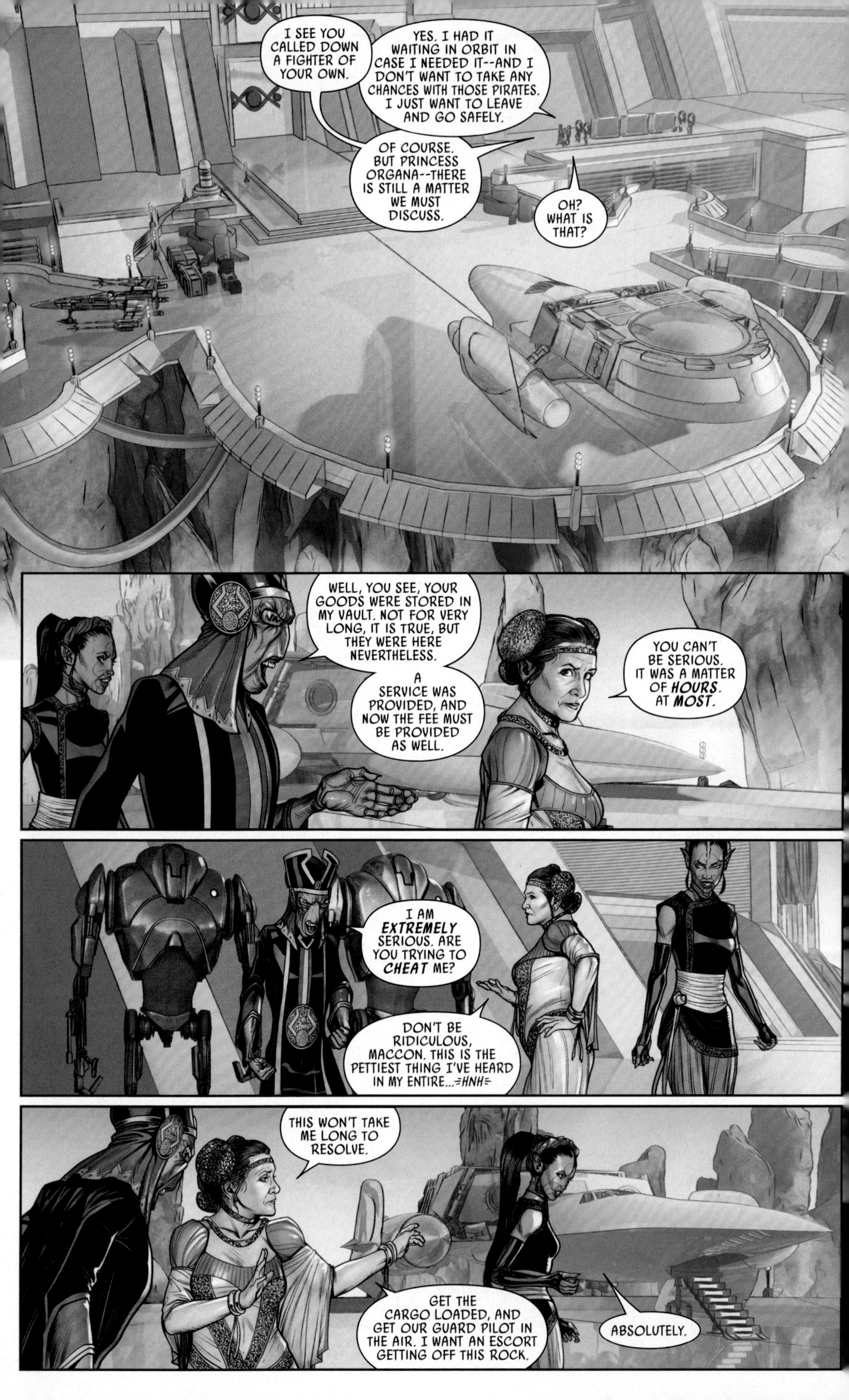
I SEE YOU CALLED DOWN A FIGHTER OF YOUR OWN.
YES. I HAD IT WAITING IN ORBIT IN CASE I NEEDED IT--AND I DON'T WANT TO TAKE ANY CHANCES WITH THOSE PIRATES. I JUST WANT TO LEAVE AND GO SAFELY.
OF COURSE. BUT PRINCESS ORGANA--THERE IS STILL A MATTER WE MUST DISCUSS.
OH? WHAT IS THAT?
WELL, YOU SEE, YOUR GOODS WERE STORED IN MY VAULT. NOT FOR VERY LONG, IT IS TRUE, BUT THEY WERE HERE NEVERTHELESS.
A SERVICE WAS PROVIDED, AND NOW THE FEE MUST BE PROVIDED AS WELL.
YOU CAN'T BE SERIOUS. IT WAS A MATTER OF *HOURS*. AT *MOST*.
I AM *EXTREMELY* SERIOUS. ARE YOU TRYING TO *CHEAT* ME?
DON'T BE RIDICULOUS, MACCON. THIS IS THE PETTIEST THING I'VE HEARD IN MY ENTIRE... =HNH=
THIS WON'T TAKE ME LONG TO RESOLVE.
GET THE CARGO LOADED, AND GET OUR GUARD PILOT IN THE AIR. I WANT AN ESCORT GETTING OFF THIS ROCK.
ABSOLUTELY.

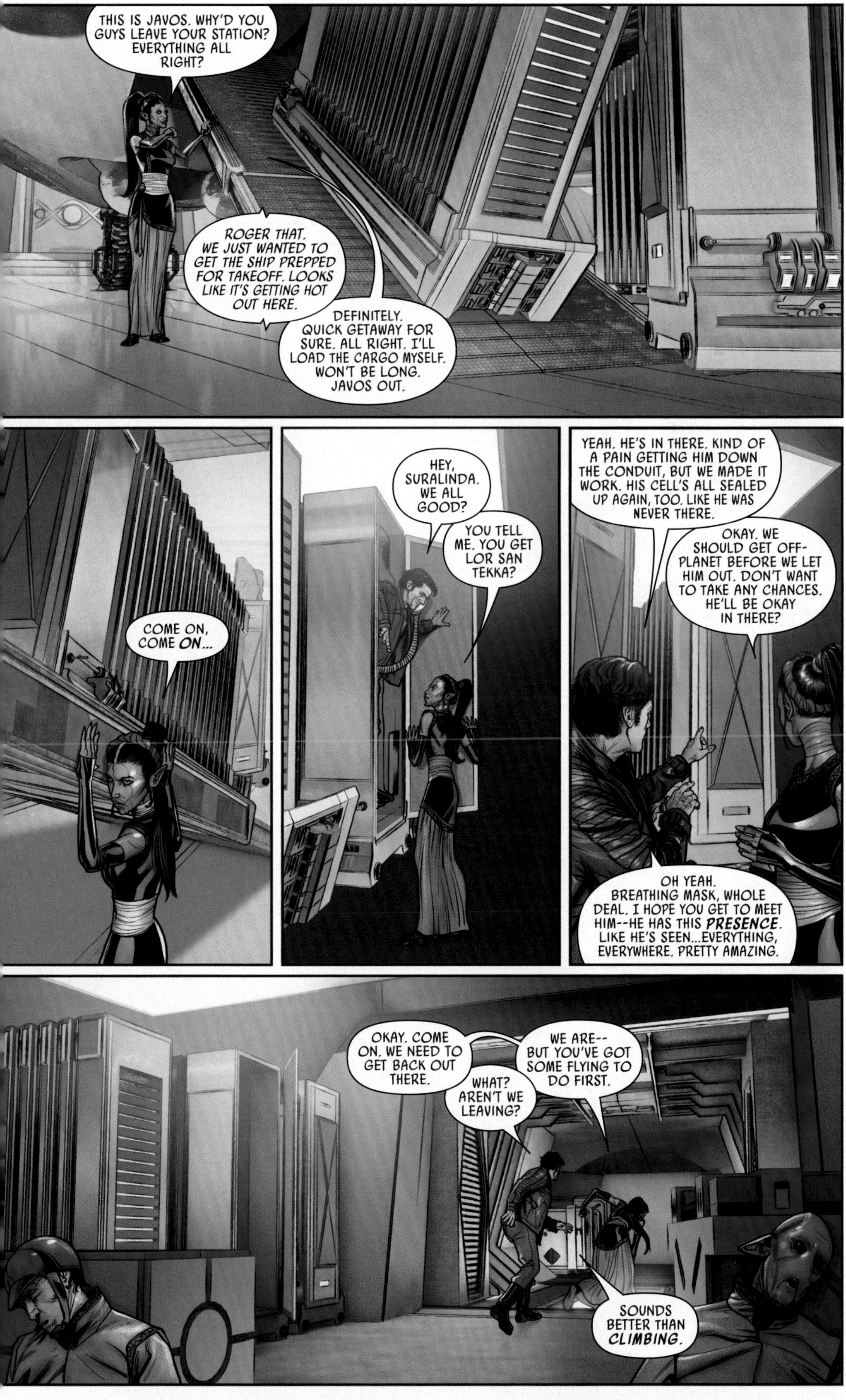
THIS IS JAVOS. WHY'D YOU GUYS LEAVE YOUR STATION? EVERYTHING ALL RIGHT?
ROGER THAT. WE JUST WANTED TO GET THE SHIP PREPPED FOR TAKEOFF. LOOKS LIKE IT'S GETTING HOT OUT HERE.
DEFINITELY. QUICK GETAWAY FOR SURE. ALL RIGHT. I'LL LOAD THE CARGO MYSELF. WON'T BE LONG. JAVOS OUT.
COME ON, COME ON...
HEY, SURALINDA. WE ALL GOOD?
YOU TELL ME. YOU GET LOR SAN TEKKA?
YEAH. HE'S IN THERE. KIND OF A PAIN GETTING HIM DOWN THE CONDUIT, BUT WE MADE IT WORK. HIS CELL'S ALL SEALED UP AGAIN, TOO. LIKE HE WAS NEVER THERE.
OKAY. WE SHOULD GET OFF-PLANET BEFORE WE LET HIM OUT. DON'T WANT TO TAKE ANY CHANCES. HE'LL BE OKAY IN THERE?
OH YEAH. BREATHING MASK, WHOLE DEAL. I HOPE YOU GET TO MEET HIM--HE HAS THIS PRESENCE. LIKE HE'S SEEN...EVERYTHING, EVERYWHERE. PRETTY AMAZING.
OKAY. COME ON. WE NEED TO GET BACK OUT THERE.
WHAT? AREN'T WE LEAVING?
WE ARE--BUT YOU'VE GOT SOME FLYING TO DO FIRST.
SOUNDS BETTER THAN CLIMBING.

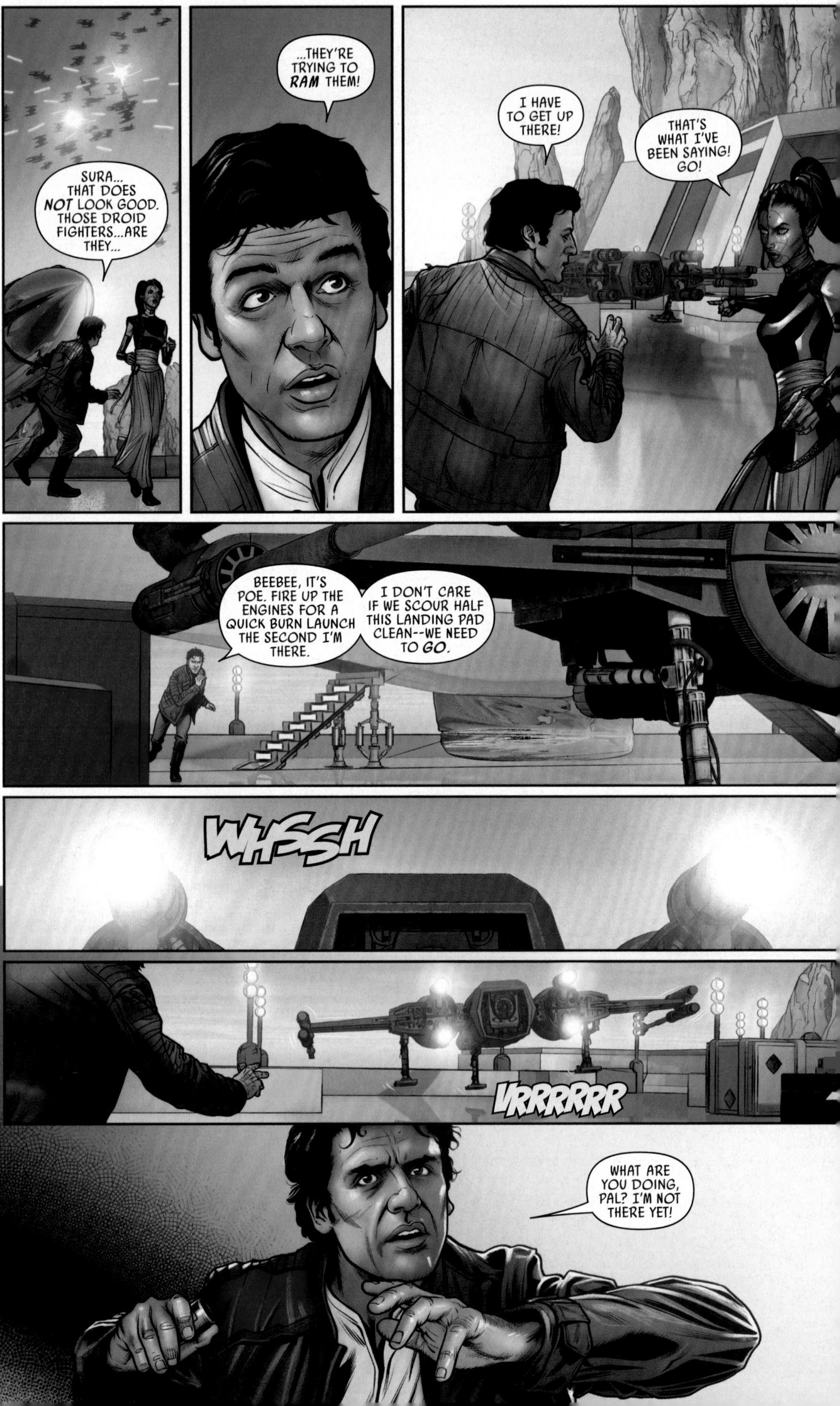
SURA... THAT DOES NOT LOOK GOOD. THOSE DROID FIGHTERS...ARE THEY...
...THEY'RE TRYING TO RAM THEM!
I HAVE TO GET UP THERE!
THAT'S WHAT I'VE BEEN SAYING! GO!
BEEBEE, IT'S POE. FIRE UP THE ENGINES FOR A QUICK BURN LAUNCH THE SECOND I'M THERE.
I DON'T CARE IF WE SCOUR HALF THIS LANDING PAD CLEAN--WE NEED TO GO.
WHSSH
VRRRRRR
WHAT ARE YOU DOING, PAL? I'M NOT THERE YET!

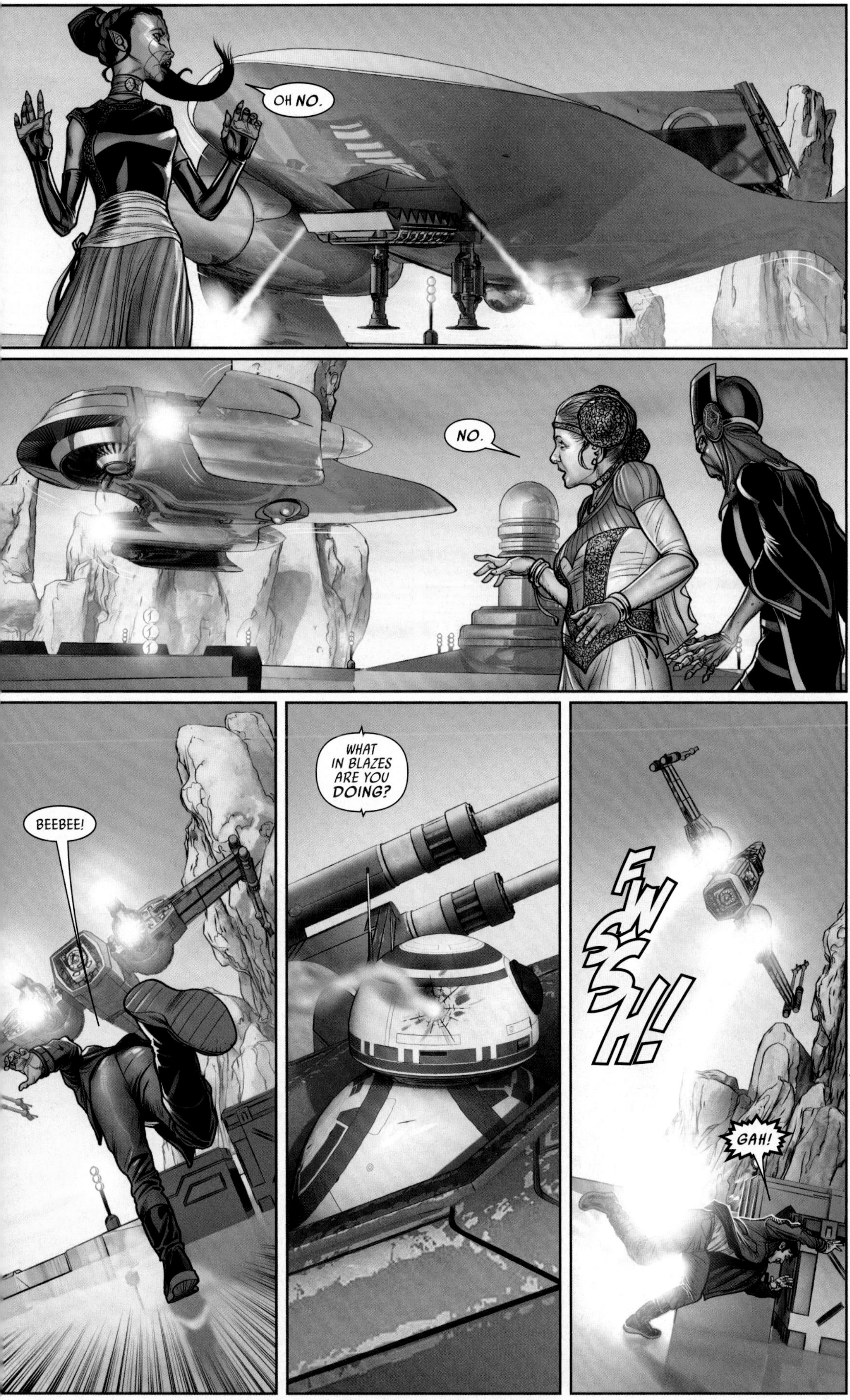
OH NO.
NO.
BEEBEE!
WHAT IN BLAZES ARE YOU DOING?
FWSSH!
GAH!

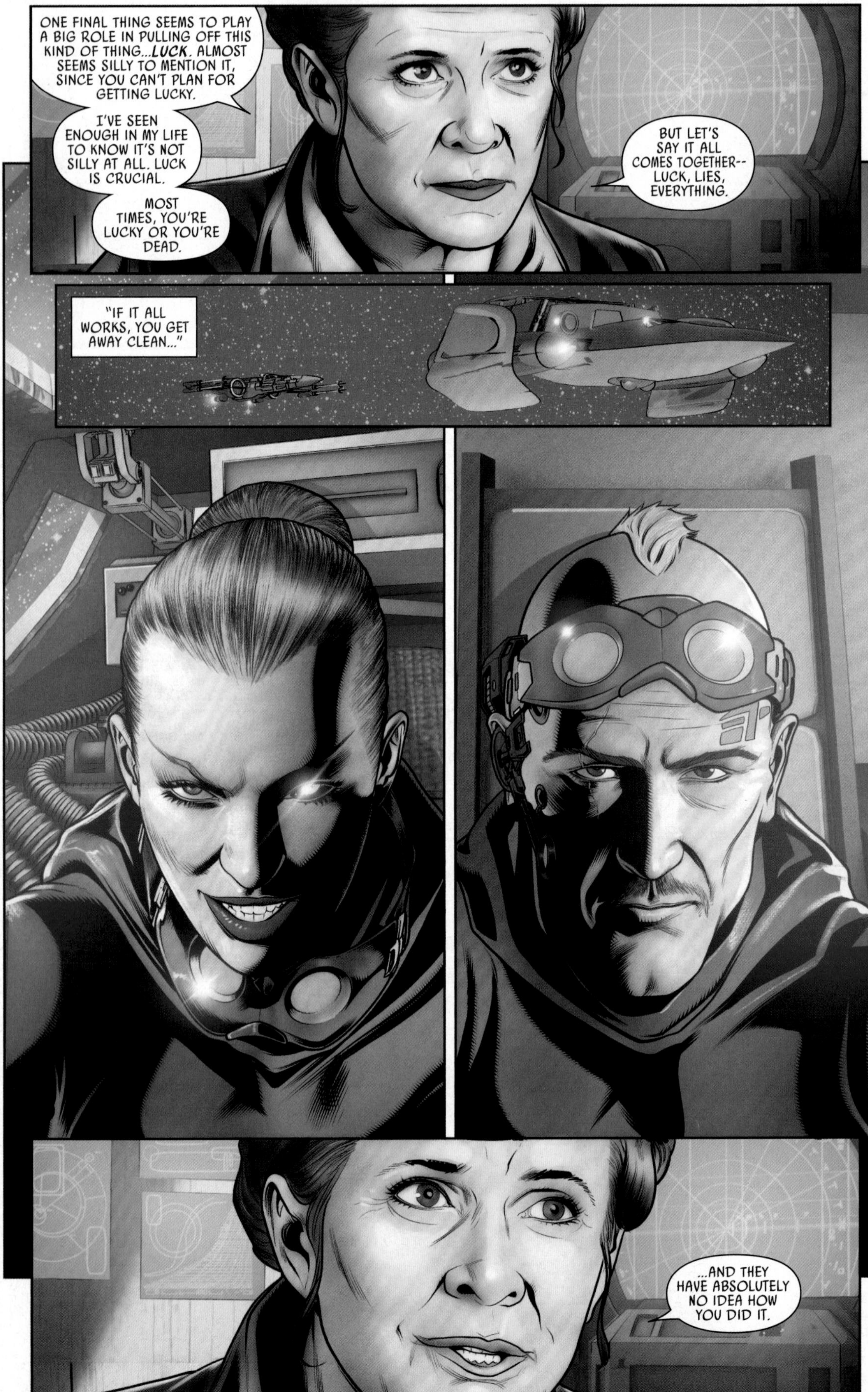
ONE FINAL THING SEEMS TO PLAY A BIG ROLE IN PULLING OFF THIS KIND OF THING...**LUCK**. ALMOST SEEMS SILLY TO MENTION IT, SINCE YOU CAN'T PLAN FOR GETTING LUCKY.
I'VE SEEN ENOUGH IN MY LIFE TO KNOW IT'S NOT SILLY AT ALL. LUCK IS CRUCIAL.
MOST TIMES, YOU'RE LUCKY OR YOU'RE DEAD.
BUT LET'S SAY IT ALL COMES TOGETHER-- LUCK, LIES, EVERYTHING.
"IF IT ALL WORKS, YOU GET AWAY CLEAN..."
...AND THEY HAVE ABSOLUTELY NO IDEA HOW YOU DID IT.

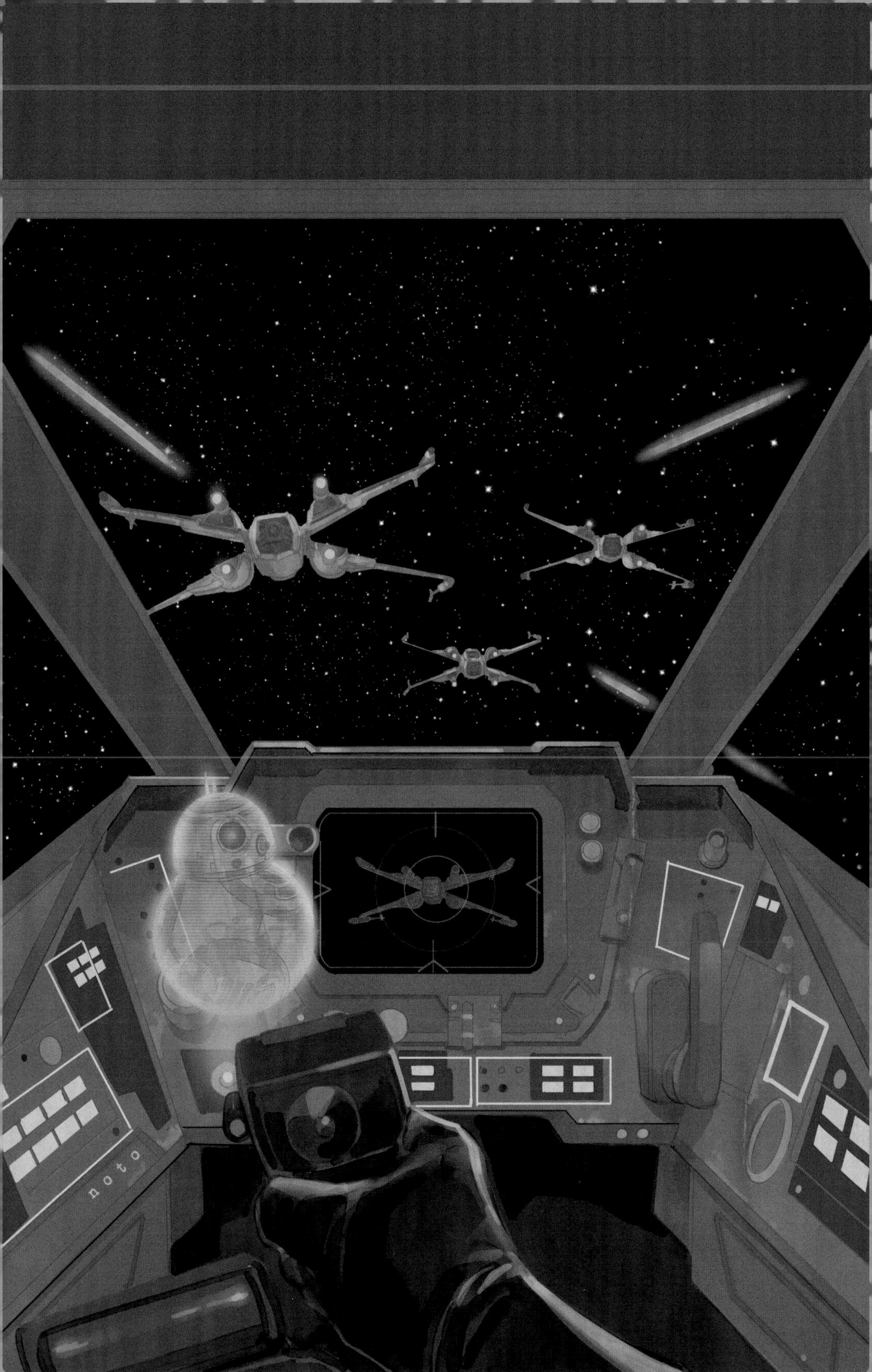
noto

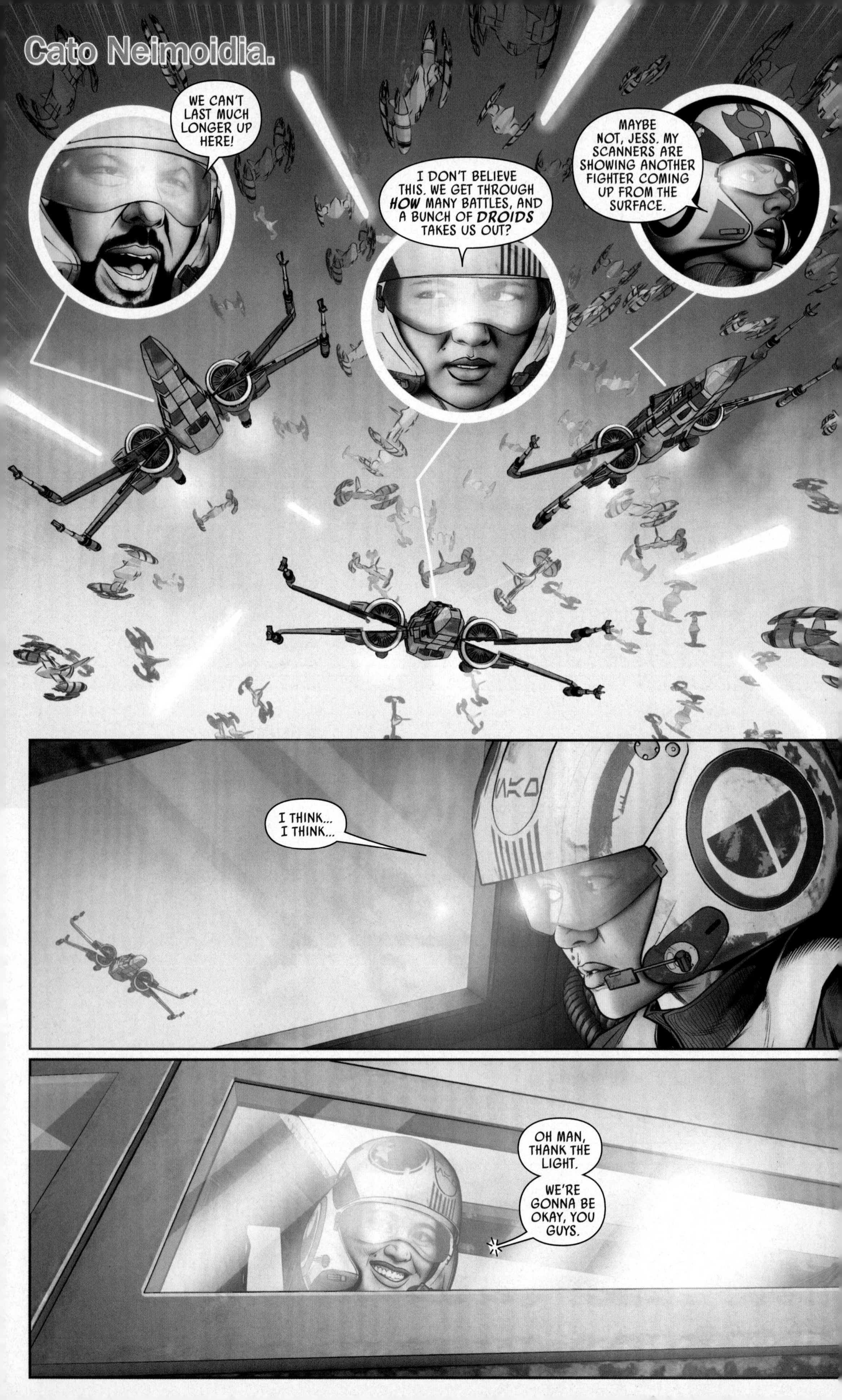
Cato Neimoidia.
WE CAN'T LAST MUCH LONGER UP HERE!
I DON'T BELIEVE THIS. WE GET THROUGH HOW MANY BATTLES, AND A BUNCH OF DROIDS TAKES US OUT?
MAYBE NOT, JESS. MY SCANNERS ARE SHOWING ANOTHER FIGHTER COMING UP FROM THE SURFACE.
I THINK... I THINK...
OH MAN, THANK THE LIGHT.
WE'RE GONNA BE OKAY, YOU GUYS.

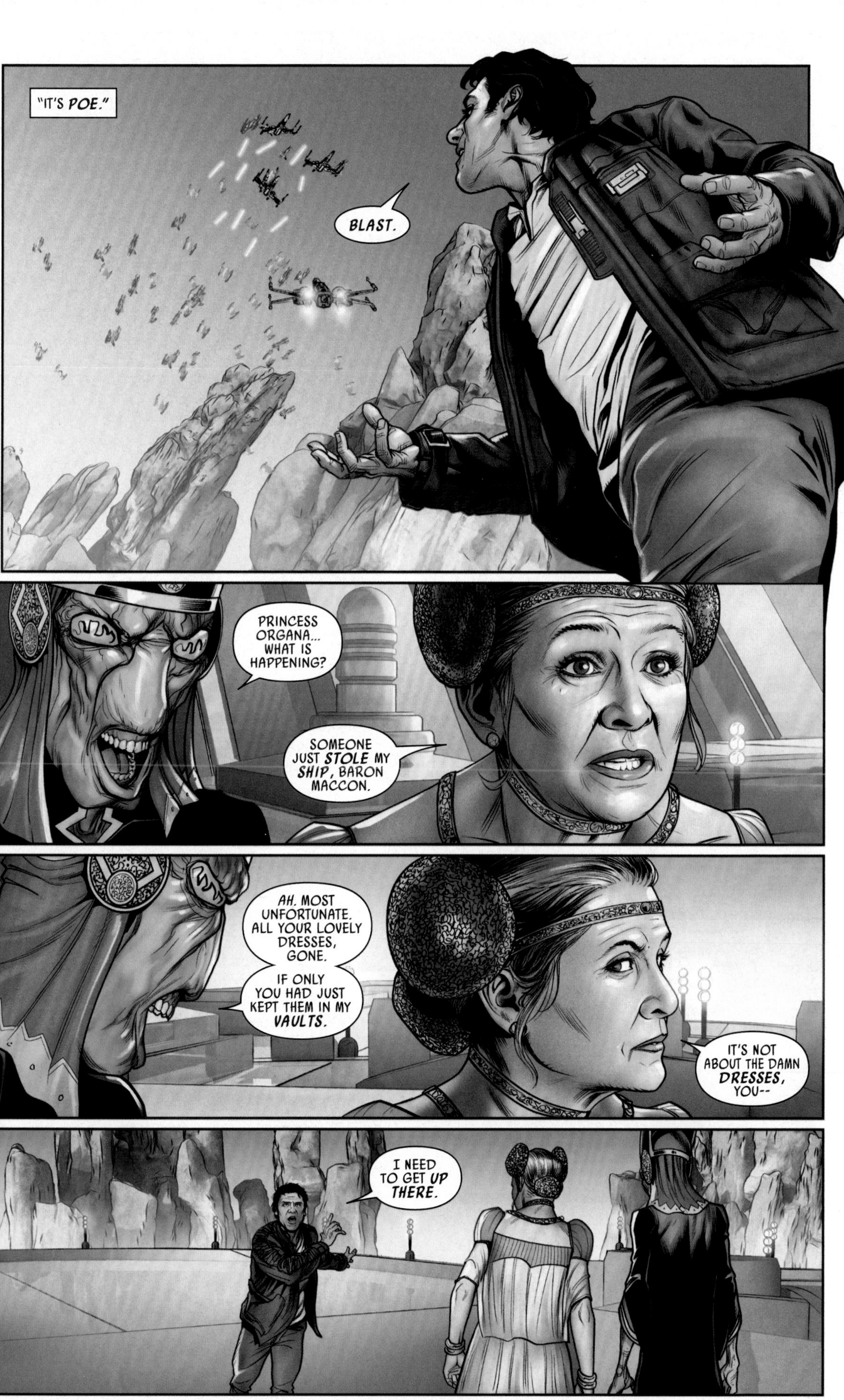
"IT'S POE."
BLAST.
PRINCESS ORGANA... WHAT IS HAPPENING?
SOMEONE JUST STOLE MY SHIP, BARON MACCON.
AH. MOST UNFORTUNATE. ALL YOUR LOVELY DRESSES, GONE.
IF ONLY YOU HAD JUST KEPT THEM IN MY VAULTS.
IT'S NOT ABOUT THE DAMN DRESSES, YOU--
I NEED TO GET UP THERE.

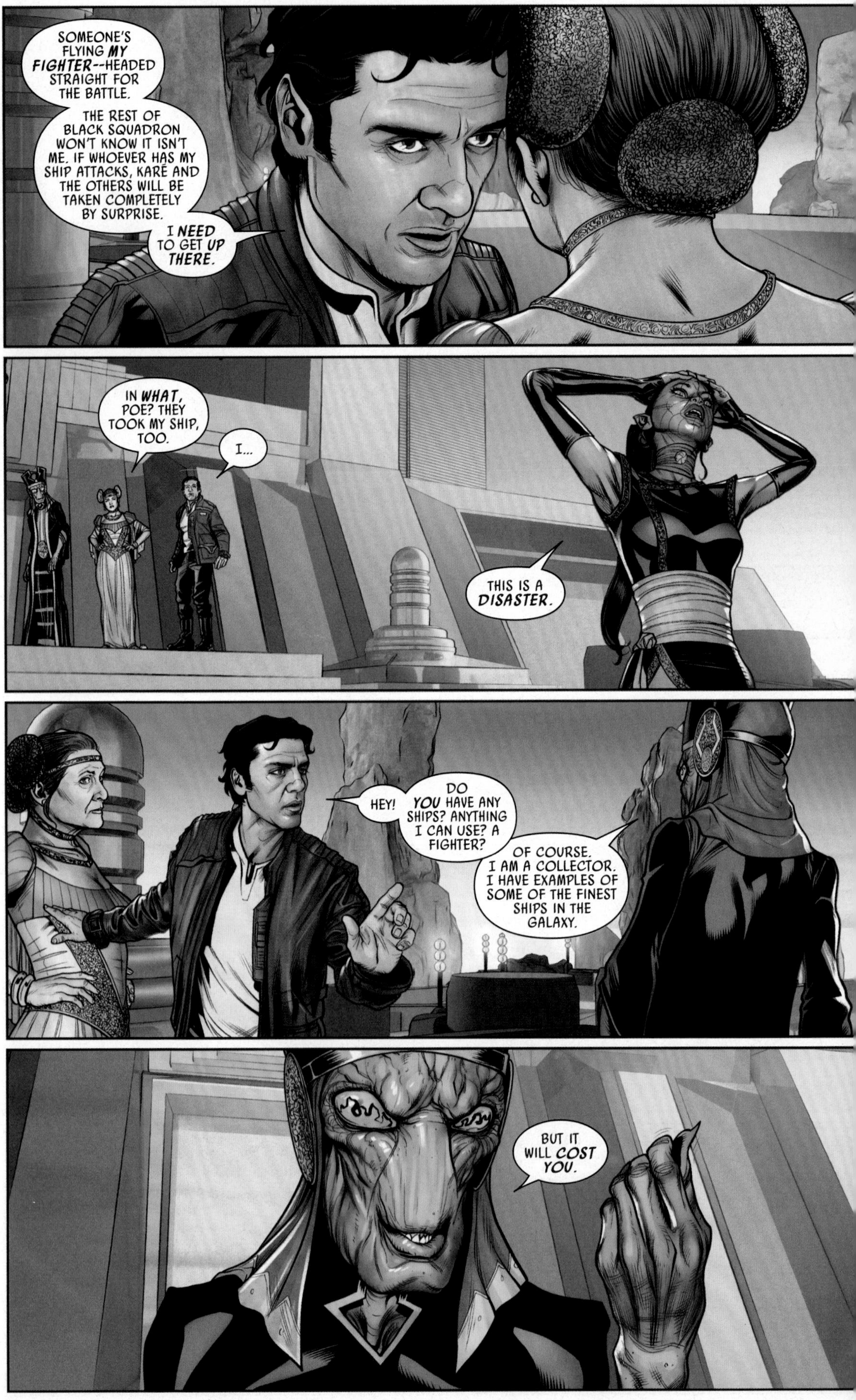

SOMEONE'S FLYING MY FIGHTER--HEADED STRAIGHT FOR THE BATTLE.
THE REST OF BLACK SQUADRON WON'T KNOW IT ISN'T ME. IF WHOEVER HAS MY SHIP ATTACKS, KARÉ AND THE OTHERS WILL BE TAKEN COMPLETELY BY SURPRISE.
I NEED TO GET UP THERE.
IN WHAT, POE? THEY TOOK MY SHIP, TOO.
I...
THIS IS A DISASTER.
HEY!
DO YOU HAVE ANY SHIPS? ANYTHING I CAN USE? A FIGHTER?
OF COURSE. I AM A COLLECTOR. I HAVE EXAMPLES OF SOME OF THE FINEST SHIPS IN THE GALAXY.
BUT IT WILL COST YOU.

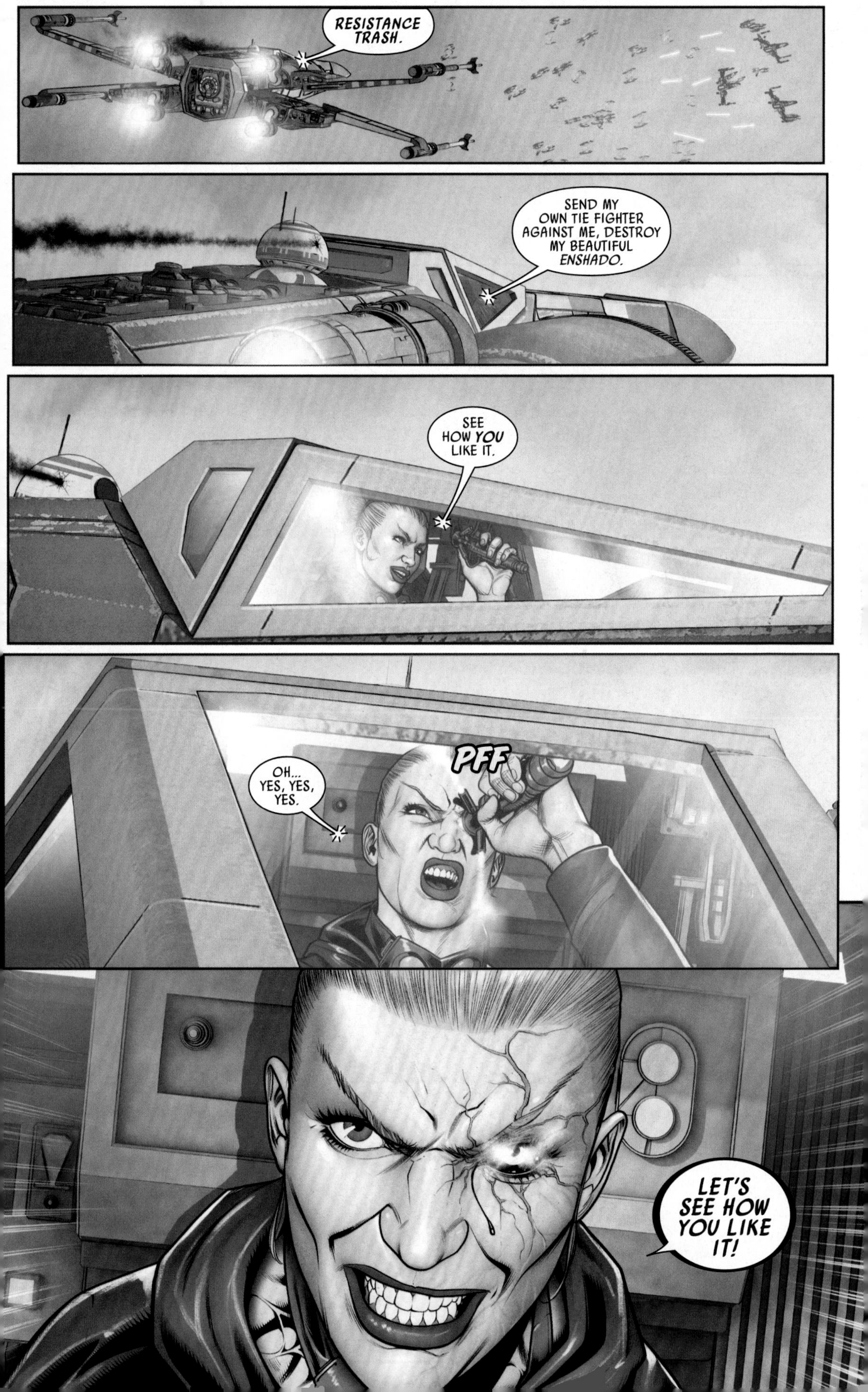
RESISTANCE TRASH.
SEND MY OWN TIE FIGHTER AGAINST ME, DESTROY MY BEAUTIFUL ENSHADO.
SEE HOW YOU LIKE IT.
PFF
OH... YES, YES, YES.
LET'S SEE HOW YOU LIKE IT!

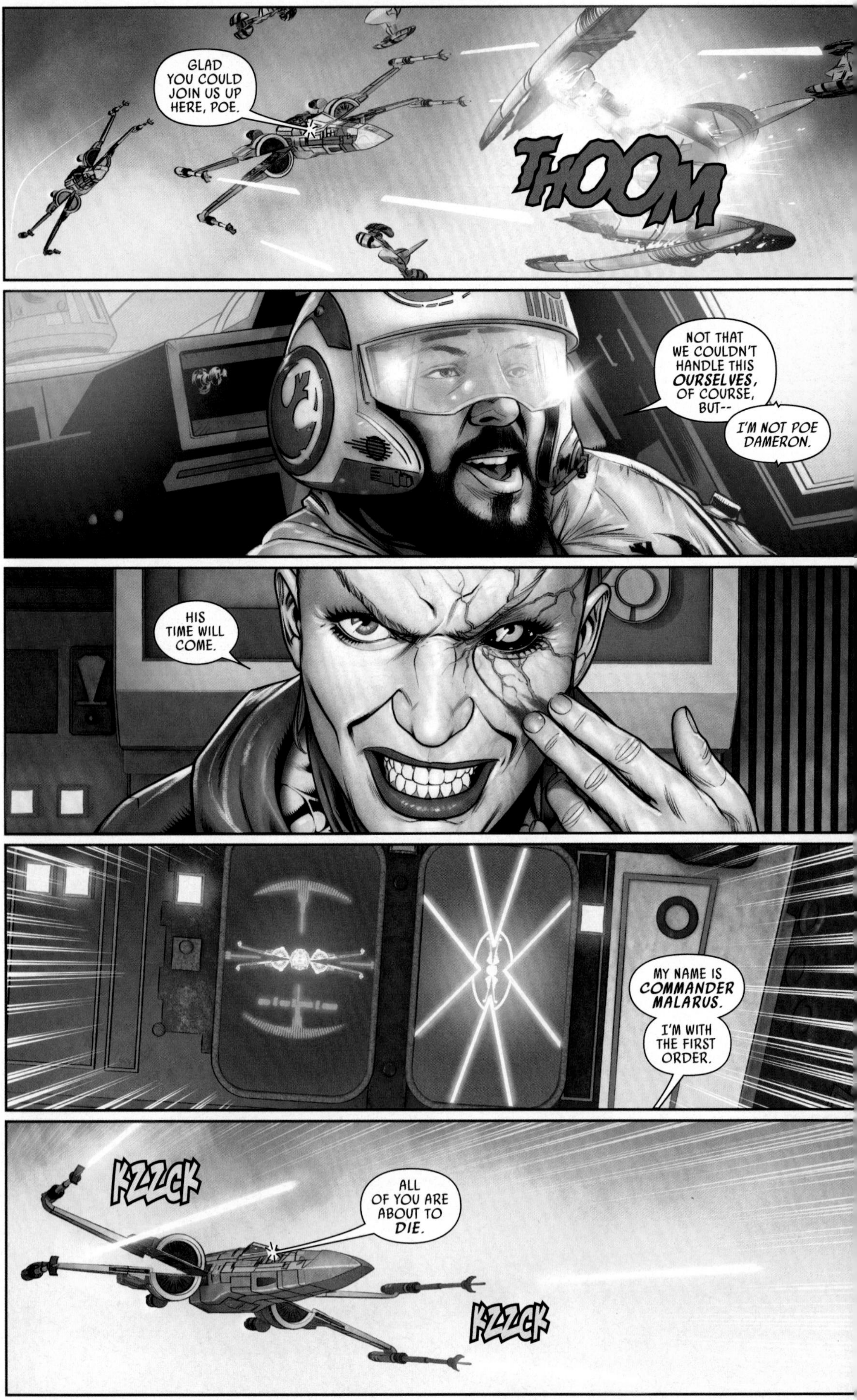
GLAD YOU COULD JOIN US UP HERE, POE.
THOOM
NOT THAT WE COULDN'T HANDLE THIS OURSELVES, OF COURSE, BUT--
I'M NOT POE DAMERON.
HIS TIME WILL COME.
MY NAME IS COMMANDER MALARUS.
I'M WITH THE FIRST ORDER.
KZZCK
ALL OF YOU ARE ABOUT TO DIE.
KZZCK

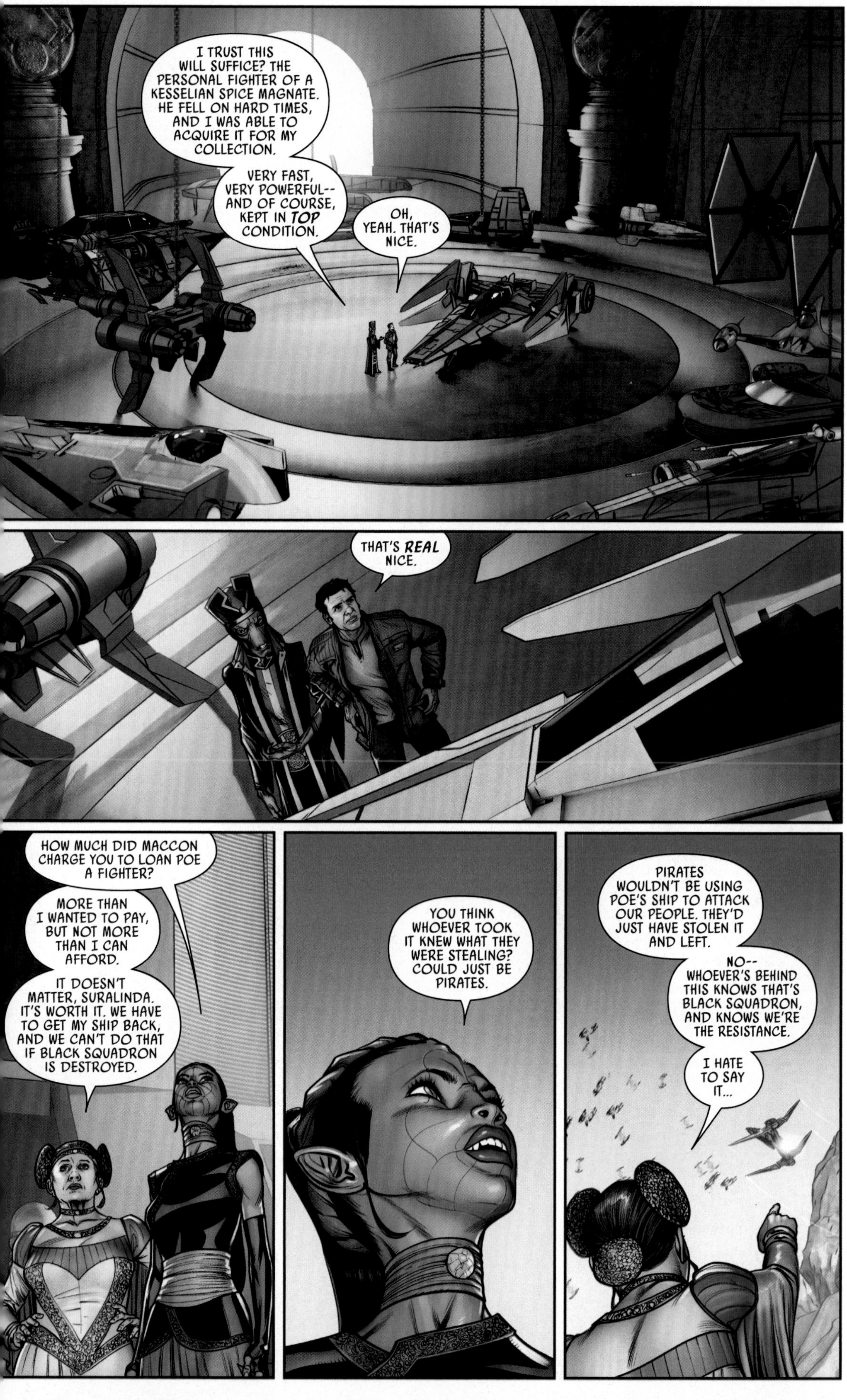
I TRUST THIS WILL SUFFICE? THE PERSONAL FIGHTER OF A KESSELIAN SPICE MAGNATE. HE FELL ON HARD TIMES, AND I WAS ABLE TO ACQUIRE IT FOR MY COLLECTION.
VERY FAST, VERY POWERFUL-- AND OF COURSE, KEPT IN *TOP* CONDITION.
OH, YEAH. THAT'S NICE.
THAT'S *REAL* NICE.
HOW MUCH DID MACCON CHARGE YOU TO LOAN POE A FIGHTER?
MORE THAN I WANTED TO PAY, BUT NOT MORE THAN I CAN AFFORD.
IT DOESN'T MATTER, SURALINDA. IT'S WORTH IT. WE HAVE TO GET MY SHIP BACK, AND WE CAN'T DO THAT IF BLACK SQUADRON IS DESTROYED.
YOU THINK WHOEVER TOOK IT KNEW WHAT THEY WERE STEALING? COULD JUST BE PIRATES.
PIRATES WOULDN'T BE USING POE'S SHIP TO ATTACK OUR PEOPLE. THEY'D JUST HAVE STOLEN IT AND LEFT.
NO-- WHOEVER'S BEHIND THIS KNOWS THAT'S BLACK SQUADRON, AND KNOWS WE'RE THE RESISTANCE.
I HATE TO SAY IT...

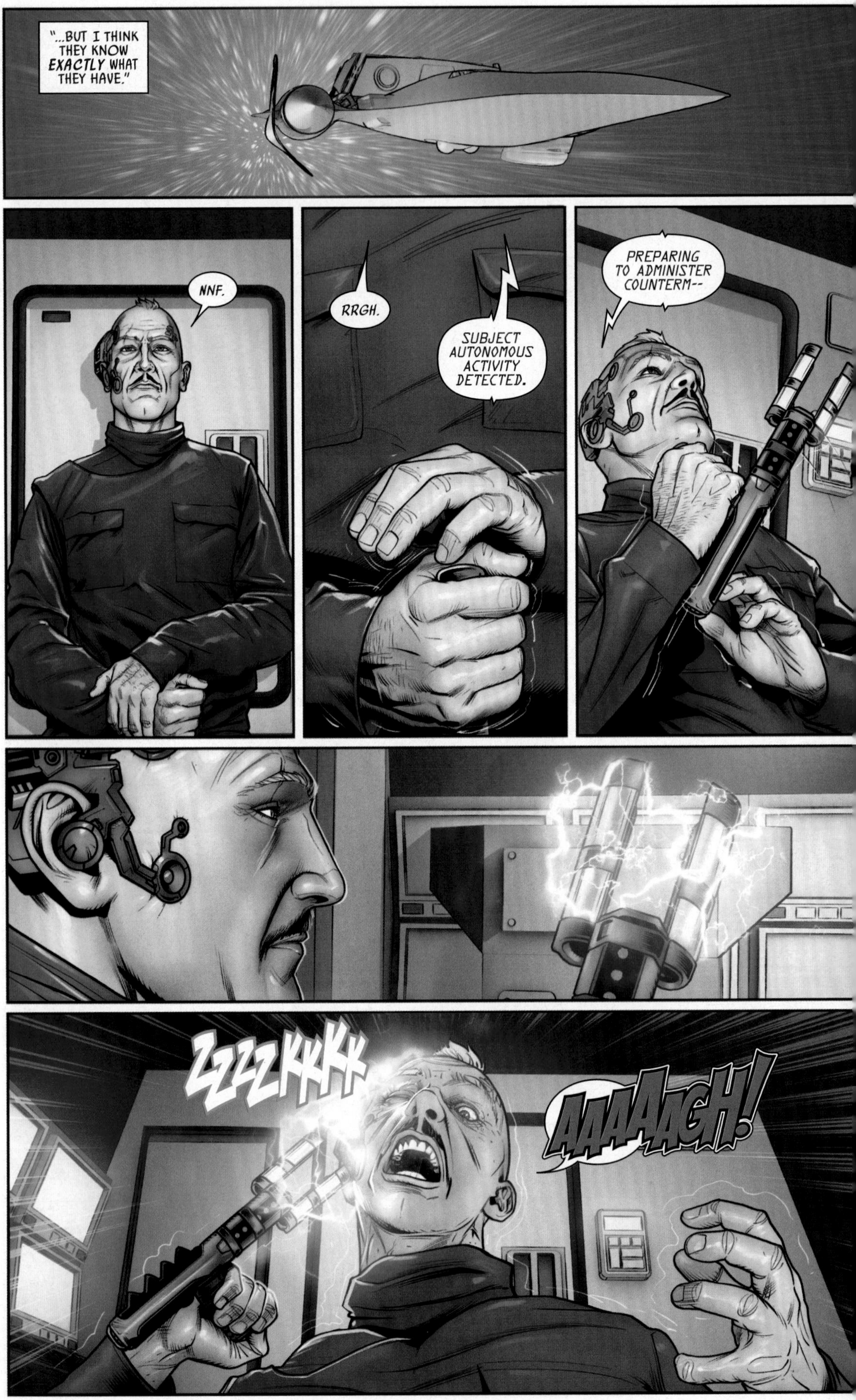
"...BUT I THINK THEY KNOW EXACTLY WHAT THEY HAVE."
NNF.
RRGH.
SUBJECT AUTONOMOUS ACTIVITY DETECTED.
PREPARING TO ADMINISTER COUNTERM--
ZZZZKKKK
AAAAAGH!

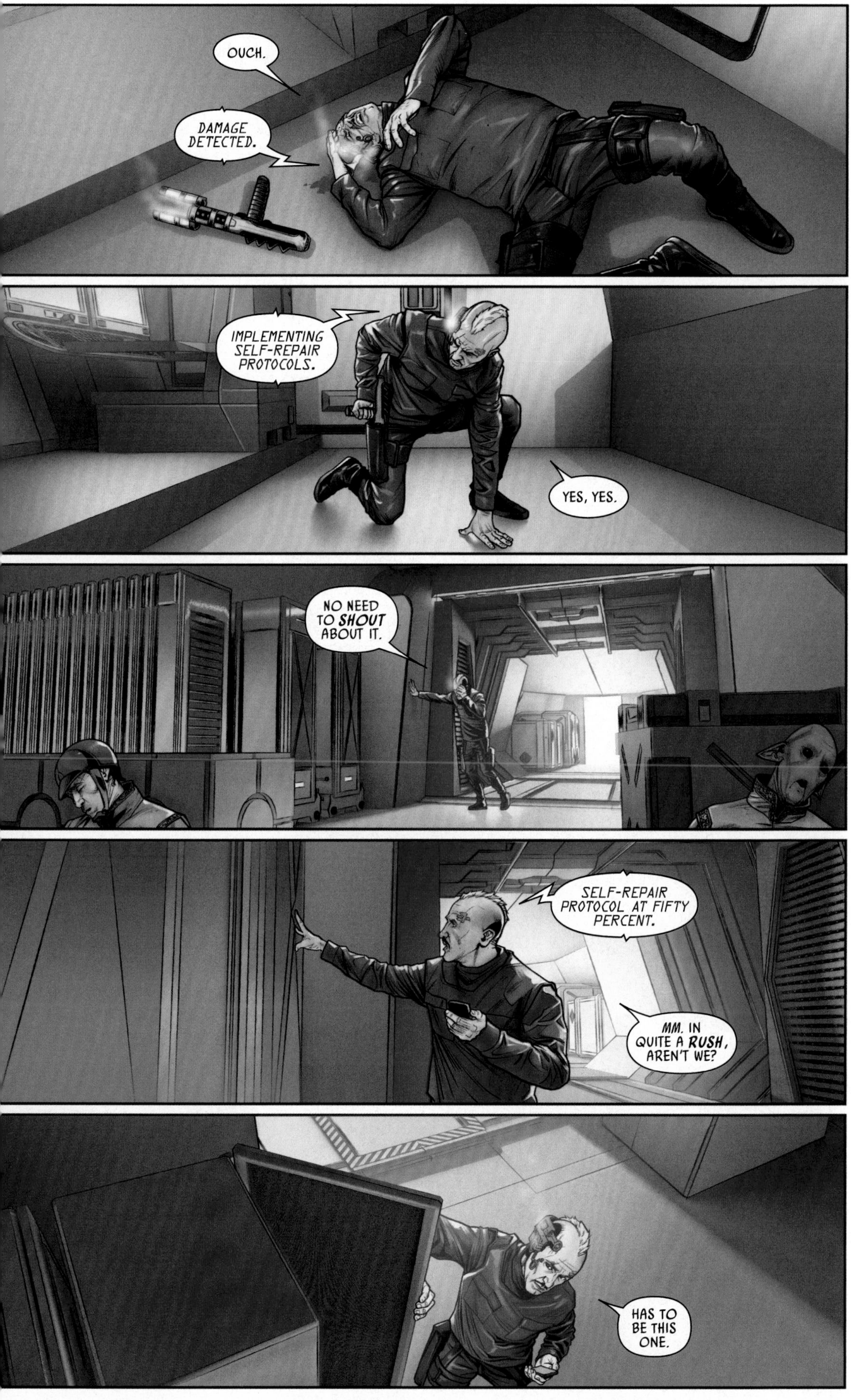
OUCH.
DAMAGE DETECTED.
IMPLEMENTING SELF-REPAIR PROTOCOLS.
YES, YES.
NO NEED TO SHOUT ABOUT IT.
SELF-REPAIR PROTOCOL AT FIFTY PERCENT.
MM. IN QUITE A RUSH, AREN'T WE?
HAS TO BE THIS ONE.

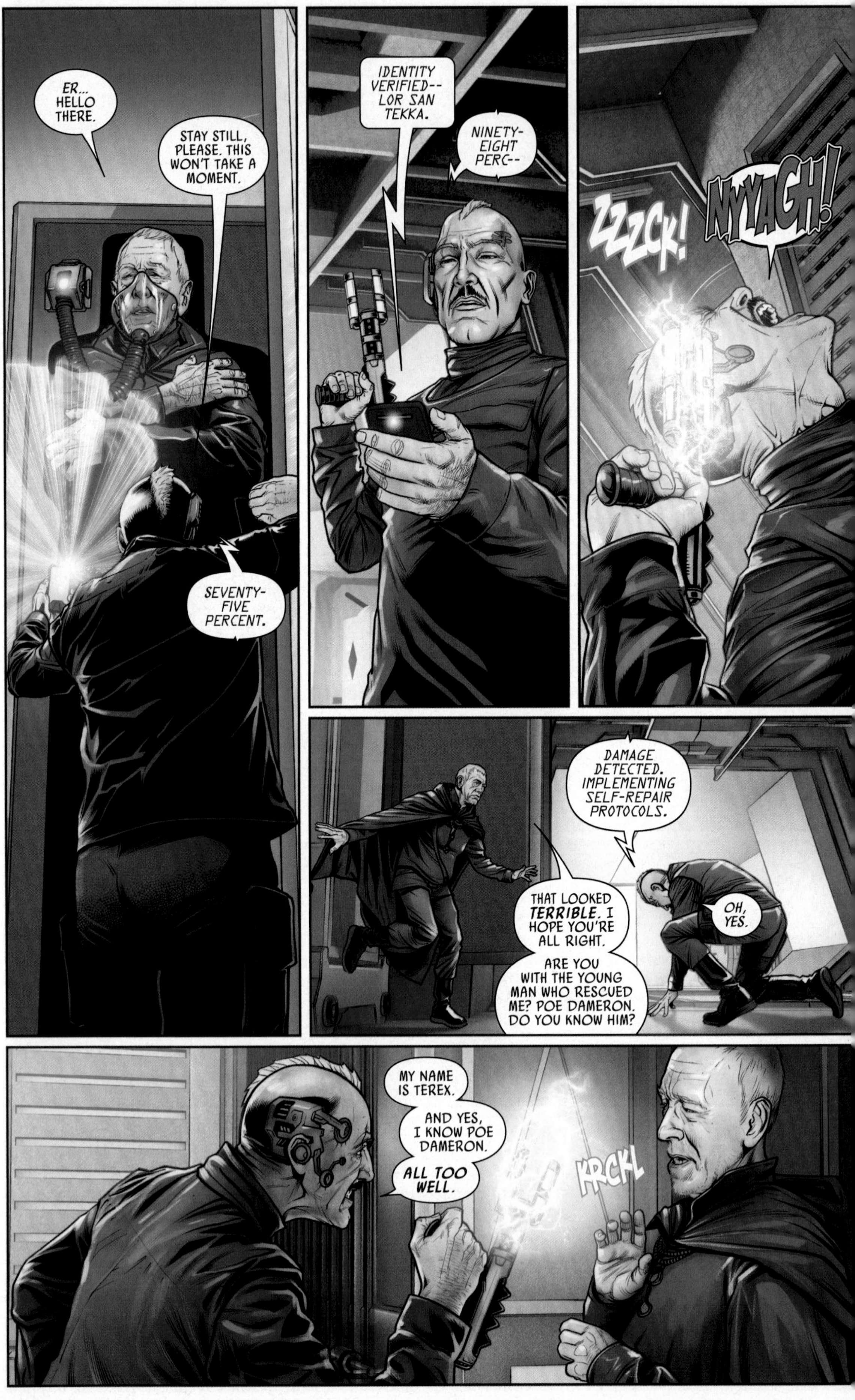

ER... HELLO THERE.
STAY STILL, PLEASE. THIS WON'T TAKE A MOMENT.
SEVENTY-FIVE PERCENT.
IDENTITY VERIFIED-- LOR SAN TEKKA.
NINETY-EIGHT PERC--
ZZZCK!
NYYAGH!
DAMAGE DETECTED. IMPLEMENTING SELF-REPAIR PROTOCOLS.
THAT LOOKED **TERRIBLE.** I HOPE YOU'RE ALL RIGHT.
ARE YOU WITH THE YOUNG MAN WHO RESCUED ME? POE DAMERON. DO YOU KNOW HIM?
OH, YES.
MY NAME IS TEREX.
AND YES, I KNOW POE DAMERON.
ALL TOO WELL.
KRCKL

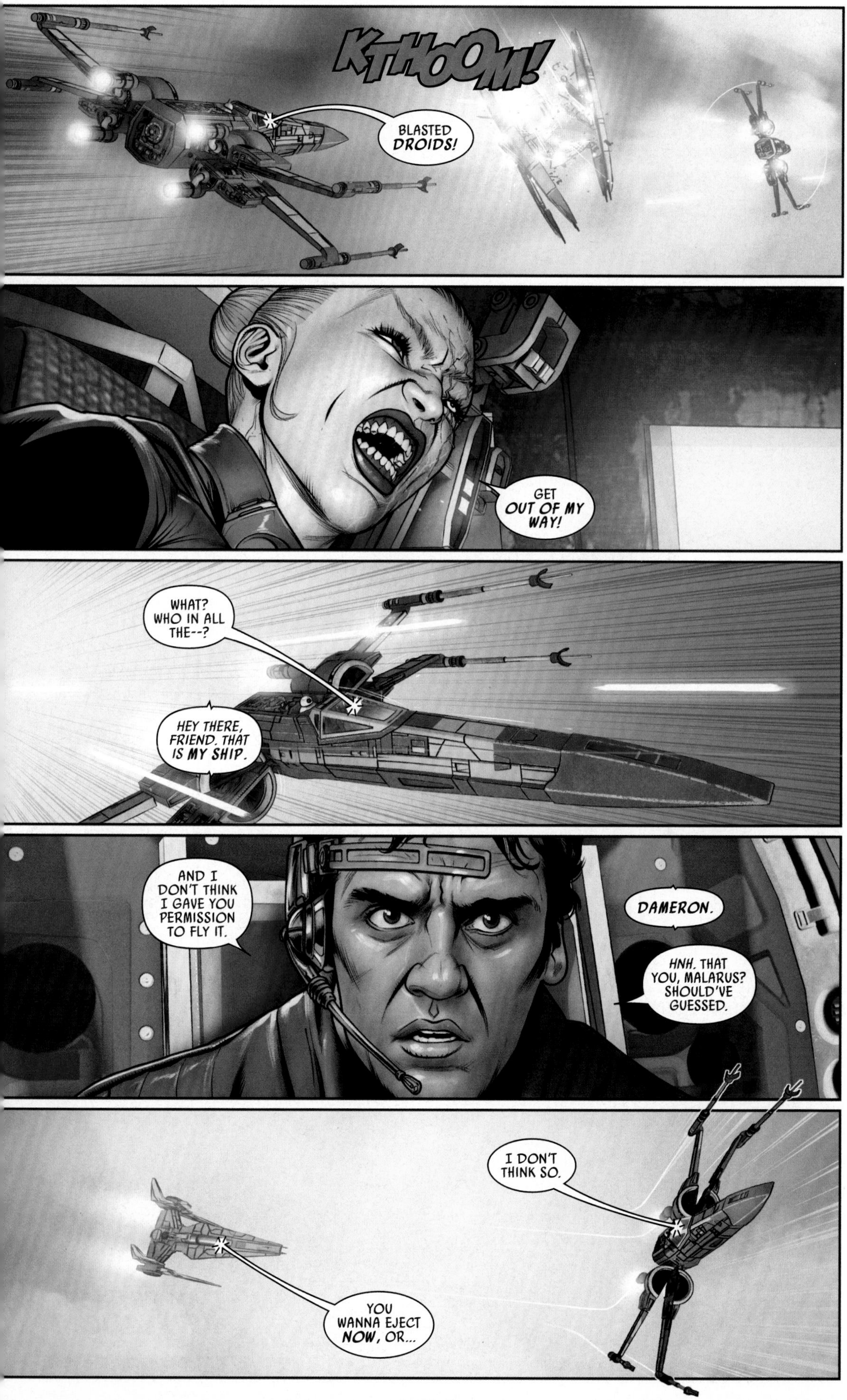
KTHOOM!
BLASTED DROIDS!
GET OUT OF MY WAY!
WHAT? WHO IN ALL THE--?
HEY THERE, FRIEND. THAT IS MY SHIP.
AND I DON'T THINK I GAVE YOU PERMISSION TO FLY IT.
DAMERON.
HNH. THAT YOU, MALARUS? SHOULD'VE GUESSED.
YOU WANNA EJECT NOW, OR...
I DON'T THINK SO.

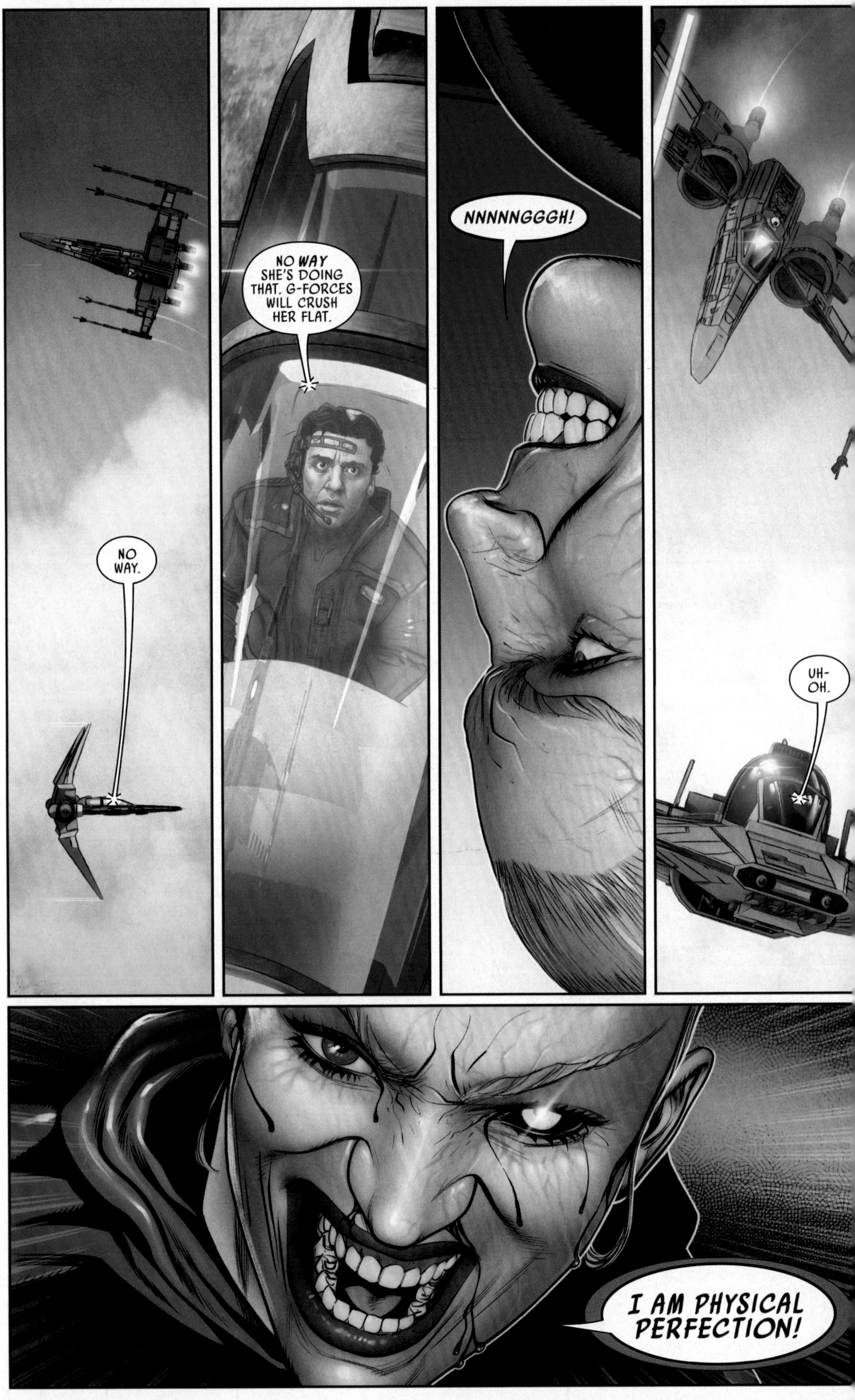
NO WAY.
NO WAY SHE'S DOING THAT. G-FORCES WILL CRUSH HER FLAT.
NNNNNGGGH!
UH-OH.
I AM PHYSICAL PERFECTION!

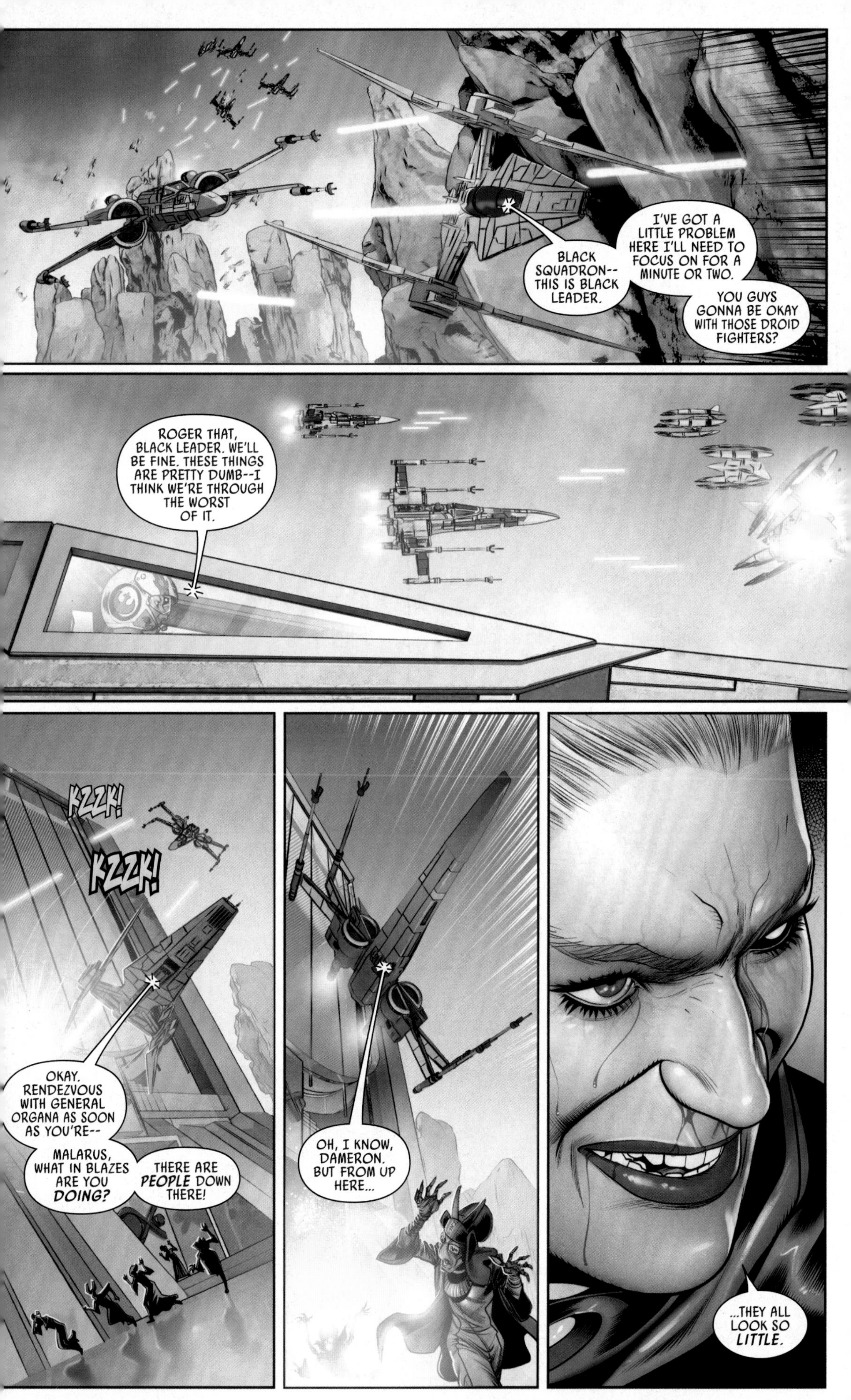

BLACK SQUADRON-- THIS IS BLACK LEADER.
I'VE GOT A LITTLE PROBLEM HERE I'LL NEED TO FOCUS ON FOR A MINUTE OR TWO.
YOU GUYS GONNA BE OKAY WITH THOSE DROID FIGHTERS?
ROGER THAT, BLACK LEADER. WE'LL BE FINE. THESE THINGS ARE PRETTY DUMB--I THINK WE'RE THROUGH THE WORST OF IT.
KZZK!
KZZK!
OKAY. RENDEZVOUS WITH GENERAL ORGANA AS SOON AS YOU'RE--
MALARUS, WHAT IN BLAZES ARE YOU *DOING?*
THERE ARE *PEOPLE* DOWN THERE!
OH, I KNOW, DAMERON. BUT FROM UP HERE...
...THEY ALL LOOK SO *LITTLE.*

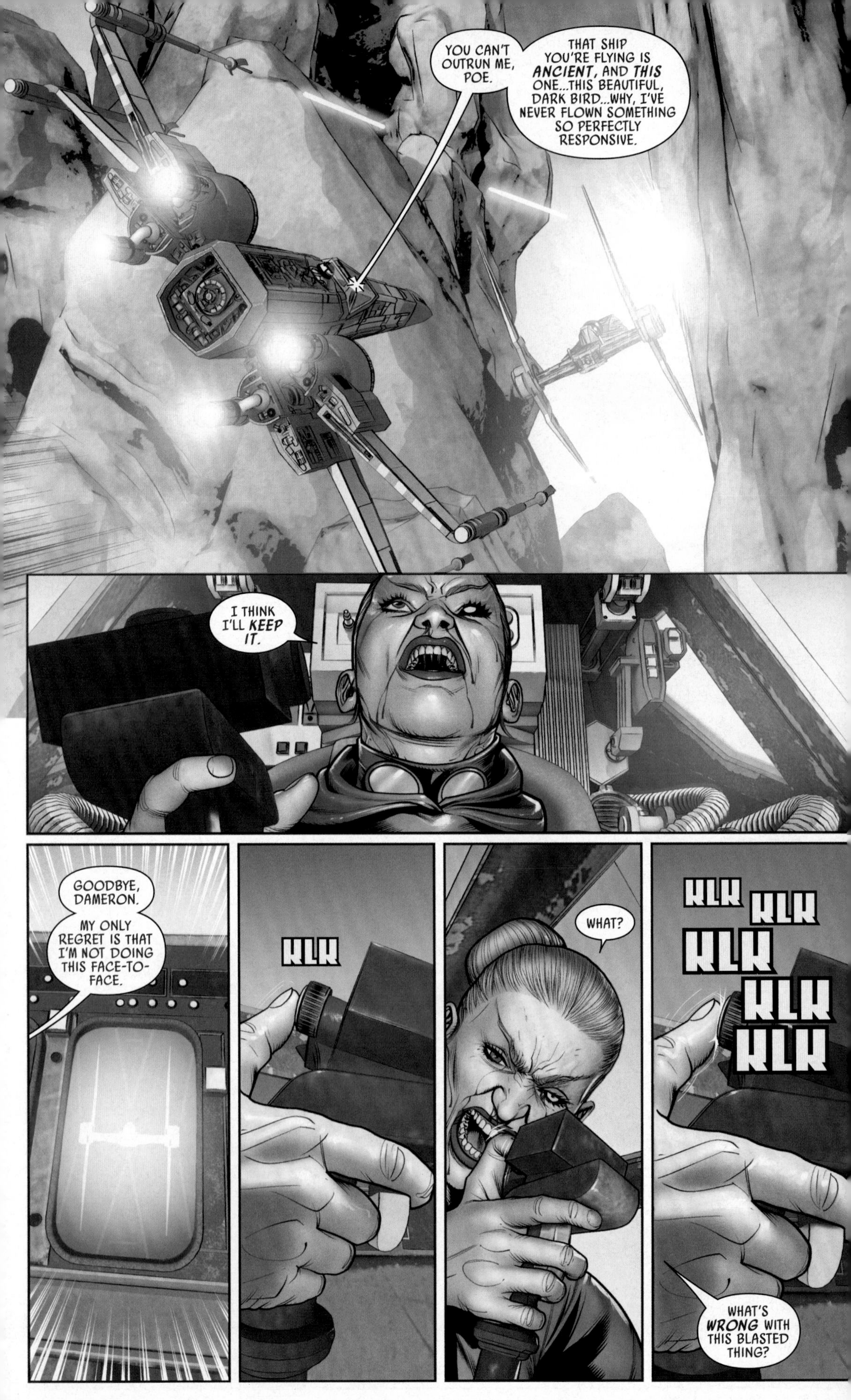
YOU CAN'T OUTRUN ME, POE.
THAT SHIP YOU'RE FLYING IS ANCIENT, AND THIS ONE...THIS BEAUTIFUL, DARK BIRD...WHY, I'VE NEVER FLOWN SOMETHING SO PERFECTLY RESPONSIVE.
I THINK I'LL KEEP IT.
GOODBYE, DAMERON.
MY ONLY REGRET IS THAT I'M NOT DOING THIS FACE-TO-FACE.
KLK
WHAT?
KLK KLK KLK KLK KLK
WHAT'S WRONG WITH THIS BLASTED THING?

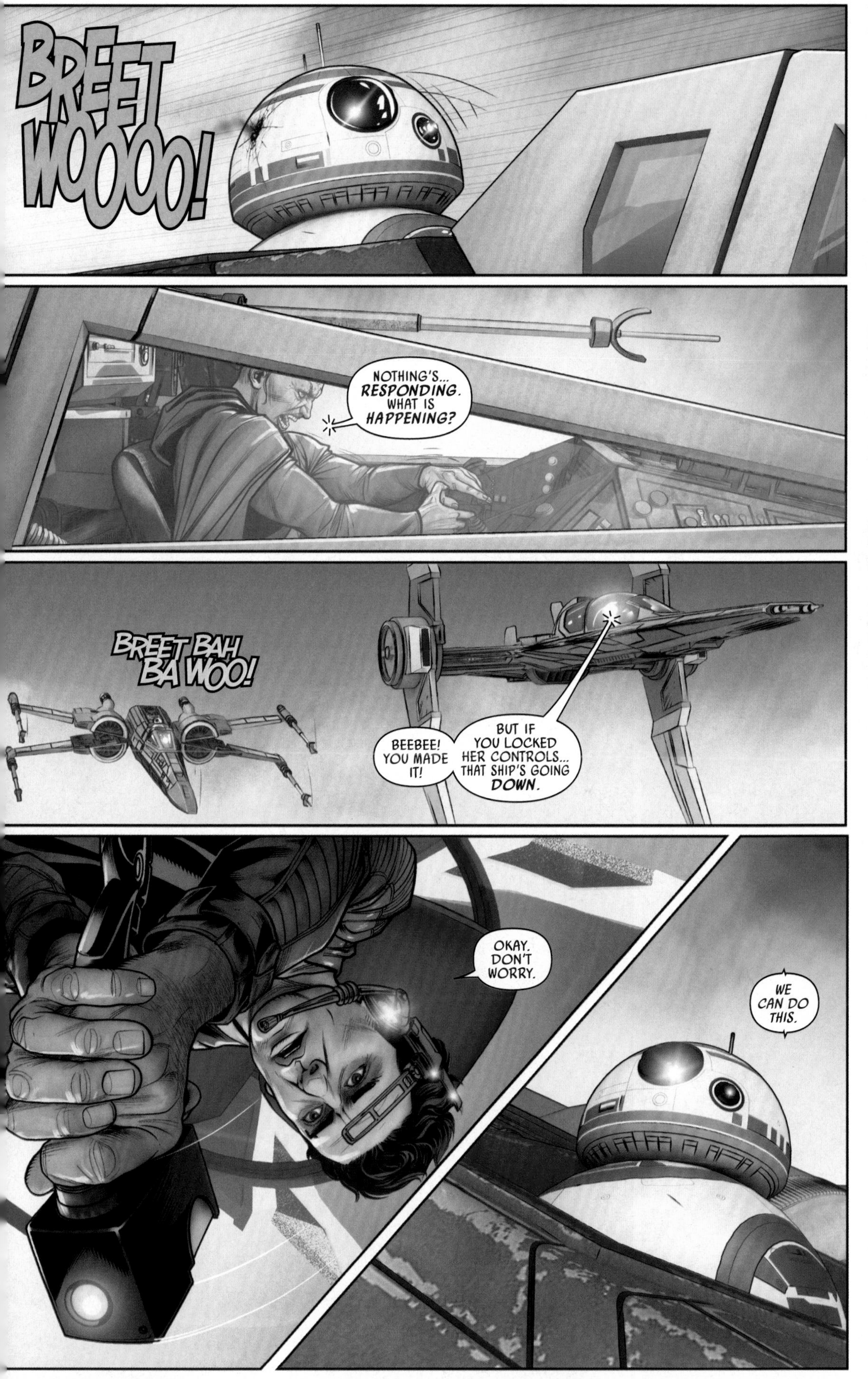
BREET WOOOO!
NOTHING'S... RESPONDING. WHAT IS HAPPENING?
BREET BAH BA WOO!
BEEBEE! YOU MADE IT!
BUT IF YOU LOCKED HER CONTROLS... THAT SHIP'S GOING DOWN.
OKAY. DON'T WORRY.
WE CAN DO THIS.

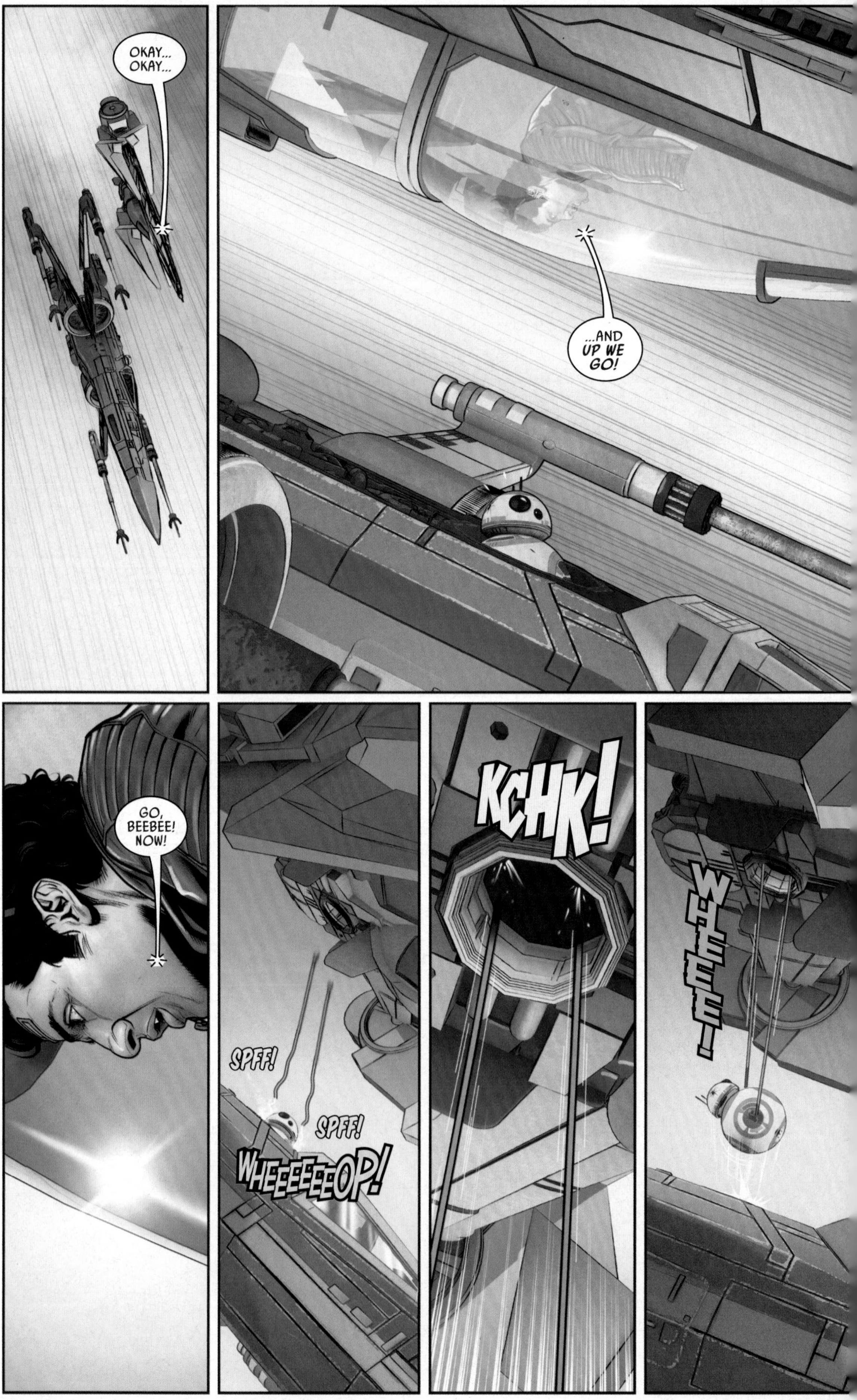
OKAY... OKAY...
...AND UP WE GO!
GO, BEEBEE! NOW!
SPFF!
SPFF!
WHEEEEEEEOP!
KCHK!
WHEEE!

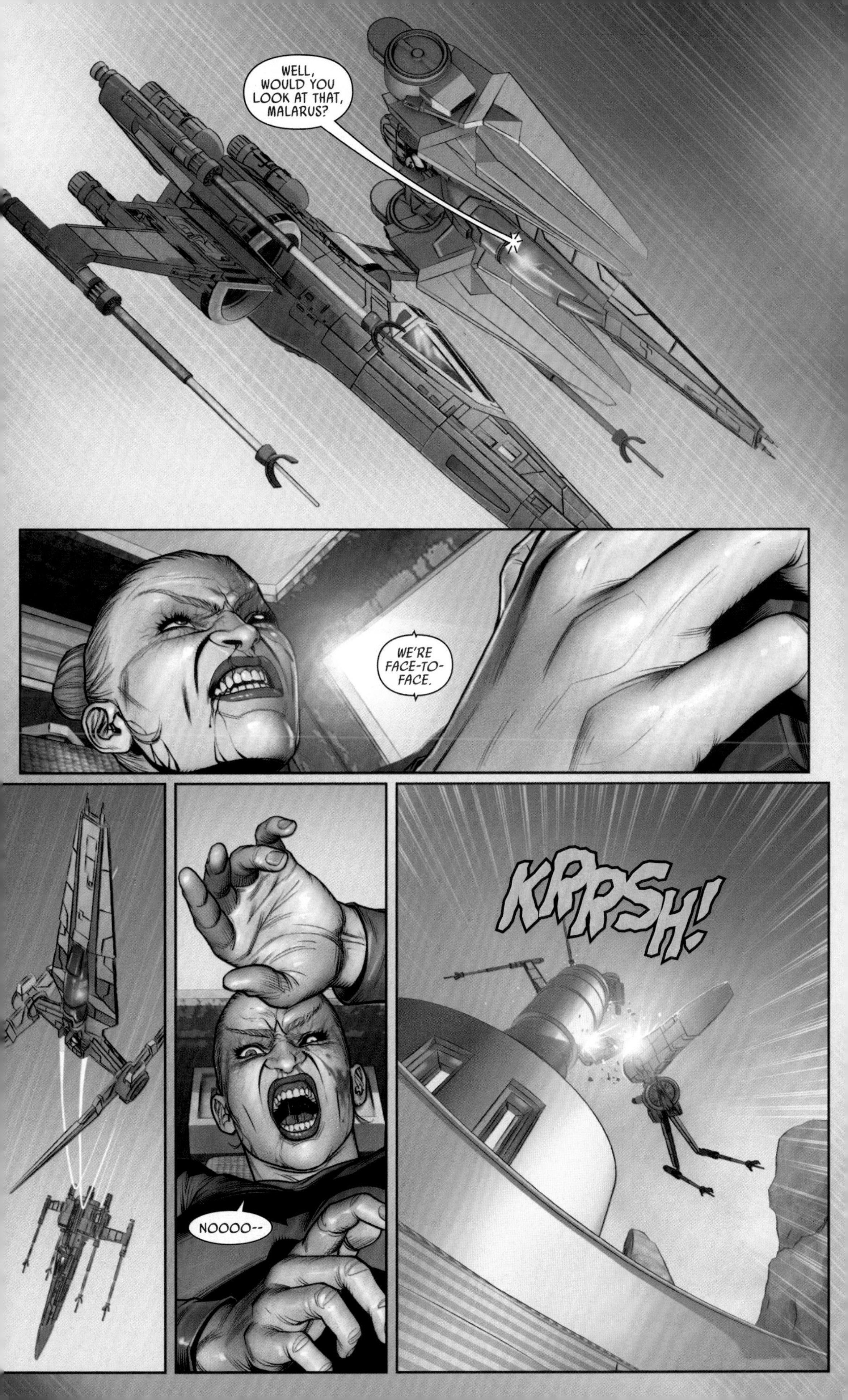
WELL, WOULD YOU LOOK AT THAT, MALARUS?
WE'RE FACE-TO-FACE.
NOOOO--
KRRSH!

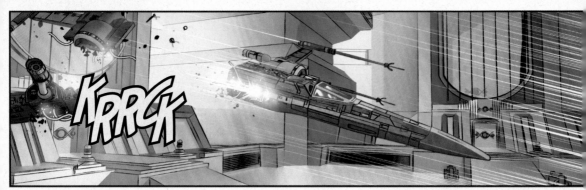

KRRCK

KSSSSS

AAAGH!

SO...YOU ATTACK HOUSE REYA, YOU SHOOT AT MY PEOPLE, YOU CRASH YOUR SHIP INTO MY PALACE.

SO MANY TERRIBLE CRIMES... BUT I CAN PROMISE YOU THIS--YOU WILL RECEIVE A FAIR TRIAL.

THE JUSTICE OF HOUSE REYA IS THE FINEST ON ALL OF CATO NEIMOIDIA.

WHY, I BELIEVE OUR CONVICTION RATE IS ONE HUNDRED PERCENT.

NNNGH!

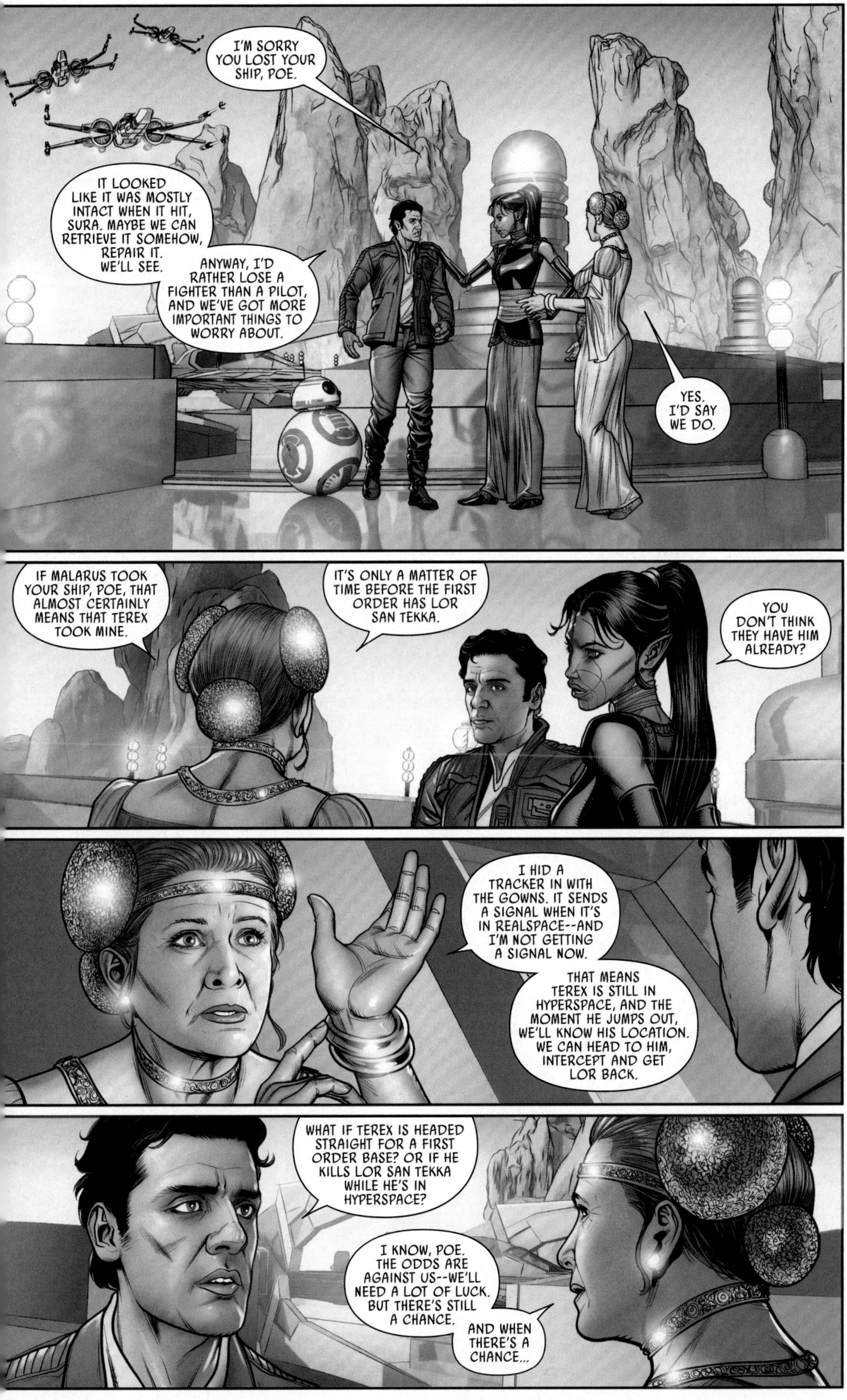
I'M SORRY YOU LOST YOUR SHIP, POE.
IT LOOKED LIKE IT WAS MOSTLY INTACT WHEN IT HIT, SURA. MAYBE WE CAN RETRIEVE IT SOMEHOW, REPAIR IT. WE'LL SEE.
ANYWAY, I'D RATHER LOSE A FIGHTER THAN A PILOT, AND WE'VE GOT MORE IMPORTANT THINGS TO WORRY ABOUT.
YES. I'D SAY WE DO.
IF MALARUS TOOK YOUR SHIP, POE, THAT ALMOST CERTAINLY MEANS THAT TEREX TOOK MINE.
IT'S ONLY A MATTER OF TIME BEFORE THE FIRST ORDER HAS LOR SAN TEKKA.
YOU DON'T THINK THEY HAVE HIM ALREADY?
I HID A TRACKER IN WITH THE GOWNS. IT SENDS A SIGNAL WHEN IT'S IN REALSPACE--AND I'M NOT GETTING A SIGNAL NOW.
THAT MEANS TEREX IS STILL IN HYPERSPACE, AND THE MOMENT HE JUMPS OUT, WE'LL KNOW HIS LOCATION. WE CAN HEAD TO HIM, INTERCEPT AND GET LOR BACK.
WHAT IF TEREX IS HEADED STRAIGHT FOR A FIRST ORDER BASE? OR IF HE KILLS LOR SAN TEKKA WHILE HE'S IN HYPERSPACE?
I KNOW, POE. THE ODDS ARE AGAINST US--WE'LL NEED A LOT OF LUCK. BUT THERE'S STILL A CHANCE.
AND WHEN THERE'S A CHANCE...

"...THERE'S HOPE."

ZZZICK!

NYYARGH!

I TRY NOT TO JUDGE ANYONE, EVER--BUT I MUST SAY, MY FRIEND--I THINK YOU ARE DOING YOURSELF SOME SERIOUS DAMAGE.

ARE YOU SURE THOSE SHOCKS ARE A GOOD IDEA?

THEY'RE BETTER THAN THE ALTERNATIVE.

NOW, BE QUIET, OLD MAN. I HAVE A DEAL TO MAKE.

THIS IS A PRIORITY COMMUNICATION-- AUTHORIZATION CODE XXT-9018.

PUT ME THROUGH.

AUTHORIZATION CODE ACKNOWLEDGED. STAND BY.

HELLO THERE, PHASMA.

AGENT TEREX? WHAT IS THIS? WHERE IS COMMANDER MALARUS?

NO IDEA. DEAD, I PRESUME. SHE WAS ALWAYS PICKING FIGHTS WITH PEOPLE. IT WAS BOUND TO CATCH UP WITH HER EVENTUALLY.

I DON'T WANT TO TALK ABOUT HER.

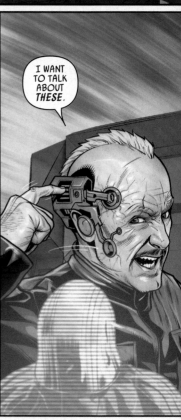

I WANT TO TALK ABOUT THESE.

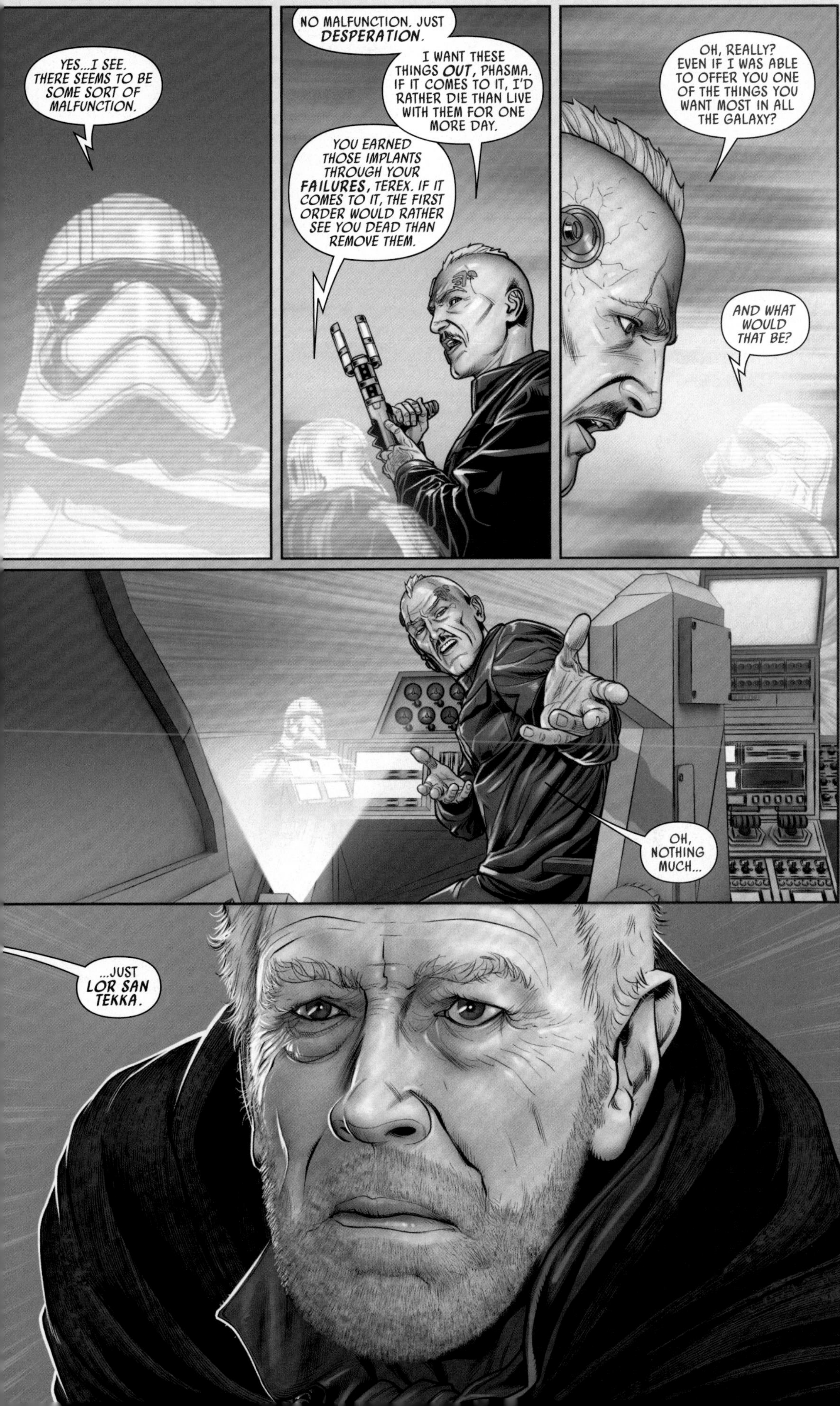
YES...I SEE. THERE SEEMS TO BE SOME SORT OF MALFUNCTION.
NO MALFUNCTION. JUST DESPERATION.
I WANT THESE THINGS OUT, PHASMA. IF IT COMES TO IT, I'D RATHER DIE THAN LIVE WITH THEM FOR ONE MORE DAY.
YOU EARNED THOSE IMPLANTS THROUGH YOUR FAILURES, TEREX. IF IT COMES TO IT, THE FIRST ORDER WOULD RATHER SEE YOU DEAD THAN REMOVE THEM.
OH, REALLY? EVEN IF I WAS ABLE TO OFFER YOU ONE OF THE THINGS YOU WANT MOST IN ALL THE GALAXY?
AND WHAT WOULD THAT BE?
OH, NOTHING MUCH...
...JUST LOR SAN TEKKA.

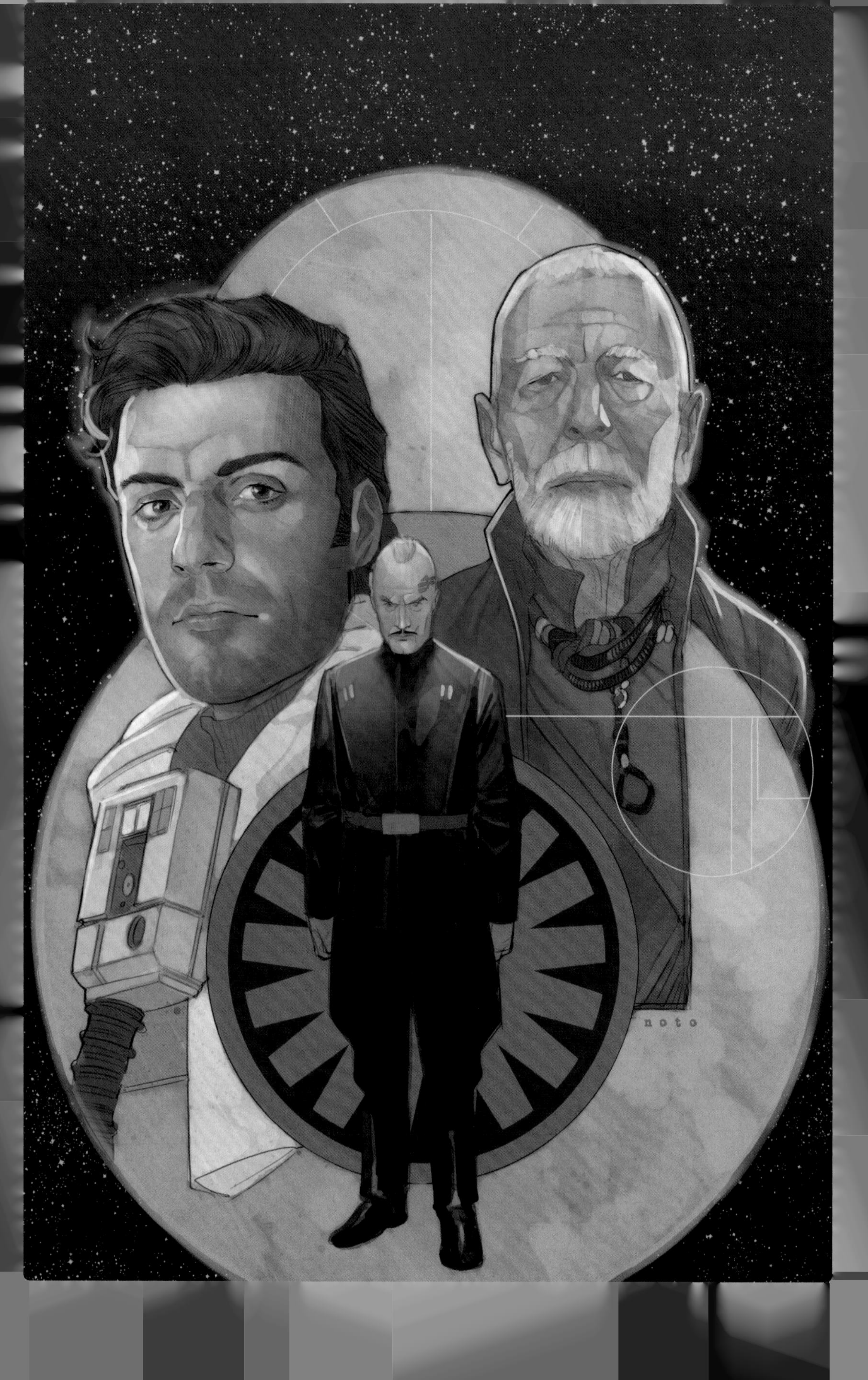
noto

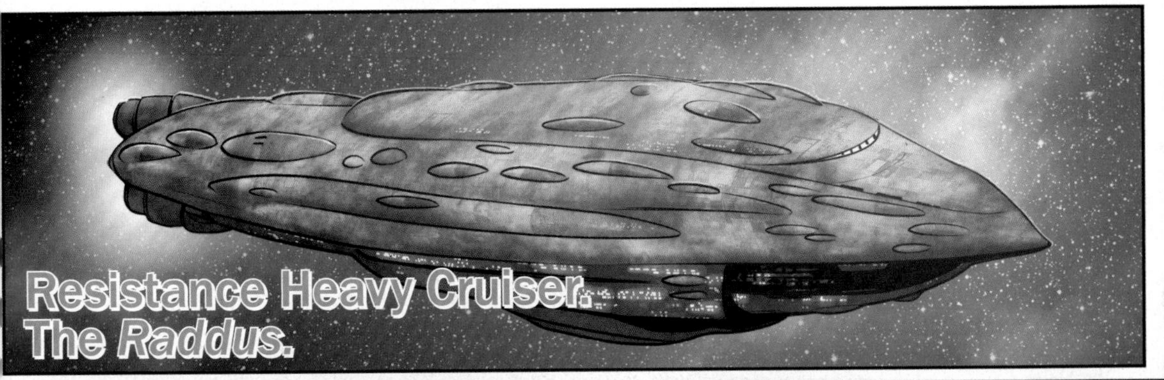
Resistance Heavy Cruiser.
The Raddus.

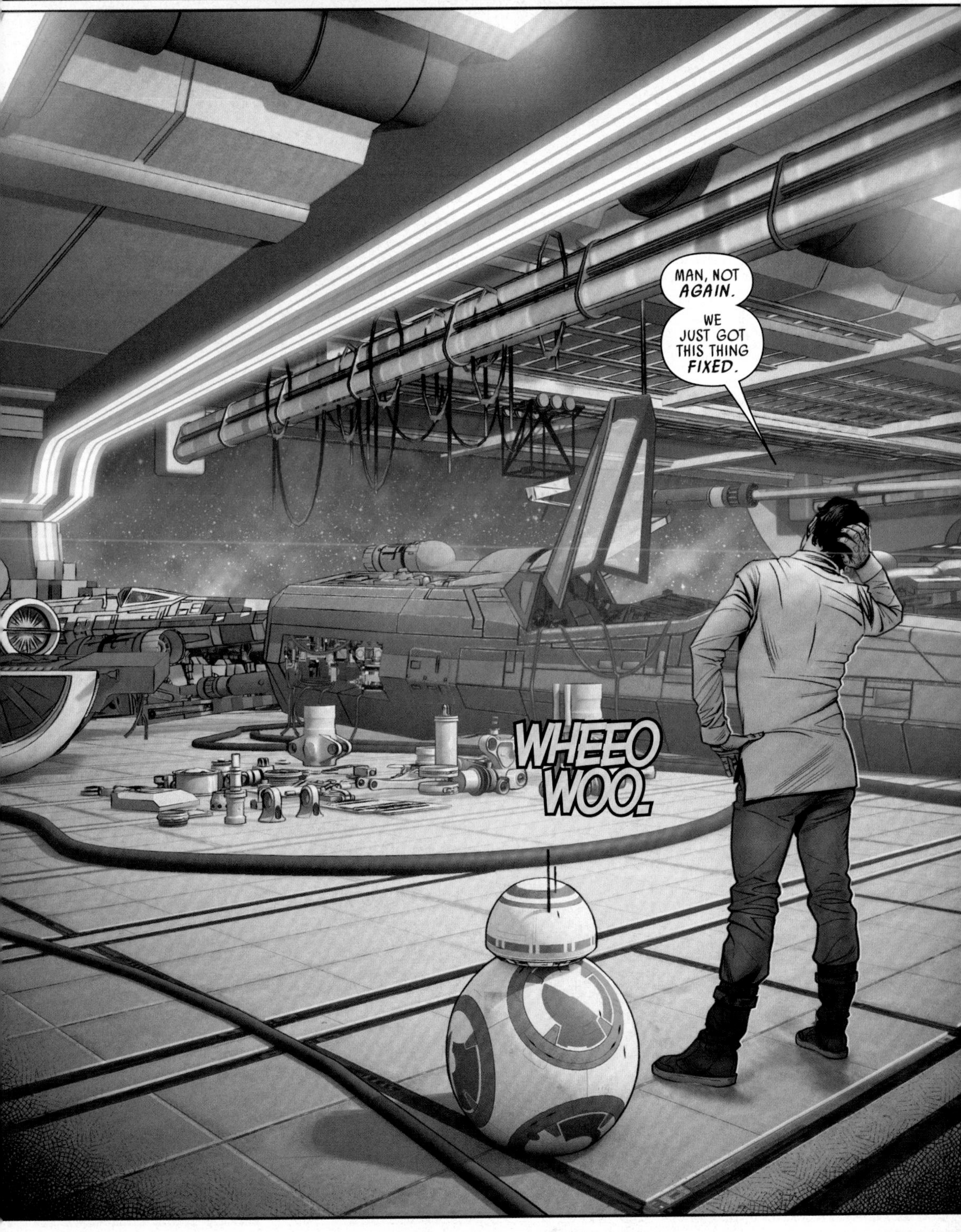
MAN, NOT AGAIN.
WE JUST GOT THIS THING FIXED.
WHEEO WOO.

YOU THINK YOU COULD ASK YOUR FRIEND IVEE TO HELP PUT HER BACK TOGETHER, BEEBEE?

I KNOW SHE SORT OF ALREADY *DID*, AND IT WAS SORT OF A FAVOR TO YOU, BUT...

BREE...

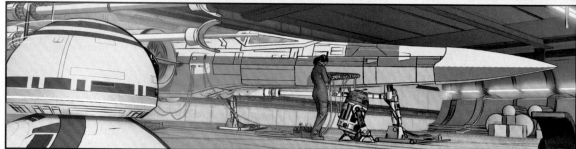

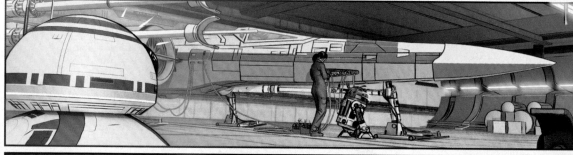

EVENTUALLY, HUH? THAT'S WHAT SHE SAID?

IVEE'S NOT ALL THAT THRILLED WE DIDN'T TAKE BETTER CARE OF HER NICE REPAIR JOB. I GET IT.

OH, WELL.

WE WOP.

GUESS IT'S JUST ME AND YOU, PAL.

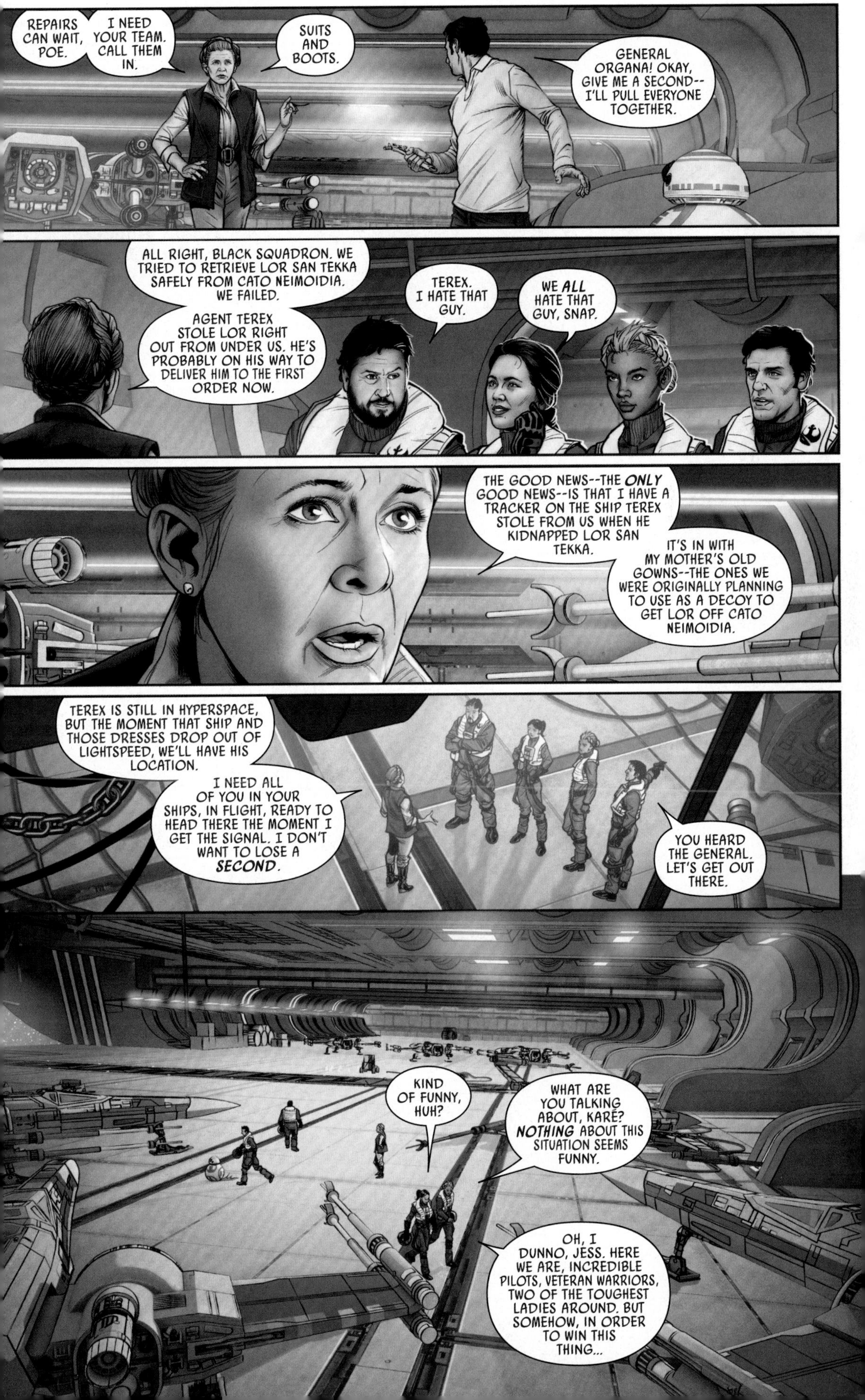
REPAIRS CAN WAIT, POE.
I NEED YOUR TEAM. CALL THEM IN.
SUITS AND BOOTS.
GENERAL ORGANA! OKAY, GIVE ME A SECOND-- I'LL PULL EVERYONE TOGETHER.
ALL RIGHT, BLACK SQUADRON. WE TRIED TO RETRIEVE LOR SAN TEKKA SAFELY FROM CATO NEIMOIDIA. WE FAILED.
AGENT TEREX STOLE LOR RIGHT OUT FROM UNDER US. HE'S PROBABLY ON HIS WAY TO DELIVER HIM TO THE FIRST ORDER NOW.
TEREX. I HATE THAT GUY.
WE ALL HATE THAT GUY, SNAP.
THE GOOD NEWS--THE ONLY GOOD NEWS--IS THAT I HAVE A TRACKER ON THE SHIP TEREX STOLE FROM US WHEN HE KIDNAPPED LOR SAN TEKKA.
IT'S IN WITH MY MOTHER'S OLD GOWNS--THE ONES WE WERE ORIGINALLY PLANNING TO USE AS A DECOY TO GET LOR OFF CATO NEIMOIDIA.
TEREX IS STILL IN HYPERSPACE, BUT THE MOMENT THAT SHIP AND THOSE DRESSES DROP OUT OF LIGHTSPEED, WE'LL HAVE HIS LOCATION.
I NEED ALL OF YOU IN YOUR SHIPS, IN FLIGHT, READY TO HEAD THERE THE MOMENT I GET THE SIGNAL. I DON'T WANT TO LOSE A SECOND.
YOU HEARD THE GENERAL. LET'S GET OUT THERE.
KIND OF FUNNY, HUH?
WHAT ARE YOU TALKING ABOUT, KARÉ? NOTHING ABOUT THIS SITUATION SEEMS FUNNY.
OH, I DUNNO, JESS. HERE WE ARE, INCREDIBLE PILOTS, VETERAN WARRIORS, TWO OF THE TOUGHEST LADIES AROUND. BUT SOMEHOW, IN ORDER TO WIN THIS THING...

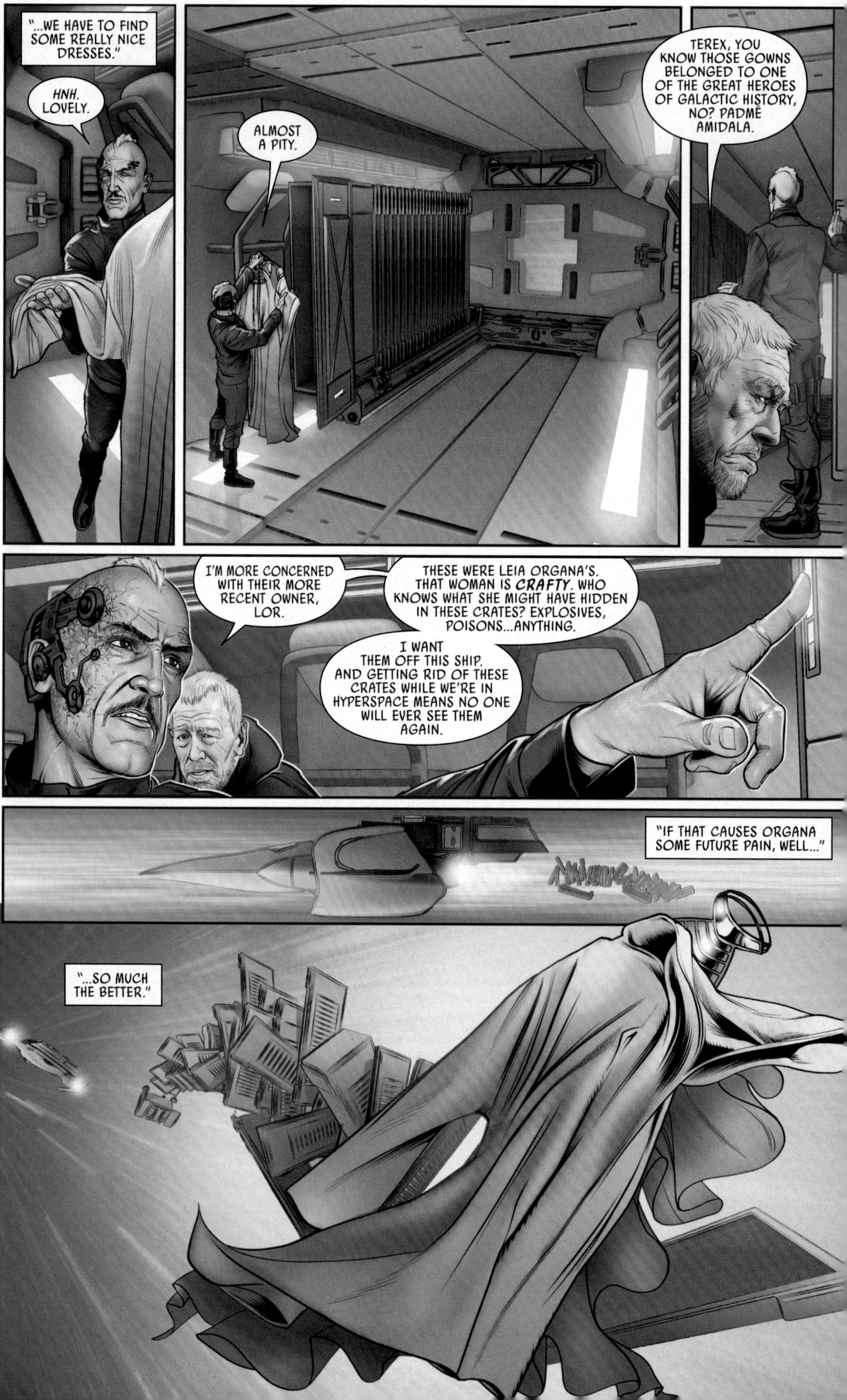
"...WE HAVE TO FIND SOME REALLY NICE DRESSES."
HNH. LOVELY.
ALMOST A PITY.
TEREX, YOU KNOW THOSE GOWNS BELONGED TO ONE OF THE GREAT HEROES OF GALACTIC HISTORY, NO? PADMÉ AMIDALA.
I'M MORE CONCERNED WITH THEIR MORE RECENT OWNER, LOR.
THESE WERE LEIA ORGANA'S. THAT WOMAN IS CRAFTY. WHO KNOWS WHAT SHE MIGHT HAVE HIDDEN IN THESE CRATES? EXPLOSIVES, POISONS...ANYTHING.
I WANT THEM OFF THIS SHIP. AND GETTING RID OF THESE CRATES WHILE WE'RE IN HYPERSPACE MEANS NO ONE WILL EVER SEE THEM AGAIN.
"IF THAT CAUSES ORGANA SOME FUTURE PAIN, WELL..."
"...SO MUCH THE BETTER."

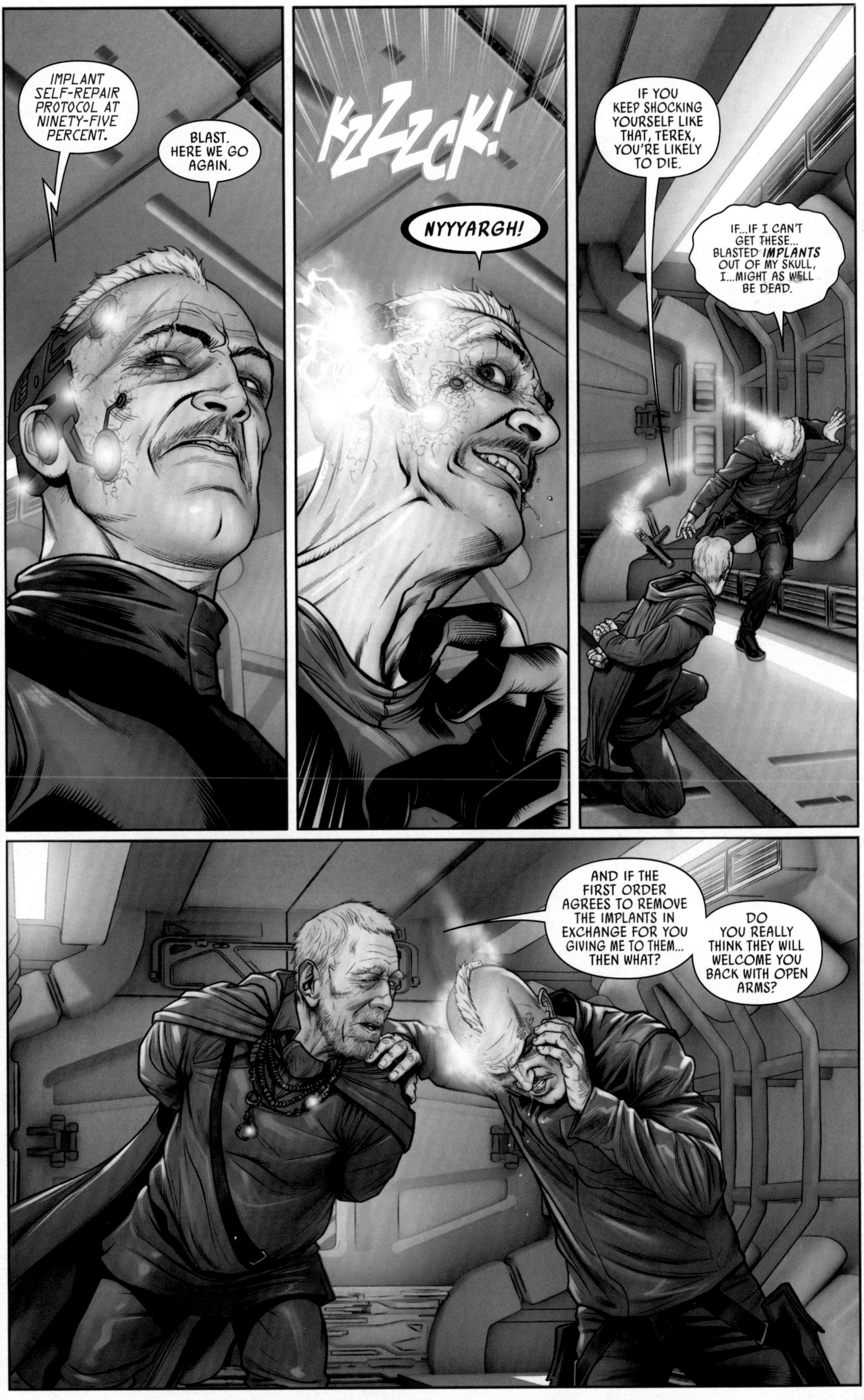
IMPLANT SELF-REPAIR PROTOCOL AT NINETY-FIVE PERCENT.
BLAST. HERE WE GO AGAIN.
KZZZZCK!
NYYYARGH!
IF YOU KEEP SHOCKING YOURSELF LIKE THAT, TEREX, YOU'RE LIKELY TO DIE.
IF...IF I CAN'T GET THESE... BLASTED IMPLANTS OUT OF MY SKULL, I...MIGHT AS WELL BE DEAD.
AND IF THE FIRST ORDER AGREES TO REMOVE THE IMPLANTS IN EXCHANGE FOR YOU GIVING ME TO THEM... THEN WHAT?
DO YOU REALLY THINK THEY WILL WELCOME YOU BACK WITH OPEN ARMS?

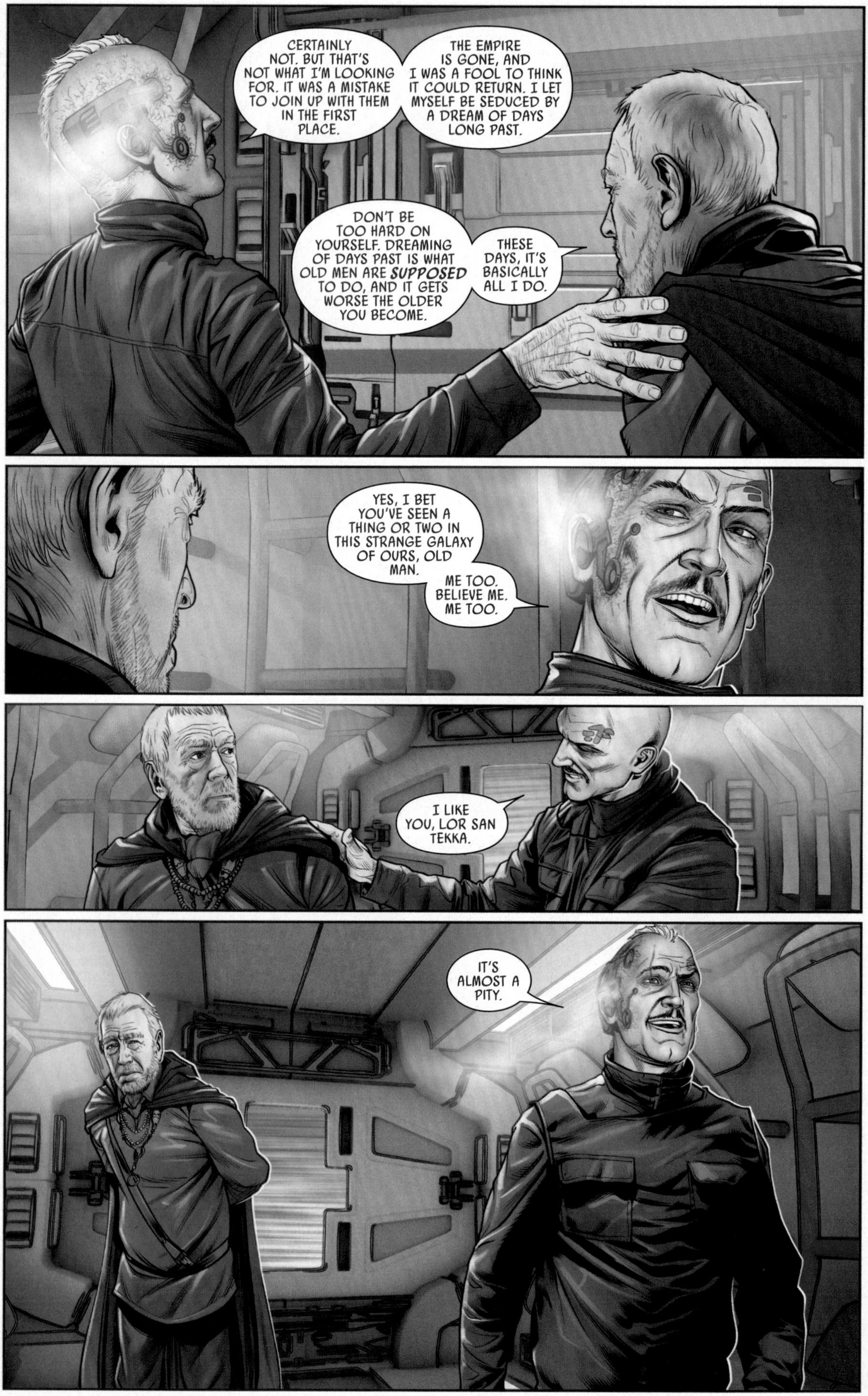
CERTAINLY NOT. BUT THAT'S NOT WHAT I'M LOOKING FOR. IT WAS A MISTAKE TO JOIN UP WITH THEM IN THE FIRST PLACE.
THE EMPIRE IS GONE, AND I WAS A FOOL TO THINK IT COULD RETURN. I LET MYSELF BE SEDUCED BY A DREAM OF DAYS LONG PAST.
DON'T BE TOO HARD ON YOURSELF. DREAMING OF DAYS PAST IS WHAT OLD MEN ARE *SUPPOSED* TO DO, AND IT GETS WORSE THE OLDER YOU BECOME.
THESE DAYS, IT'S BASICALLY ALL I DO.
YES, I BET YOU'VE SEEN A THING OR TWO IN THIS STRANGE GALAXY OF OURS, OLD MAN.
ME TOO. BELIEVE ME. ME TOO.
I LIKE YOU, LOR SAN TEKKA.
IT'S ALMOST A PITY.

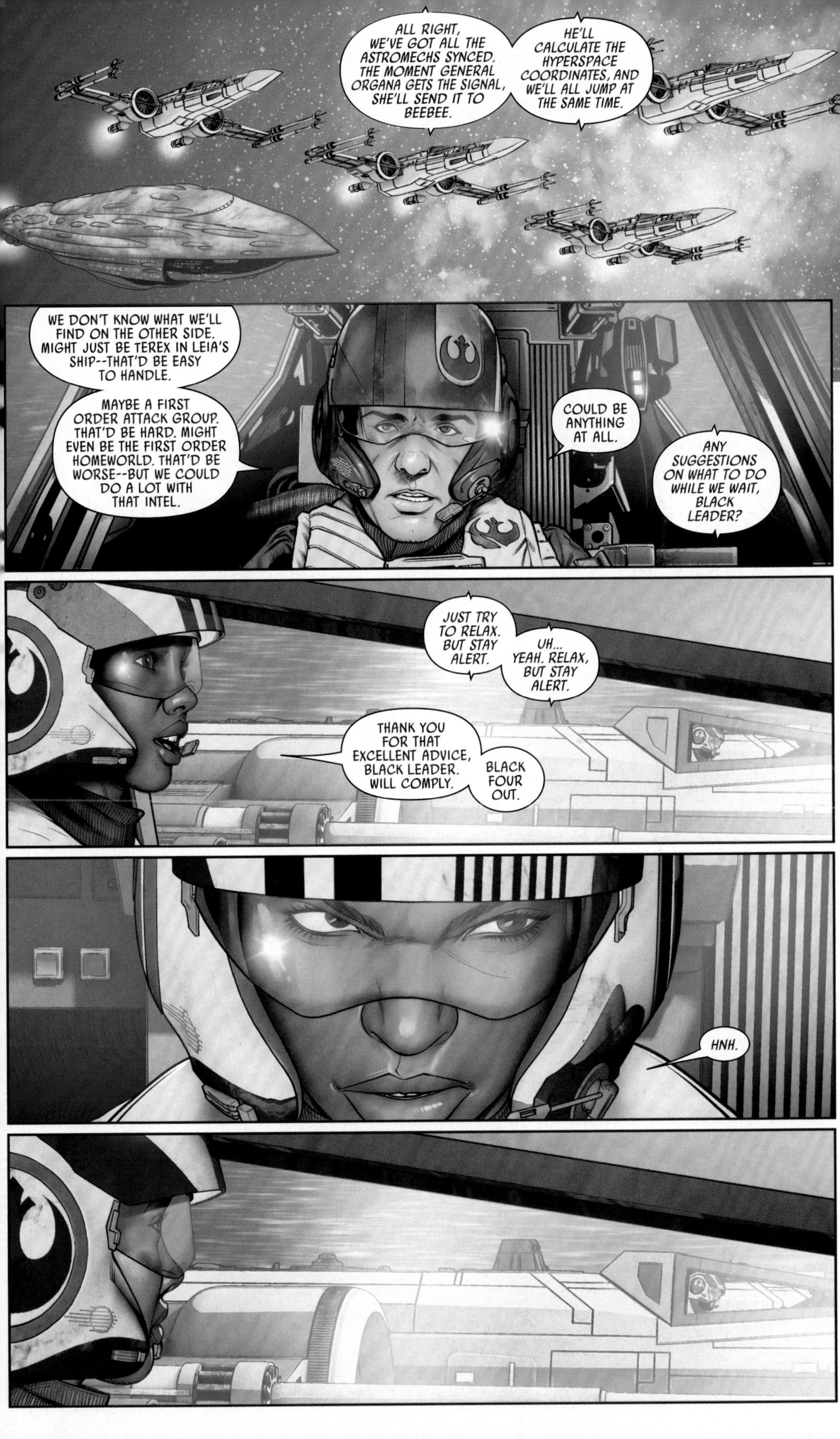
ALL RIGHT, WE'VE GOT ALL THE ASTROMECHS SYNCED. THE MOMENT GENERAL ORGANA GETS THE SIGNAL, SHE'LL SEND IT TO BEEBEE.
HE'LL CALCULATE THE HYPERSPACE COORDINATES, AND WE'LL ALL JUMP AT THE SAME TIME.
WE DON'T KNOW WHAT WE'LL FIND ON THE OTHER SIDE. MIGHT JUST BE TEREX IN LEIA'S SHIP--THAT'D BE EASY TO HANDLE.
MAYBE A FIRST ORDER ATTACK GROUP. THAT'D BE HARD. MIGHT EVEN BE THE FIRST ORDER HOMEWORLD. THAT'D BE WORSE--BUT WE COULD DO A LOT WITH THAT INTEL.
COULD BE ANYTHING AT ALL.
ANY SUGGESTIONS ON WHAT TO DO WHILE WE WAIT, BLACK LEADER?
JUST TRY TO RELAX. BUT STAY ALERT.
UH... YEAH. RELAX, BUT STAY ALERT.
THANK YOU FOR THAT EXCELLENT ADVICE, BLACK LEADER. WILL COMPLY.
BLACK FOUR OUT.
HNH.

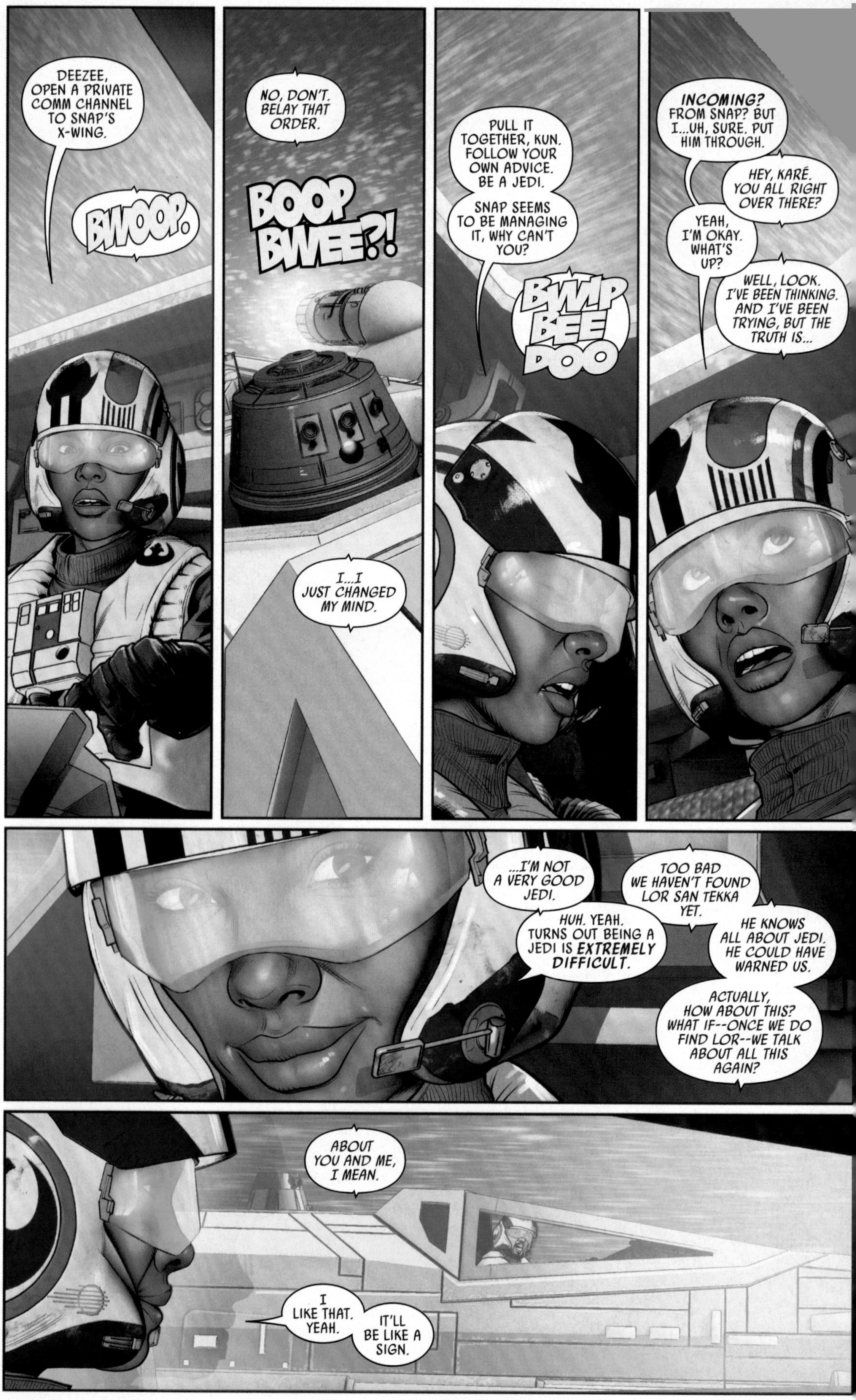
DEEZEE, OPEN A PRIVATE COMM CHANNEL TO SNAP'S X-WING.
BWOOP.
NO, DON'T. BELAY THAT ORDER.
BOOP BWEE?!
I...I JUST CHANGED MY MIND.
PULL IT TOGETHER, KUN. FOLLOW YOUR OWN ADVICE. BE A JEDI.
SNAP SEEMS TO BE MANAGING IT, WHY CAN'T YOU?
BWIP BEE DOO
INCOMING? FROM SNAP? BUT I...UH, SURE. PUT HIM THROUGH.
HEY, KARÉ. YOU ALL RIGHT OVER THERE?
YEAH, I'M OKAY. WHAT'S UP?
WELL, LOOK. I'VE BEEN THINKING. AND I'VE BEEN TRYING, BUT THE TRUTH IS...
...I'M NOT A VERY GOOD JEDI.
HUH. YEAH. TURNS OUT BEING A JEDI IS EXTREMELY DIFFICULT.
TOO BAD WE HAVEN'T FOUND LOR SAN TEKKA YET.
HE KNOWS ALL ABOUT JEDI. HE COULD HAVE WARNED US.
ACTUALLY, HOW ABOUT THIS? WHAT IF--ONCE WE DO FIND LOR--WE TALK ABOUT ALL THIS AGAIN?
ABOUT YOU AND ME, I MEAN.
I LIKE THAT. YEAH.
IT'LL BE LIKE A SIGN.

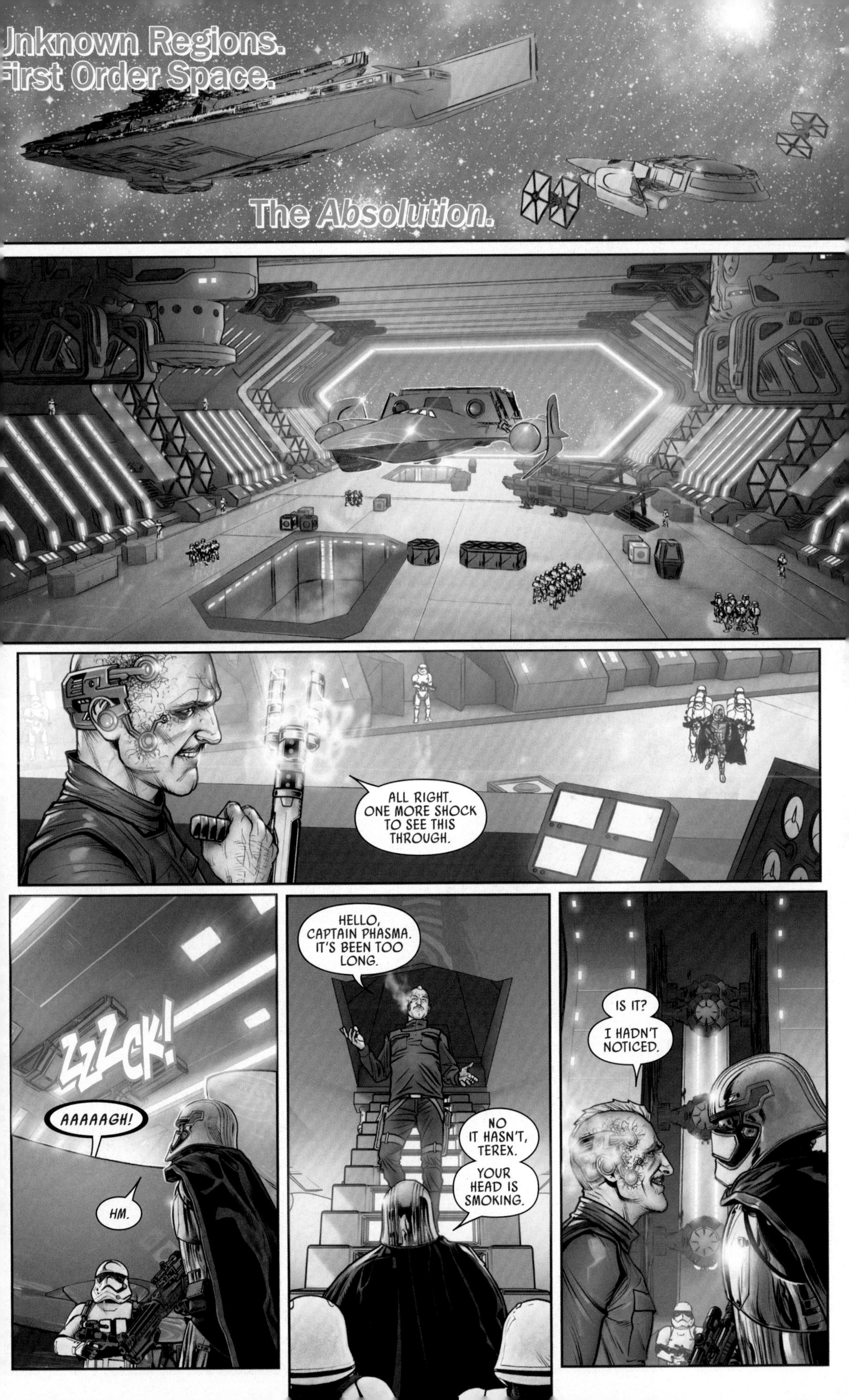
Unknown Regions.
First Order Space.
The Absolution.
ALL RIGHT. ONE MORE SHOCK TO SEE THIS THROUGH.
ZZZCK!
AAAAAGH!
HM.
HELLO, CAPTAIN PHASMA. IT'S BEEN TOO LONG.
NO IT HASN'T, TEREX.
YOUR HEAD IS SMOKING.
IS IT?
I HADN'T NOTICED.

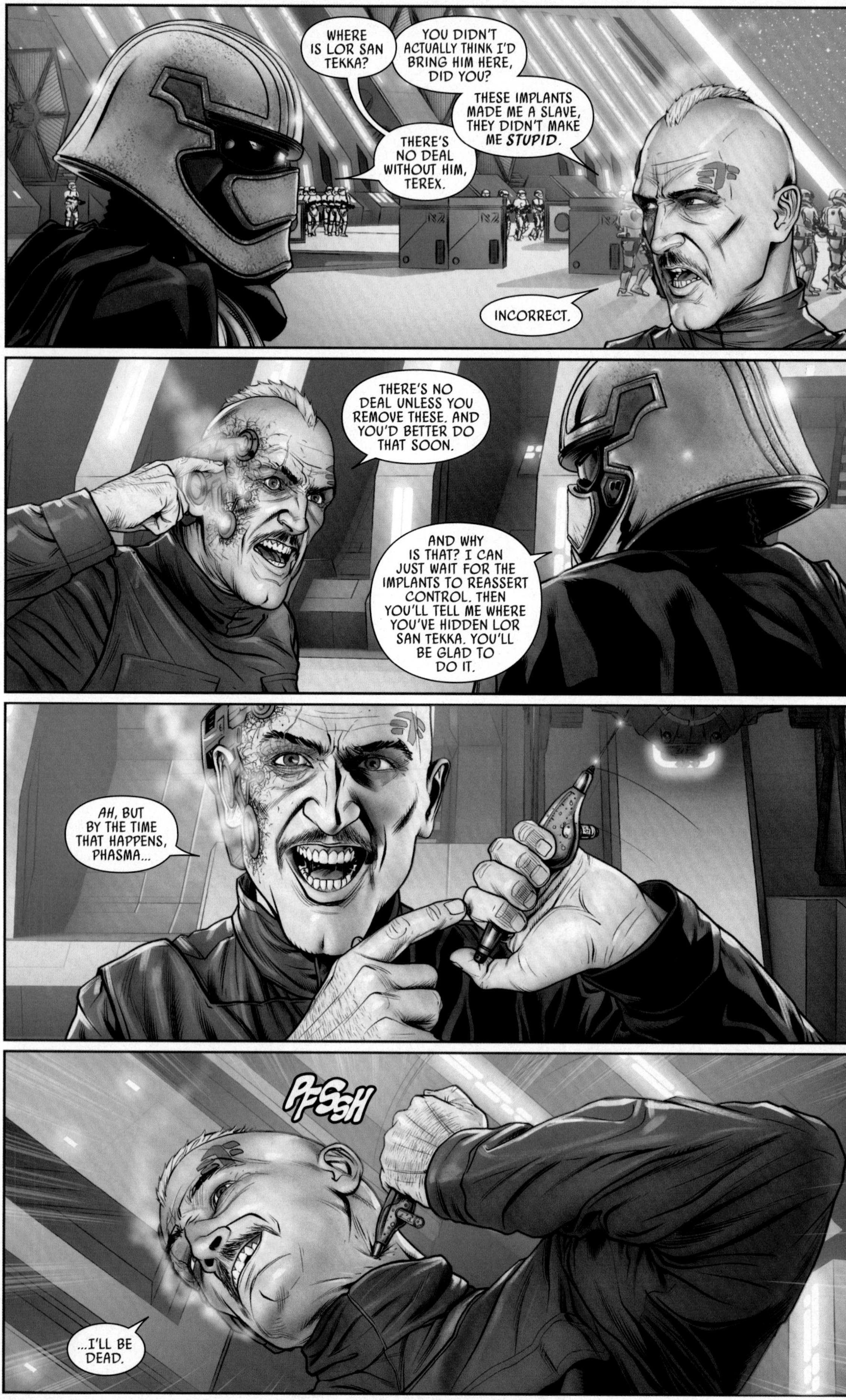
WHERE IS LOR SAN TEKKA?
YOU DIDN'T ACTUALLY THINK I'D BRING HIM HERE, DID YOU?
THESE IMPLANTS MADE ME A SLAVE, THEY DIDN'T MAKE ME STUPID.
THERE'S NO DEAL WITHOUT HIM, TEREX.
INCORRECT.
THERE'S NO DEAL UNLESS YOU REMOVE THESE. AND YOU'D BETTER DO THAT SOON.
AND WHY IS THAT? I CAN JUST WAIT FOR THE IMPLANTS TO REASSERT CONTROL. THEN YOU'LL TELL ME WHERE YOU'VE HIDDEN LOR SAN TEKKA. YOU'LL BE GLAD TO DO IT.
AH, BUT BY THE TIME THAT HAPPENS, PHASMA...
PFSSH
...I'LL BE DEAD.

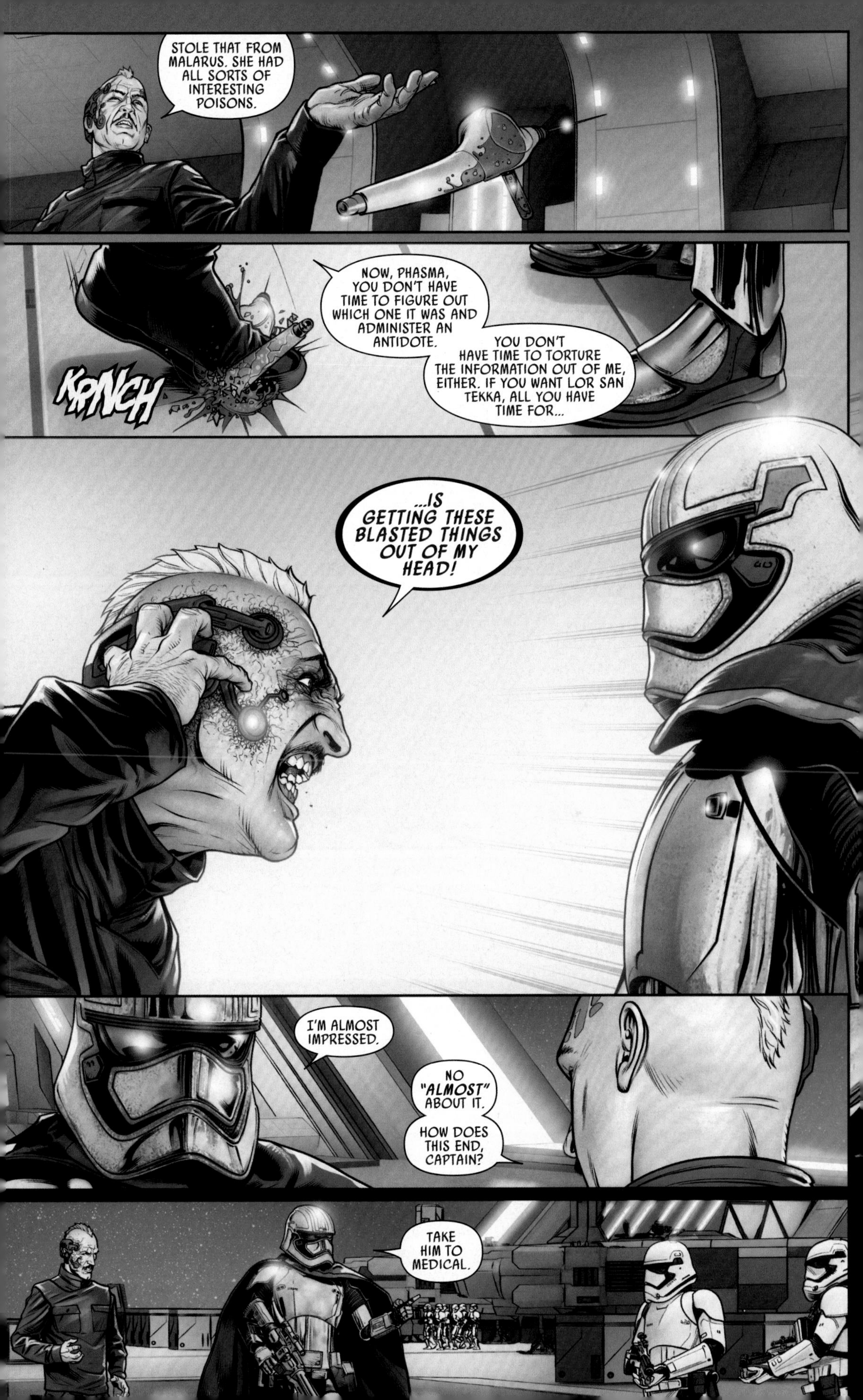
STOLE THAT FROM MALARUS. SHE HAD ALL SORTS OF INTERESTING POISONS.
KRNCH
NOW, PHASMA, YOU DON'T HAVE TIME TO FIGURE OUT WHICH ONE IT WAS AND ADMINISTER AN ANTIDOTE.
YOU DON'T HAVE TIME TO TORTURE THE INFORMATION OUT OF ME, EITHER. IF YOU WANT LOR SAN TEKKA, ALL YOU HAVE TIME FOR...
...IS GETTING THESE BLASTED THINGS OUT OF MY HEAD!
I'M ALMOST IMPRESSED.
NO "ALMOST" ABOUT IT.
HOW DOES THIS END, CAPTAIN?
TAKE HIM TO MEDICAL.

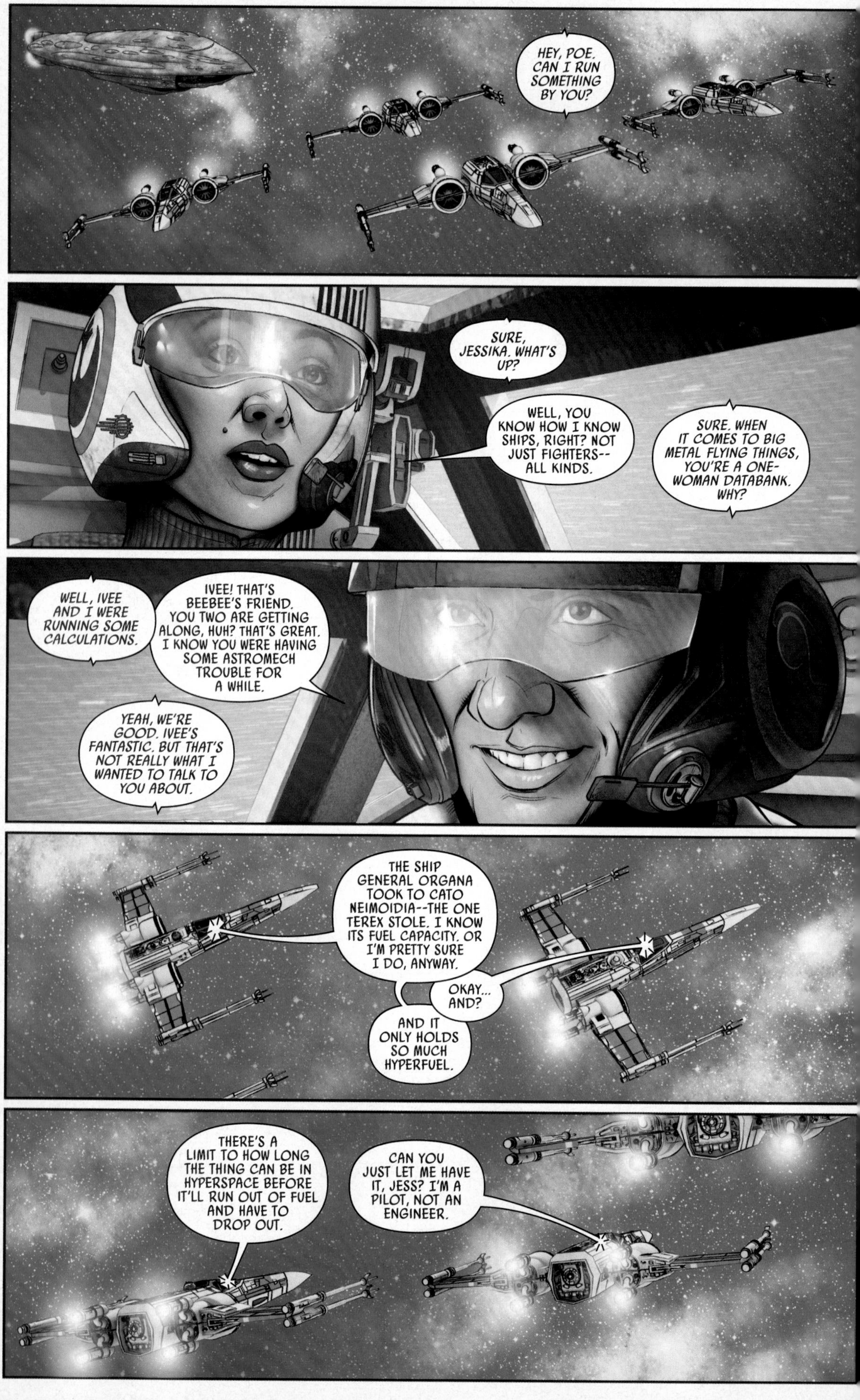
HEY, POE. CAN I RUN SOMETHING BY YOU?
SURE, JESSIKA. WHAT'S UP?
WELL, YOU KNOW HOW I KNOW SHIPS, RIGHT? NOT JUST FIGHTERS--ALL KINDS.
SURE. WHEN IT COMES TO BIG METAL FLYING THINGS, YOU'RE A ONE-WOMAN DATABANK. WHY?
WELL, IVEE AND I WERE RUNNING SOME CALCULATIONS.
IVEE! THAT'S BEEBEE'S FRIEND. YOU TWO ARE GETTING ALONG, HUH? THAT'S GREAT. I KNOW YOU WERE HAVING SOME ASTROMECH TROUBLE FOR A WHILE.
YEAH, WE'RE GOOD. IVEE'S FANTASTIC. BUT THAT'S NOT REALLY WHAT I WANTED TO TALK TO YOU ABOUT.
THE SHIP GENERAL ORGANA TOOK TO CATO NEIMOIDIA--THE ONE TEREX STOLE. I KNOW ITS FUEL CAPACITY. OR I'M PRETTY SURE I DO, ANYWAY.
OKAY... AND?
AND IT ONLY HOLDS SO MUCH HYPERFUEL.
THERE'S A LIMIT TO HOW LONG THE THING CAN BE IN HYPERSPACE BEFORE IT'LL RUN OUT OF FUEL AND HAVE TO DROP OUT.
CAN YOU JUST LET ME HAVE IT, JESS? I'M A PILOT, NOT AN ENGINEER.

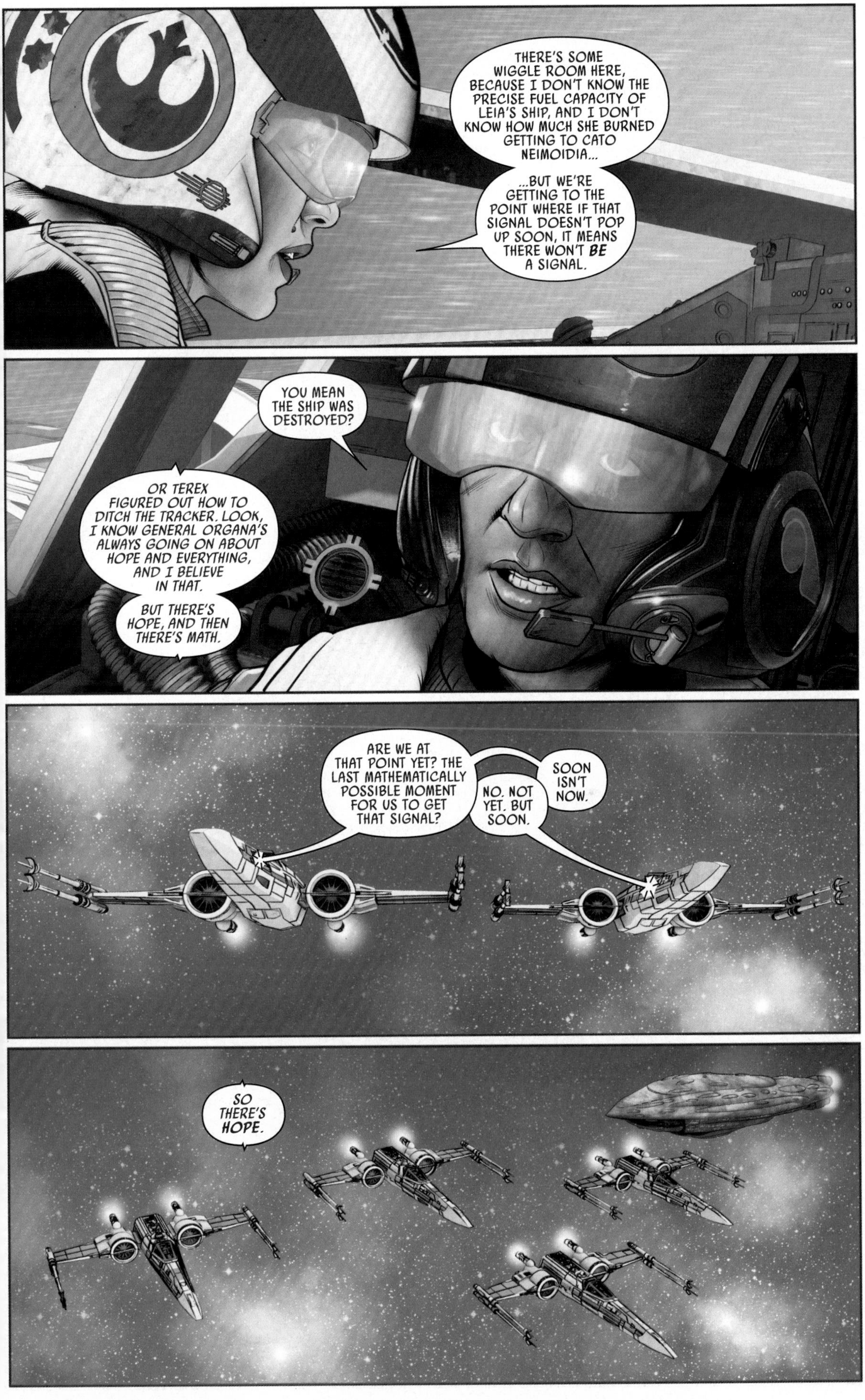
THERE'S SOME WIGGLE ROOM HERE, BECAUSE I DON'T KNOW THE PRECISE FUEL CAPACITY OF LEIA'S SHIP, AND I DON'T KNOW HOW MUCH SHE BURNED GETTING TO CATO NEIMOIDIA...
...BUT WE'RE GETTING TO THE POINT WHERE IF THAT SIGNAL DOESN'T POP UP SOON, IT MEANS THERE WON'T BE A SIGNAL.
YOU MEAN THE SHIP WAS DESTROYED?
OR TEREX FIGURED OUT HOW TO DITCH THE TRACKER. LOOK, I KNOW GENERAL ORGANA'S ALWAYS GOING ON ABOUT HOPE AND EVERYTHING, AND I BELIEVE IN THAT.
BUT THERE'S HOPE, AND THEN THERE'S MATH.
ARE WE AT THAT POINT YET? THE LAST MATHEMATICALLY POSSIBLE MOMENT FOR US TO GET THAT SIGNAL?
NO. NOT YET. BUT SOON.
SOON ISN'T NOW.
SO THERE'S HOPE.

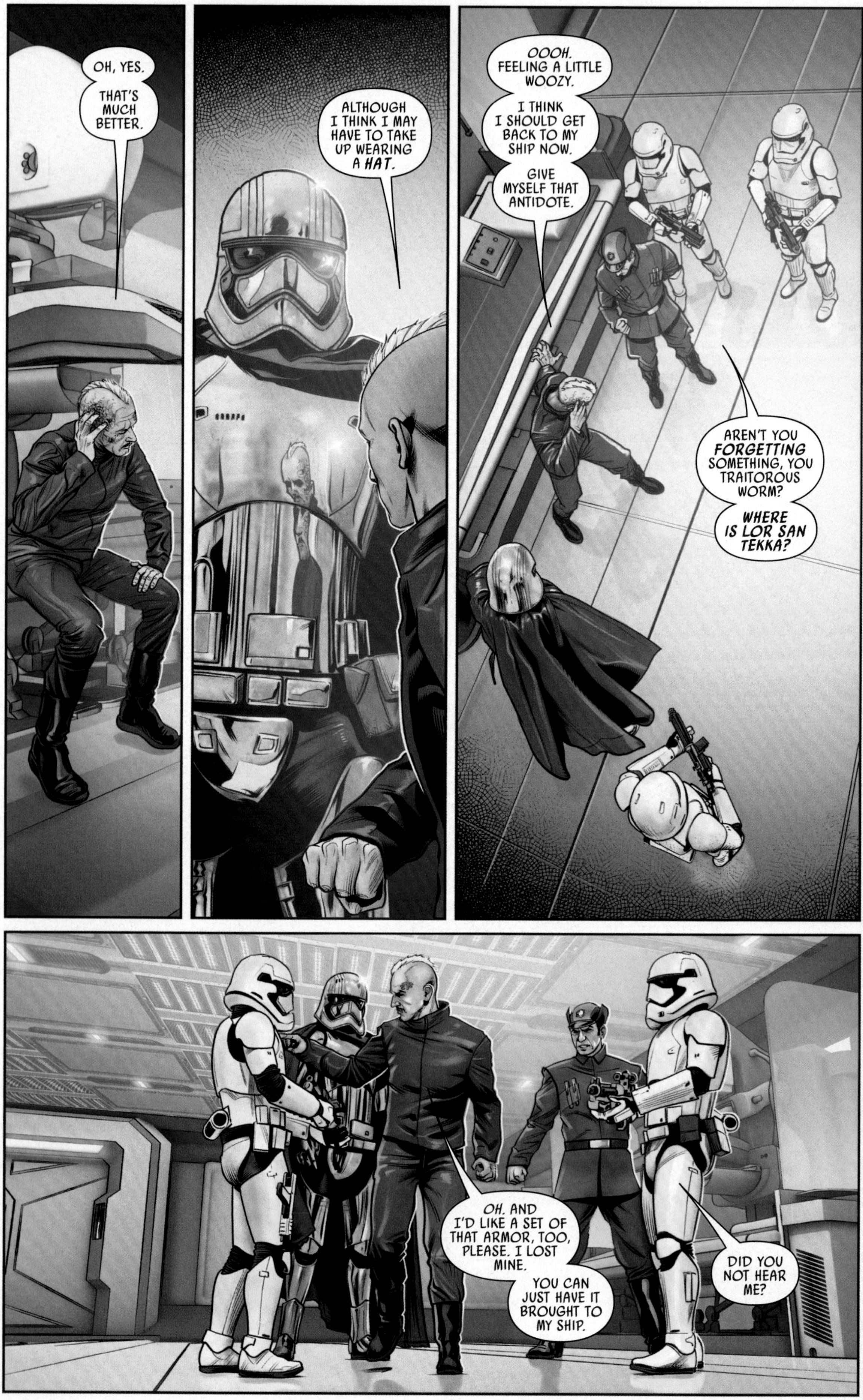
OH, YES.
THAT'S MUCH BETTER.
ALTHOUGH I THINK I MAY HAVE TO TAKE UP WEARING A HAT.
OOOH. FEELING A LITTLE WOOZY.
I THINK I SHOULD GET BACK TO MY SHIP NOW.
GIVE MYSELF THAT ANTIDOTE.
AREN'T YOU FORGETTING SOMETHING, YOU TRAITOROUS WORM?
WHERE IS LOR SAN TEKKA?
OH. AND I'D LIKE A SET OF THAT ARMOR, TOO, PLEASE. I LOST MINE.
YOU CAN JUST HAVE IT BROUGHT TO MY SHIP.
DID YOU NOT HEAR ME?

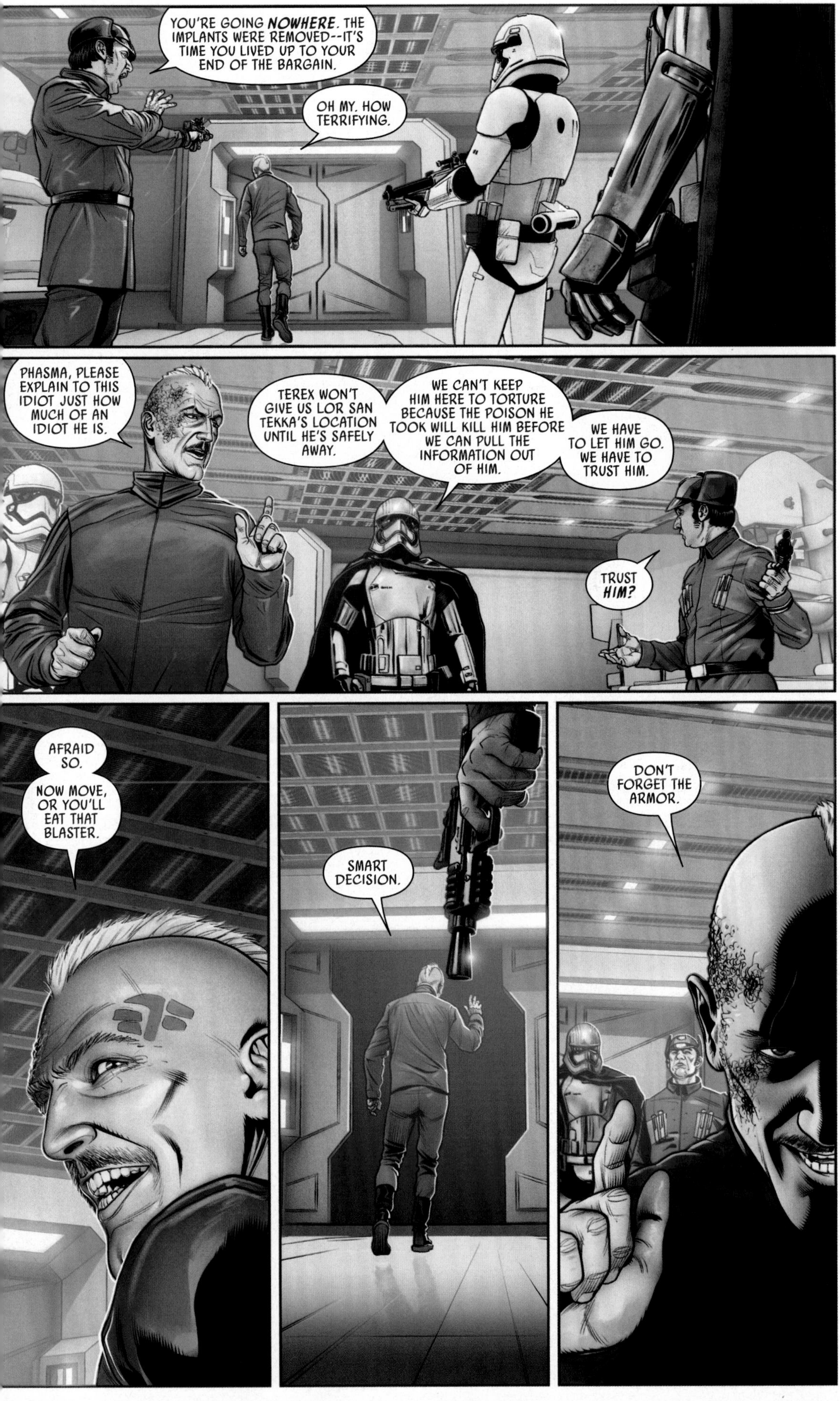
YOU'RE GOING NOWHERE. THE IMPLANTS WERE REMOVED--IT'S TIME YOU LIVED UP TO YOUR END OF THE BARGAIN.
OH MY. HOW TERRIFYING.
PHASMA, PLEASE EXPLAIN TO THIS IDIOT JUST HOW MUCH OF AN IDIOT HE IS.
TEREX WON'T GIVE US LOR SAN TEKKA'S LOCATION UNTIL HE'S SAFELY AWAY.
WE CAN'T KEEP HIM HERE TO TORTURE BECAUSE THE POISON HE TOOK WILL KILL HIM BEFORE WE CAN PULL THE INFORMATION OUT OF HIM.
WE HAVE TO LET HIM GO. WE HAVE TO TRUST HIM.
TRUST HIM?
AFRAID SO.
NOW MOVE, OR YOU'LL EAT THAT BLASTER.
SMART DECISION.
DON'T FORGET THE ARMOR.

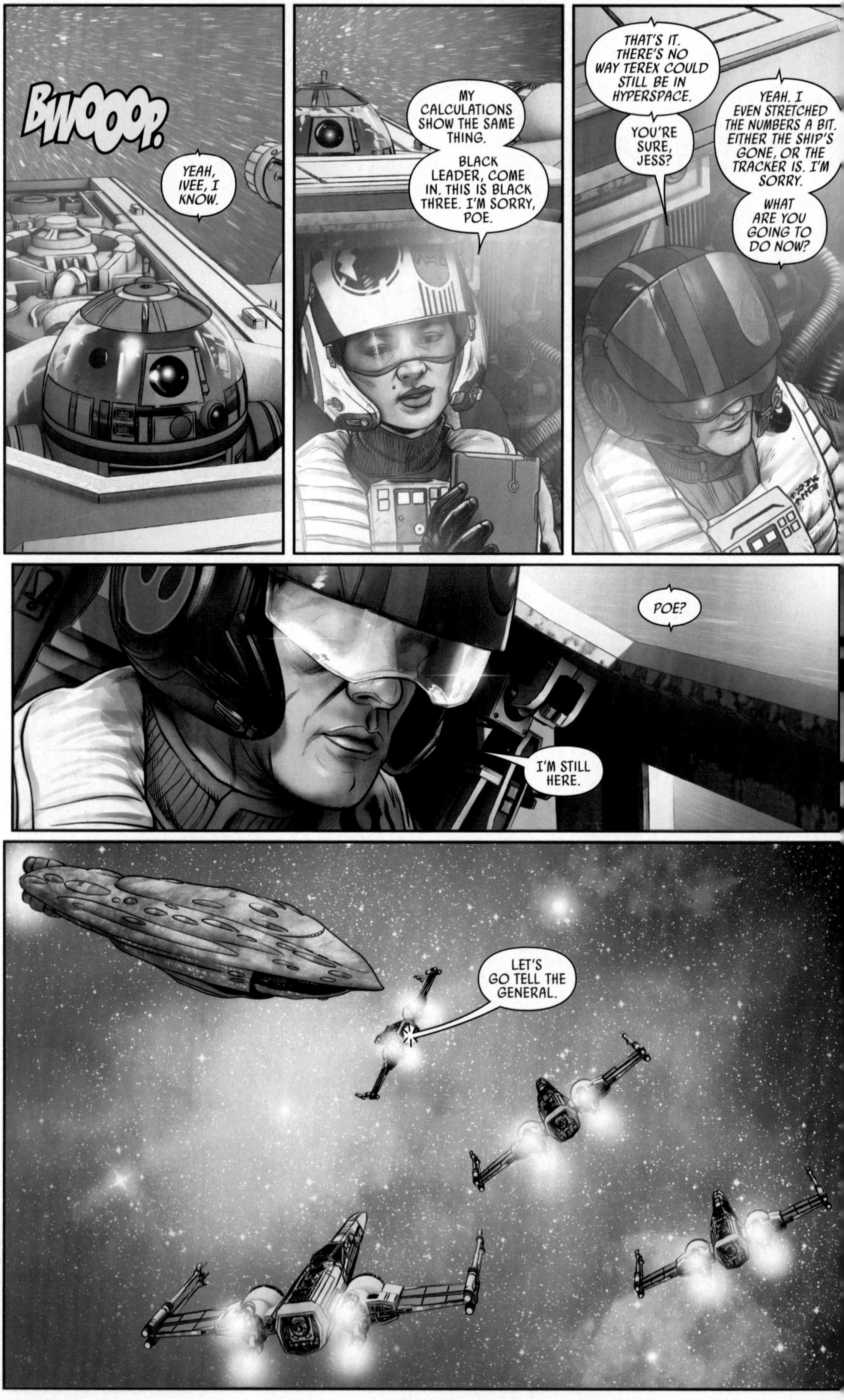
BWOOOP.
YEAH, IVEE, I KNOW.
MY CALCULATIONS SHOW THE SAME THING.
BLACK LEADER, COME IN. THIS IS BLACK THREE. I'M SORRY, POE.
THAT'S IT. THERE'S NO WAY TEREX COULD STILL BE IN HYPERSPACE.
YOU'RE SURE, JESS?
YEAH. I EVEN STRETCHED THE NUMBERS A BIT. EITHER THE SHIP'S GONE, OR THE TRACKER IS. I'M SORRY.
WHAT ARE YOU GOING TO DO NOW?
POE?
I'M STILL HERE.
LET'S GO TELL THE GENERAL.

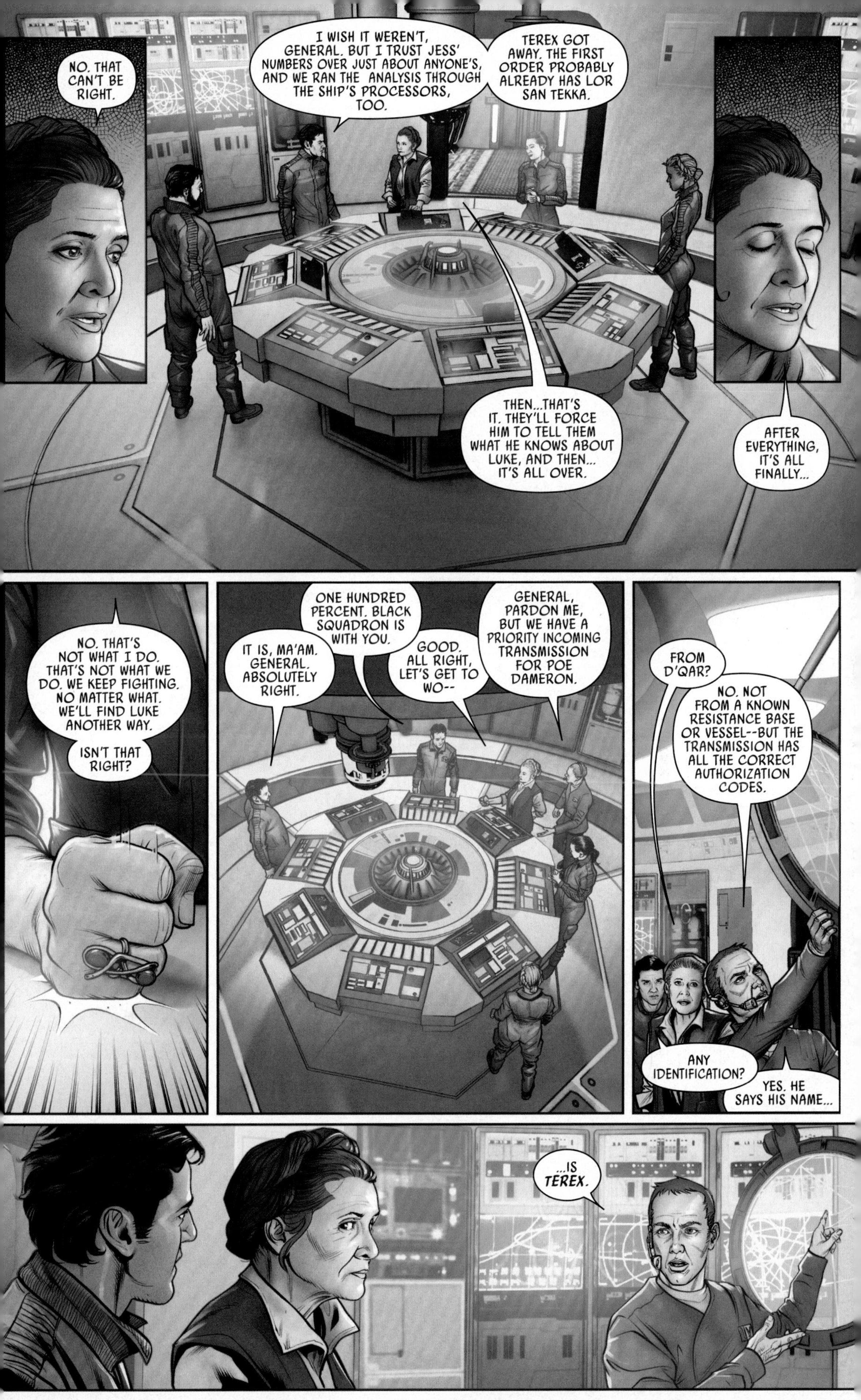
NO. THAT CAN'T BE RIGHT.
I WISH IT WEREN'T, GENERAL. BUT I TRUST JESS' NUMBERS OVER JUST ABOUT ANYONE'S, AND WE RAN THE ANALYSIS THROUGH THE SHIP'S PROCESSORS, TOO.
TEREX GOT AWAY. THE FIRST ORDER PROBABLY ALREADY HAS LOR SAN TEKKA.
THEN...THAT'S IT. THEY'LL FORCE HIM TO TELL THEM WHAT HE KNOWS ABOUT LUKE, AND THEN... IT'S ALL OVER.
AFTER EVERYTHING, IT'S ALL FINALLY...
NO. THAT'S NOT WHAT I DO. THAT'S NOT WHAT WE DO. WE KEEP FIGHTING. NO MATTER WHAT. WE'LL FIND LUKE ANOTHER WAY.
ISN'T THAT RIGHT?
IT IS, MA'AM. GENERAL. ABSOLUTELY RIGHT.
ONE HUNDRED PERCENT. BLACK SQUADRON IS WITH YOU.
GOOD. ALL RIGHT, LET'S GET TO WO--
GENERAL, PARDON ME, BUT WE HAVE A PRIORITY INCOMING TRANSMISSION FOR POE DAMERON.
FROM D'QAR?
NO. NOT FROM A KNOWN RESISTANCE BASE OR VESSEL--BUT THE TRANSMISSION HAS ALL THE CORRECT AUTHORIZATION CODES.
ANY IDENTIFICATION?
YES. HE SAYS HIS NAME...
...IS *TEREX*.

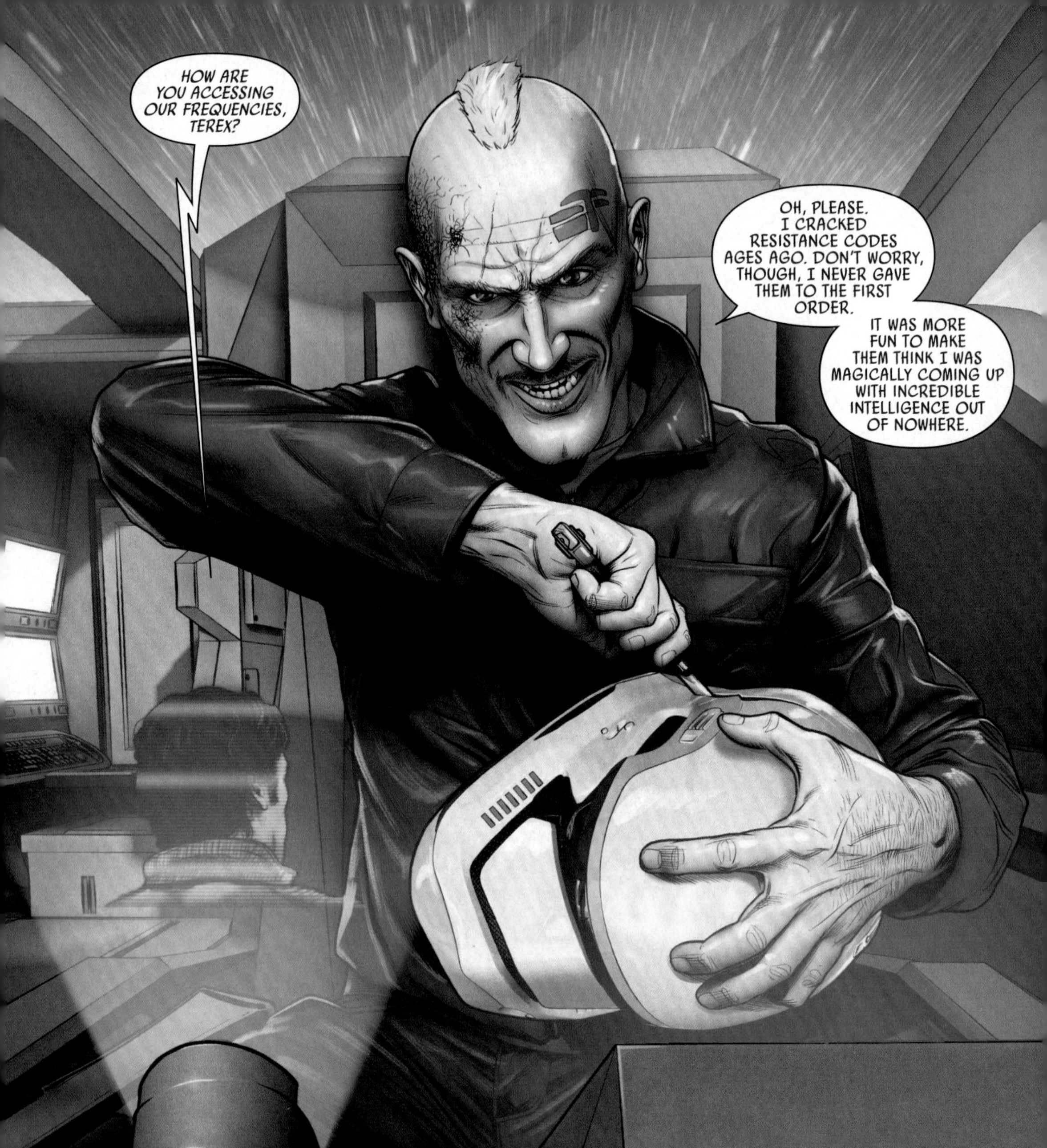
HOW ARE YOU ACCESSING OUR FREQUENCIES, TEREX?
OH, PLEASE. I CRACKED RESISTANCE CODES AGES AGO. DON'T WORRY, THOUGH, I NEVER GAVE THEM TO THE FIRST ORDER.
IT WAS MORE FUN TO MAKE THEM THINK I WAS MAGICALLY COMING UP WITH INCREDIBLE INTELLIGENCE OUT OF NOWHERE.
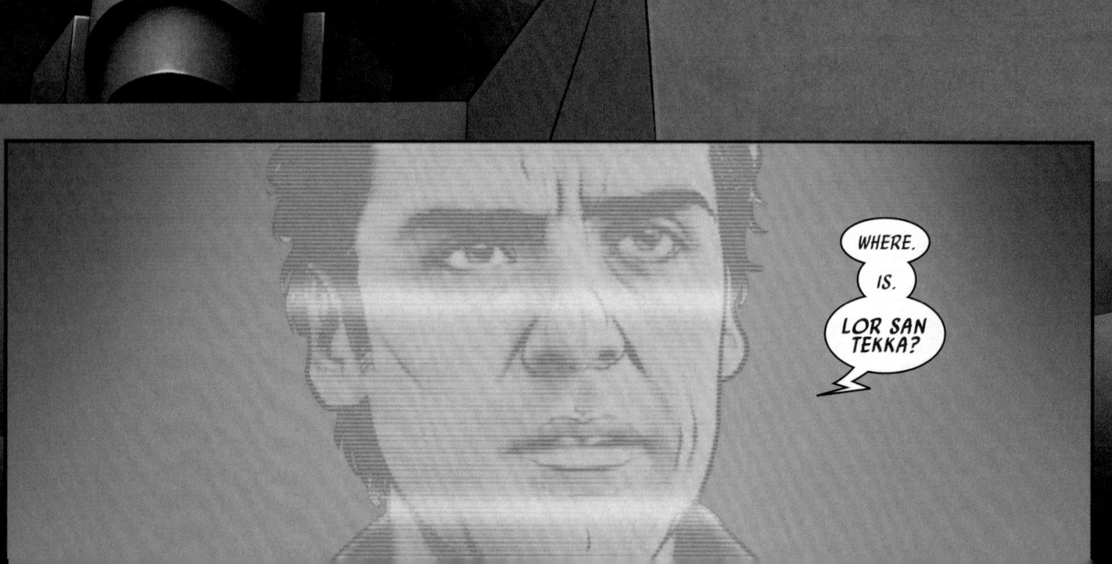
WHERE.
IS.
LOR SAN TEKKA?

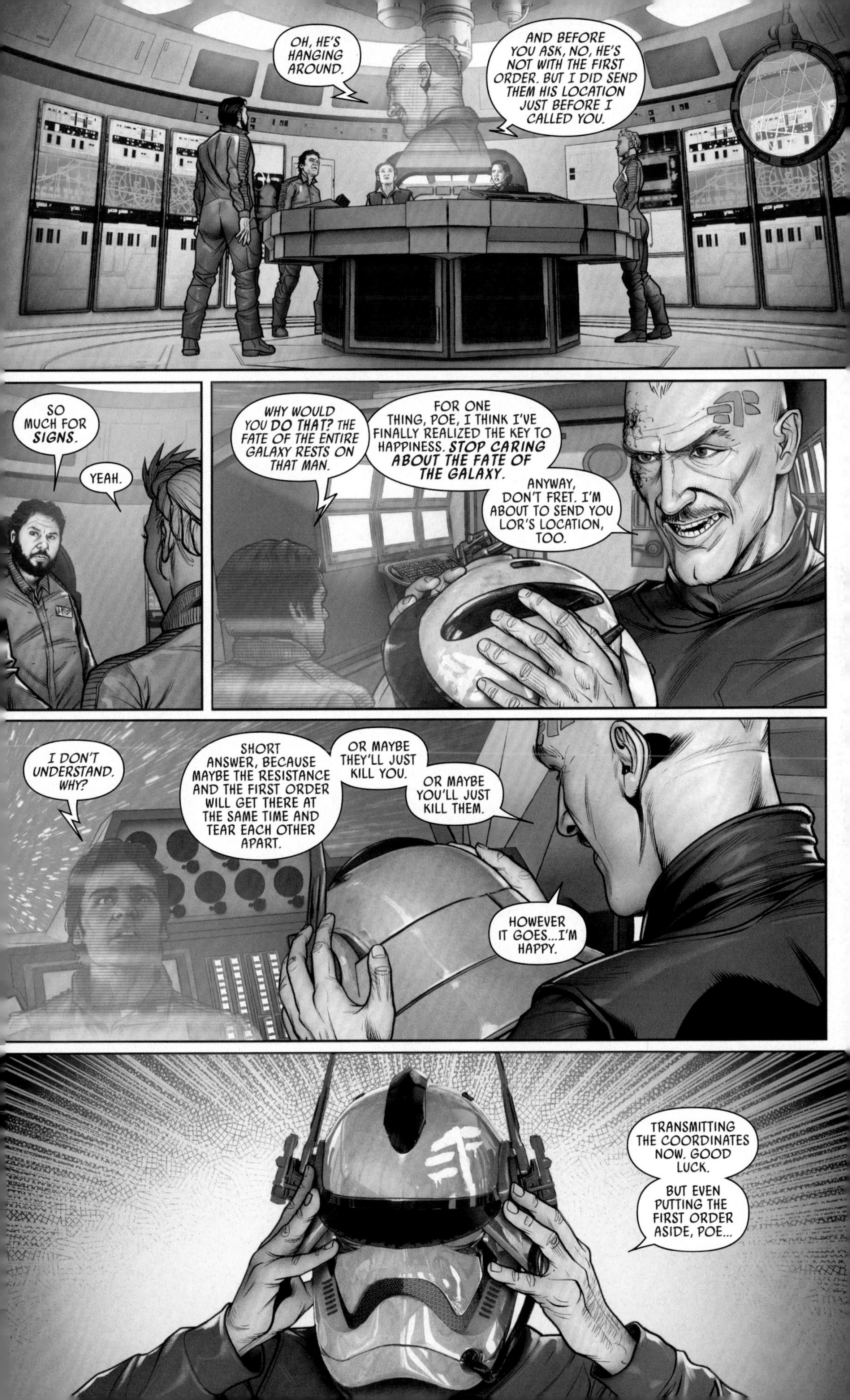
OH, HE'S HANGING AROUND.
AND BEFORE YOU ASK, NO, HE'S NOT WITH THE FIRST ORDER. BUT I DID SEND THEM HIS LOCATION JUST BEFORE I CALLED YOU.
SO MUCH FOR SIGNS.
YEAH.
WHY WOULD YOU DO THAT? THE FATE OF THE ENTIRE GALAXY RESTS ON THAT MAN.
FOR ONE THING, POE, I THINK I'VE FINALLY REALIZED THE KEY TO HAPPINESS. STOP CARING ABOUT THE FATE OF THE GALAXY.
ANYWAY, DON'T FRET. I'M ABOUT TO SEND YOU LOR'S LOCATION, TOO.
I DON'T UNDERSTAND. WHY?
SHORT ANSWER, BECAUSE MAYBE THE RESISTANCE AND THE FIRST ORDER WILL GET THERE AT THE SAME TIME AND TEAR EACH OTHER APART.
OR MAYBE THEY'LL JUST KILL YOU.
OR MAYBE YOU'LL JUST KILL THEM.
HOWEVER IT GOES...I'M HAPPY.
TRANSMITTING THE COORDINATES NOW. GOOD LUCK.
BUT EVEN PUTTING THE FIRST ORDER ASIDE, POE...

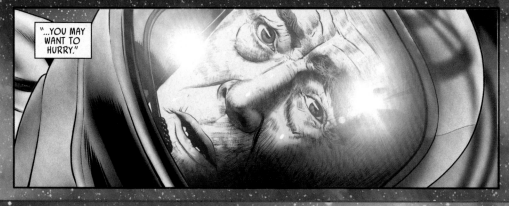

"...YOU MAY WANT TO HURRY."

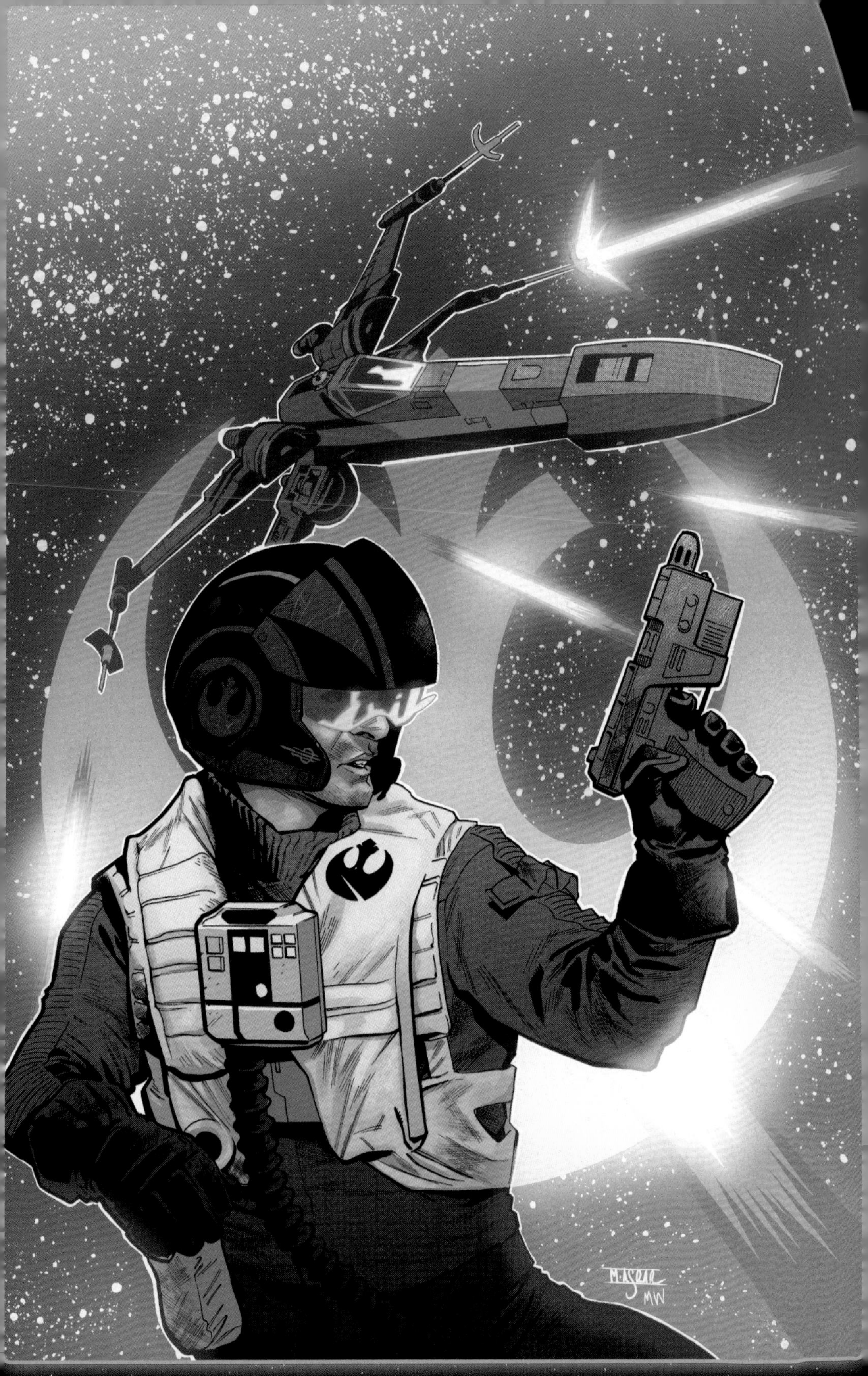
M. ASRAR
MW

STAR WARS: POE DAMERON ANNUAL 1
VARIANT BY MAHMUD ASRAR & MATTHEW WILSON

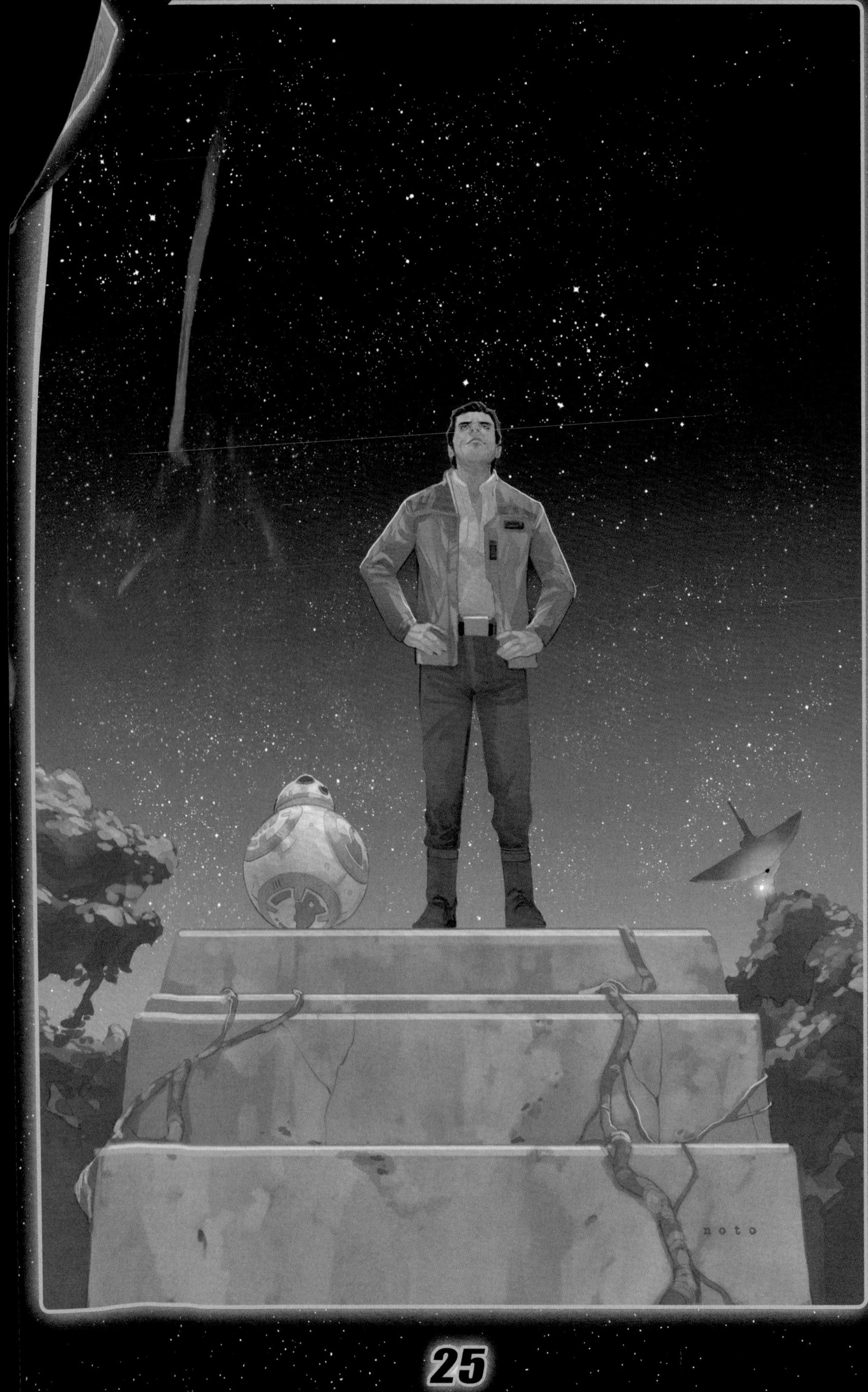
noto
25

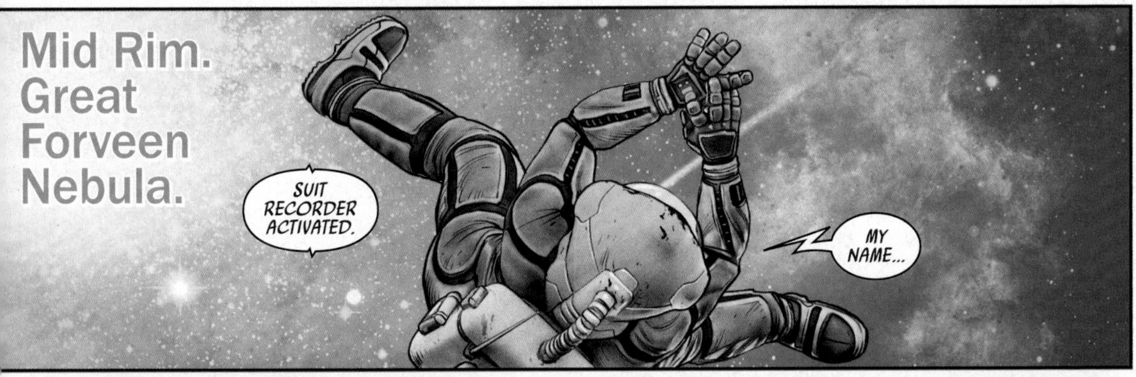
Mid Rim. Great Forveen Nebula.
SUIT RECORDER ACTIVATED.
MY NAME...

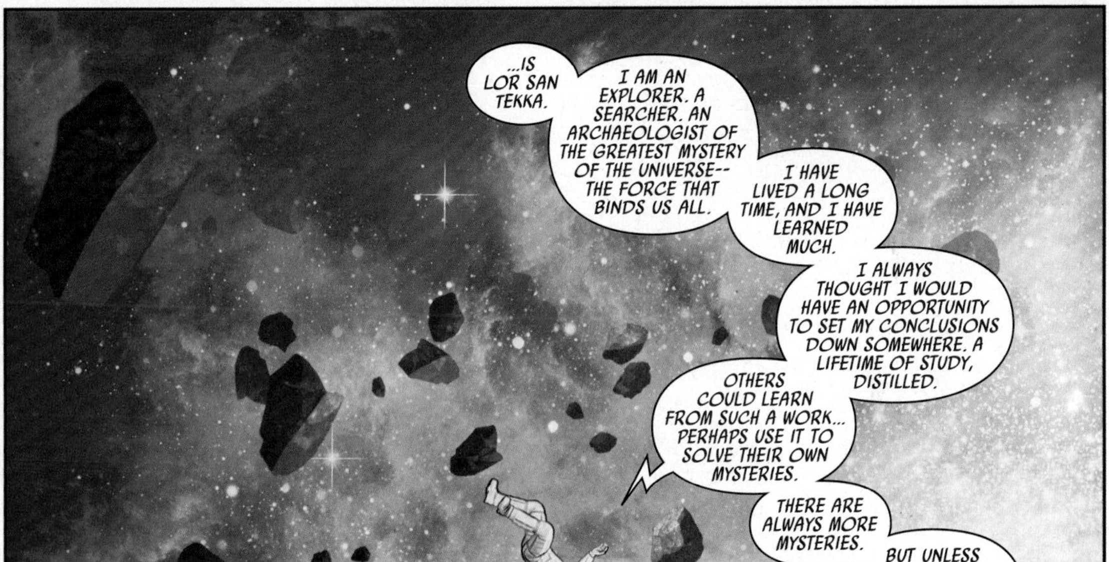
...IS LOR SAN TEKKA.
I AM AN EXPLORER. A SEARCHER. AN ARCHAEOLOGIST OF THE GREATEST MYSTERY OF THE UNIVERSE-- THE FORCE THAT BINDS US ALL.
I HAVE LIVED A LONG TIME, AND I HAVE LEARNED MUCH.
I ALWAYS THOUGHT I WOULD HAVE AN OPPORTUNITY TO SET MY CONCLUSIONS DOWN SOMEWHERE. A LIFETIME OF STUDY, DISTILLED.
OTHERS COULD LEARN FROM SUCH A WORK... PERHAPS USE IT TO SOLVE THEIR OWN MYSTERIES.
THERE ARE ALWAYS MORE MYSTERIES.
BUT UNLESS I AM MISTAKEN, THERE WILL BE NO GREAT SCHOLARLY RECORD FROM ME.
JUST THIS MEAGER TESTAMENT, SPOKEN INTO A SPACESUIT DATA RECORDER AS I DRIFT, ALONE IN THE IMMENSITY OF THE COSMOS.
AGAINST IT, I AM AS NOTHING.
BUT YET... HERE I AM, STILL.
I AM LOR SAN TEKKA.

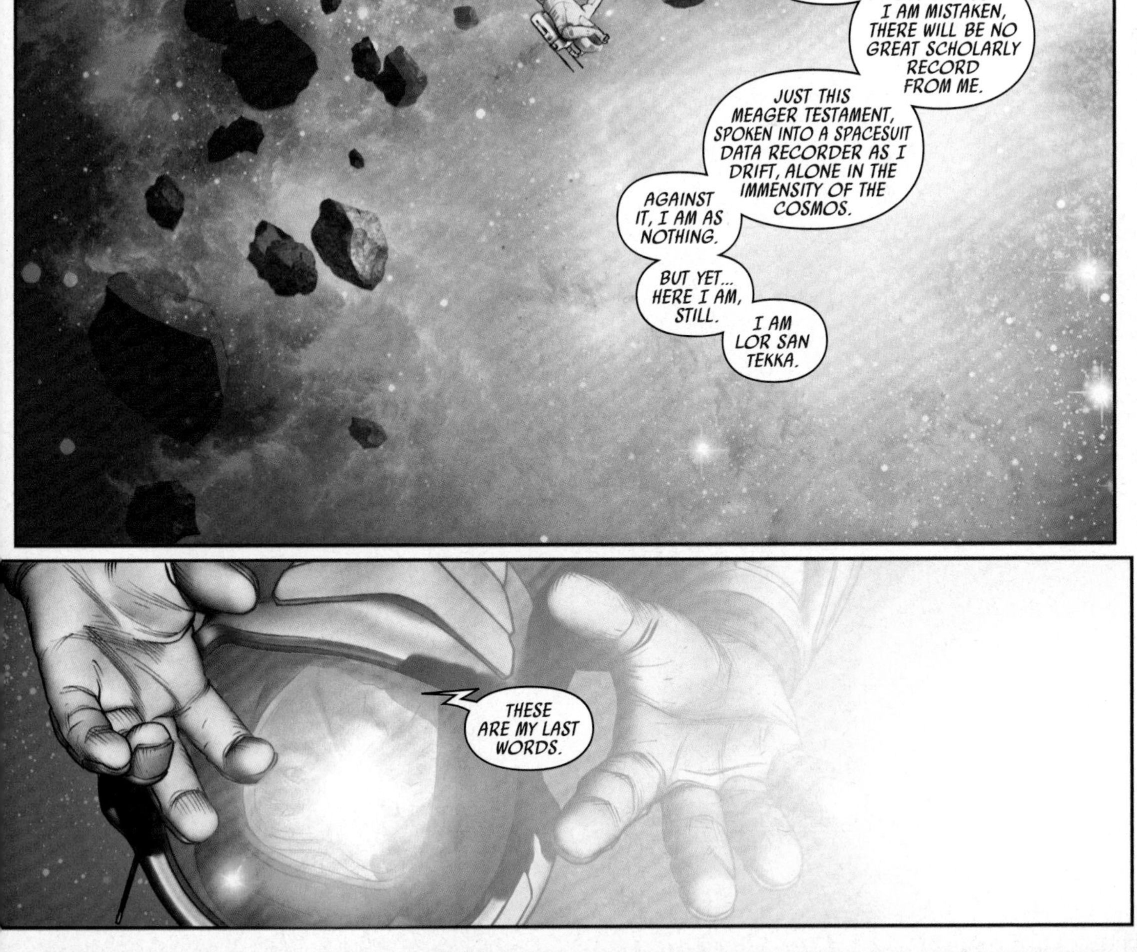
THESE ARE MY LAST WORDS.

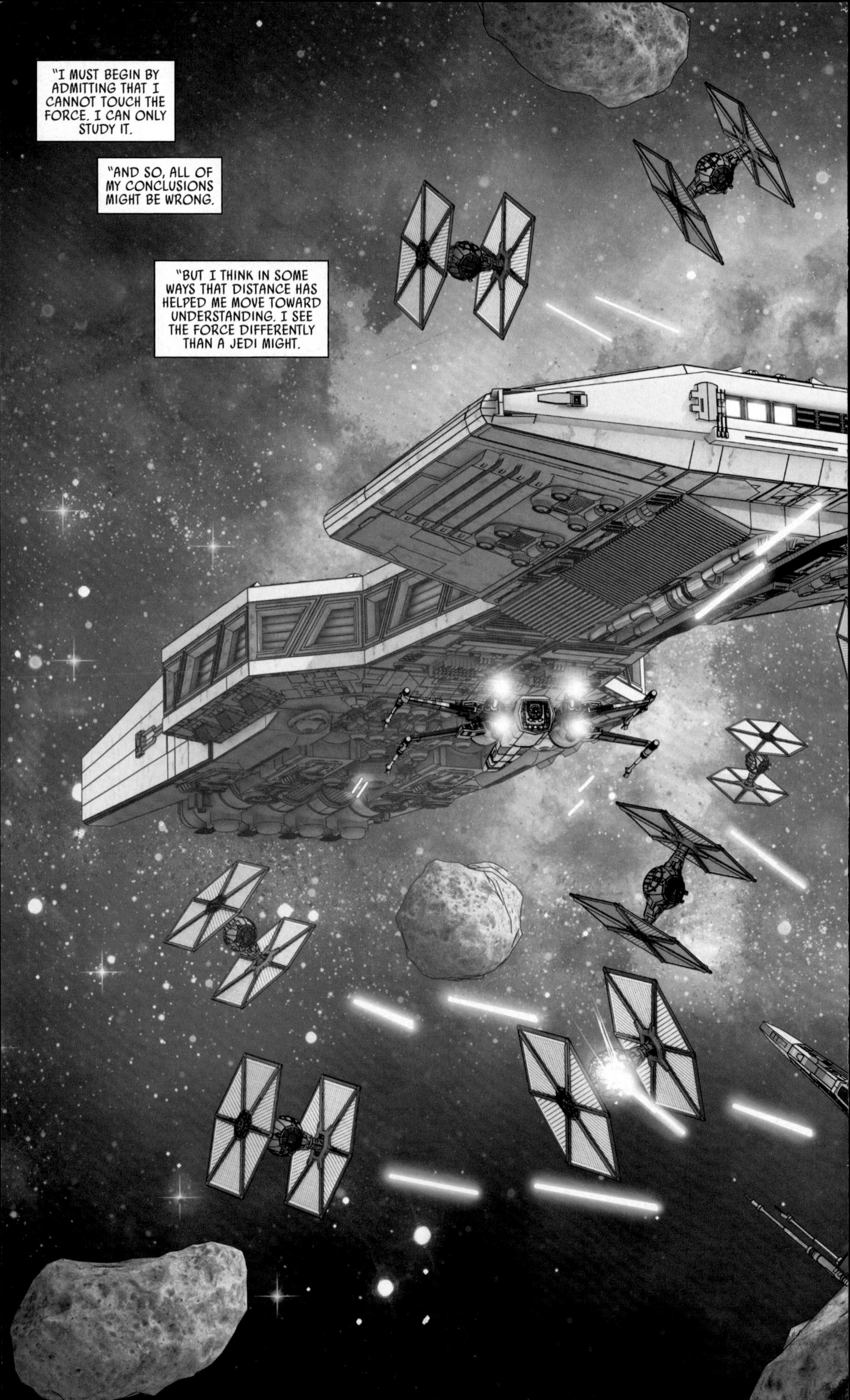
"I MUST BEGIN BY ADMITTING THAT I CANNOT TOUCH THE FORCE. I CAN ONLY STUDY IT.
"AND SO, ALL OF MY CONCLUSIONS MIGHT BE WRONG.
"BUT I THINK IN SOME WAYS THAT DISTANCE HAS HELPED ME MOVE TOWARD UNDERSTANDING. I SEE THE FORCE DIFFERENTLY THAN A JEDI MIGHT.

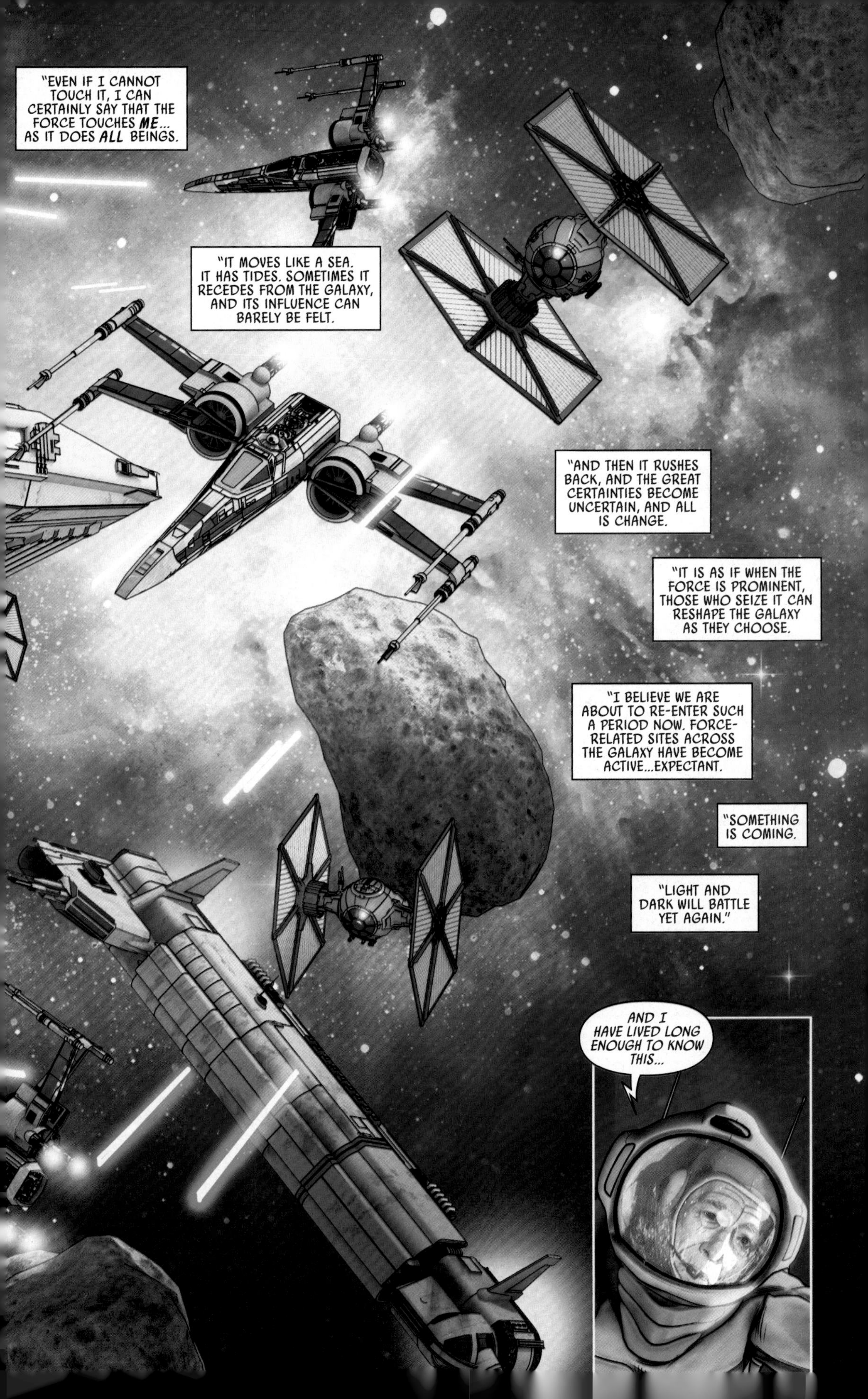
"EVEN IF I CANNOT TOUCH IT, I CAN CERTAINLY SAY THAT THE FORCE TOUCHES *ME*... AS IT DOES *ALL* BEINGS.
"IT MOVES LIKE A SEA. IT HAS TIDES. SOMETIMES IT RECEDES FROM THE GALAXY, AND ITS INFLUENCE CAN BARELY BE FELT.
"AND THEN IT RUSHES BACK, AND THE GREAT CERTAINTIES BECOME UNCERTAIN, AND ALL IS CHANGE.
"IT IS AS IF WHEN THE FORCE IS PROMINENT, THOSE WHO SEIZE IT CAN RESHAPE THE GALAXY AS THEY CHOOSE.
"I BELIEVE WE ARE ABOUT TO RE-ENTER SUCH A PERIOD NOW. FORCE-RELATED SITES ACROSS THE GALAXY HAVE BECOME ACTIVE...EXPECTANT.
"SOMETHING IS COMING.
"LIGHT AND DARK WILL BATTLE YET AGAIN."
AND I HAVE LIVED LONG ENOUGH TO KNOW THIS...

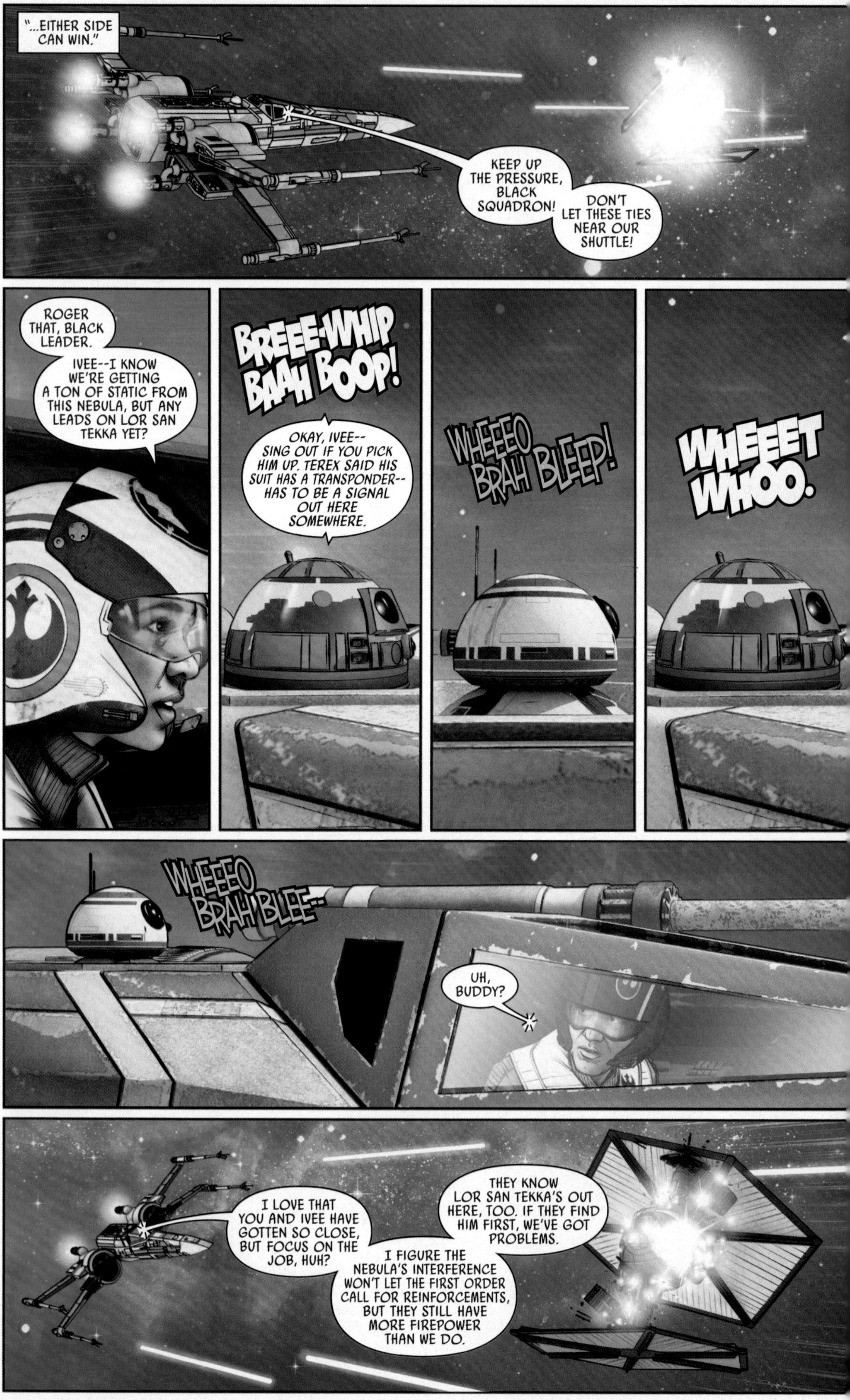
"...EITHER SIDE CAN WIN."
KEEP UP THE PRESSURE, BLACK SQUADRON!
DON'T LET THESE TIES NEAR OUR SHUTTLE!
ROGER THAT, BLACK LEADER.
IVEE--I KNOW WE'RE GETTING A TON OF STATIC FROM THIS NEBULA, BUT ANY LEADS ON LOR SAN TEKKA YET?
BREEE-WHIP BAAH BOOP!
OKAY, IVEE-- SING OUT IF YOU PICK HIM UP. TEREX SAID HIS SUIT HAS A TRANSPONDER-- HAS TO BE A SIGNAL OUT HERE SOMEWHERE.
WHEEEO BRAH BLEEP!
WHEEET WHOO.
WHEEEO BRAH BLEE--
UH, BUDDY?
I LOVE THAT YOU AND IVEE HAVE GOTTEN SO CLOSE, BUT FOCUS ON THE JOB, HUH?
THEY KNOW LOR SAN TEKKA'S OUT HERE, TOO. IF THEY FIND HIM FIRST, WE'VE GOT PROBLEMS.
I FIGURE THE NEBULA'S INTERFERENCE WON'T LET THE FIRST ORDER CALL FOR REINFORCEMENTS, BUT THEY STILL HAVE MORE FIREPOWER THAN WE DO.

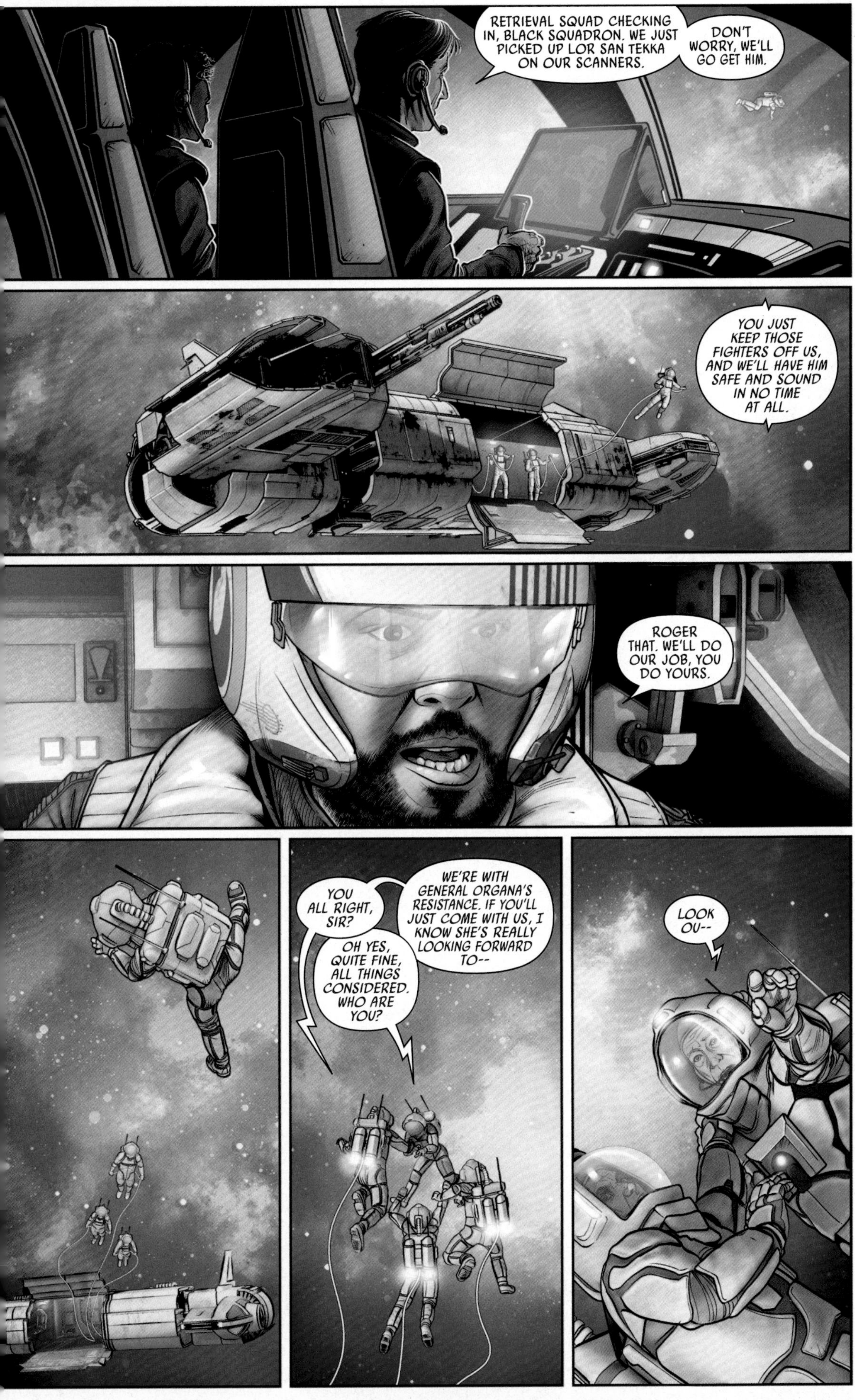
RETRIEVAL SQUAD CHECKING IN, BLACK SQUADRON. WE JUST PICKED UP LOR SAN TEKKA ON OUR SCANNERS.
DON'T WORRY, WE'LL GO GET HIM.
YOU JUST KEEP THOSE FIGHTERS OFF US, AND WE'LL HAVE HIM SAFE AND SOUND IN NO TIME AT ALL.
ROGER THAT. WE'LL DO OUR JOB, YOU DO YOURS.
YOU ALL RIGHT, SIR?
OH YES, QUITE FINE, ALL THINGS CONSIDERED. WHO ARE YOU?
WE'RE WITH GENERAL ORGANA'S RESISTANCE. IF YOU'LL JUST COME WITH US, I KNOW SHE'S REALLY LOOKING FORWARD TO--
LOOK OU--

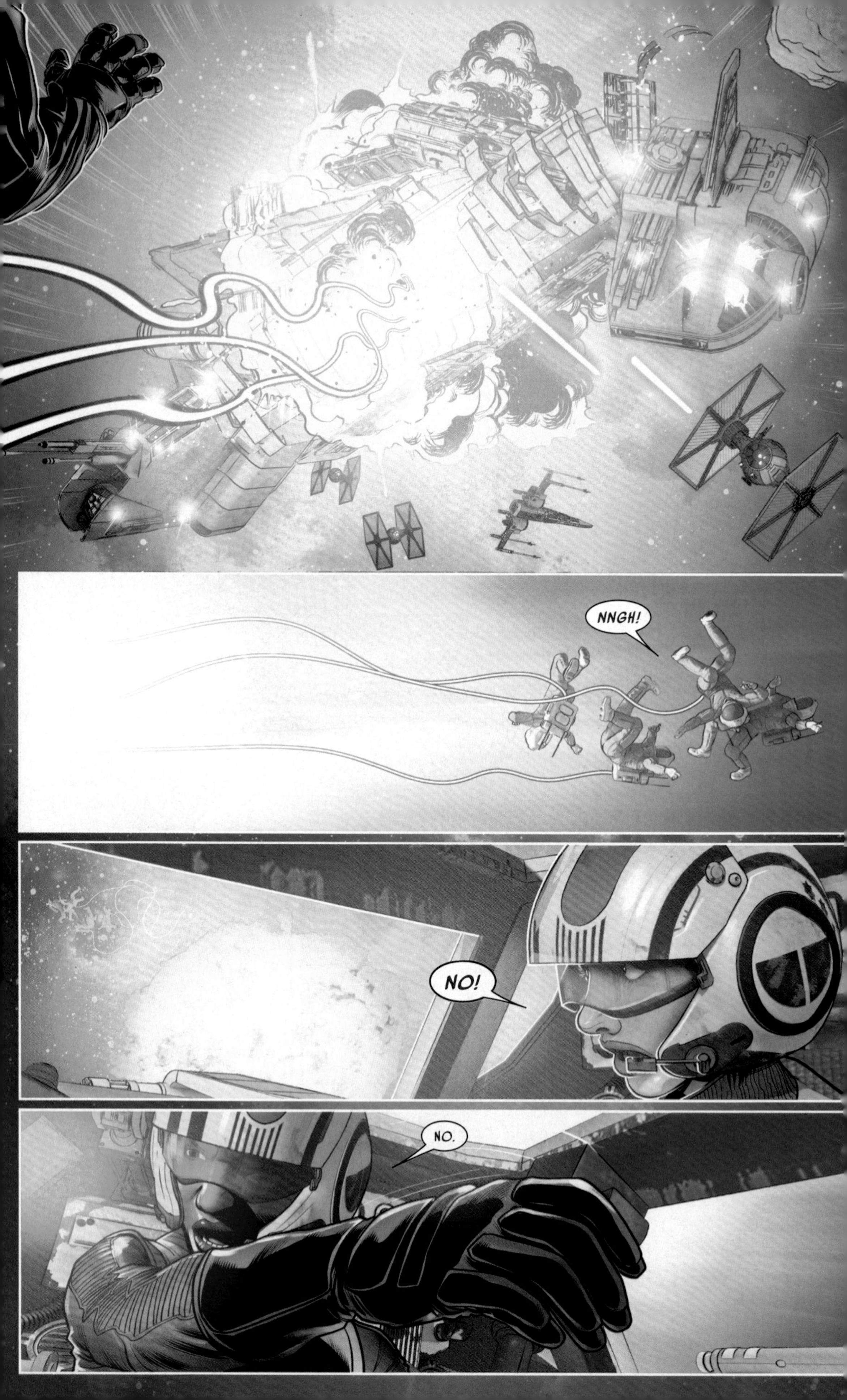
NNGH!
NO!
NO.

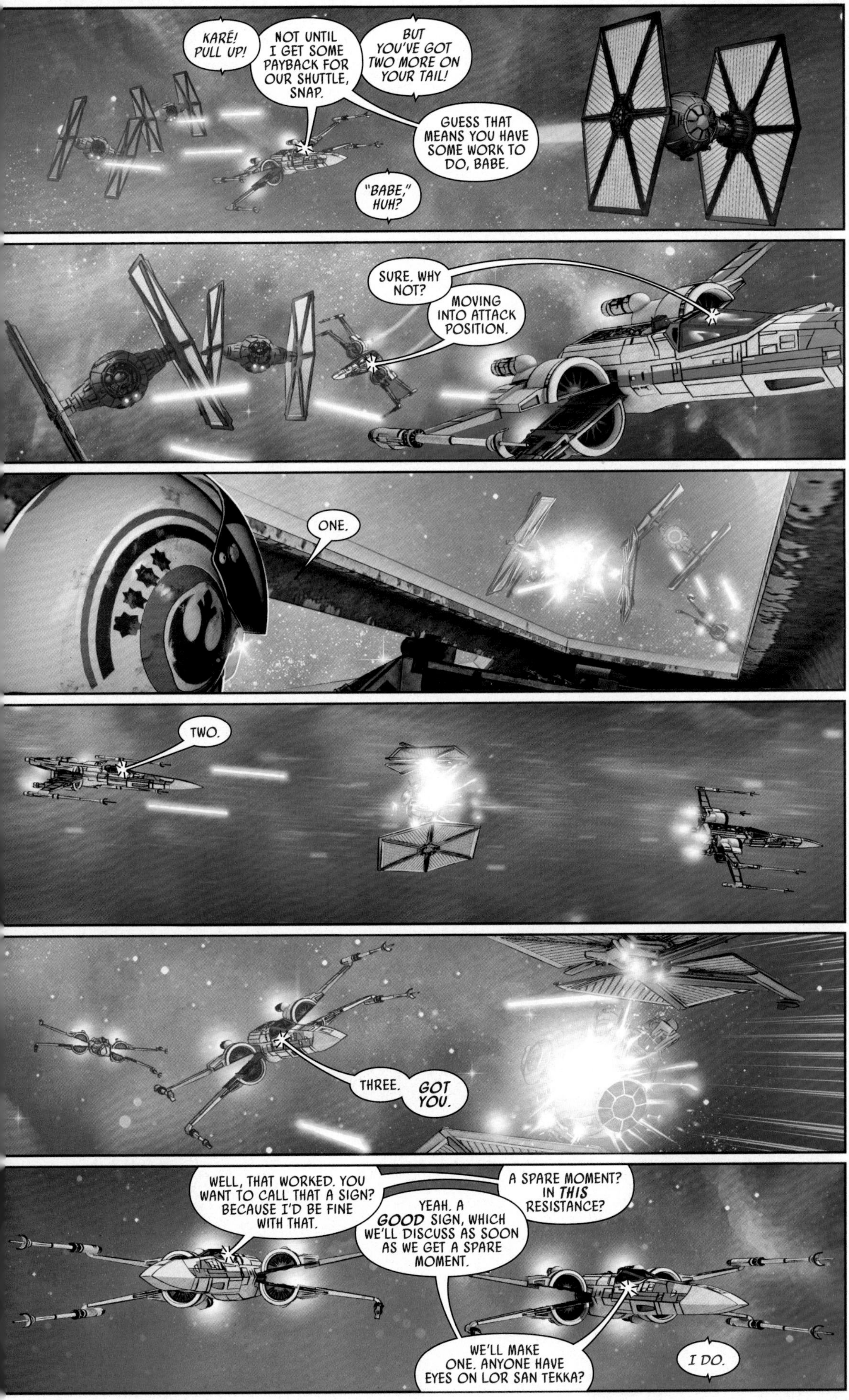
KARÉ! PULL UP!
NOT UNTIL I GET SOME PAYBACK FOR OUR SHUTTLE, SNAP.
BUT YOU'VE GOT TWO MORE ON YOUR TAIL!
GUESS THAT MEANS YOU HAVE SOME WORK TO DO, BABE.
"BABE," HUH?
SURE. WHY NOT?
MOVING INTO ATTACK POSITION.
ONE.
TWO.
THREE.
GOT YOU.
WELL, THAT WORKED. YOU WANT TO CALL THAT A SIGN? BECAUSE I'D BE FINE WITH THAT.
YEAH. A GOOD SIGN, WHICH WE'LL DISCUSS AS SOON AS WE GET A SPARE MOMENT.
A SPARE MOMENT? IN THIS RESISTANCE?
WE'LL MAKE ONE. ANYONE HAVE EYES ON LOR SAN TEKKA?
I DO.

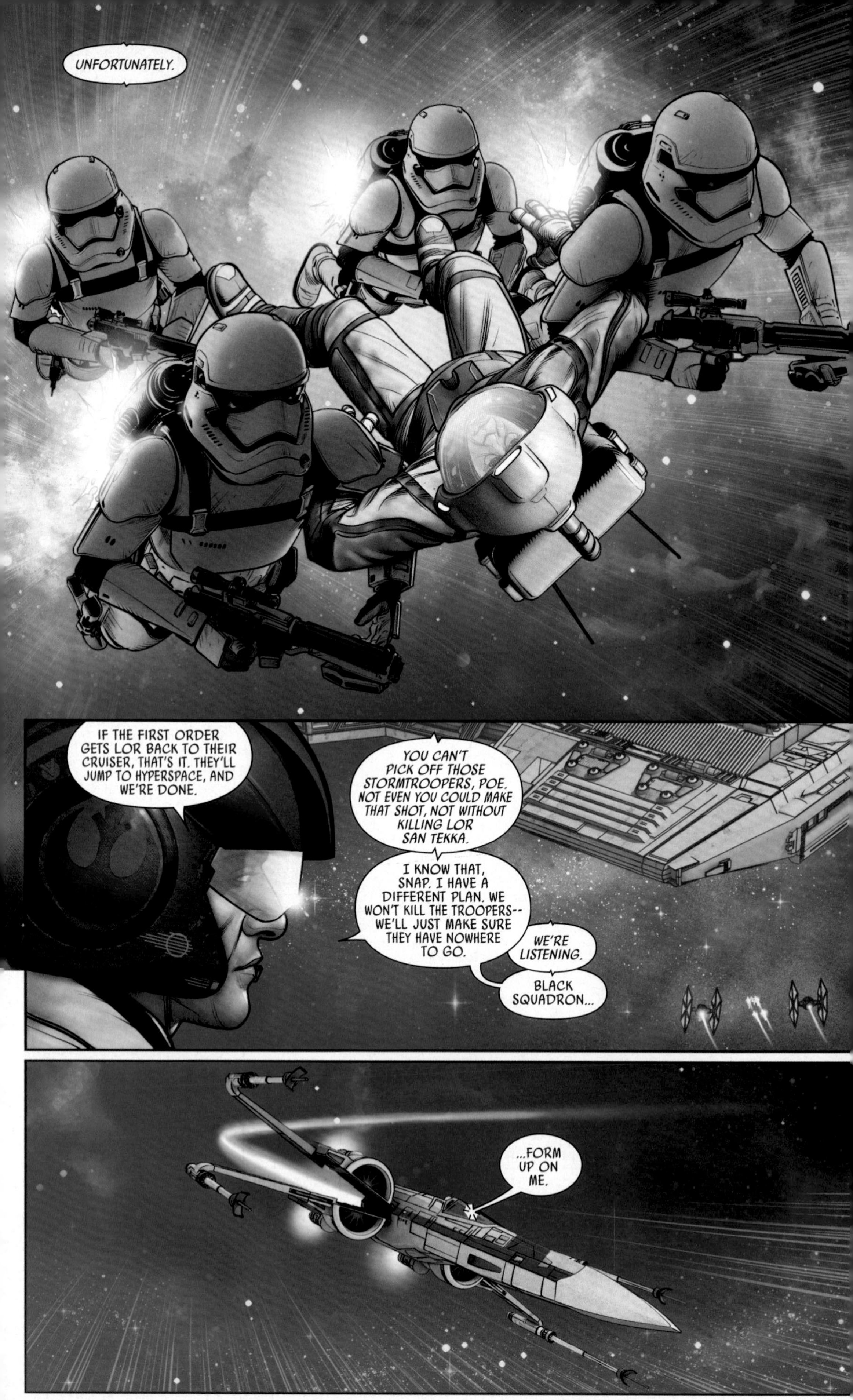
UNFORTUNATELY.
IF THE FIRST ORDER GETS LOR BACK TO THEIR CRUISER, THAT'S IT. THEY'LL JUMP TO HYPERSPACE, AND WE'RE DONE.
YOU CAN'T PICK OFF THOSE STORMTROOPERS, POE. NOT EVEN YOU COULD MAKE THAT SHOT, NOT WITHOUT KILLING LOR SAN TEKKA.
I KNOW THAT, SNAP. I HAVE A DIFFERENT PLAN. WE WON'T KILL THE TROOPERS-- WE'LL JUST MAKE SURE THEY HAVE NOWHERE TO GO.
WE'RE LISTENING.
BLACK SQUADRON...
...FORM UP ON ME.

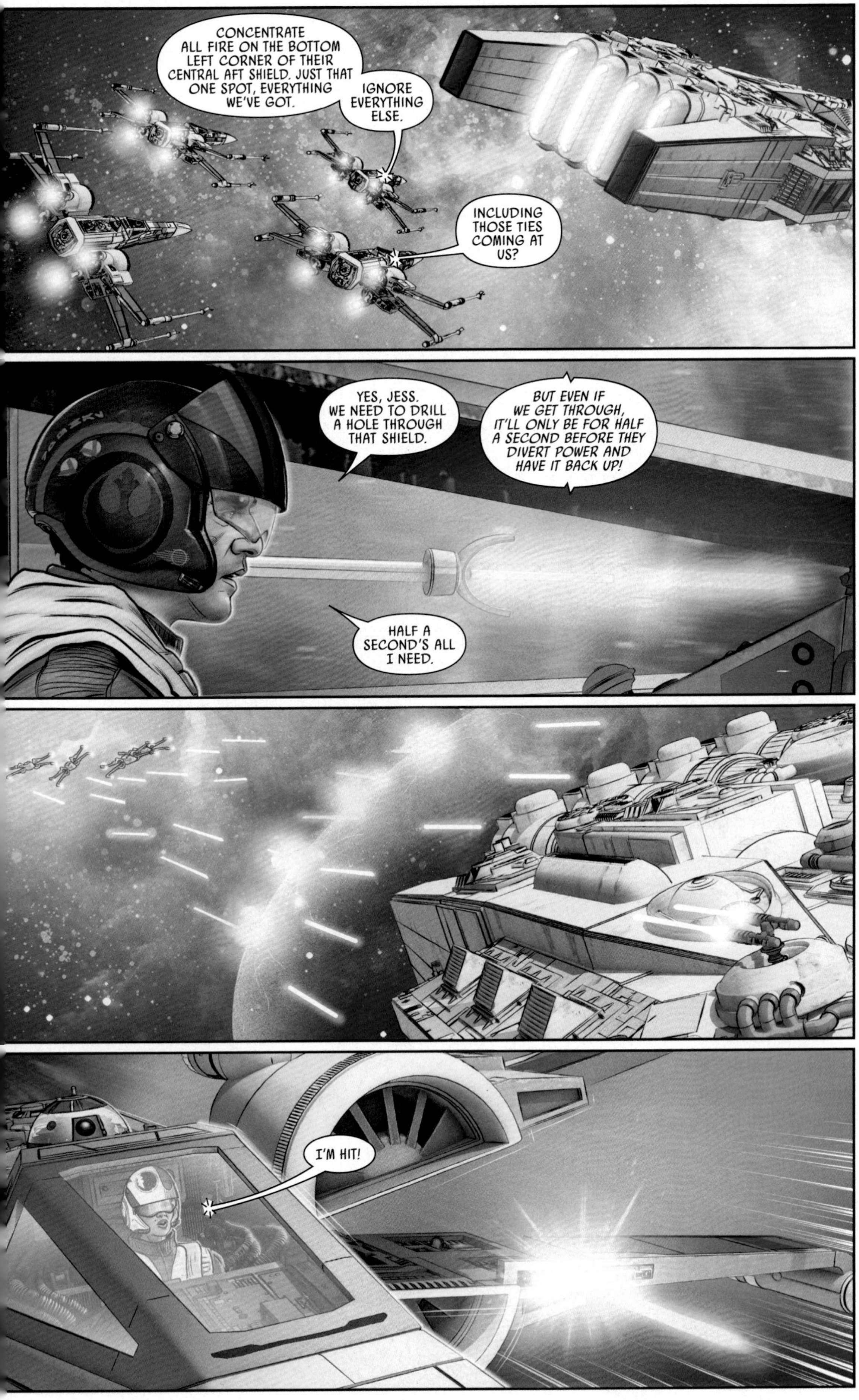
CONCENTRATE ALL FIRE ON THE BOTTOM LEFT CORNER OF THEIR CENTRAL AFT SHIELD. JUST THAT ONE SPOT, EVERYTHING WE'VE GOT.
IGNORE EVERYTHING ELSE.
INCLUDING THOSE TIES COMING AT US?
YES, JESS. WE NEED TO DRILL A HOLE THROUGH THAT SHIELD.
BUT EVEN IF WE GET THROUGH, IT'LL ONLY BE FOR HALF A SECOND BEFORE THEY DIVERT POWER AND HAVE IT BACK UP!
HALF A SECOND'S ALL I NEED.
I'M HIT!

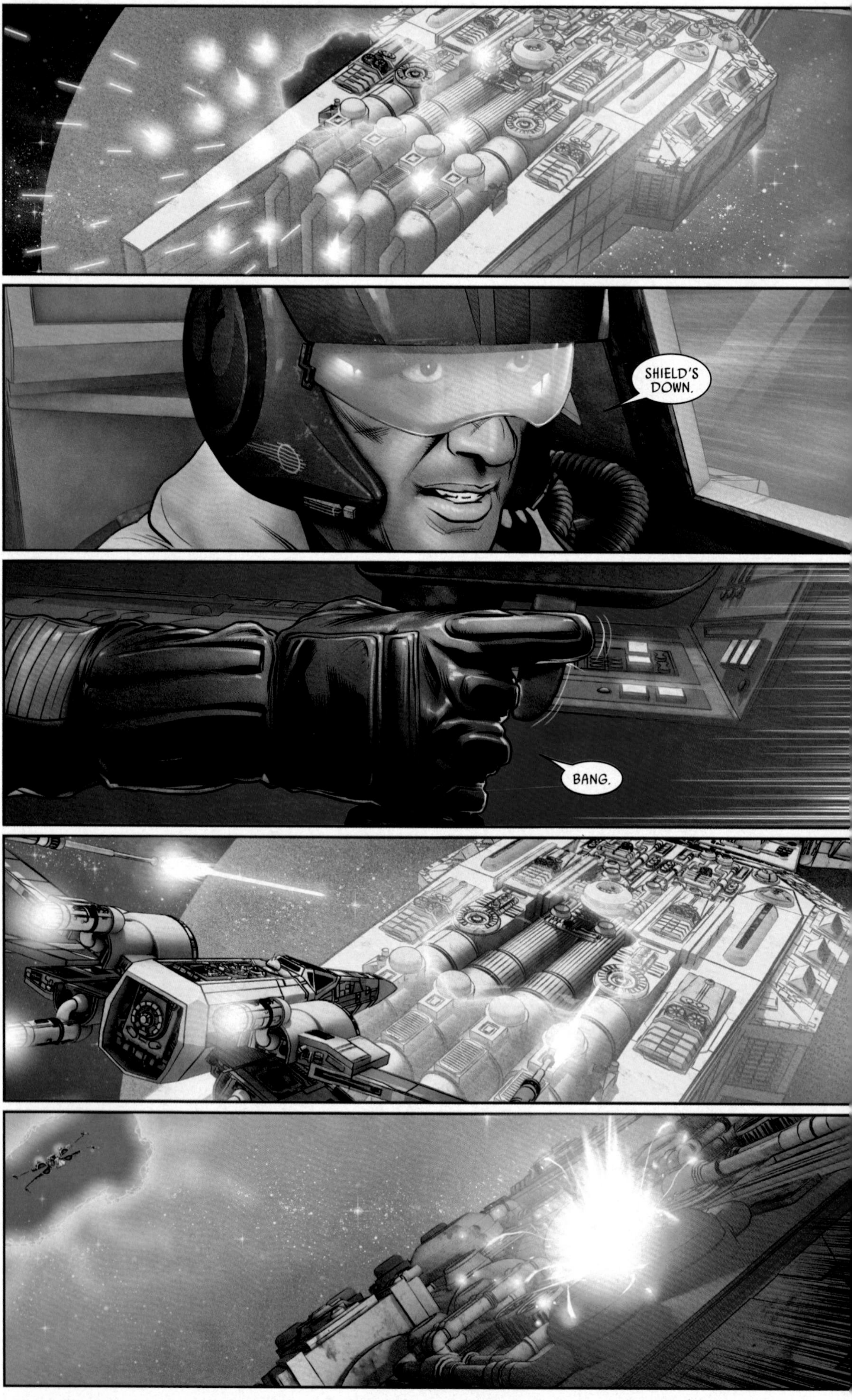

SHIELD'S DOWN.
BANG.

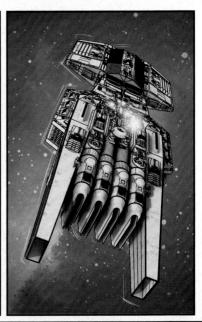

CRUISER'S POWER'S OWN. TAKE IT OUT, BLACK SQUADRON.

HOW DID YOU DO THAT, POE?

THANK THREEPIO AND HIS DROID SPIES. THEY FOUND A DESIGN FLAW IN THESE FIRST ORDER LIGHT CRUISERS--A POWER CONDUIT BUILT TOO CLOSE TO THE HULL.

NOT THE KIND OF THING ONE FIGHTER COULD EXPLOIT ALONE, BUT WHEN YOU'VE GOT THE RIGHT TEAM... WELL, THE RESULTS SPEAK FOR THEMSELVES, EH?

GUYS, I'M VERY PROUD OF YOU, BUT MY PROPULSION'S OUT. THAT CRUISER GOT IN A LUCKY HIT. I'M ON THE DRIFT HERE. IVEE'S WORKING ON IT, BUT IT MIGHT BE--

WHEEEEEO!

OH... BLAST. NOT GOOD.

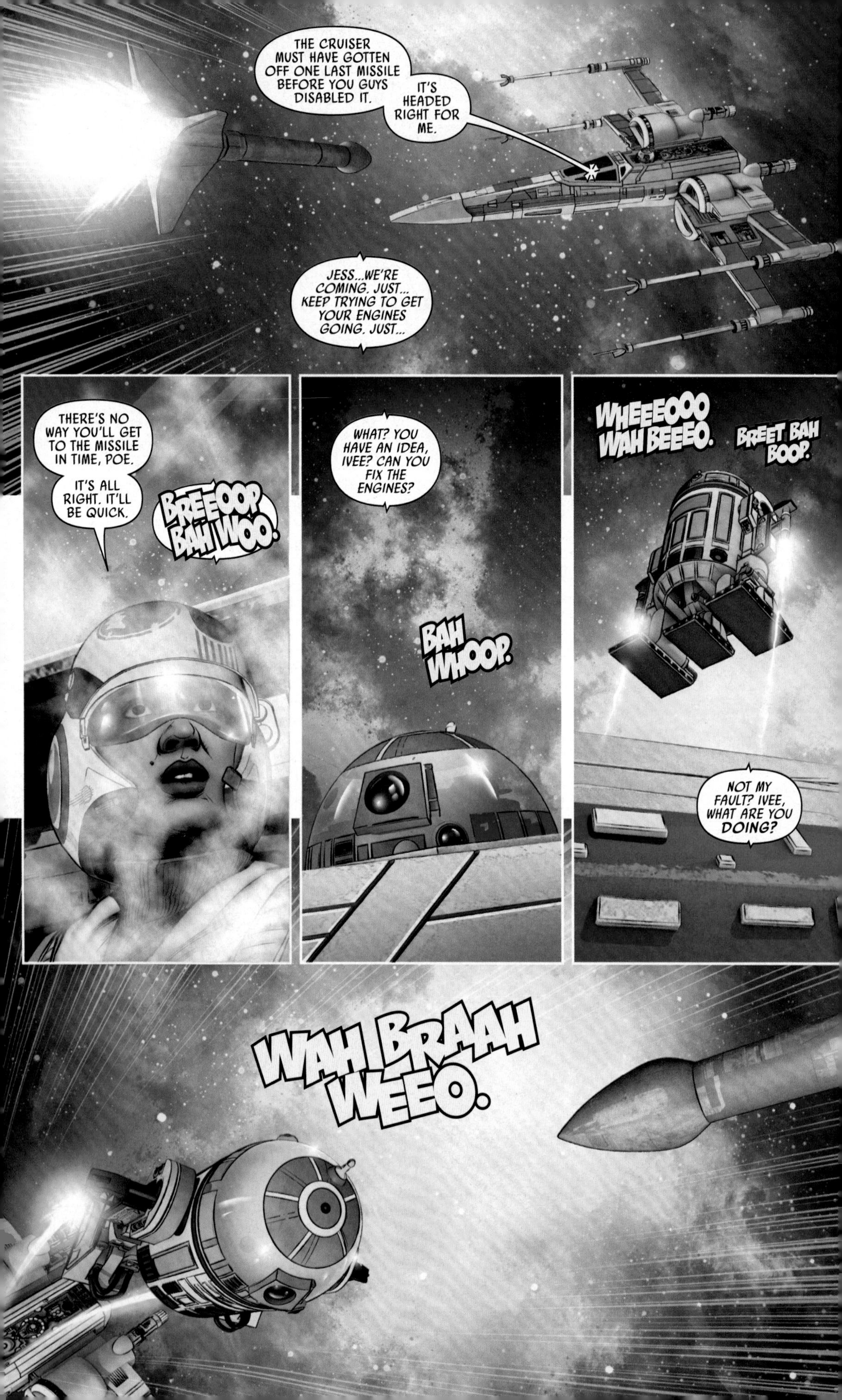

THE CRUISER MUST HAVE GOTTEN OFF ONE LAST MISSILE BEFORE YOU GUYS DISABLED IT.
IT'S HEADED RIGHT FOR ME.
JESS...WE'RE COMING. JUST... KEEP TRYING TO GET YOUR ENGINES GOING. JUST...
THERE'S NO WAY YOU'LL GET TO THE MISSILE IN TIME, POE.
IT'S ALL RIGHT. IT'LL BE QUICK.
BREEOOP BAH WOO.
WHAT? YOU HAVE AN IDEA, IVEE? CAN YOU FIX THE ENGINES?
BAH WHOOP.
WHEEEOOO WAH BEEEO.
BREET BAH BOOP.
NOT MY FAULT? IVEE, WHAT ARE YOU DOING?
WAH BRAAH WEEO.

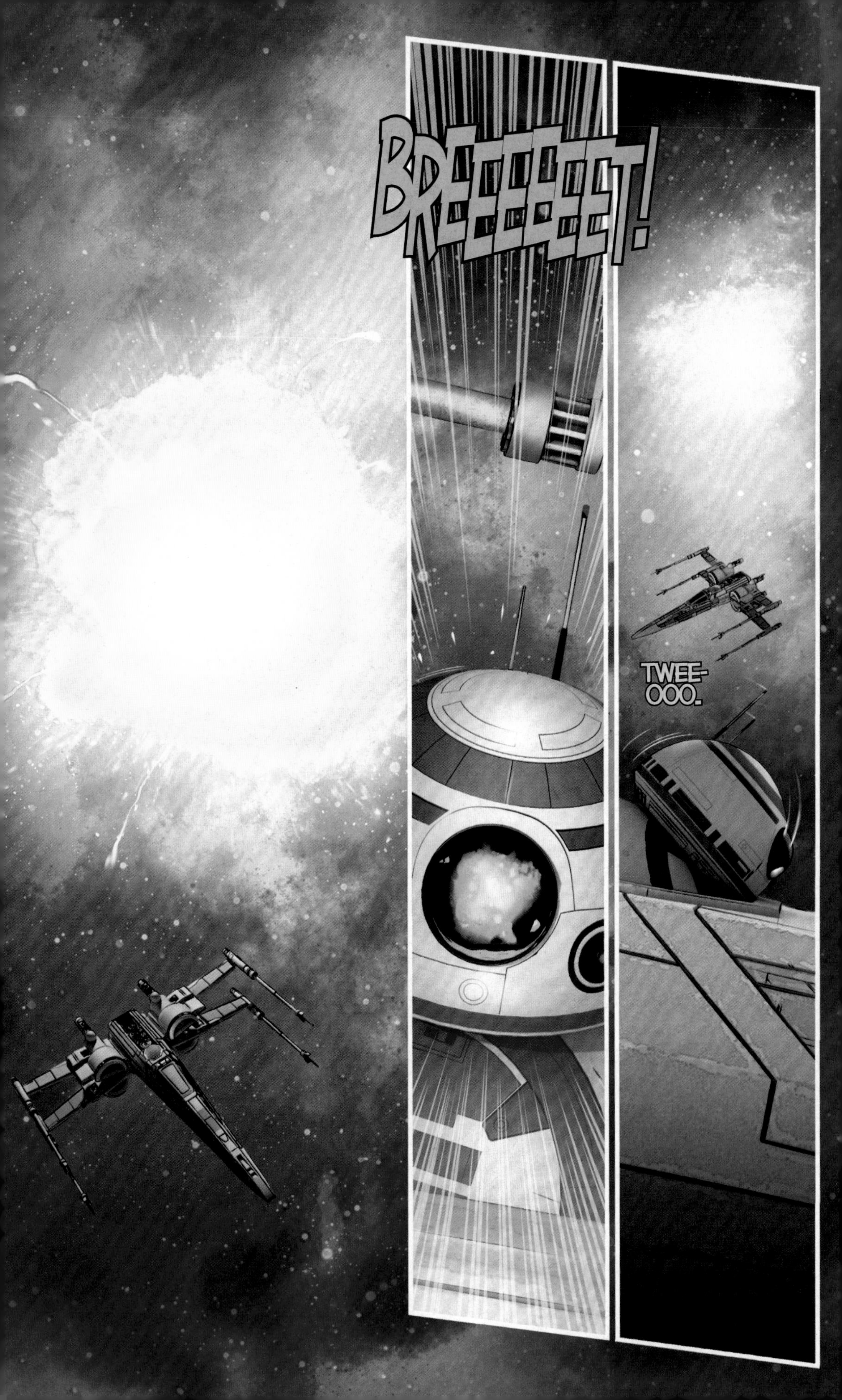
BREEEEEET!
TWEE-
OOO.

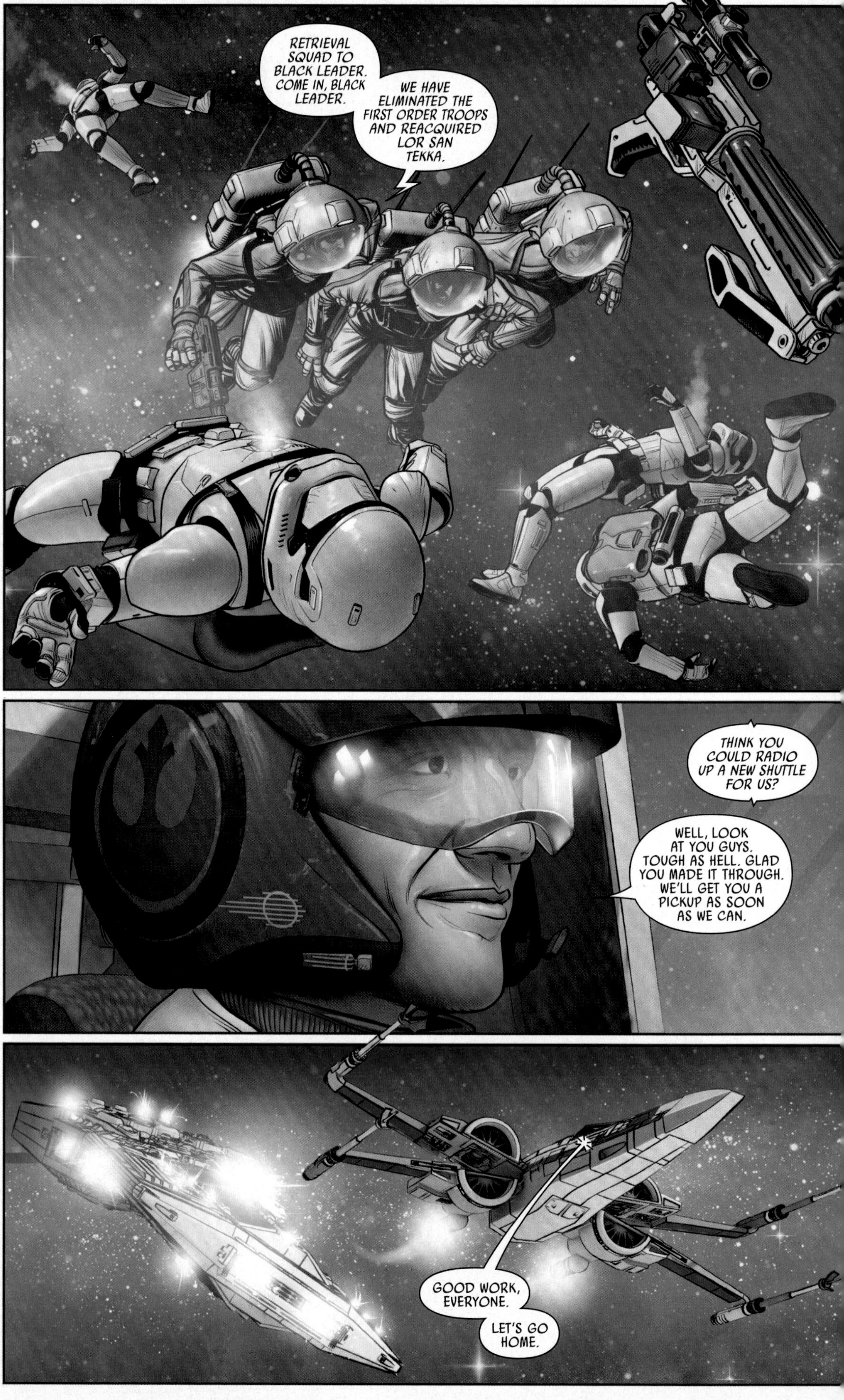
RETRIEVAL SQUAD TO BLACK LEADER. COME IN, BLACK LEADER.
WE HAVE ELIMINATED THE FIRST ORDER TROOPS AND REACQUIRED LOR SAN TEKKA.
THINK YOU COULD RADIO UP A NEW SHUTTLE FOR US?
WELL, LOOK AT YOU GUYS. TOUGH AS HELL. GLAD YOU MADE IT THROUGH. WE'LL GET YOU A PICKUP AS SOON AS WE CAN.
GOOD WORK, EVERYONE.
LET'S GO HOME.

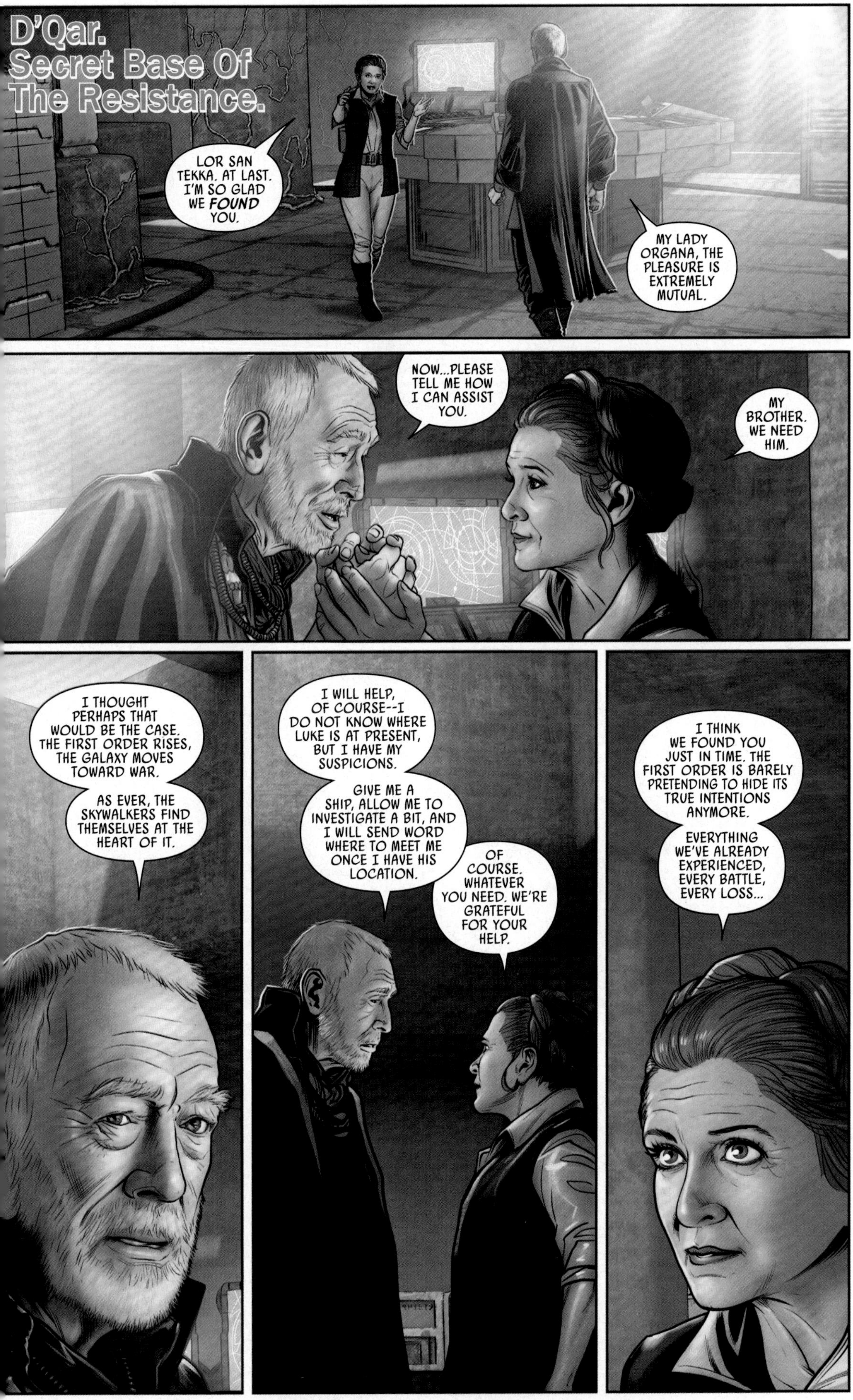
D'Qar. Secret Base Of The Resistance.
LOR SAN TEKKA. AT LAST. I'M SO GLAD WE FOUND YOU.
MY LADY ORGANA, THE PLEASURE IS EXTREMELY MUTUAL.
NOW...PLEASE TELL ME HOW I CAN ASSIST YOU.
MY BROTHER. WE NEED HIM.
I THOUGHT PERHAPS THAT WOULD BE THE CASE. THE FIRST ORDER RISES, THE GALAXY MOVES TOWARD WAR.
AS EVER, THE SKYWALKERS FIND THEMSELVES AT THE HEART OF IT.
I WILL HELP, OF COURSE--I DO NOT KNOW WHERE LUKE IS AT PRESENT, BUT I HAVE MY SUSPICIONS.
GIVE ME A SHIP, ALLOW ME TO INVESTIGATE A BIT, AND I WILL SEND WORD WHERE TO MEET ME ONCE I HAVE HIS LOCATION.
OF COURSE. WHATEVER YOU NEED. WE'RE GRATEFUL FOR YOUR HELP.
I THINK WE FOUND YOU JUST IN TIME. THE FIRST ORDER IS BARELY PRETENDING TO HIDE ITS TRUE INTENTIONS ANYMORE.
EVERYTHING WE'VE ALREADY EXPERIENCED, EVERY BATTLE, EVERY LOSS...

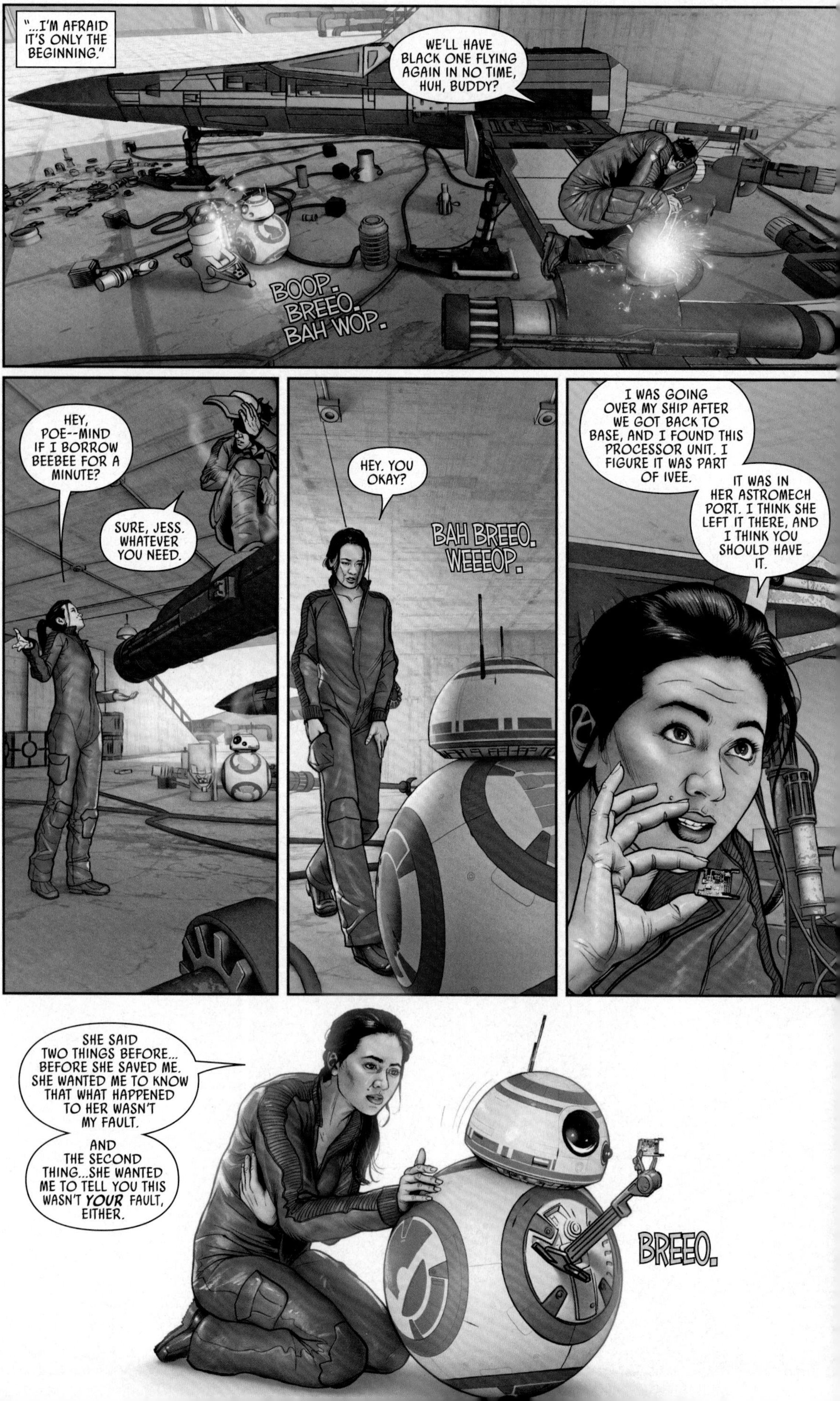
"...I'M AFRAID IT'S ONLY THE BEGINNING."
WE'LL HAVE BLACK ONE FLYING AGAIN IN NO TIME, HUH, BUDDY?
BOOP. BREEO. BAH WOP.
HEY, POE--MIND IF I BORROW BEEBEE FOR A MINUTE?
SURE, JESS. WHATEVER YOU NEED.
HEY. YOU OKAY?
BAH BREEO. WEEEOP.
I WAS GOING OVER MY SHIP AFTER WE GOT BACK TO BASE, AND I FOUND THIS PROCESSOR UNIT. I FIGURE IT WAS PART OF IVEE.
IT WAS IN HER ASTROMECH PORT. I THINK SHE LEFT IT THERE, AND I THINK YOU SHOULD HAVE IT.
SHE SAID TWO THINGS BEFORE... BEFORE SHE SAVED ME. SHE WANTED ME TO KNOW THAT WHAT HAPPENED TO HER WASN'T MY FAULT.
AND THE SECOND THING...SHE WANTED ME TO TELL YOU THIS WASN'T *YOUR* FAULT, EITHER.
BREEO.

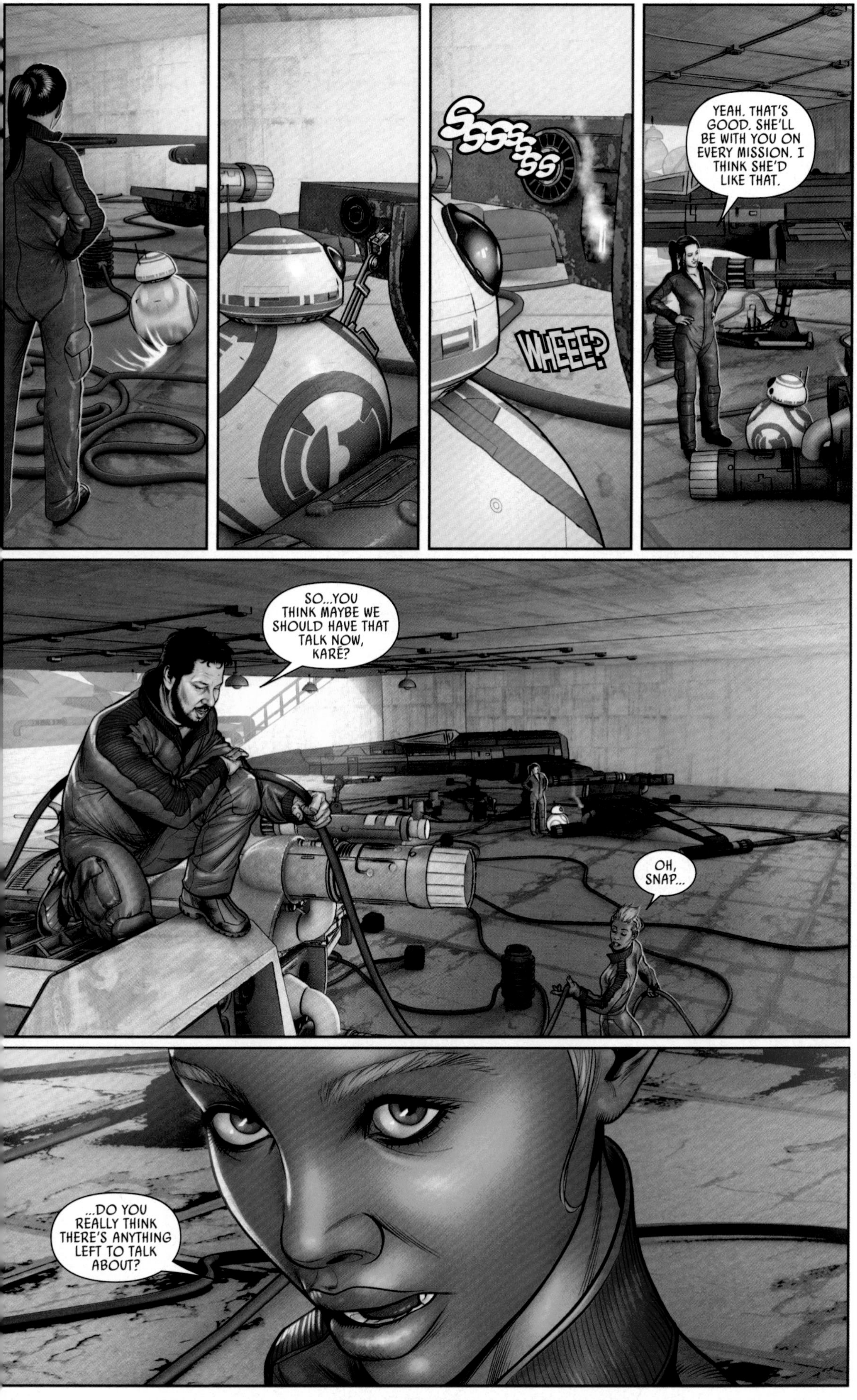
SSSSSSS
WHEEE?
YEAH. THAT'S GOOD. SHE'LL BE WITH YOU ON EVERY MISSION. I THINK SHE'D LIKE THAT.
SO...YOU THINK MAYBE WE SHOULD HAVE THAT TALK NOW, KARÉ?
OH, SNAP...
...DO YOU REALLY THINK THERE'S ANYTHING LEFT TO TALK ABOUT?

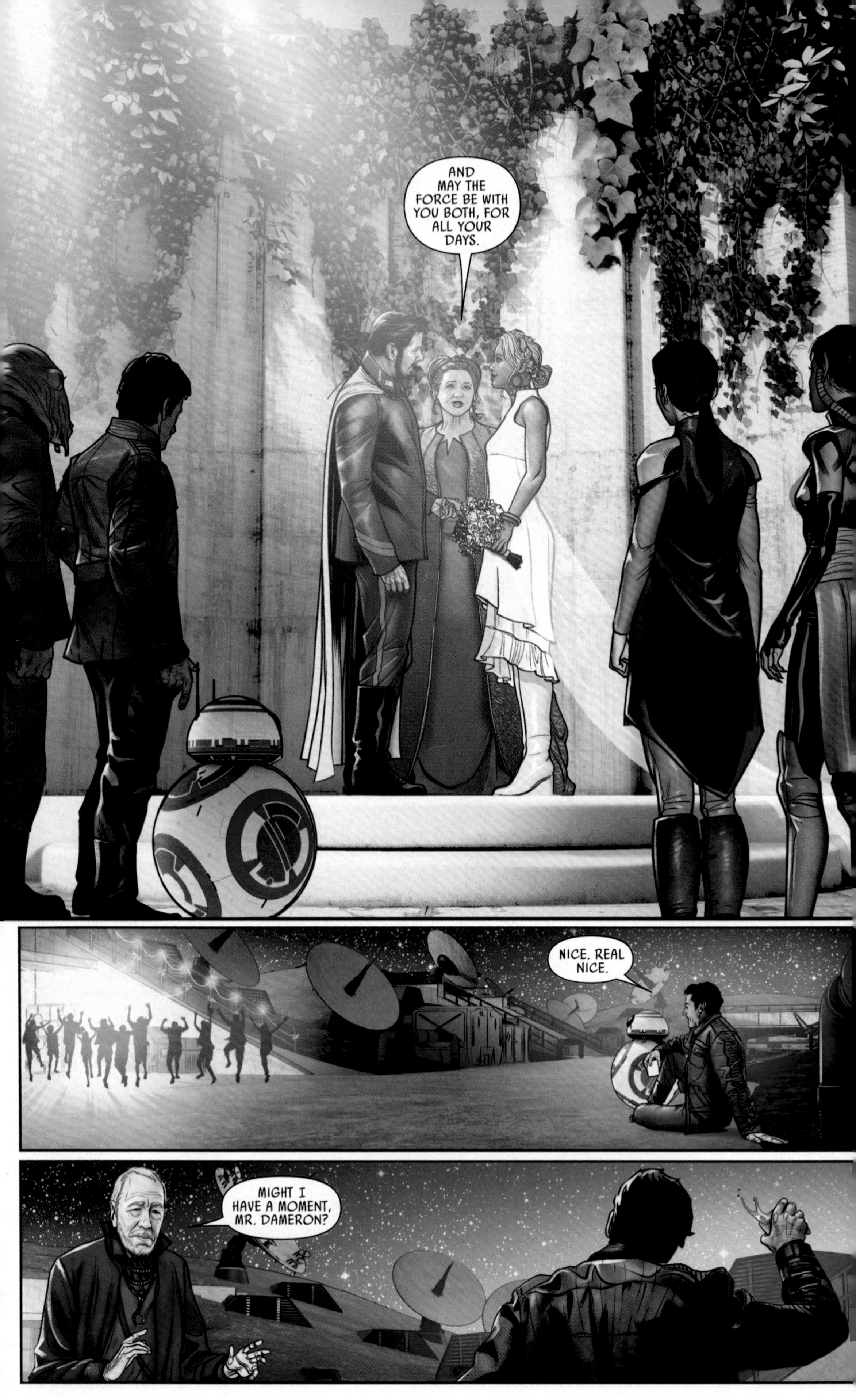
AND MAY THE FORCE BE WITH YOU BOTH, FOR ALL YOUR DAYS.
NICE. REAL NICE.
MIGHT I HAVE A MOMENT, MR. DAMERON?

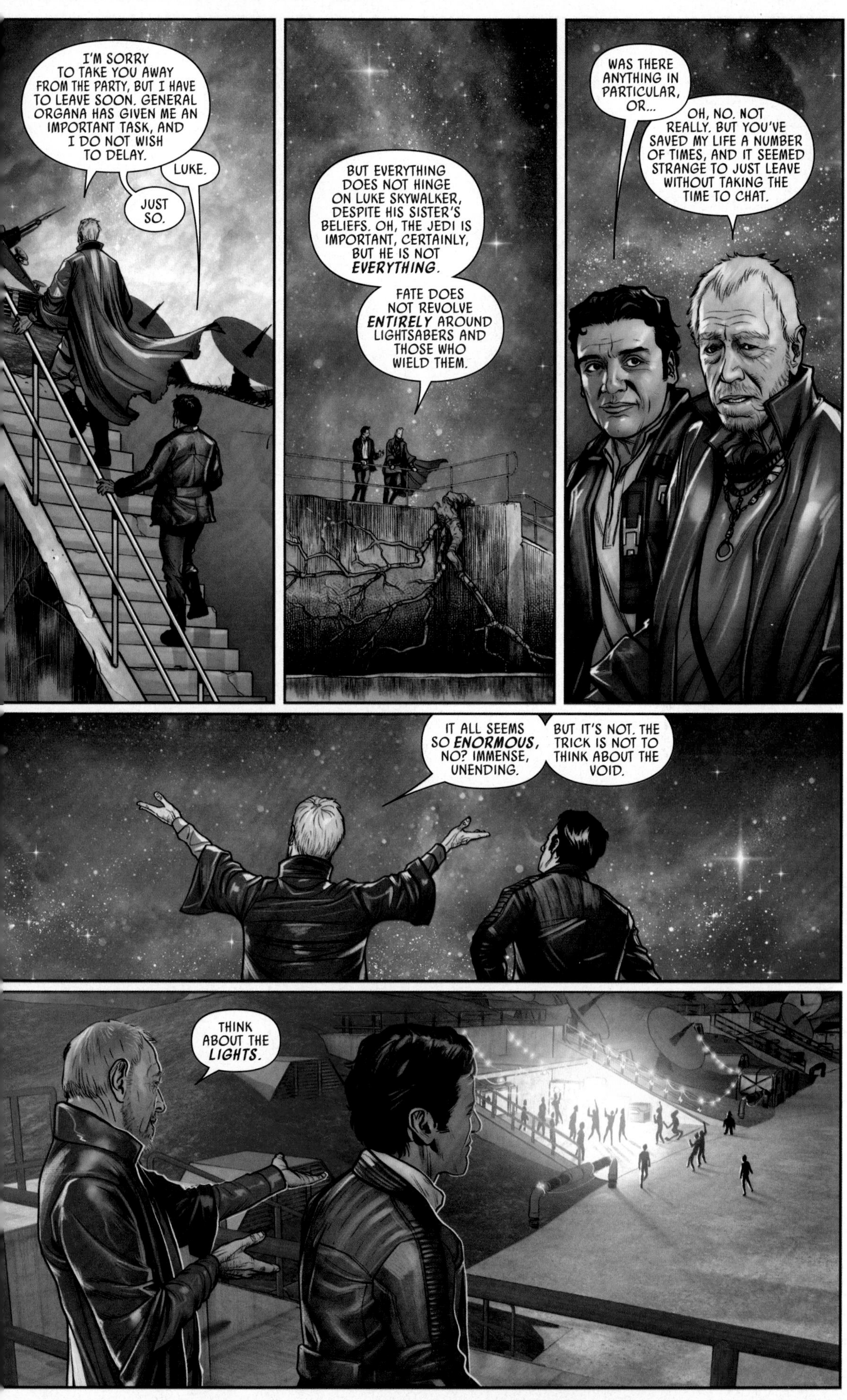
I'M SORRY TO TAKE YOU AWAY FROM THE PARTY, BUT I HAVE TO LEAVE SOON. GENERAL ORGANA HAS GIVEN ME AN IMPORTANT TASK, AND I DO NOT WISH TO DELAY.
LUKE.
JUST SO.
BUT EVERYTHING DOES NOT HINGE ON LUKE SKYWALKER, DESPITE HIS SISTER'S BELIEFS. OH, THE JEDI IS IMPORTANT, CERTAINLY, BUT HE IS NOT EVERYTHING.
FATE DOES NOT REVOLVE ENTIRELY AROUND LIGHTSABERS AND THOSE WHO WIELD THEM.
WAS THERE ANYTHING IN PARTICULAR, OR...
OH, NO. NOT REALLY. BUT YOU'VE SAVED MY LIFE A NUMBER OF TIMES, AND IT SEEMED STRANGE TO JUST LEAVE WITHOUT TAKING THE TIME TO CHAT.
IT ALL SEEMS SO ENORMOUS, NO? IMMENSE, UNENDING.
BUT IT'S NOT. THE TRICK IS NOT TO THINK ABOUT THE VOID.
THINK ABOUT THE LIGHTS.

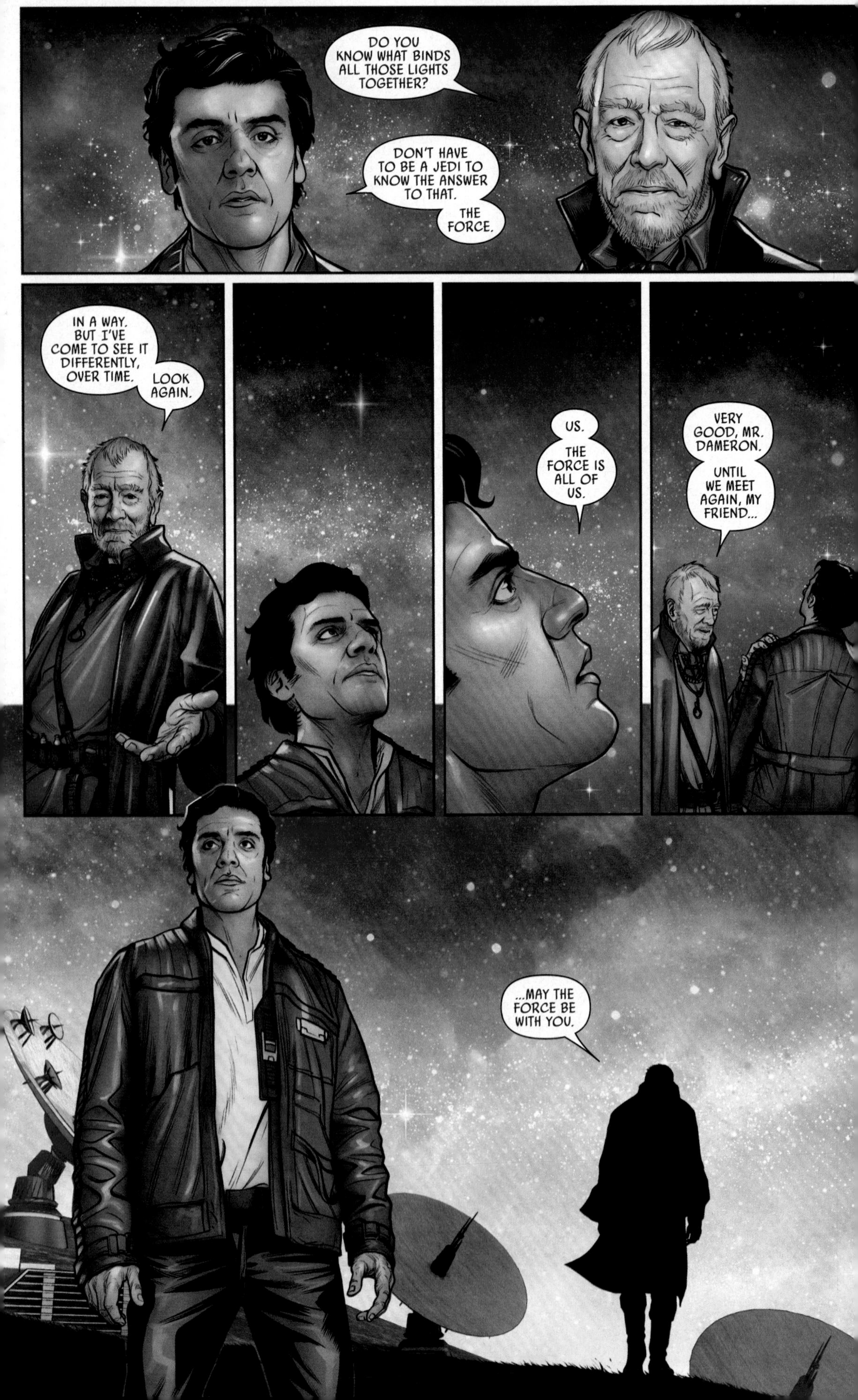
DO YOU KNOW WHAT BINDS ALL THOSE LIGHTS TOGETHER?
DON'T HAVE TO BE A JEDI TO KNOW THE ANSWER TO THAT.
THE FORCE.
IN A WAY. BUT I'VE COME TO SEE IT DIFFERENTLY, OVER TIME.
LOOK AGAIN.
US.
THE FORCE IS ALL OF US.
VERY GOOD, MR. DAMERON.
UNTIL WE MEET AGAIN, MY FRIEND...
...MAY THE FORCE BE WITH YOU.

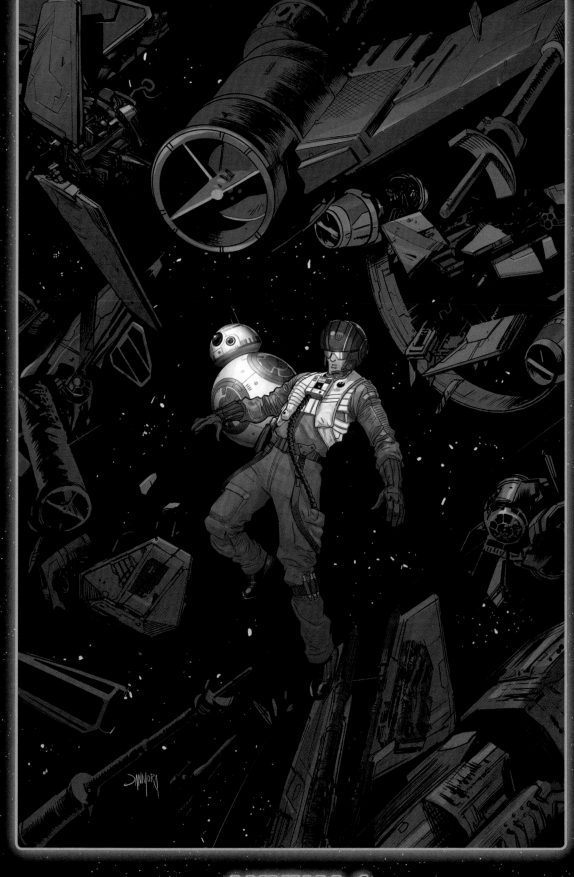

ANNUAL 1

ANNUAL

It is a time of uncertainty in the galaxy. Standing against the brutal oppression of the First Order is General Organa's Resistance, including Poe Dameron and his droid named Beebee-Ate.

Poe Dameron and his team have recently emerged from a bittersweet victory. Through a combination of luck and skill, they defeated the ruthless crime lord Terex, although in the process they suffered the loss of grizzled veteran pilot L'ulo.

In the wake of this loss, Poe is more dedicated than ever to defeating the First Order — no matter the cost. But the same rebellious spirit that makes Poe a great pilot often causes tension in the Resistance....

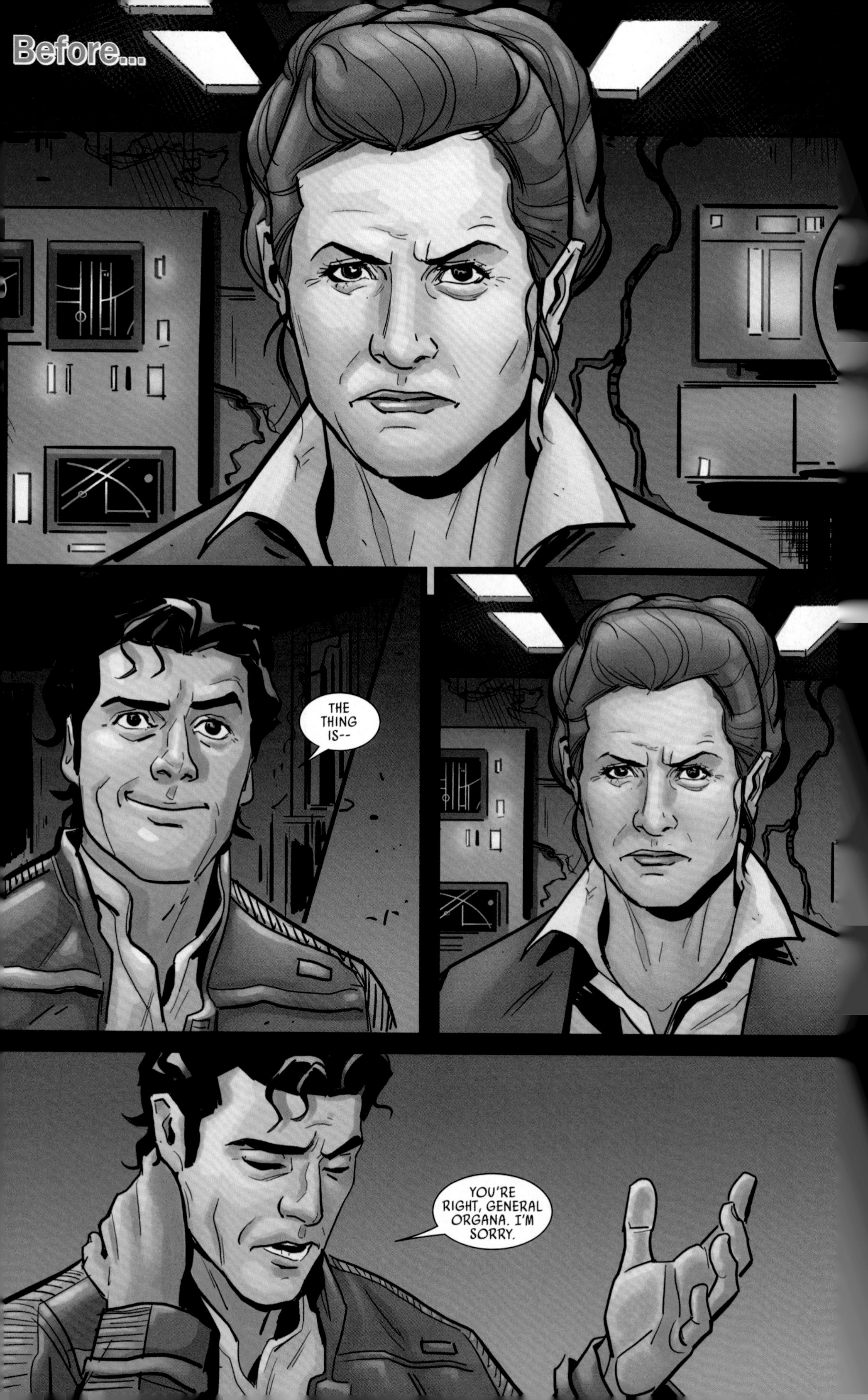
Before...
THE THING IS--
YOU'RE RIGHT, GENERAL ORGANA. I'M SORRY.

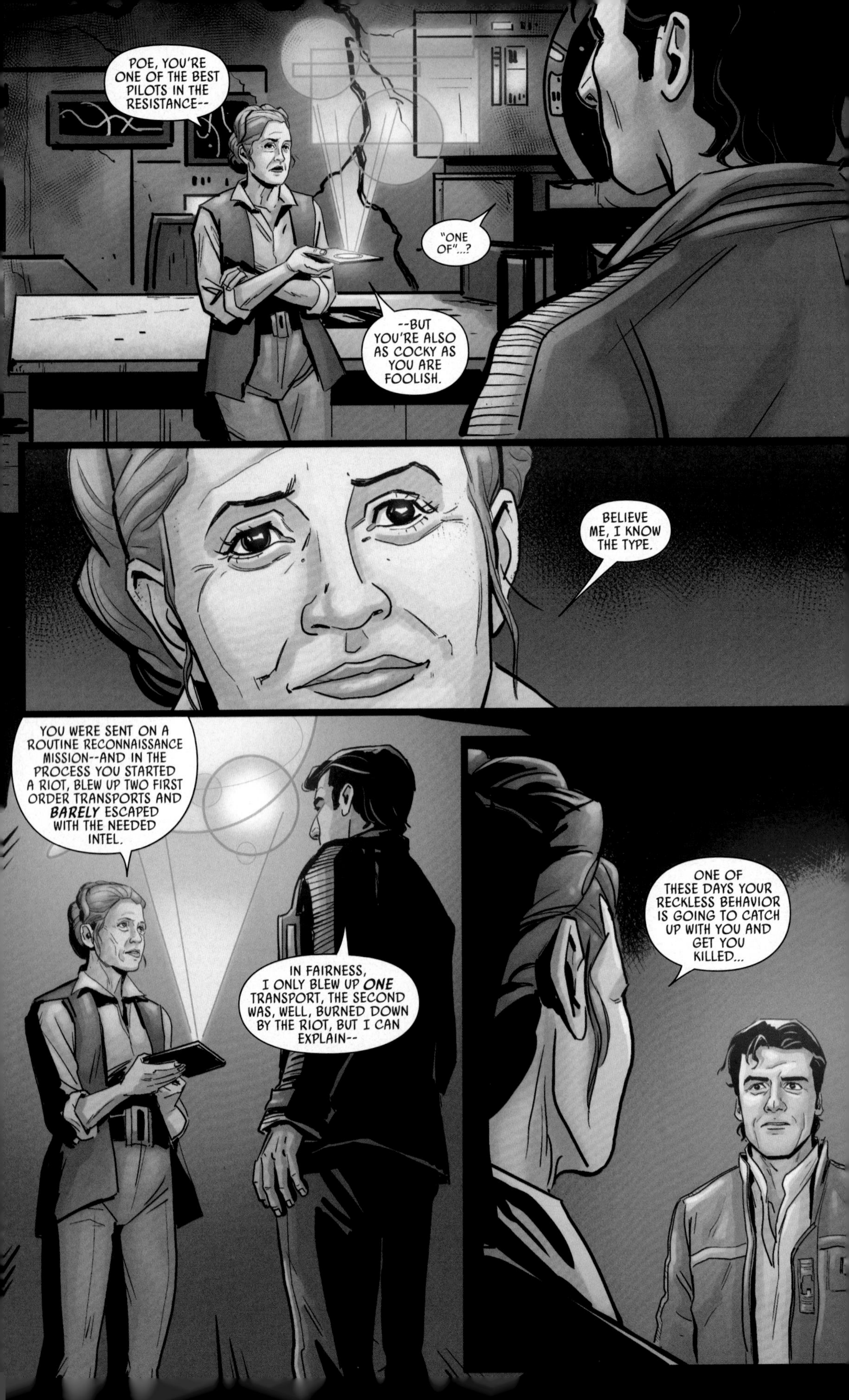
POE, YOU'RE ONE OF THE BEST PILOTS IN THE RESISTANCE--
"ONE OF"...?
--BUT YOU'RE ALSO AS COCKY AS YOU ARE FOOLISH.
BELIEVE ME, I KNOW THE TYPE.
YOU WERE SENT ON A ROUTINE RECONNAISSANCE MISSION--AND IN THE PROCESS YOU STARTED A RIOT, BLEW UP TWO FIRST ORDER TRANSPORTS AND BARELY ESCAPED WITH THE NEEDED INTEL.
IN FAIRNESS, I ONLY BLEW UP ONE TRANSPORT, THE SECOND WAS, WELL, BURNED DOWN BY THE RIOT, BUT I CAN EXPLAIN--
ONE OF THESE DAYS YOUR RECKLESS BEHAVIOR IS GOING TO CATCH UP WITH YOU AND GET YOU KILLED...

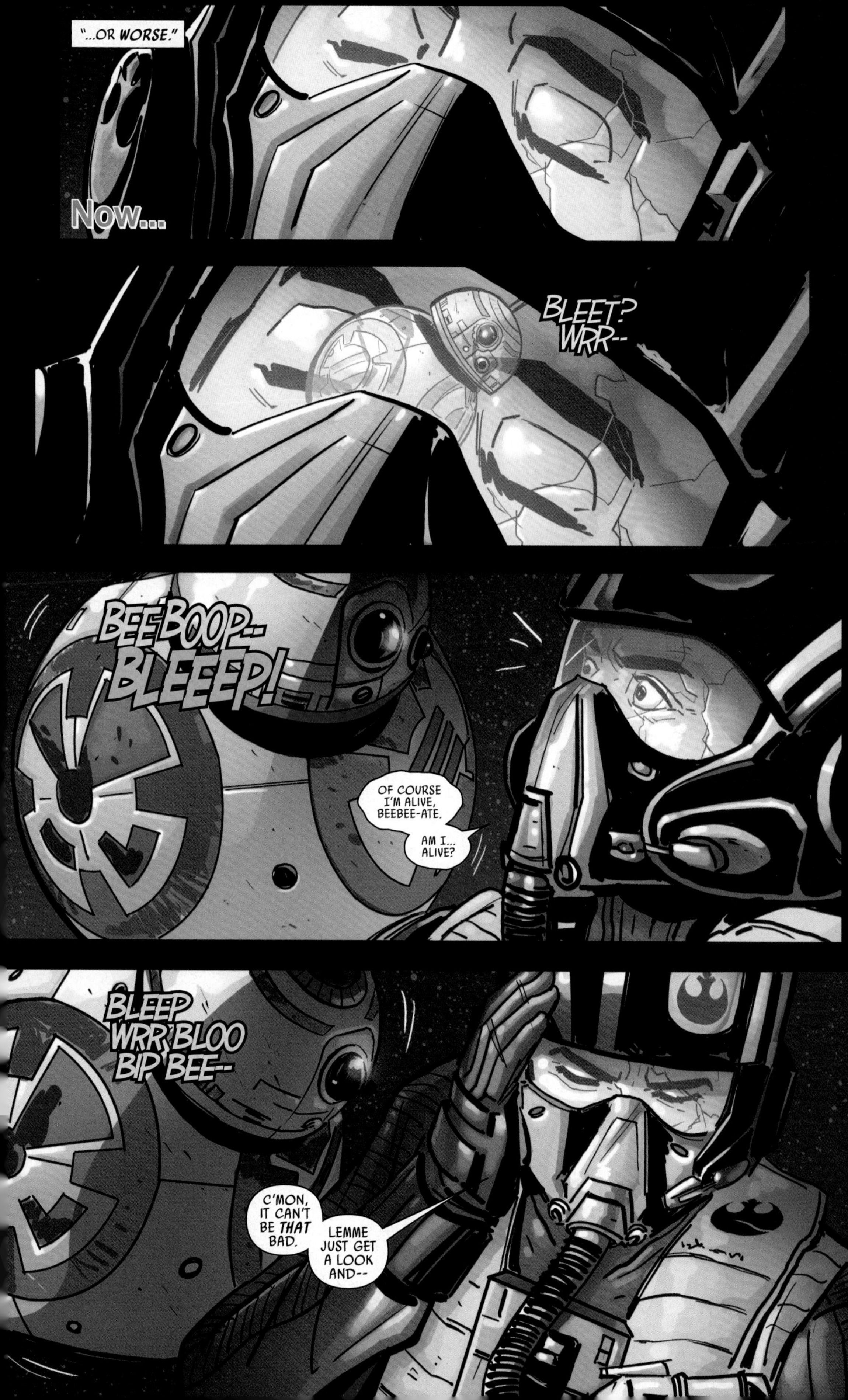
"...OR WORSE."
NOW...
BLEET? WRR--
BEE BOOP-- BLEEEP!
OF COURSE I'M ALIVE, BEEBEE-ATE.
AM I... ALIVE?
BLEEP WRR BLOO BIP BEE--
C'MON, IT CAN'T BE THAT BAD.
LEMME JUST GET A LOOK AND--

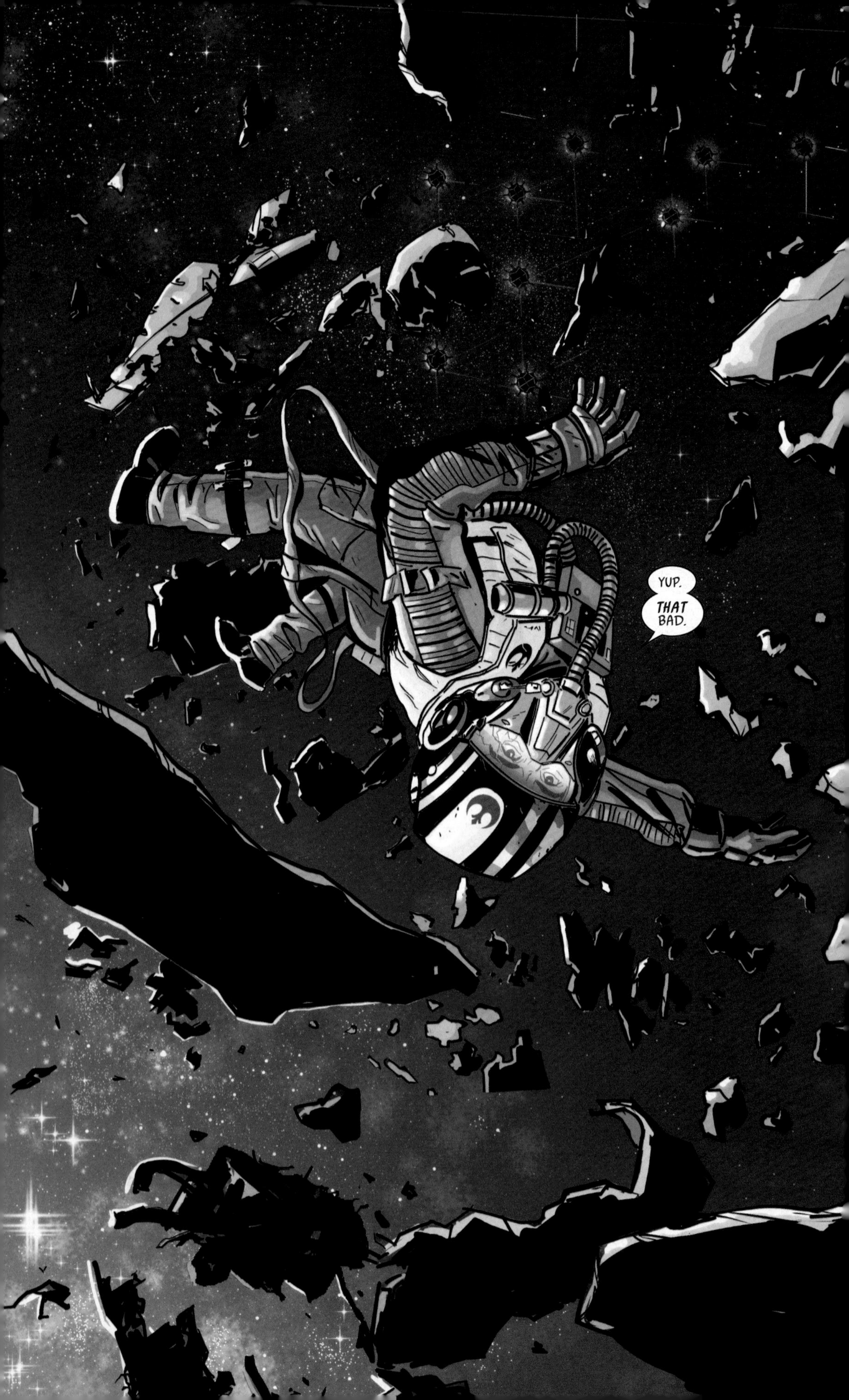
YUP. THAT BAD.

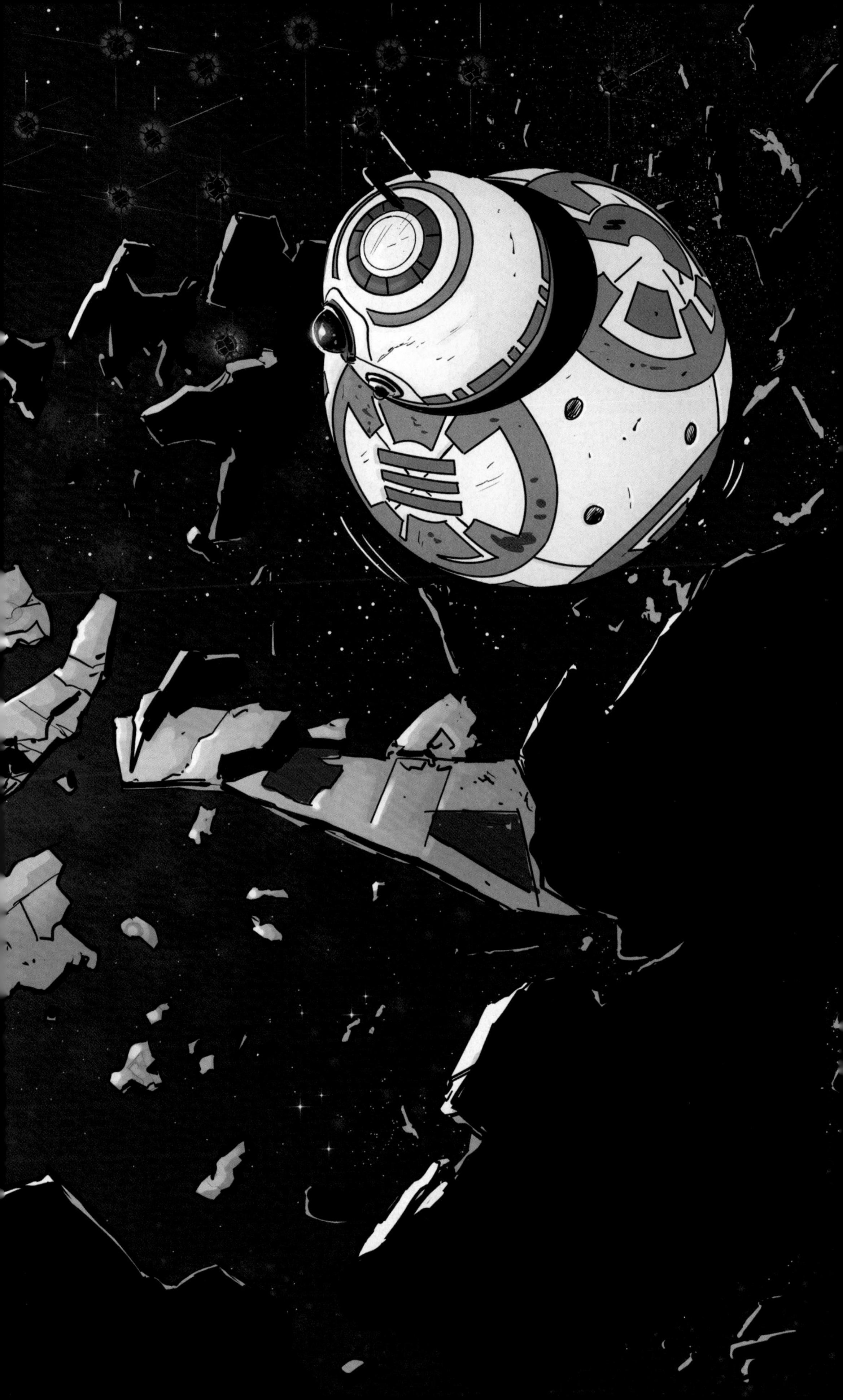

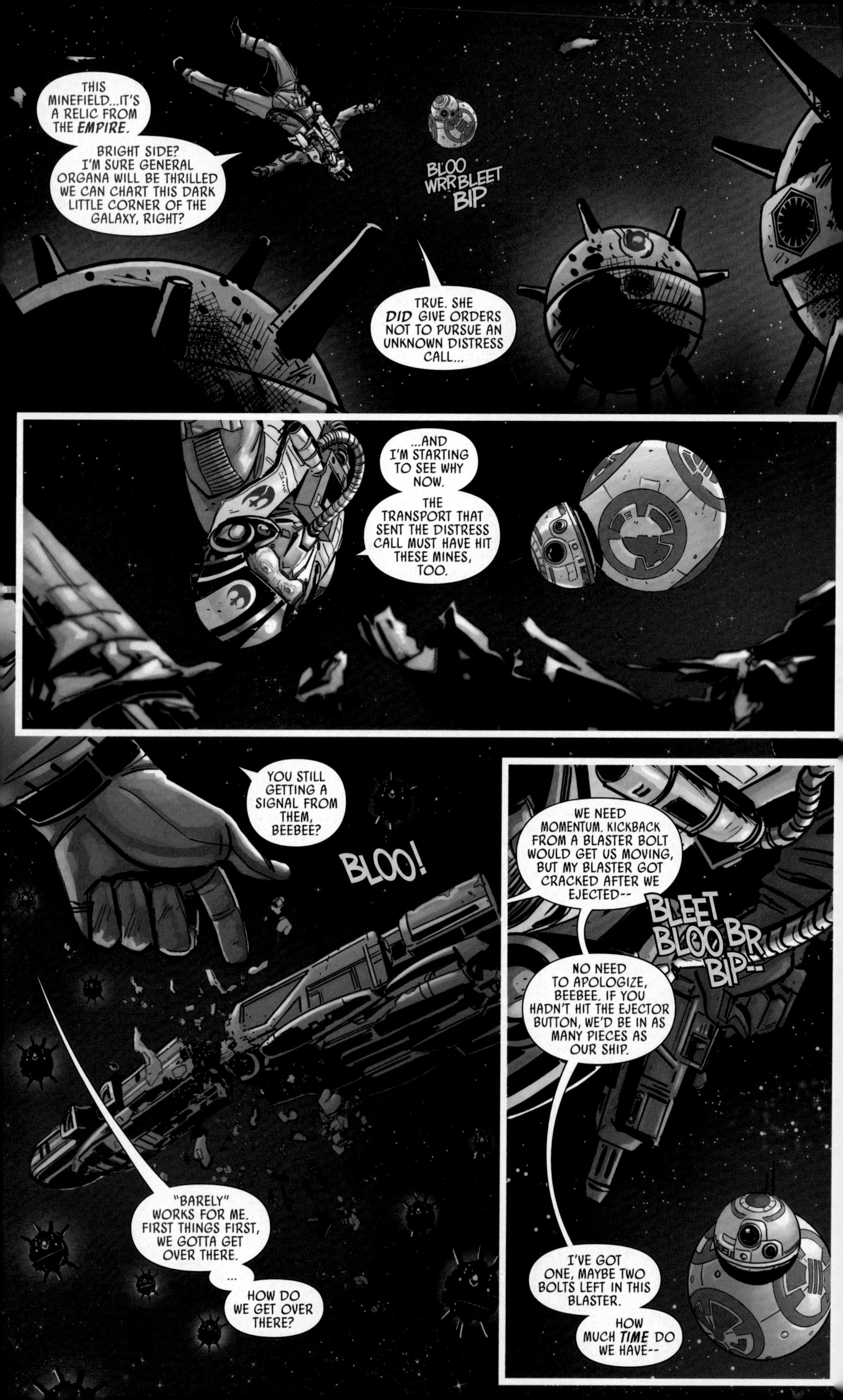
THIS MINEFIELD...IT'S A RELIC FROM THE EMPIRE.
BRIGHT SIDE? I'M SURE GENERAL ORGANA WILL BE THRILLED WE CAN CHART THIS DARK LITTLE CORNER OF THE GALAXY, RIGHT?
BLOO WRRBLEET BIP.
TRUE. SHE DID GIVE ORDERS NOT TO PURSUE AN UNKNOWN DISTRESS CALL...
...AND I'M STARTING TO SEE WHY NOW.
THE TRANSPORT THAT SENT THE DISTRESS CALL MUST HAVE HIT THESE MINES, TOO.
YOU STILL GETTING A SIGNAL FROM THEM, BEEBEE?
BLOO!
"BARELY" WORKS FOR ME. FIRST THINGS FIRST, WE GOTTA GET OVER THERE.
...
HOW DO WE GET OVER THERE?
WE NEED MOMENTUM. KICKBACK FROM A BLASTER BOLT WOULD GET US MOVING, BUT MY BLASTER GOT CRACKED AFTER WE EJECTED--
BLEET BLOO BR BIP--
NO NEED TO APOLOGIZE, BEEBEE. IF YOU HADN'T HIT THE EJECTOR BUTTON, WE'D BE IN AS MANY PIECES AS OUR SHIP.
I'VE GOT ONE, MAYBE TWO BOLTS LEFT IN THIS BLASTER.
HOW MUCH TIME DO WE HAVE--

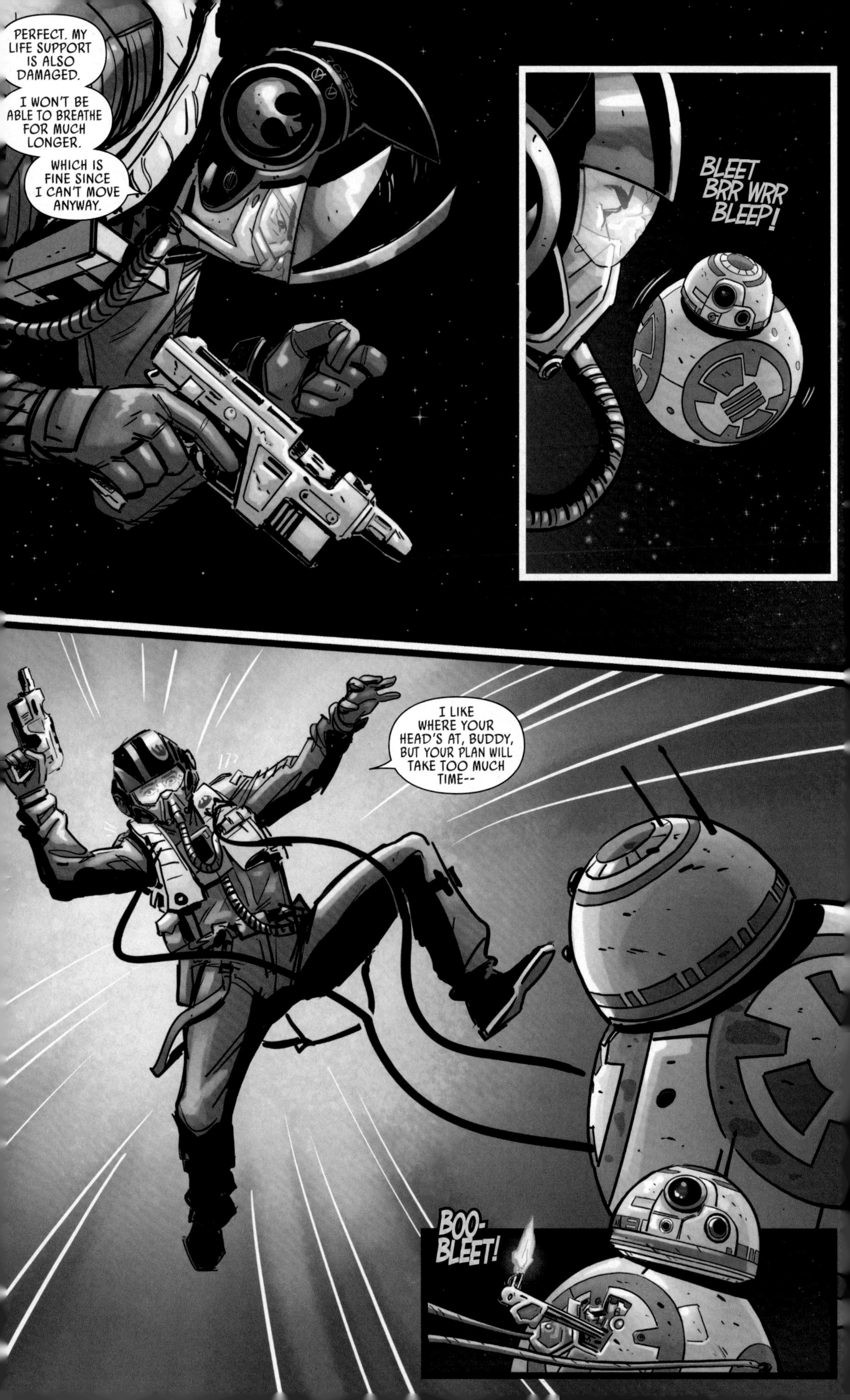
PERFECT. MY LIFE SUPPORT IS ALSO DAMAGED.
I WON'T BE ABLE TO BREATHE FOR MUCH LONGER.
WHICH IS FINE SINCE I CAN'T MOVE ANYWAY.
BLEET BRR WRR BLEEP!
I LIKE WHERE YOUR HEAD'S AT, BUDDY, BUT YOUR PLAN WILL TAKE TOO MUCH TIME--
BOO-BLEET!

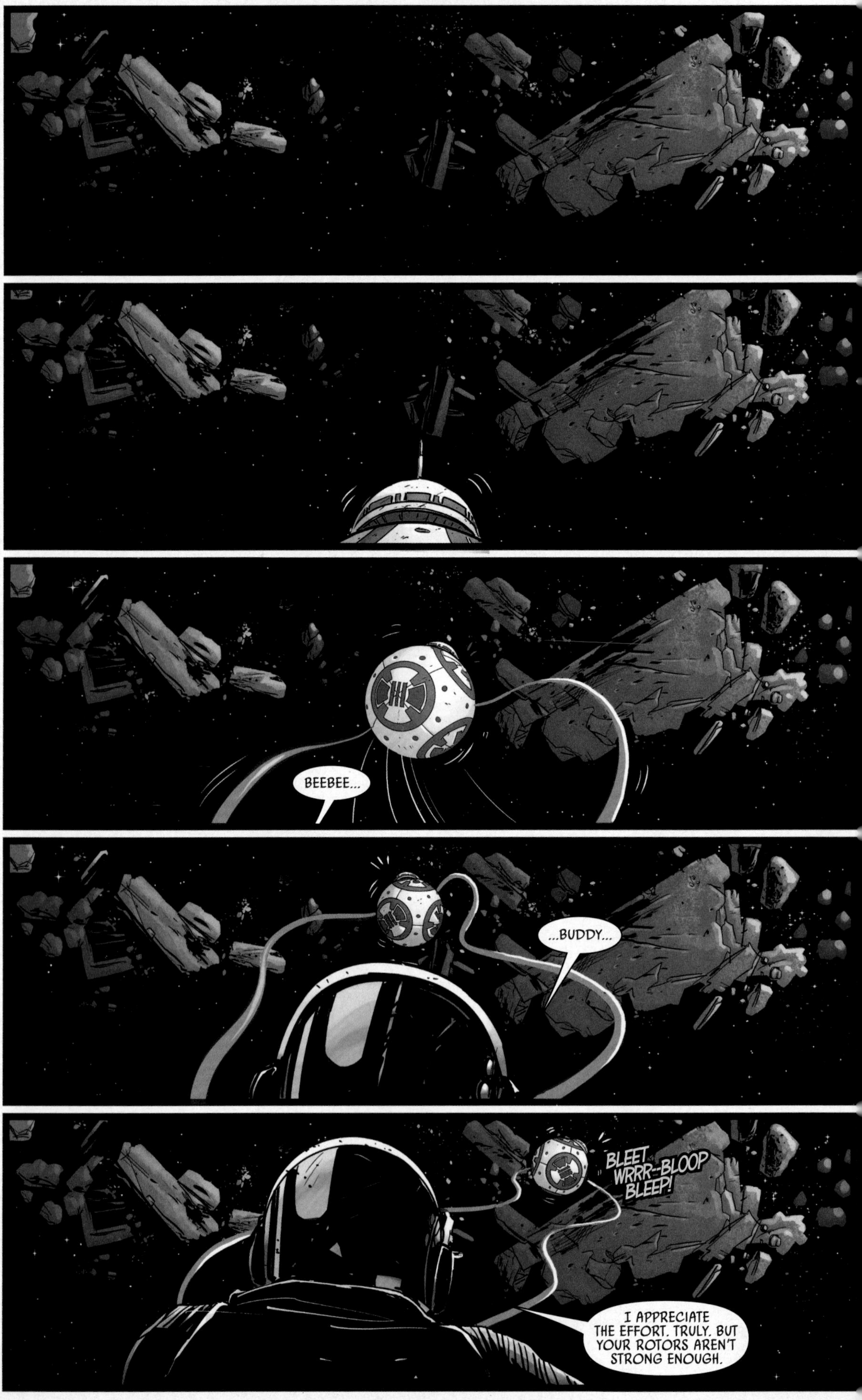
BEEBEE...
...BUDDY...
BLEET WRRR--BLOOP BLEEP!
I APPRECIATE THE EFFORT. TRULY. BUT YOUR ROTORS AREN'T STRONG ENOUGH.

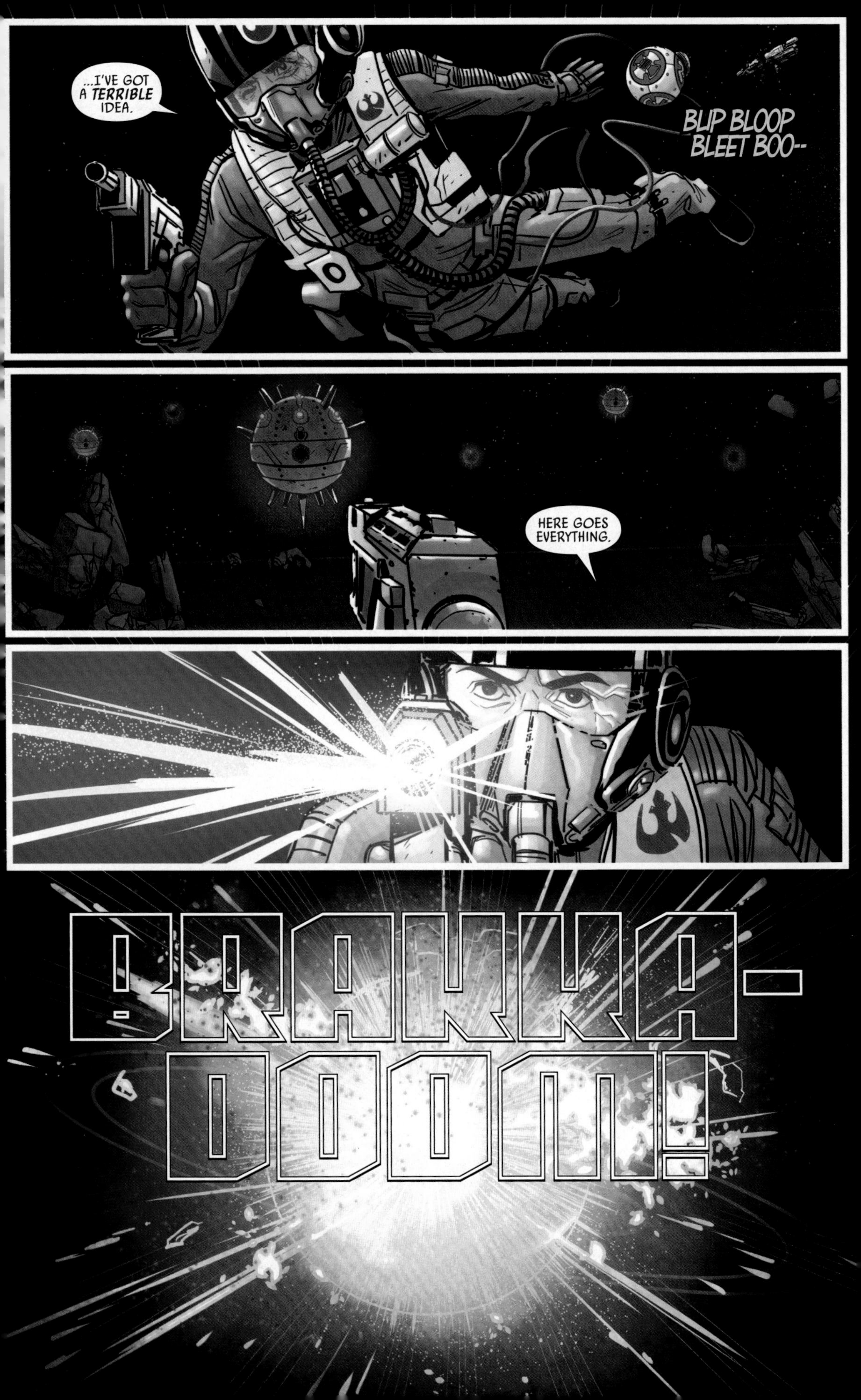

...I'VE GOT A TERRIBLE IDEA.
BLIP BLOOP BLEET BOO--
HERE GOES EVERYTHING.
BRAKKA-DOOM!

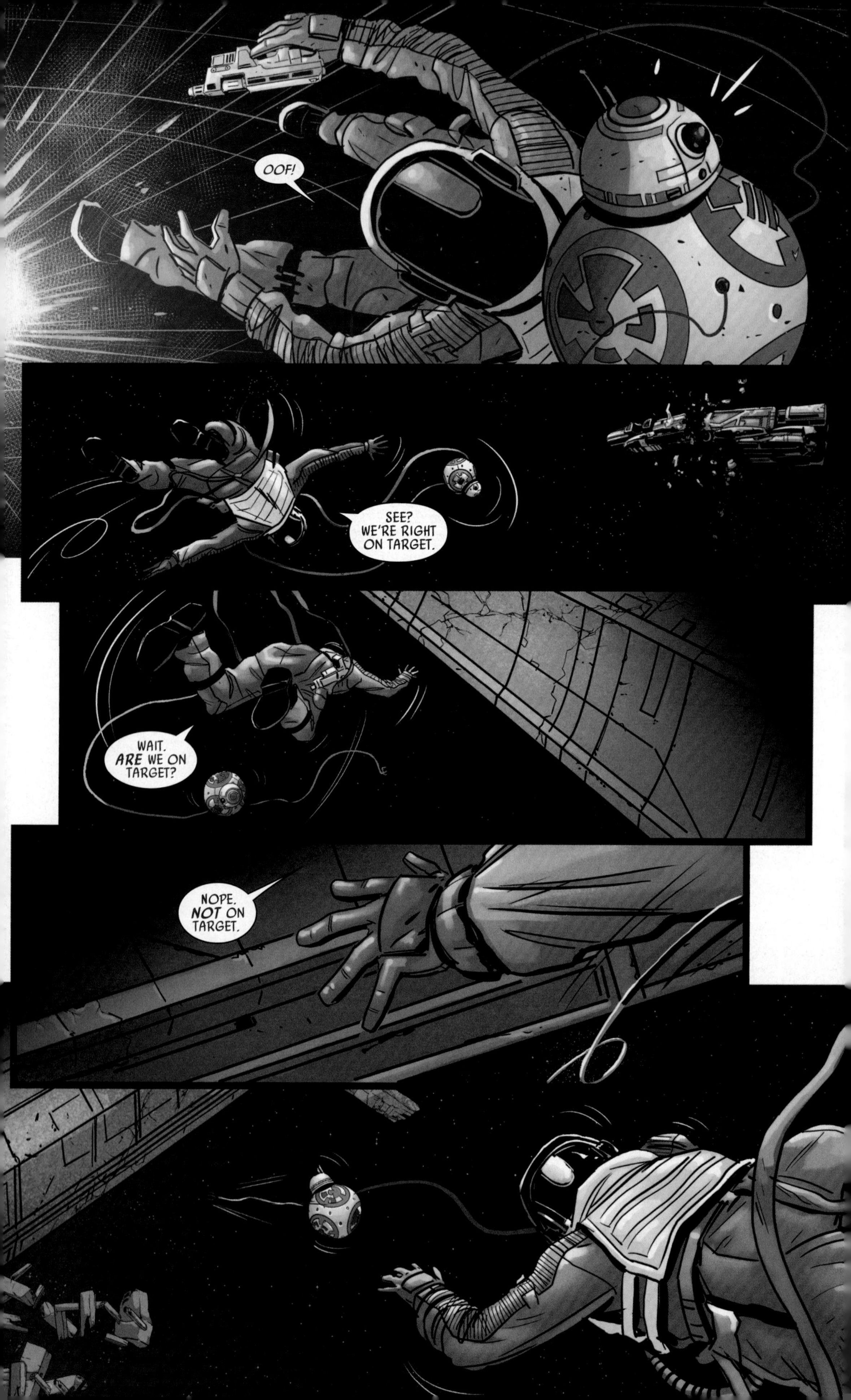
OOF!
SEE? WE'RE RIGHT ON TARGET.
WAIT. ARE WE ON TARGET?
NOPE. NOT ON TARGET.

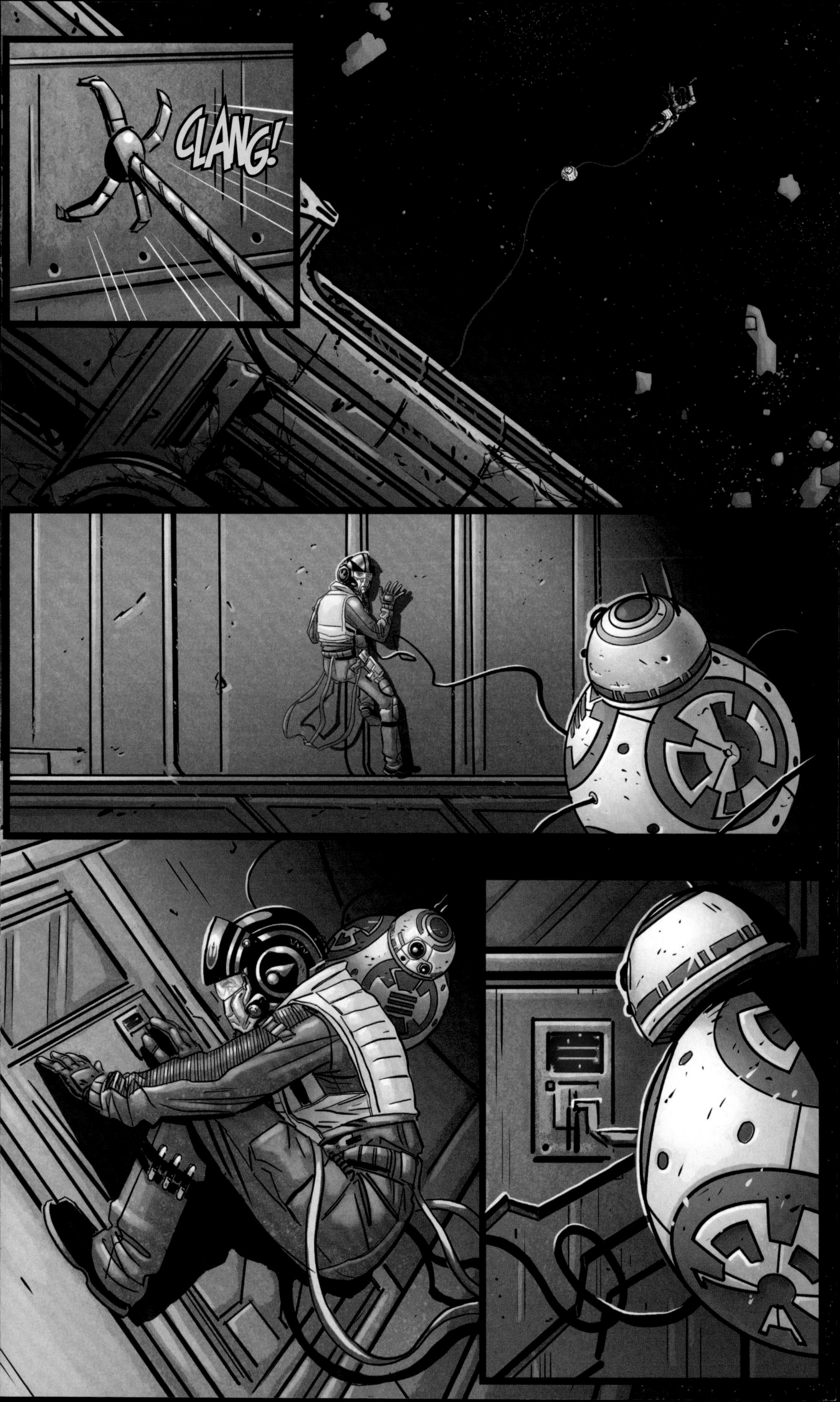
CLANG!

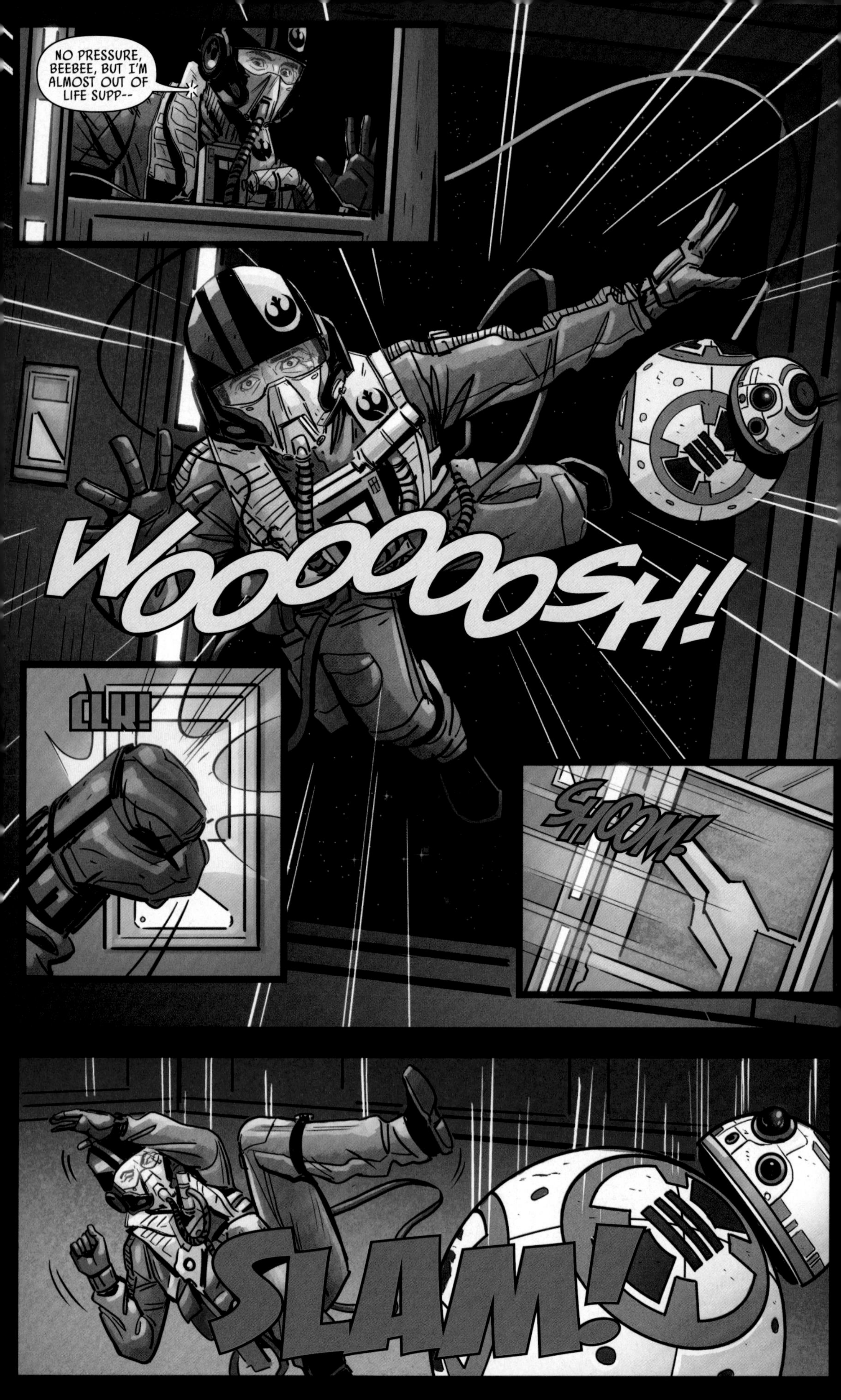
NO PRESSURE, BEEBEE, BUT I'M ALMOST OUT OF LIFE SUPP--
WOOOOOOSH!
CLK!
SHOOM!
SLAM!

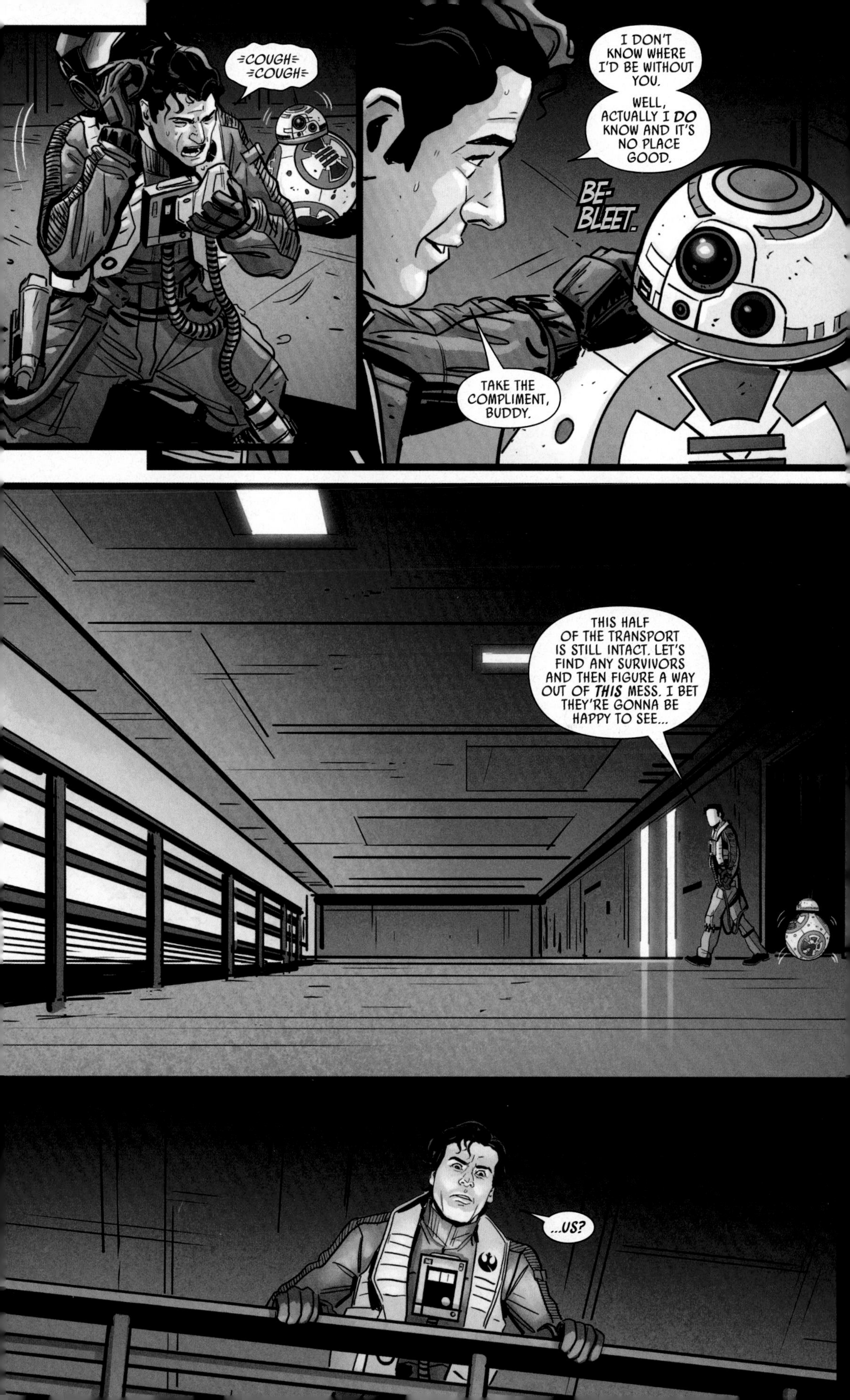

COUGH COUGH
I DON'T KNOW WHERE I'D BE WITHOUT YOU.
WELL, ACTUALLY I DO KNOW AND IT'S NO PLACE GOOD.
BE-BLEET.
TAKE THE COMPLIMENT, BUDDY.
THIS HALF OF THE TRANSPORT IS STILL INTACT. LET'S FIND ANY SURVIVORS AND THEN FIGURE A WAY OUT OF THIS MESS. I BET THEY'RE GONNA BE HAPPY TO SEE...
...US?

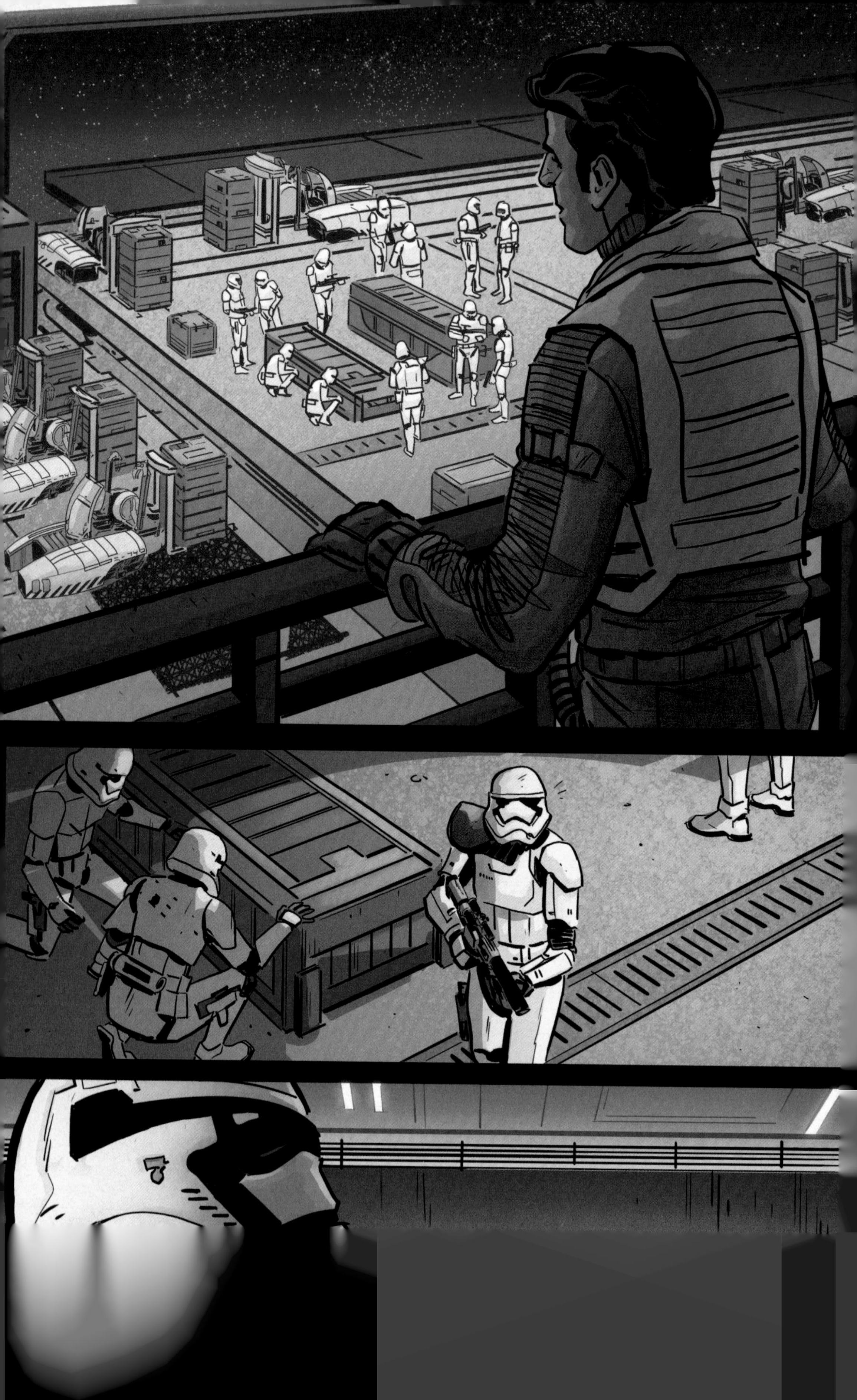

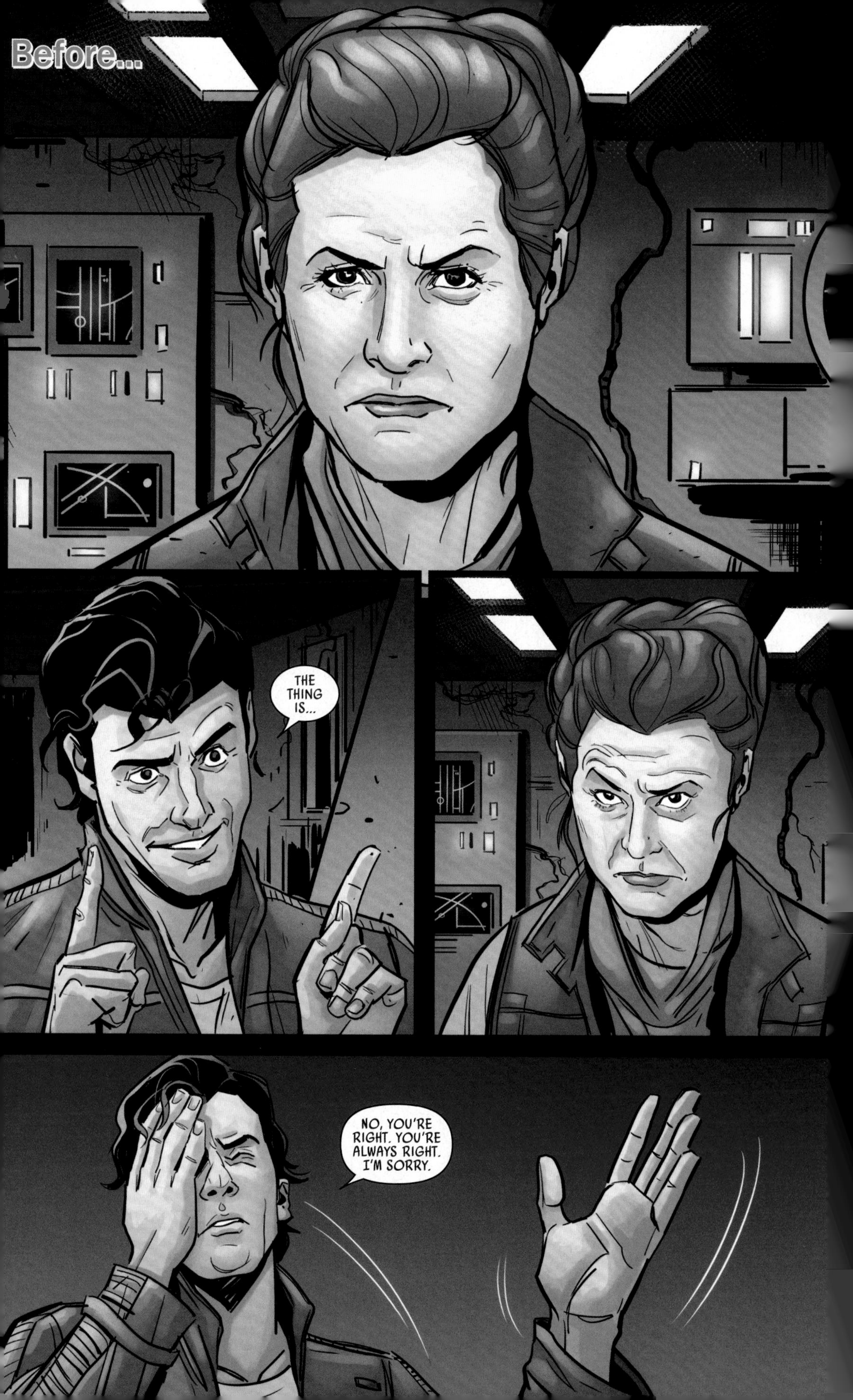
Before...
THE THING IS...
NO, YOU'RE RIGHT. YOU'RE ALWAYS RIGHT. I'M SORRY.

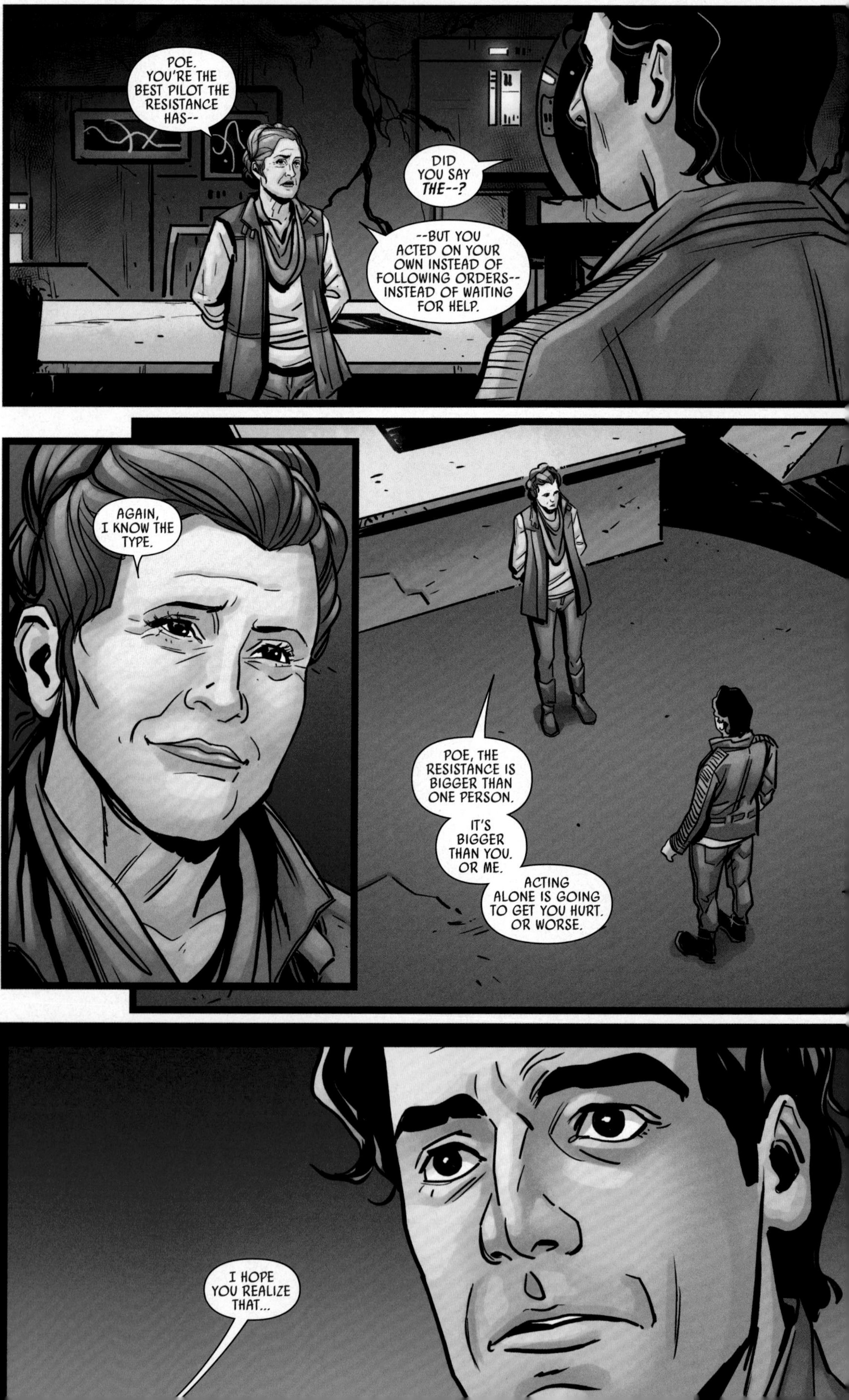
POE. YOU'RE THE BEST PILOT THE RESISTANCE HAS--
DID YOU SAY *THE*--?
--BUT YOU ACTED ON YOUR OWN INSTEAD OF FOLLOWING ORDERS-- INSTEAD OF WAITING FOR HELP.
AGAIN, I KNOW THE TYPE.
POE, THE RESISTANCE IS BIGGER THAN ONE PERSON.
IT'S BIGGER THAN YOU. OR ME.
ACTING ALONE IS GOING TO GET YOU HURT. OR WORSE.
I HOPE YOU REALIZE THAT...

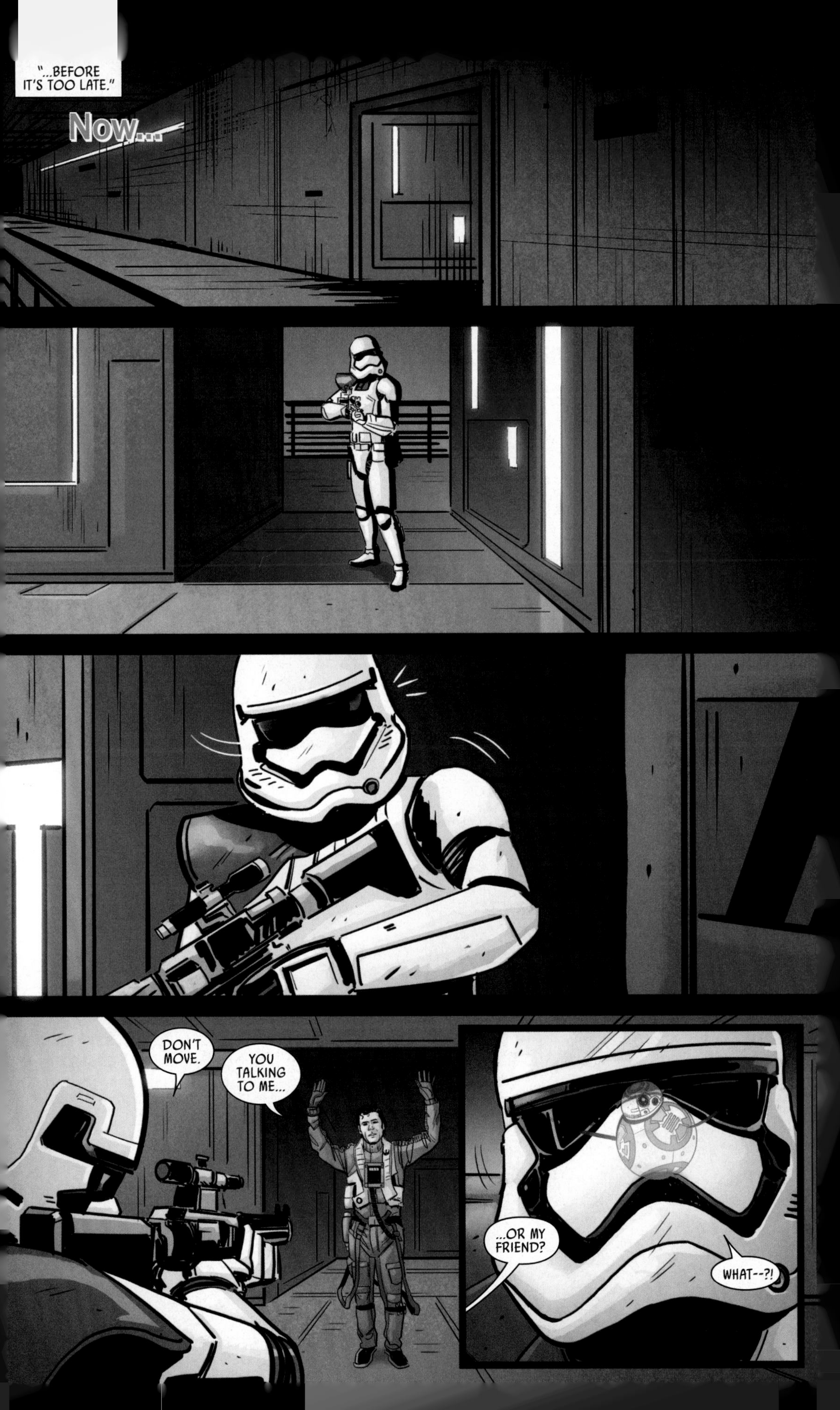
"...BEFORE IT'S TOO LATE."
Now...
DON'T MOVE.
YOU TALKING TO ME...
...OR MY FRIEND?
WHAT--?!

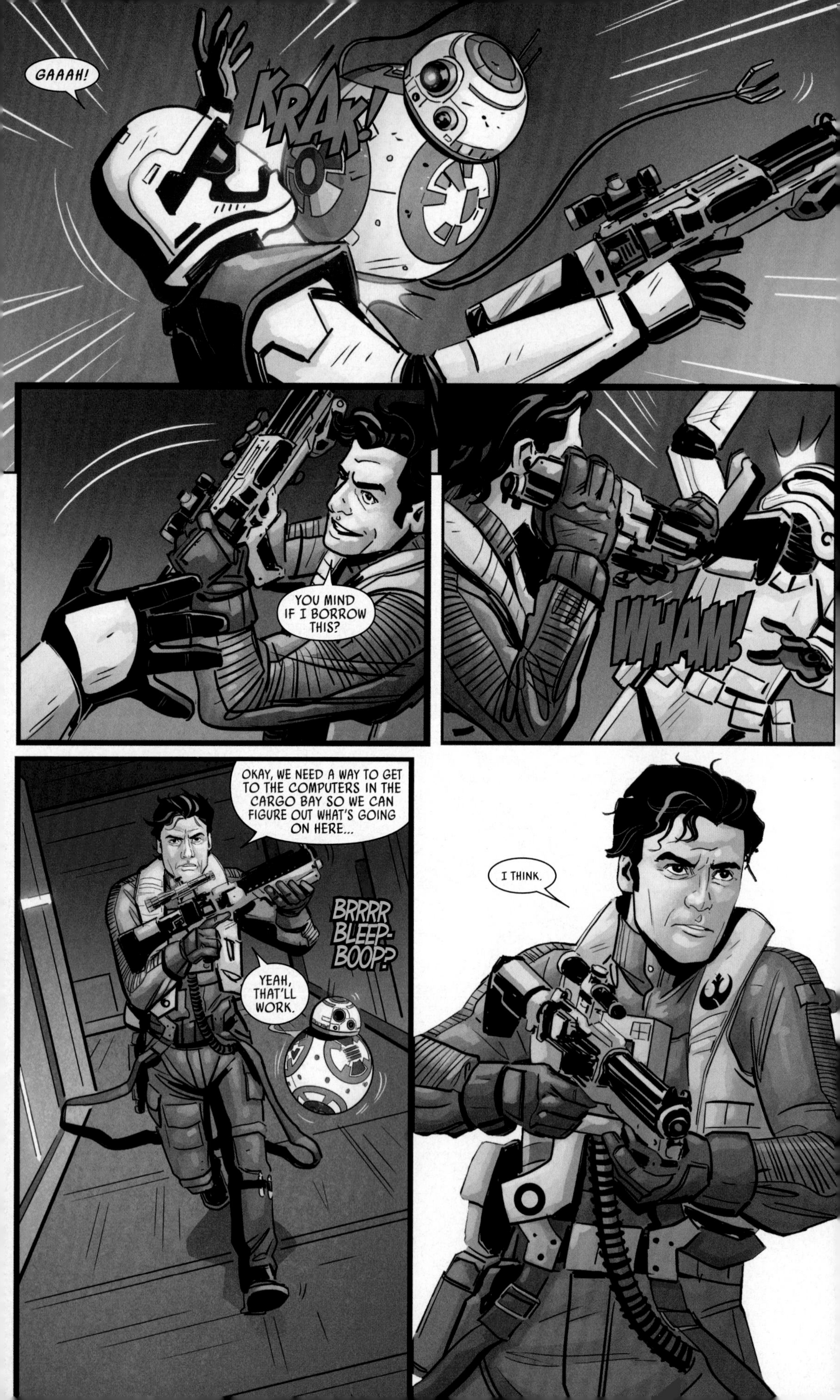
GAAAH!
KRAK!
YOU MIND IF I BORROW THIS?
WHAM!
OKAY, WE NEED A WAY TO GET TO THE COMPUTERS IN THE CARGO BAY SO WE CAN FIGURE OUT WHAT'S GOING ON HERE...
BRRRR BLEEP-BOOP?
YEAH, THAT'LL WORK.
I THINK.

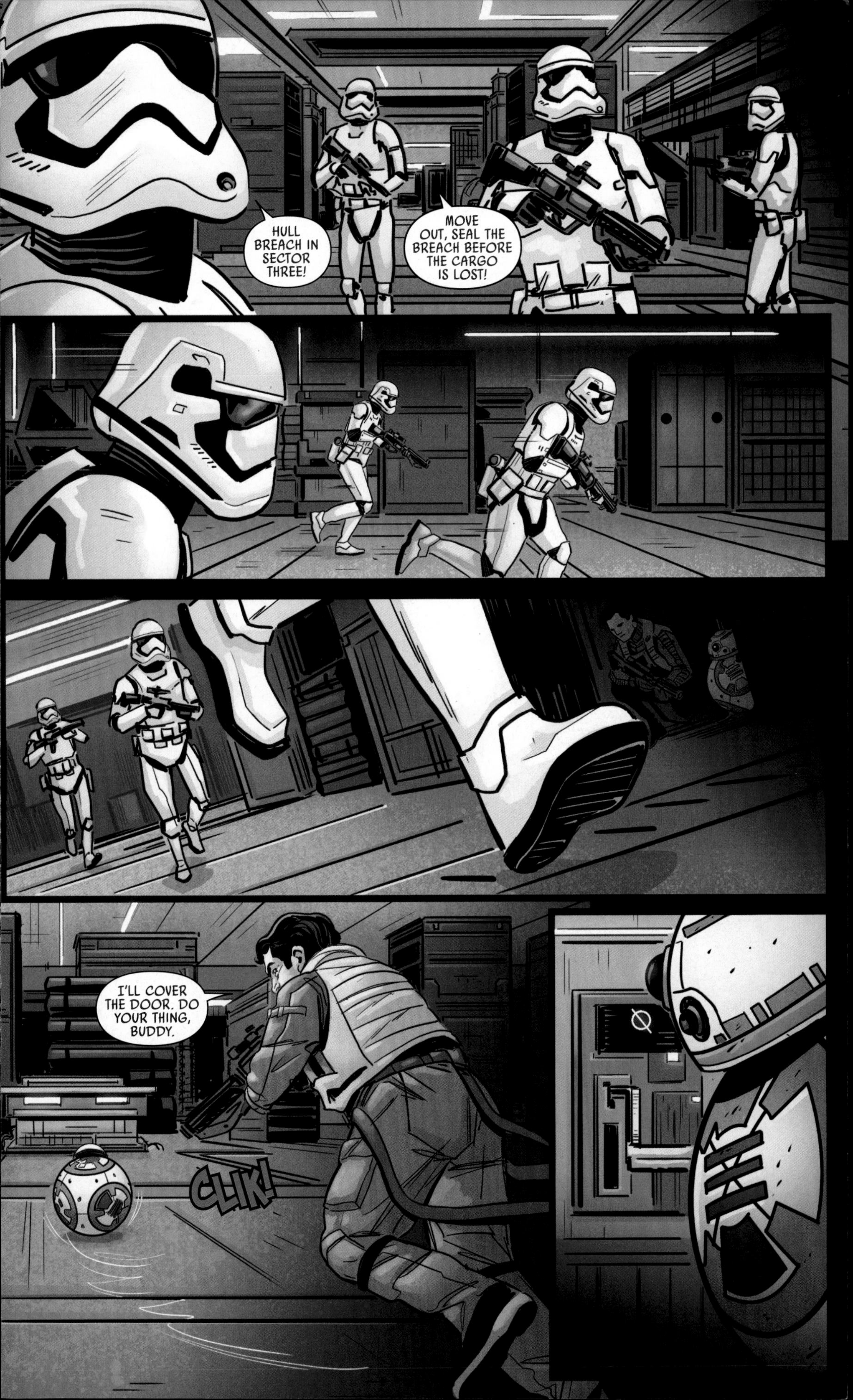
HULL BREACH IN SECTOR THREE!
MOVE OUT, SEAL THE BREACH BEFORE THE CARGO IS LOST!
I'LL COVER THE DOOR. DO YOUR THING, BUDDY.
CLIK!

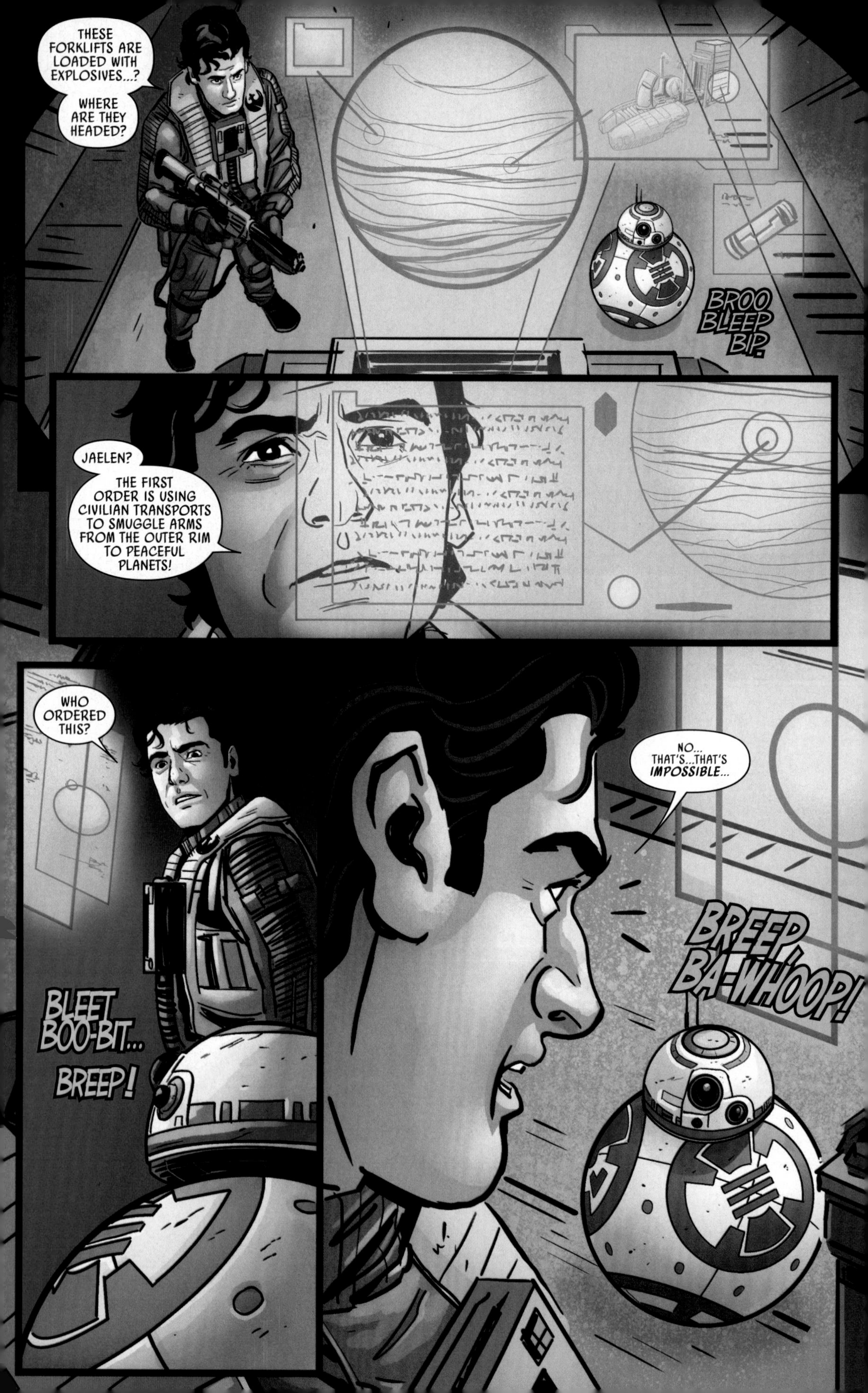
THESE FORKLIFTS ARE LOADED WITH EXPLOSIVES...?
WHERE ARE THEY HEADED?
BROO BLEEP BIP.
JAELEN?
THE FIRST ORDER IS USING CIVILIAN TRANSPORTS TO SMUGGLE ARMS FROM THE OUTER RIM TO PEACEFUL PLANETS!
WHO ORDERED THIS?
BLEET BOO-BIT... BREEP!
NO... THAT'S...THAT'S IMPOSSIBLE...
BREEP BA-WHOOP!

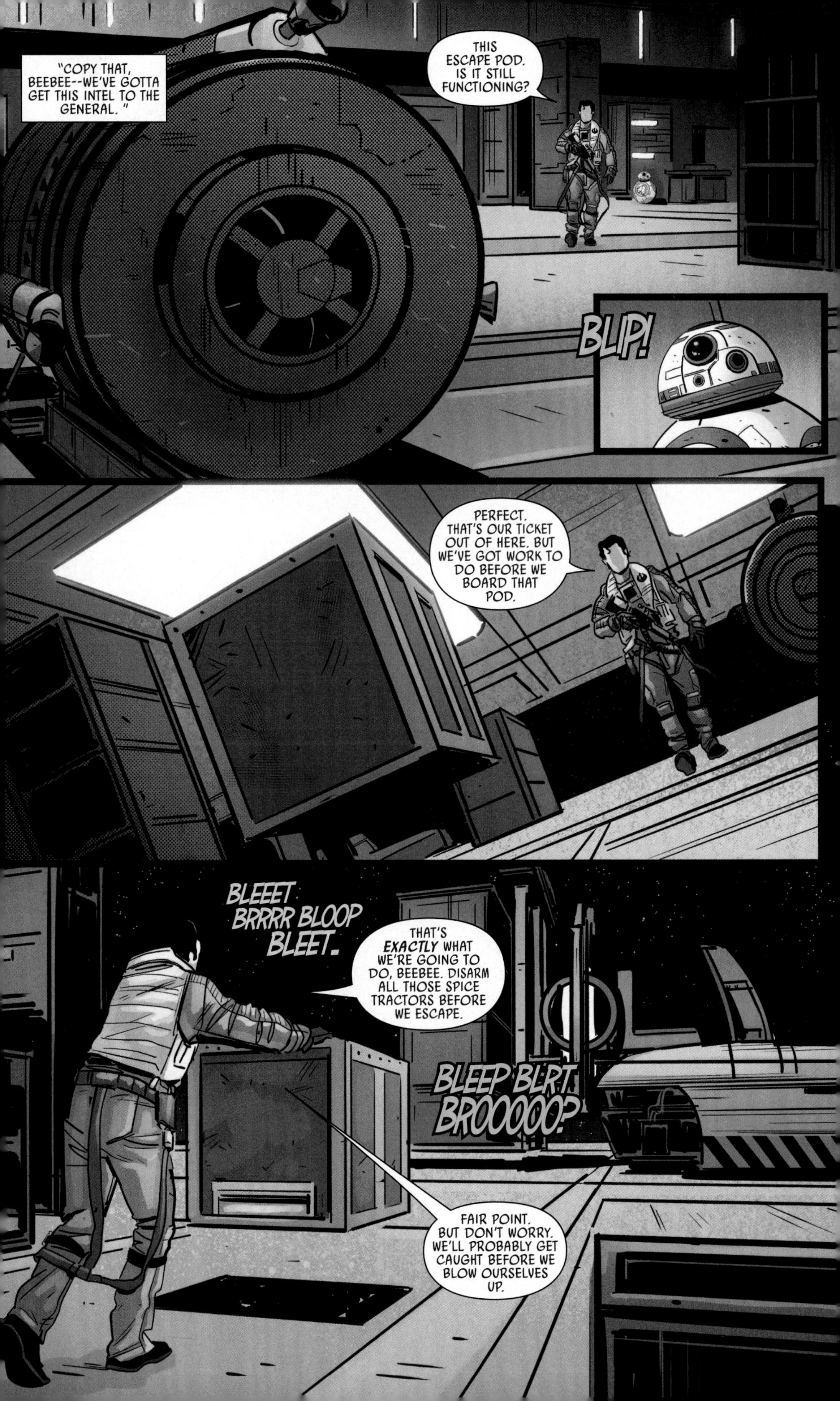
"COPY THAT, BEEBEE--WE'VE GOTTA GET THIS INTEL TO THE GENERAL."
THIS ESCAPE POD. IS IT STILL FUNCTIONING?
BLIP!
PERFECT. THAT'S OUR TICKET OUT OF HERE. BUT WE'VE GOT WORK TO DO BEFORE WE BOARD THAT POD.
BLEEET BRRRR BLOOP BLEET..
THAT'S *EXACTLY* WHAT WE'RE GOING TO DO, BEEBEE. DISARM ALL THOSE SPICE TRACTORS BEFORE WE ESCAPE.
BLEEP BLRT BROOOOO?
FAIR POINT. BUT DON'T WORRY. WE'LL PROBABLY GET CAUGHT BEFORE WE BLOW OURSELVES UP.

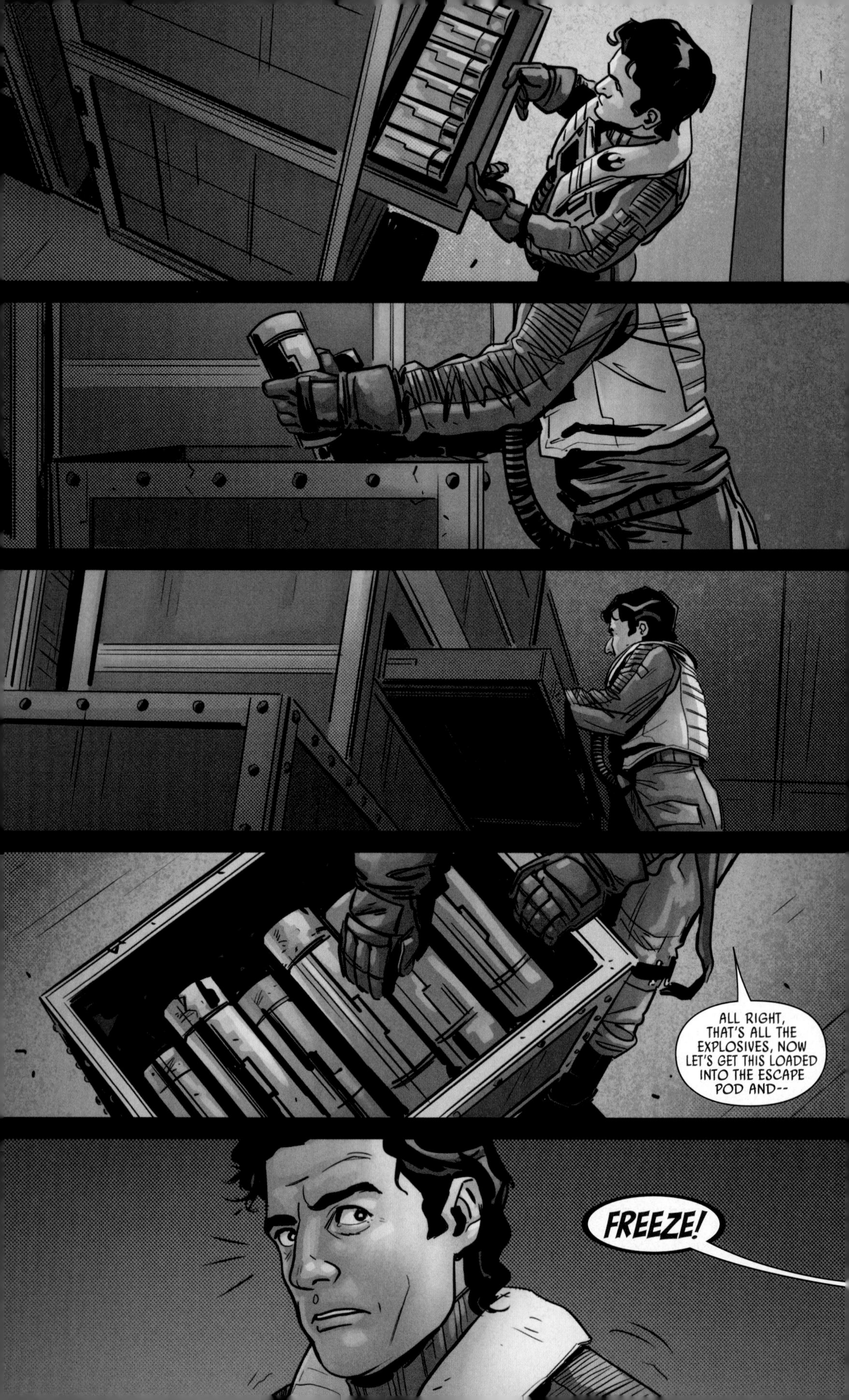
ALL RIGHT, THAT'S ALL THE EXPLOSIVES, NOW LET'S GET THIS LOADED INTO THE ESCAPE POD AND--
FREEZE!

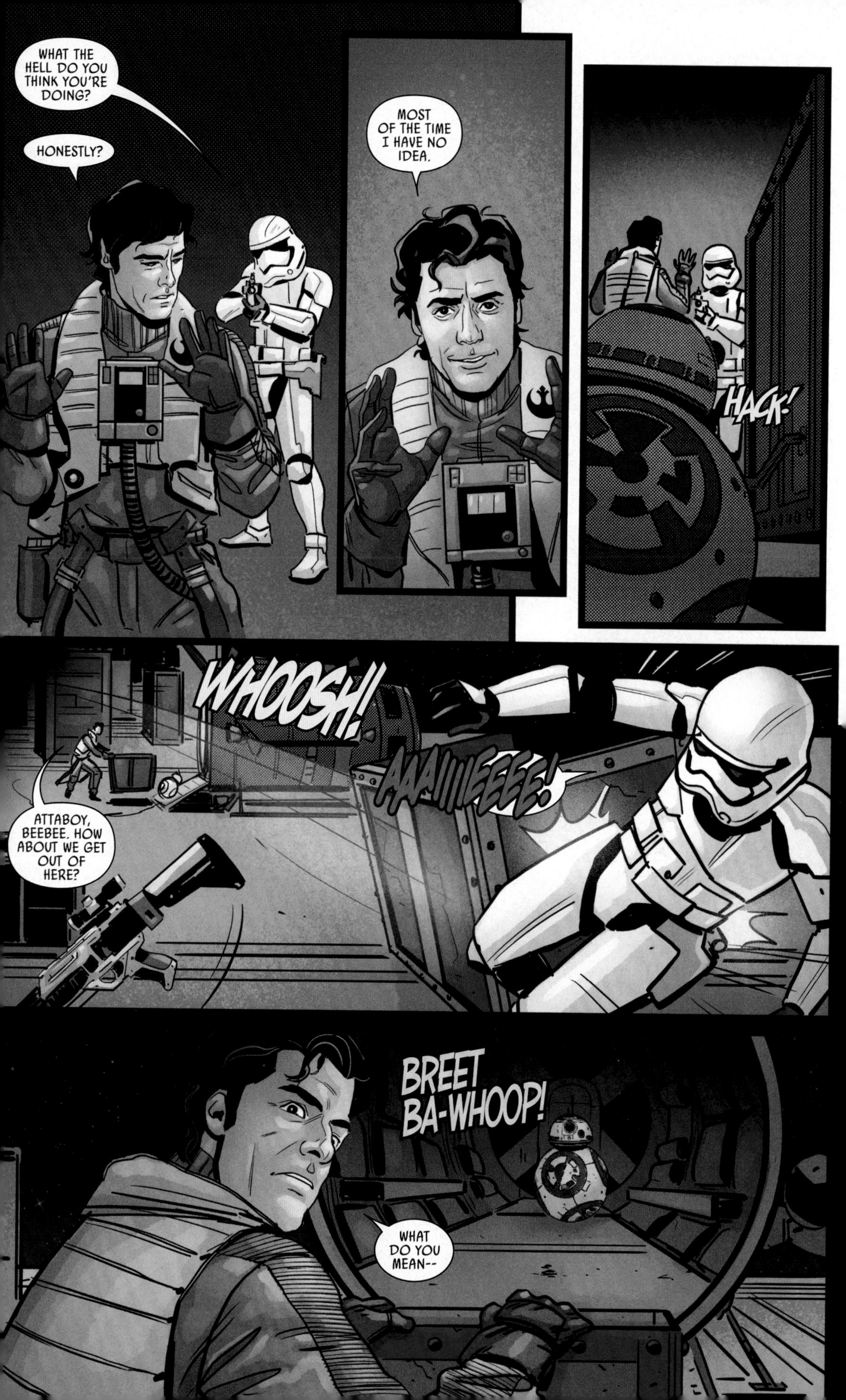
WHAT THE HELL DO YOU THINK YOU'RE DOING?
HONESTLY?
MOST OF THE TIME I HAVE NO IDEA.
HACK!
WHOOSH!
AAAIIIIEEEE!
ATTABOY, BEEBEE. HOW ABOUT WE GET OUT OF HERE?
BREET BA-WHOOP!
WHAT DO YOU MEAN--

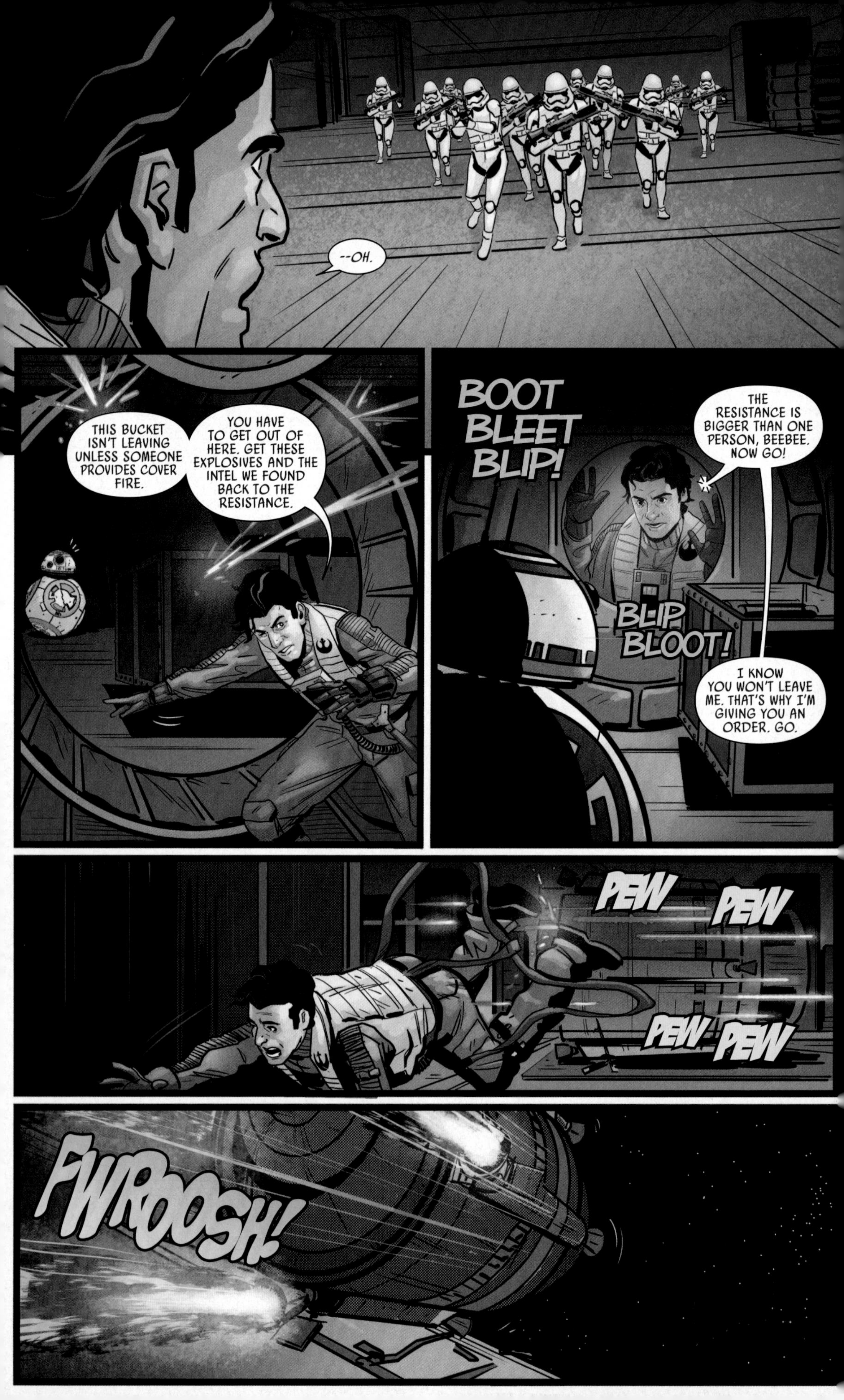
--OH.
THIS BUCKET ISN'T LEAVING UNLESS SOMEONE PROVIDES COVER FIRE.
YOU HAVE TO GET OUT OF HERE. GET THESE EXPLOSIVES AND THE INTEL WE FOUND BACK TO THE RESISTANCE.
BOOT BLEET BLIP!
THE RESISTANCE IS BIGGER THAN ONE PERSON, BEEBEE. NOW GO!
BLIP BLOOT!
I KNOW YOU WON'T LEAVE ME. THAT'S WHY I'M GIVING YOU AN ORDER. GO.
PEW PEW
PEW PEW
FWROOSH!

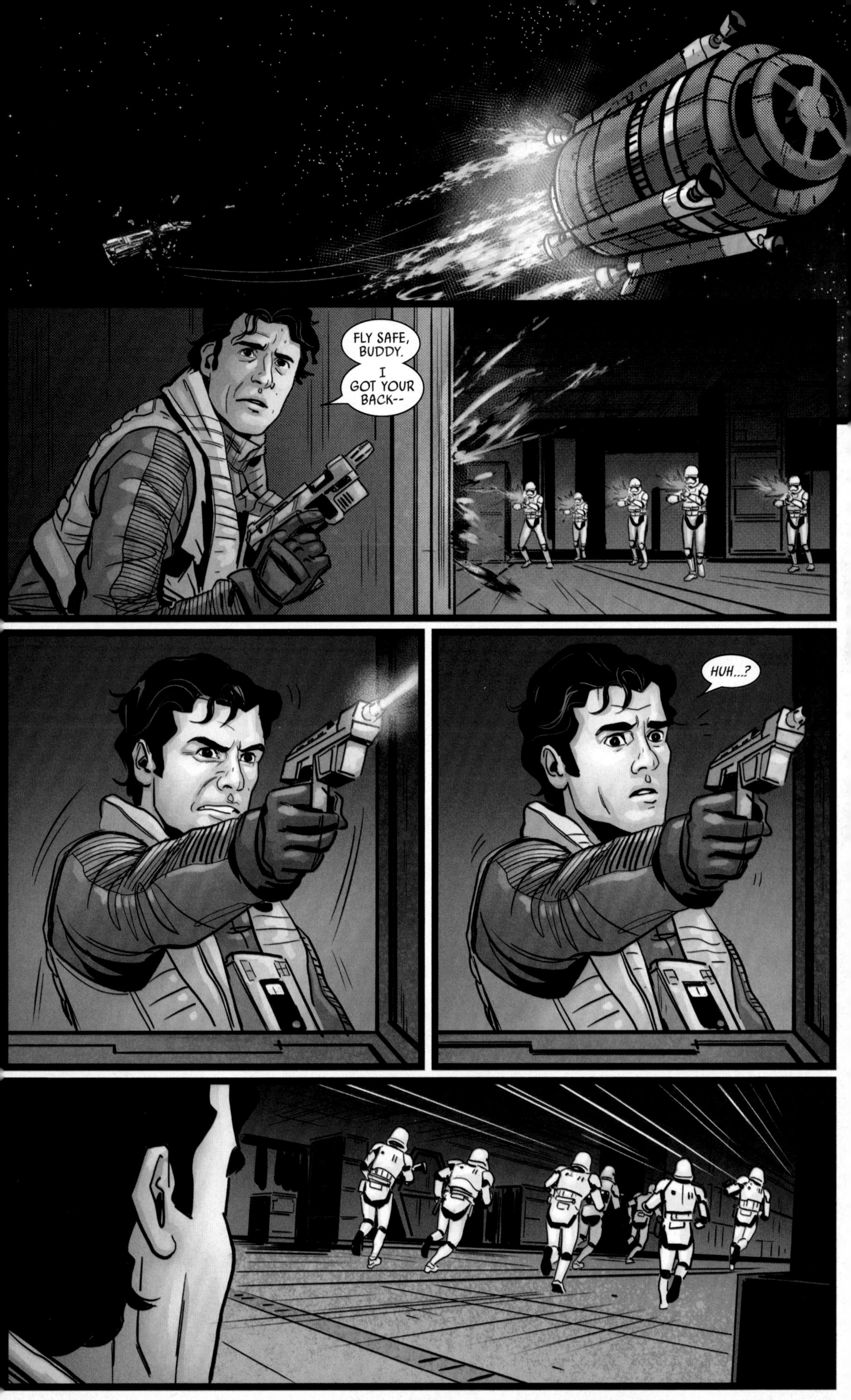
FLY SAFE, BUDDY.
I GOT YOUR BACK--
HUH...?

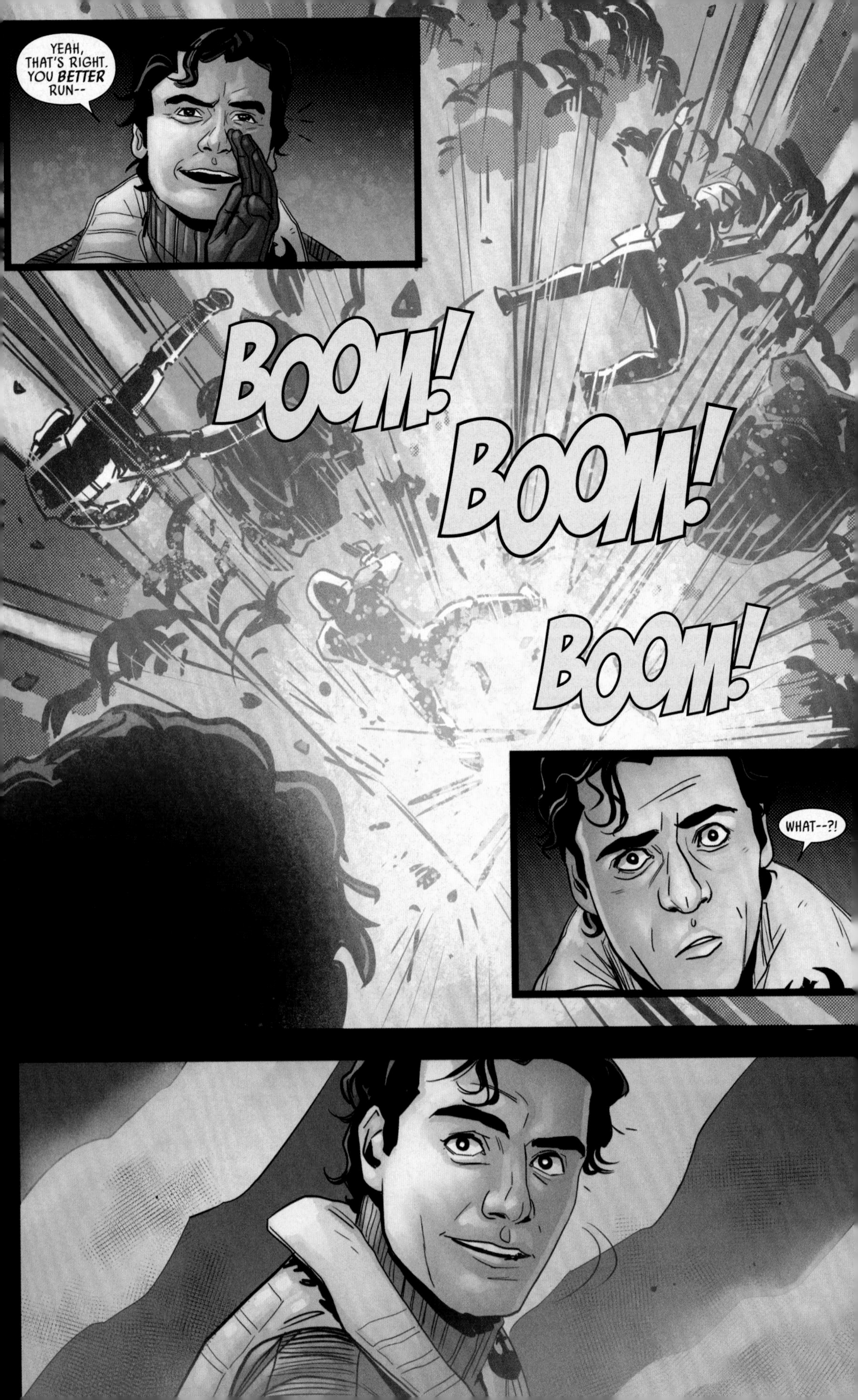
YEAH, THAT'S RIGHT. YOU BETTER RUN--
BOOM!
BOOM!
BOOM!
WHAT--?!

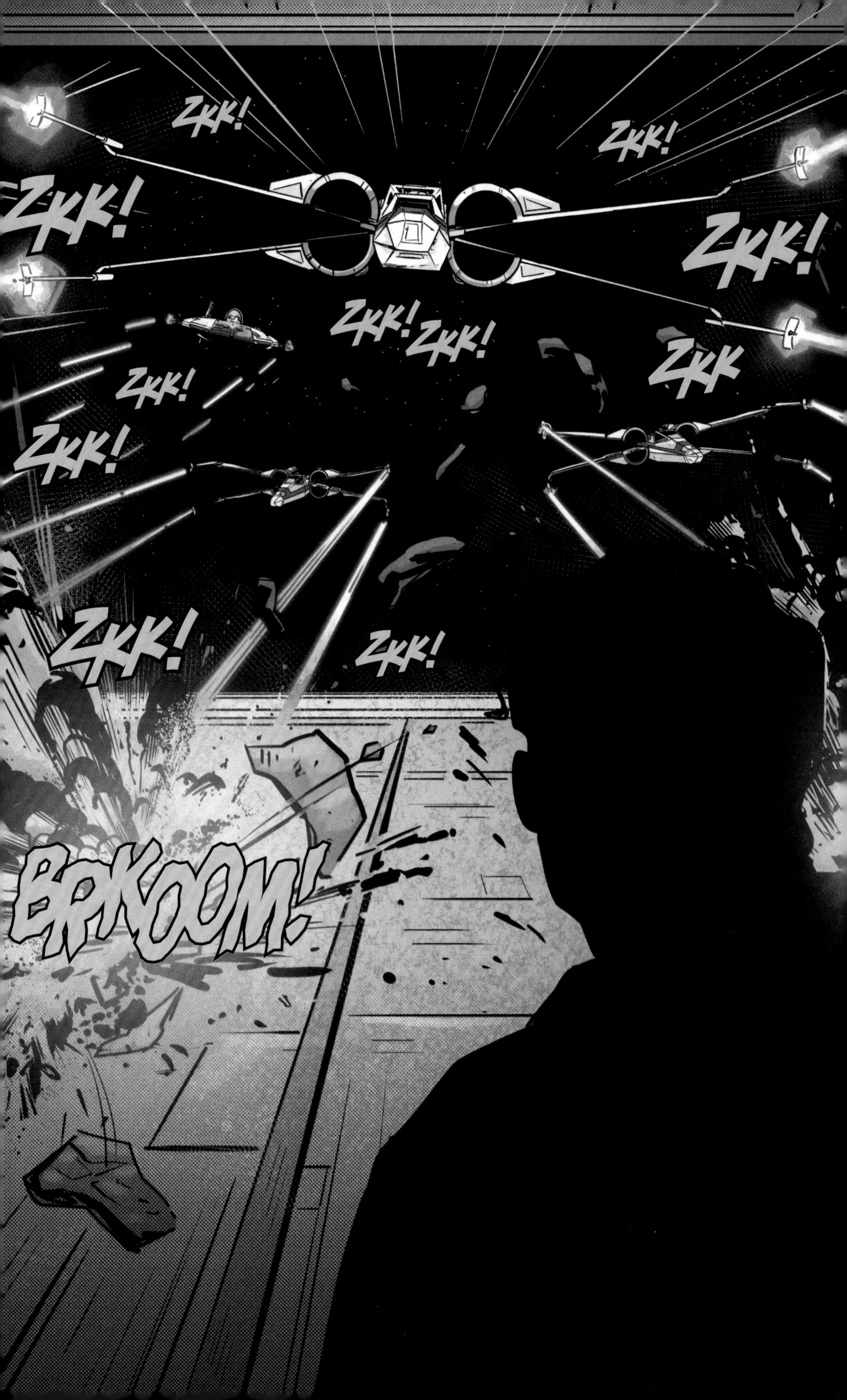
ZKK!
ZKK!
ZKK!
ZKK!
ZKK!
ZKK!
ZKK
ZKK!
ZKK!
ZKK!
ZKK!
BRKOOM!

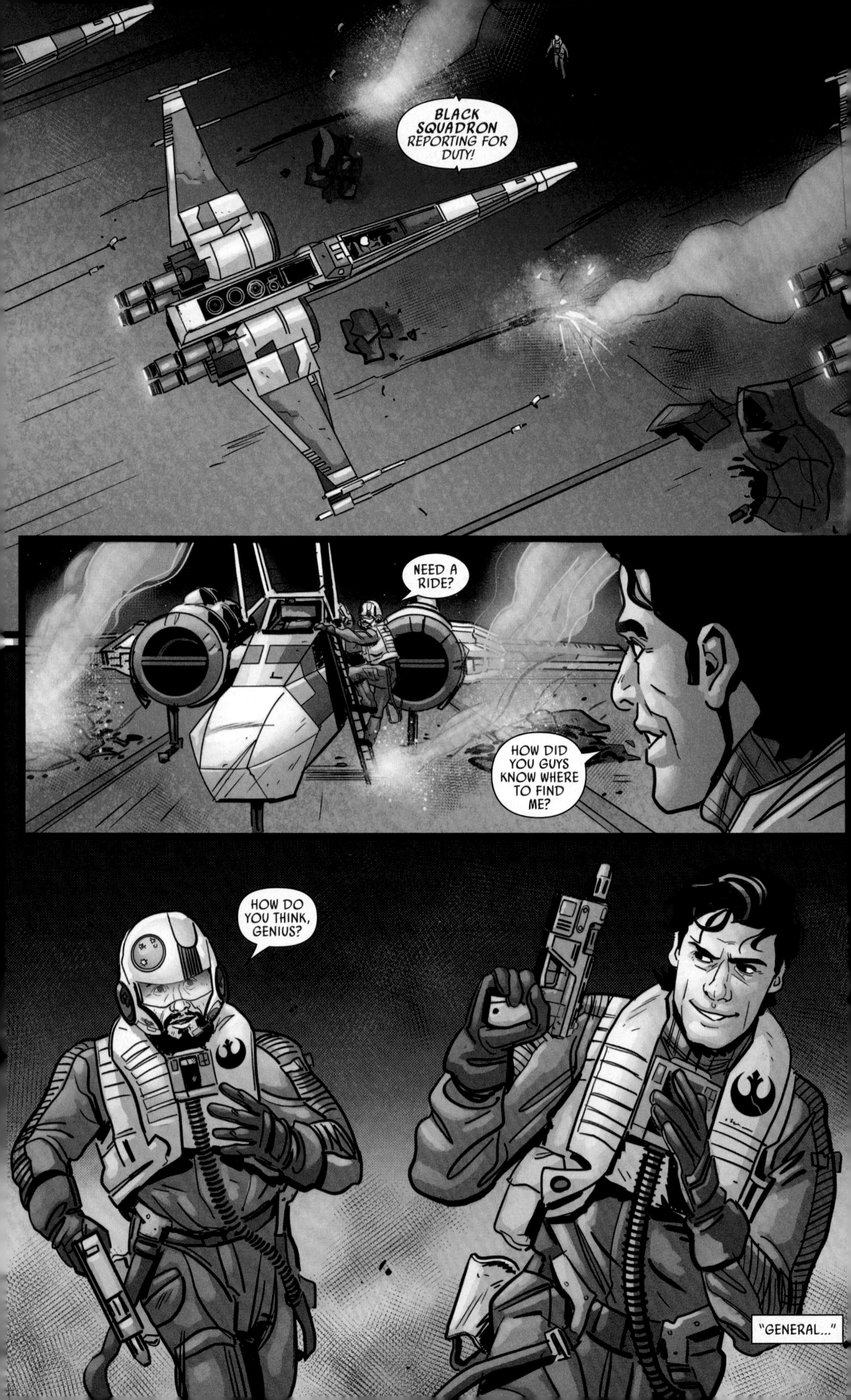
BLACK SQUADRON REPORTING FOR DUTY!
NEED A RIDE?
HOW DID YOU GUYS KNOW WHERE TO FIND ME?
HOW DO YOU THINK, GENIUS?
"GENERAL..."

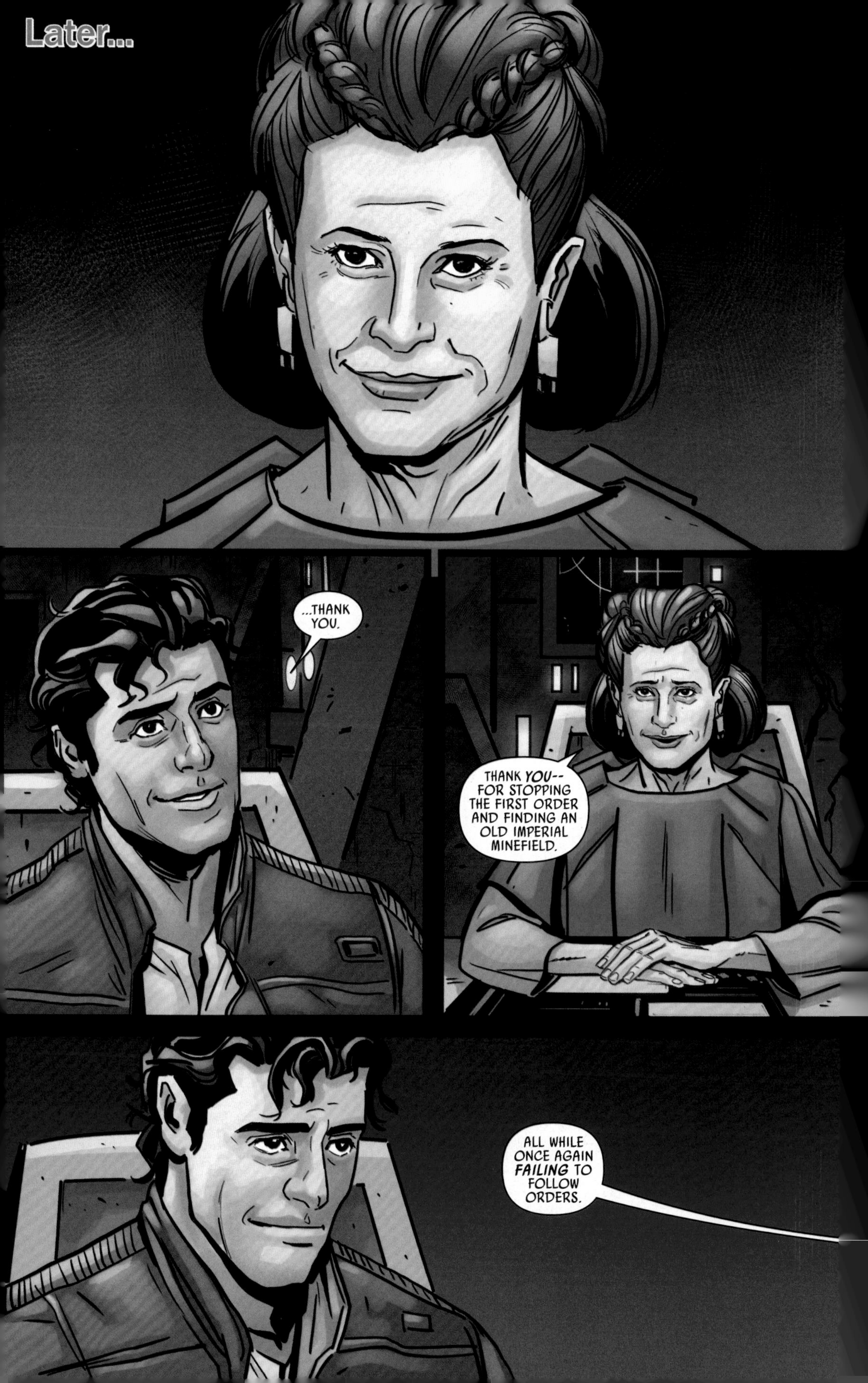
Later...
...THANK YOU.
THANK YOU-- FOR STOPPING THE FIRST ORDER AND FINDING AN OLD IMPERIAL MINEFIELD.
ALL WHILE ONCE AGAIN FAILING TO FOLLOW ORDERS.

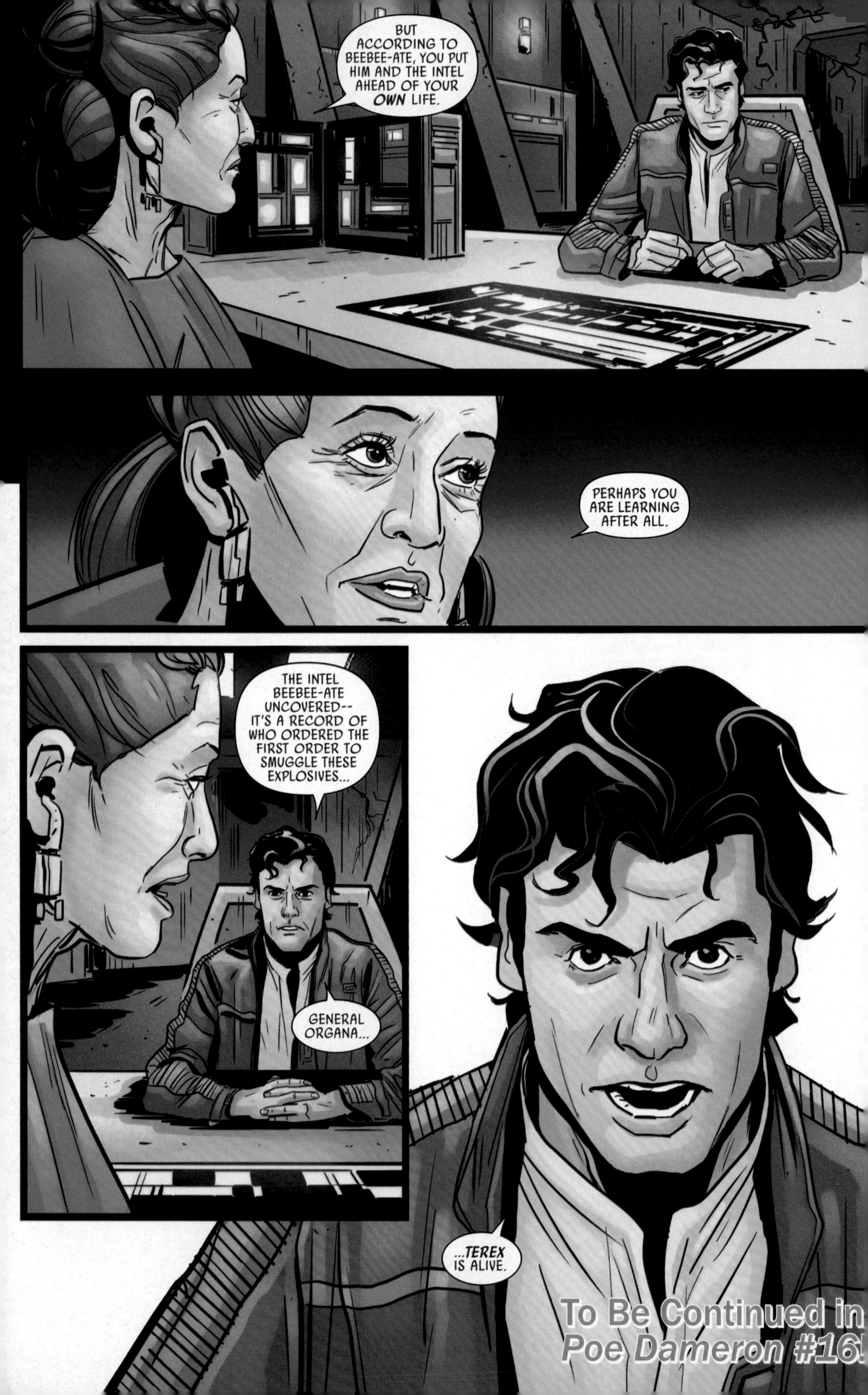
BUT ACCORDING TO BEEBEE-ATE, YOU PUT HIM AND THE INTEL AHEAD OF YOUR OWN LIFE.
PERHAPS YOU ARE LEARNING AFTER ALL.
THE INTEL BEEBEE-ATE UNCOVERED-- IT'S A RECORD OF WHO ORDERED THE FIRST ORDER TO SMUGGLE THESE EXPLOSIVES...
GENERAL ORGANA...
...TEREX IS ALIVE.
To Be Continued in Poe Dameron #16!

RETURN TO A GALAXY FAR, FAR AWAY!

STAR WARS: THE FORCE AWAKENS ADAPTATION TPB
978-1302902032

ON SALE NOW
WHEREVER BOOKS ARE SOLD

TO FIND A COMIC SHOP NEAR YOU, VISIT COMICSHOPLOCATOR.COM

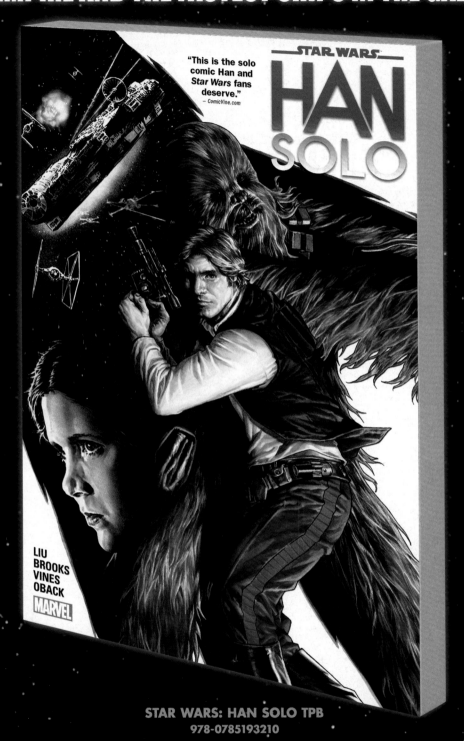

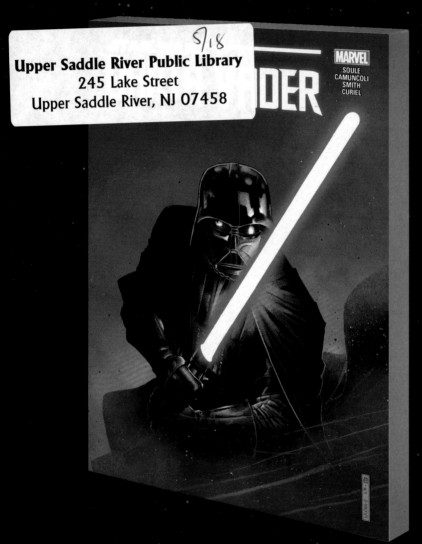

THE DARK LORD OF THE SITH'S FIRST DEADLY MISSION

**STAR WARS: DARTH VADER: DARK LORD OF THE SITH
VOL. 1: IMPERIAL MACHINE TPB**
978-1302907440

ON SALE NOW
WHEREVER BOOKS ARE SOLD

TO FIND A COMIC SHOP NEAR YOU, VISIT COMICSHOPLOCATOR.COM